MOVING PICTURES

Moving Pictures

A History of American Animation from Gertie to Pixar and Beyond

Darl Larsen

ROWMAN & LITTLEFIELD
Lanham • Boulder • New York • London

Published by Rowman & Littlefield
An imprint of The Rowman & Littlefield Publishing Group, Inc.
4501 Forbes Boulevard, Suite 200, Lanham, Maryland 20706
www.rowman.com

86-90 Paul Street, London EC2A 4NE

British Library Cataloguing in Publication Information Available

Library of Congress Cataloging-in-Publication Data
Names: Larsen, Darl, 1963– author.
Title: Moving pictures : a history of American animation from Gertie to Pixar and beyond / Darl Larsen.
Description: Lanham : Rowman & Littlefield, [2024] | Includes bibliographical references and index. | Summary: "A fascinating look at the history of film and television animation in the United States, from the animated comic strips of the early 1900s to the proliferation of animation companies and hit films of the present"— Provided by publisher.
Identifiers: LCCN 2023054529 (print) | LCCN 2023054530 (ebook) | ISBN 9781538160374 (cloth) | ISBN 9781538160381 (epub)
Subjects: LCSH: Animated films—United States—History and criticism | Animated film industry—United States—History.
Classification: LCC NC1766.U5 L37 2024 (print) | LCC NC1766.U5 (ebook) | DDC 791.43/340973—dc23/eng/20240206
LC record available at https://lccn.loc.gov/2023054529
LC ebook record available at https://lccn.loc.gov/2023054530

For Hayden, Linc, Yomi, Moon, and AJ—
We love cartoons!

CONTENTS

Abbreviations

AAC	*The American Animated Cartoon* (G. Peary)
AC	*American Cinematographer*
AMG	*The Animated Movie Guide* (J. Beck)
BM	*Before Mickey* (D. Crafton)
BSM	*Business Screen Magazine*
DV	*The Disney Version* (R. Schickel)
ED	*Enchanted Drawings* (C. Solomon)
EDR	*Exhibitors Daily Review*
EH	*Exhibitors Herald*
ETR	*Exhibitor's Trade Review*
FD	*The Film Daily*
FDY	*Film Daily Yearbook*
HC	*Hollywood Cartoons* (M. Barrier)
HR	*The Hollywood Reporter*
HSS	*The Hollywood Studio System* (D. Gomery)
LAT	*Los Angeles Times*
MPD	*Motion Picture Distributor*
MPE	*Motion Picture Exhibitor*
MPH	*Motion Picture Herald*
MPN	*Motion Picture News*
MPW	*Motion Picture World*
NYT	*New York Times*
OMM	*Of Mice and Magic* (L. Maltin)

Abbreviations

SM   Seven Minutes (N. Klein)
STR   Showmen's Trade Review
WSJ   Wall Street Journal
WMF   When Magoo Flew (A. Abraham)
WMLA   Winsor McCay: His Life and Art
              (J. Canemaker)

ACKNOWLEDGMENTS

Thanks to department chairs Wade Hollingshaus and Megan Sanborn Jones and the entire Theatre & Media Arts Department; thanks to our front-desk help for their patience and work honoring odd requests; thanks to Kyle Stapley and Grant Gomm; thanks to the College of Fine Arts and Communications; and thanks to the Harold B. Lee Library and especially the Interlibrary Loan services.

Thanks to my animation students who had to hear more than once about some book project they fortunately didn't have to purchase.

Thanks across the years to Dana Driskel, who taught me my first animation course at University of California, Santa Barbara; to April Chabries Makgoeng, who nudged me into teaching animation history in the first place; and to Kelly Loosli, who made me feel welcome with the animation faculty and who drove me around greater Los Angeles so I could point out obscure motion-picture landmarks.

And a special thanks to my family—Nycole, Keir, Hayden, and Lincoln; Emrys, Cat, and AJ; Brynmor, Chad, Yomi, and Moon; and Eamonn, Dathyl, Ransom, and Cuchulainn.

You make all this easier.

Introduction

IN 1936, CARTOONIST MAX FLEISCHER WAS CERTAIN FEATURE-LENGTH cartoons were coming.[1] Max may have sounded a bit crazy in 1936, when Europe was darkening and the Depression gripped America. The first feature-length animated film hadn't even been released, and many in the Hollywood cartoon and film industries were certain that Walt Disney, spending thousands of dollars and artist hours on a forthcoming "folly" called *Snow White and the Seven Dwarfs*, was going to lose everything Mickey, Donald, and the Silly Symphonies had built. Now, almost ninety years later, audiences can go to a local cinema for a *selection* of cartoon features, a *Minions* or a *Sonic the Hedgehog* or something entirely new. A feature cartoon has become a feature film.

Moving Pictures is a history of US animation, shorts and features, produced for release in theaters (cinemas). Along the way, we will see as follows:

- that, for nearly fifty years, entertainment cartoons were made for the only venue available—the cinema;
- that world wars and a depression helped canalize some cartoons and studios into information, education, and propaganda;
- that animated characters endured across time and societal change;
- that generations were introduced to and influenced by theatrical animation as studio back catalogs appeared on television;
- that, by the 1970s, theatrical animation was consumptive at best, struggling to find its breath and audience; and

- that creative and market forces helped turn a corner in the late 1980s, such that the animated feature became synonymous with the Hollywood blockbuster.

Which is where we are today. The year 2022, for example, was a drag on Hollywood, thanks to the lingering effects of a pandemic. Several animated projects switched distribution from theatrical to streaming, and Disney and Pixar produced expensive flops (*Lightyear*, *Strange World*); still, American feature animated films managed to contribute $1.8 billion to box office coffers. In 2019, prior to cinemas being shuttered, Hollywood theatrical animation was able to gross more than $5 billion.

So why this précis on American cinematic animation? A simple exercise: Think of your favorite cartoon characters from the major cartoon studio Bray-Hurd. How about from Raoul Barré or Pat Sullivan? Nothing yet? Maybe Paul Terry, Amedee Van Beuren, and the Fleischer Brothers, all leading cartoon producers in the 1910s and 1920s? Then how about Disney? This is benign sophistry of a sort—a trick question. Before Mickey, Walt had Alice, Julius, and Oswald, secondary characters and cartoon series for the most part (Alice wasn't even a *cartoon* character). Walt Disney was no bigger or better than competitors of the 1920s and well behind several. He more than once told his associates that if they could just reach the (relentlessly average) level of Terry's Aesop's Fables cartoons, they'd have succeeded[2]—but Disney's name echoes in the pantheon; others merit a whisper. Still, Farmer Al Falfa, Koko the Clown, and Felix the Cat ruled their days. As we'll discover, until November 1928, Disney's were earnest, pleasant cartoon diversions in a sea of cartoon diversions.

What is this young art form, animation, then? For frame-by-frame imagery that produces the illusion of motion, a minimum level of technology, including the recording of a photographed image and a method and device to display or project that image, was necessary. Before animated film was possible, a camera, a projector, and flexible film stock needed to be in hand. Animation was predated by photography and by optical experiments and toys, including camera obscura, magic lanterns, flip books, the thaumatrope, the zoetrope, and the phenakistoscope—these devices tantalized many who sought projection and the illusion of motion using still images.³ I distinctly remember as a child leafing through a hymnal only to find crude stick-figure drawings defacing the bottom white space, page after page. Some wannabe Aragonés⁴ had drawn a marginal figure—in location and quality—with a bow and arrow in one page corner, and a target in the opposite corner, creating a diverting flip book. A quick thumb-flip of dog-eared pages sent the arrow along its herky-jerky path and into the target. And, apocryphal or not, the first American comics and animation master Winsor McCay credits the flip books that fascinated his son with being the seed for his own experiments in moving pictures.⁵

The newspaper publishing industry, and especially the comics, were key for early animation. The comic strip provided willing artists; a simple visual aesthetic; broad, often stereotyped continuing characters; and a shorthand style of humor—a notational entertainment form easily adaptable to "moving" drawings. Newspaper comic creators like Winsor McCay and J. R. Bray were some of the earliest animated cartoon contributors. Live-performance vaudeville houses were already entertaining large crowds, and, after debuting in smaller, makeshift storefronts, movies became a natural part of many vaudeville theaters' programs. Soon the "flickers" were more popular and programmable (and affordable, easily replaceable) than live acts. These vaudeville houses transitioned into theater chains, like the Keith-Albee and Orpheum circuit, controlling theaters across the country. The beginning of the movies in the United States was intertwined with regional and national circuits, outlets that would soon demand a continuous supply of new product. With the coming of sound, movies exploded in popularity; burgeoning chains like Keith-Albee-Orpheum merged with film- and radio-related entities to form an early Hollywood studio, RKO (Radio-Keith-Orpheum). RKO would later distribute Disney's *Snow White*. Others made similar associations, conglomerating the means of film production, distribution, and exhibition into single companies, becoming the giant, vertically integrated studios Paramount, Loew's (MGM), Fox, and Warner Bros. All these studios would eventually distribute cartoons.

Moving Pictures came about as a happy result of teaching a history-of-animation course in a new major to computer animation students. It is aimed at those students as well as at the general reader interested in a little industry that could and *did*—an industry that began with whatever the value of chalk and a bit of film stock might have been in 1906, when J. S. Blackton filmed himself drawing. It's also meant to be a survey, primarily, with deeper dives where it seems needful. And, even though there are critical international contributions to the art form and the specter of television looms large after World War II, this book will examine the development and rise of American *theatrical* animation— meaning animation intended for projection in cinemas—where just ten years after its beginnings it mostly transitioned to industry status, like its live-action cinema cousin, becoming a multibillion-dollar commercial phenomenon. We will *mention* television and advertising after the war since much of the declining cartoon industry went there when cinematic orders slowed and ultimately stopped. New short animation nearly disappeared at this point (the late 1960s), while feature animation limped along, trying to be done with Disney and assay audiences with more mature cartoons. Those audiences didn't wholesale materialize, and the creator of *Snow White* wasn't done with feature animation.

Speaking of Walt, we won't be able to do this properly if we treat the man and his work as anything other than a kind of categorical imperative, a sine qua non. The young Walt and his comrades started in 1919 well below even the lumpen level of the budding animation industry, their work indistinguishable from those they were aping except that it was slightly worse. Disney lost that business. By 1923, the Disney efforts with the *Alice* cartoons were palatable, even pleasant; by 1926, Oswald was likable, distributable, his animation accomplished; in late 1928, Walt, partner Ub Iwerks, and Mickey would change the animation industry forever.

There is also the thought out there that the study of American animation has been "done," that there's little left to say or show; that, or the thought that far, far too much has been credited to Walt while others are out there, awaiting their due attention. There are elements of truth on both sides of that semicolon. Many commentators across the years have opined that, prior to Disney, there was no animation.[6] The *anyone other than Disney* school also exists. That book could be written, yes, but imagine a mountain's shadow without the mountain. Disney's product was much richer for lesser-known animators and studios, as we'll discover.

And there are some good reasons for a look at animation of the United States as opposed to taking a North American or an English-speaking or a global approach, all of which could be justified and have been fruitful. In many significant ways, including the following, however, American animation history is distinct from all others:

- US animation has been baldly *commercial* in nature, almost from the start, unlike much animation from around the world. It has endured proto-industrial and then industrial lives and functions. It was always meant to be self-supporting, not subsidized by government or larger industry beneficence. American animation was sink or swim from the beginning.

- Related to the reason above, animation became an *industry* in the United States, eventually attached to Hollywood, streamlining and marshalling all productive and organizational forces to produce a sellable product at a market price with some profit presumed.

- Animation became a significant part of the filmed output of the major and minor American film studio system in which production was centralized; all majors and minors distributed cartoons along with their live-action features at some point.

- Animation has become almost indistinguishable from feature film, especially at the distribution and exhibition portals, its stand-alone films marketed and shown as "normal" feature-film releases today.

Animated shorts *and* features still matter; Oscars still go to a Best Animated Feature and Best Animated Short Film. Even during the wilderness years for theatrical animation, when new films floundered (if they were made at all), animated shorts and features survived. Across the 1950s, the short-subjects back catalogs of Warner Bros., Terrytoons, and Paramount were sold to television, reaching new generations who would in turn make their own cartoon-influenced films. Such younger-generation filmmakers ranged from George Lucas and Steven Spielberg to Jeffrey Katzenberg and Chris Meledandri to John Lasseter and Brad Bird. Disney's back catalog likewise continued to find an audience. In 1967, a rerelease of *Snow White* reached number twenty-two in box office gross in the United States; in 1975, it was released again and climbed to number fifteen, becoming the highest-ranked animated film on the list that year; and, in 1983, *Snow White* was released again, reaching number twenty-four. That year, Disney's *Sword in the Stone*, *The Rescuers*, and *Peter Pan* were also rereleased, and all charted in the top eighty films. Since then, the sales of home-video versions of these films have reached into the hundreds of millions, and, for many down periods, the popularity of these home-video versions kept the Disney studio afloat.

BRASS TACKS

Foundational texts are out there and often very good. They include Charles Solomon's *Enchanted Drawings*, Michael Barrier's *Hollywood Cartoons*, Donald Crafton's *Before Mickey*, Maureen Furniss's *A New History of Animation*, Norman Klein's *Seven Minutes*, and Leonard Maltin's *Of Mice and Magic*. There are also myriad biography-type approaches to animation, its studios and personalities, including Richard Schickel's broadside *The Disney Version*; John Canemaker's and Joe Adamson's compelling discussions of early cinema pioneers J. R. Bray, Otto Messmer, Disney, and Tex Avery and individual (and often less heralded) Disney and Fleischer artists like Richard Huemer, Grim Natwick, and Ub Iwerks; also dozens of Disney biographies or exposés, authorized and not, from Gabler, Mosley, Shale, Ryan, Merritt and Kaufman, Susanin, and Bob Thomas. There are a handful of single volumes dedicated to other leading figures not named Walt Disney, including a few about Winsor McCay or the Fleischer brothers and their studios, one monograph for the other Walt—Walter Lantz, creator of Woody Woodpecker—and one for Paul Terry, creator of nothing terribly memorable but possessing an enviable nest egg when he retired in 1953. Gaps in the scholarship are apparent immediately, with much less dedicated individually to luminaries like old-timers Bray, Earl Hurd, and Raoul Barré, scattered examinations of Messmer, Sullivan, Margaret Winkler, or, interestingly, even later titans like Hanna and Barbera (beyond their autobiographies). There's much to still explore.

In 1906, animation didn't truly exist, excepting a few filmed and presented drawings. By 1926, some Fleischer animated films were making noise like feature films would; Disney had Mickey whistling and prodding in synchronization two years later. In 1937, cartoons were "the Esperanto of the screen," thanks to universal appeal.[7] Three years after that, another pundit would rule on animation, concluding that "the animated cartoon is no longer a pawkish stepchild among the crafts; it has become an industry."[8] That industry chugged along behind Disney's lead until United Productions of America (UPA) threw a clog in the works in the late 1940s, maybe changing everything. Nope. UPA ruled the early 1950s for the literati and graphic artists, but Disney, MGM, and Warner Bros. entertained through the war and well into the 1950s—there joined by UPA's nod to commerce, Magoo—and thence to television screens to this day. And after a harrowing two decades leading into the mid-1980s, animation was given a new life, thanks to characters like Roger Rabbit, Ariel, and a blue genie. Even more unusual, an ogre named Shrek, a plumber named Mario, Manny the Mammoth, and a swarm of Minions were in the wings, waiting for their digital cue, populating colorful, antic blockbuster films since 2001. This is American animation.

We'll talk about all of this and a panda who does kung fu, too.

Blackton Begat Mccay Begat Bray Begat . . .

JAMES STUART BLACKTON, WINSOR MCCAY, JOHN RANDOLPH BRAY, and Raoul Barré kickstarted American animation from different angles and with different goals. Blackton helped McCay, McCay inspired Barré and helped Bray, and Bray helped himself. Blackton was a trailblazer, hovering around Thomas Edison for inspiration, practicing an imma- ture trade before mentoring McCay and moving off into live-action film.[1] Comic and vaudeville artist McCay wanted to translate his talents to the screen, bringing a pen-and-ink-magician's artistry to the stage—a true craftsman where others worked rough. Bray and Barré saw and seized opportunities, Bray imitating McCay's mosquito character to leech tradecraft from the man himself and spin those wisps into gold. All drew water from a common well: "Drawings that 'come to life' may be said to be the great theme of all animation. And the narrative content of many animated films, especially in the silent period, may be seen as a heroic struggle by the drawings to retain their unexpected corporeal existence."[2] As the god of both worlds, McCay would tinker with this unearned life in his stage show, where the controlling, presenting McCay enters the world of the animated image to interact with the drawn dino- saur Gertie. Later, restoration of order would be demonstrated when the Fleischers' Koko dove back into the inkwell, mayhem contained. Still later, only the end of the cartoon could contain Tex Avery's Wolf, Screwy Squirrel, or even Bugs (mostly). Blackton's Vitagraph[3] saw to the shooting and distribution of McCay's first film, *Little Nemo*; McCay explained to a mystery man (thought to have been Bray posing as a journalist) the details of the nascent art form; influenced by McCay's work, both Barré and Bray pondered and practiced those techniques; Bray patented them. Bray was trying to make the impractical practical and profitable. Blackton moved out of the cartoon business rather quickly; McCay tinkered as an artist for a few years, creating magic, but lost interest and momentum by 1921; Barré moved between animation and fine art; Bray collected licensing fees and produced affordable, occasionally interesting cartoons until 1928. All four outlived their place and time in the cartoon world. For different reasons, they earned their plinths in the pantheon of American animation. "It is probably fair to say that McCay realized the visual potential of the animated film," Conrad Smith sums up, "that Raoul Barré was the first to mass-produce animated cartoons, and that John Bray brought the mass production of cartoons the best possible compromise between quantity and quality."[4] In a nutshell, yes, but the meat within is worth a taste.

At various times, Blackton, McCay, Max Fleischer, and Bray (and Frenchman Emile Cohl) all claimed to have created cinematic animation.[5] Bray would write in July 1917 that his name had become "a household word" and that he had "conceived the idea of animating drawings" after seeing a stop-action film at a department store.[6] McCay also merits inventor's credit, his based solely on first-view knowledge: "In pure line, on a white ground, a plant is seen to grow up and unfold into a flower; a young man turns and plucks it and hands it to a girl . . . I shall never forget my excitement when I saw it . . . I was witnessing the birth of a new art."[7] This observer was remembering his introduction to McCay's cartoon exercise *Little Nemo*, no earlier than 1911, several years after the debuts of animated work from Blackton and Cohl, but prior to the appearance of Barré or Bray's first animated short. But before Nemo could cavort on screen, he gamboled on the page.

It was the success of the newspaper comic strip—at once "infantile, brutal, unsophisticated, and subliterate"—that fueled the first animated cartoons, with early practitioners like Blackton borrowing almost whole cloth from the printed page's format, humor, and caricatures.[8] Pierre

Couperie notes, "The animated cartoon, the movie, and the comic strip were born simultaneously; although each appeared independently of the other, they embodied in related forms the deep-seated trend underlying the entire nineteenth century."[9] Industry historian Terry Ramsaye writes not long after this period, "Incidentally and significantly, the strip comic is the newspaper's nearest approach to the presentation of a motion picture."[10] As will be seen, McCay's version of the strip comic ventured as near as any to the sublime, the fantastic, and the cinematic. And then he crossed those lines and made animated films. For at least the next decade or more, many comic-strip artists, including McCay, supplemented their incomes by licensing or creating their own animated versions of these strips. If the artist owned the rights to his characters, this was a steady source of additional income, and it could also help sell newspapers, so publishers (including, in a characteristically big way, William Randolph Hearst) were often involved. It was the American newspaper comics page—home of "a despised medium," according to Gilbert Seldes[11]— effectively birthing the animated film, often via the vaudeville stage and lightning-sketch phenomena. Characters created just for animated cartoons would soon follow, bringing comic-strip sensibilities and tools of the trade with them, and many looked like new versions of Krazy Kat or Ignatz the Mouse, popular comics characters of the time. By the early 1910s, dialogue and thought bubbles, sound-effects imagery, speed lines, and dashed character gaze lines all found their way from comic strips to animated shorts from Bray, Earl Hurd, Carlson, Paul Terry, Max Fleischer, and many others. But first, Blackton and McCay.

JAMES S. BLACKTON

James S. Blackton's *Humorous Phases of Funny Faces* (1906) is argu- ably the world's first animated film and is a version of Blackton's early pre-animation works advertised as "chalk-talks" or "lightning sketches," what's been termed "slow motion animation."[12] A shot sheet for this first cartoon film would note frame-by-frame titles using chalk and cutout paper, the artist's hand drawing with chalk, erasing when needed, and a man and a woman's faces being drawn, undrawn, erased, either by the artist's hand or by the "magic" of frame-by-frame animation. It would have been spectacular in 1906. In this short, filmed section, Blackton managed to provide, predict, and straitjacket the iconography for the next two decades of American animation, connecting, as Crafton has ably discussed, the artist directly to his character. We are presented with the artist, the surface on which he will draw, and the drawings themselves—all borrowed from vaudeville performances—images and icons, familiar and understood. As late as 1929, former Disney animator Rudy Ising's hand was drawing Bosko, presenting him to an unseen audience, giving birth to Warner Bros. cartoons. On the way to animation as an industry, McCay, Bray, Hurd, Walter Lantz, and Walt Disney—and many others—would embrace this iconography.

These popular performances involved either chalk and a chalkboard or a large piece of paper and a broad-tipped pencil or crayon, likely depending on the venue (variety theater or private salon).[13] The talented artist Blackton would draw to his own patter, his handwritten words like "Coon," "Cohen," or "Kelly" morphing, a deft line at a time, into a racially stereotyped caricature of a Black, a Jew, an Irishman. The casual, latent racism of the day found its way into comic strips, panel cartoons, staged comic and musical performances (including vaudeville and minstrelsy), and, ultimately, cartoons, the movies, and television. These "performances" employed recognizable ethnic stereotypes and stock figures. Fin de siècle American audiences were familiar with this visual and verbal shorthand, allowing for the joke or situation to play out against the foundation of commonly accepted racial, religious, or gendered "realities." This insensitivity would fade only slowly across the time we are studying.

Blackton's filmed version uses chalk drawings, yes, but also already employs cutouts meant to look like drawings to reduce the work between exposures—erasings on the board would leave a residue, which disappears when cutouts are used. Drawing, talking, adding to the drawing, erasing, talking, adding more, erasing a part, more drawing, and patter, patter, patter—this had become the accustomed stage practice for lightning-sketch artists; Blackton was here simply translating that process to a filmed performance.[14] Blackton achieved the effect by stopping the camera for a new drawing every three frames or so.[15] He was moving beyond the stage version when he swapped in the precut paper images, an early labor-saving device.

Blackton left animation as his interest in the "trick-film" waned, pursuing live-action film instead, inspired by D. W. Griffith.[16] Historically, early animation is where Blackton's influence has been identified, but he was also a director, a producer, a studio head, a special-effects craftsman, and an industry organizer.[17] Blackton and Griffith had been performers, both came to be production supervisors at nascent motion-picture studios and oversaw scores of films, and both made larger, more personal projects after leaving their studio confines.[18] Griffith made popular, controversial, talk-worthy film after film; Blackton made a handful of personal passion projects that were expensive and have been forgotten. Blackton didn't see his early animated efforts as anything more than camera tricks, and by 1909 most trick-films were being made only for children's matinees.[19] This may be why this period of animation—between McCay's best work and the appearance of on-screen personalities like Felix and Koko a few years later—can boast little original work; instead, there was a surfeit of rote comic-strip adaptations or continuing-character series and stagnant or declining programmability in cinemas: "*Gertie* . . . was the most accomplished animated film to date [1914] (and for many years thereafter)."[20] For some, this was the period when the cartoon was no better than a lights-up-chaser—short subjects that could clear the theater for the next showing.[21]

Though not much remembered or recognized except in history books, Blackton's was a key organizational presence, certainly laying the groundwork for what became the Hollywood studio system across the following fifteen years. He was the first studio mogul, the demands of which—"by 1910, he was supervising all the company's productions"[22]—kept him from focusing on performing and animating. After his departure, the Vitagraph studio would eventually be sold to Warner Bros.; by 1926, all the major and minor film studios were in place. Blackton had been a vital part of that construction.

WINSOR MCCAY

Winsor McCay brought his elevated, celebrated comic-strip artistry to the early animated film, and, rather than swap that artistic finesse for industry for clumsy drawing and reproducible functionality, he later left animation. The success of Cohl's *Newlyweds* cartoon series, based on George McManus's popular strip, threw open the door for distributors looking for new program package items and turned the heads of comic-strip artists toward this new revenue stream. Between McCay's *Little Nemo* and *The Sinking of the Lusitania* (1911–1918), the world of animation would develop from artistry to cottage industry to just plain industry. Animation was better than when he found(ed) it, for his unique contributions, but McCay's withdrawal left a vacuum that was immediately filled by "a host of imitators whose animation was crude and merely designed to show movement from point to point."[23] Gimcrack studios were peopled by those who could easily justify what McCay would not— weak drawing, reuse, and repetition, creating "a glut of dull animation" able to stretch meager production dollars and compete for distribution with live-action short films.[24] But even when the budgets were scanty, there was still a cost to producing crude work, according to early animator Dick Huemer: "[Early on our films] were given away with features. You got a feature, you got a newsreel, you got some other strange thing, then you got a cartoon. . . . If the exhibitor hated cartoons, he didn't run them."[25] Arguably, critics saw no return of that McCay artistry to American animation until, for most, Disney of the early 1930s, or "only by the very best animators—the top artists at Disney, Schlesinger, or MGM—at the height of their powers."[26] But first, McCay's artistic approach and attention to fine detail offers an identity to preindustrial animation.

As a young man, McCay had worked making posters and advertisements for many businesses but significantly for an in situ Cincinnati freak show, where "the grotesque left its mark on [his] style," one historian writes. "[McCay's] later work is replete with carnival motifs, including distortions based on trick mirrors, exotic animals, clowns and dancers."[27] These influences would be seen first in his very popular comic strips (or comic pages, often), including *Little Nemo in Slumberland* from 1905, in which Nemo's bed would often walk from his room and take him to visit the Man in the Moon: "Right at the outset . . . McCay grasped the one great advantage that movies made from drawings must have over movies made from photographs: that absolutely anything is possible."[28] Not artistically satisfied with his confining newspaper work, McCay took to the boards (where cartoonists Blackton, Richard Outcault, and Bud Fisher already supplemented their incomes), creating a short vaudeville lightning-sketch routine, "Seven Ages of Man" (inspired by a story in his *Dream of the Rarebit Fiend* comic strip[29]). In this popular 1906 performance, McCay metamorphosed with only chalkboard and chalk his characters from cradle to grave before the audience's eyes. By 1907, McCay's was the "extraordinary feature" of most bills. "Winsor McCay, as a cartoonist, draws two faces, and by erasing and adding lines, transforms them from youth to old age," one reporter noted. "The act is of a high class, and is appreciated."[30] McCay would also use paper for drawings on stage, reported *Variety*, seen later in the *Little Nemo* and *Gertie* films.[31] By 1909, McCay had grown "prosperous" and was performing his vaudeville shows "some fifteen or twenty weeks . . . each year."[32] On a bet[33] with fellow comic artists, including McManus, McCay took on the challenge of adding an animated element to his lightning-sketch act.[34] McCay would say later that he was most inspired to move from stage and comic graphic work to motion-picture cartoons by the flip books his son had brought into their home. Crafton reminds us that McCay had access to Blackton's work as well as Cohl's,[35] so there is probably a more involved answer than just flip books, but they did matter.

McCay had been employing unpatented paper animation processes since at least 1911, when he completed *Little Nemo*, which he might have begun in 1909.[36] McCay was almost Griffithian in his Victorian views of the significance of animation, of its artisanal nature, and the crucial place of hands-on craftsmanship in the art form.[37] That's why he himself would draw each page of animation, with the backgrounds having to be redrawn each frame, as well. (His assistant Fitzsimmons was tasked with these backgrounds using a master created by the Master.) McCay's approach couldn't usher in the animation-as-industry phase, but he did set the bar high enough for the reach of like-minded artists in the future, for experimenters, avant-gardists, and men like Disney. *Nemo* was itself primarily an experiment in filmed drawings on paper suggesting motion, and in it we see faithful, exacting dalliances with squash and stretch, cycling, of character resizing, of perspective and drawing in depth, and on.[38] But McCay's experiments weren't meant to take animation to metamorphic extremes; rather, McCay strove for a "pictorial realism" that was "a final contrast to Cohl's tendency toward openness and linear abstraction [and] virtually defined the aesthetic ground rules for all later American animation."[39] Artists from Bray through Disney and Chuck Jones absorbed and displayed this McCay aesthetic. John Canemaker sets McCay in history succinctly: "His painstaking experiments with timing, motion, characterization, and techniques, for which there were no precedents, rightfully place him as the true father of animation."[40] Seeing this work as an art form, McCay "never fully explored the commercial possibilities of animation," leaving that avenue open for more business-minded artists including Barré, Bray, Hurd, and others.[41]

Not unlike UPA some quarter of a century later, McCay is remembered for the bellwether films and aesthetics he created, not the quantity of his work. As an animator, he is best known for just four cartoons, really, produced across an eight-year period: *Little Nemo* (1911), *How a Mosquito Operates* (1912), *Gertie the Dinosaur* (1914), and *The Sinking of the Lusitania* (1918). Each one is remarkable in its way for the confident strides taken into the new art form, and each set standards that the industry followed. *Nemo* was a four-thousand-drawings advertisement for McCay's well-loved newspaper comic strip—no plot or story, just a thrilling "watch me move" invitation from one of McCay's doppelgangers. Finished in black and white, McCay would soon hand-color every drawing (of the version used in his stage show) to resemble the newspaper comic-strip versions.

It was his second film, *How a Mosquito Operates*, that set the tone for all commercial animation to follow: "McCay sought to go beyond motion-for-motion's sake experiments and magical metamorphosis," Canemaker writes. "He decided to tell a story, a moral tale in pantomime, using illusionism he pioneered in *Little Nemo*."[42] This film was announced as demanding six thousand individual sketches.[43] The mosquito is also gifted with a personality; he's a character, waving at his assumed audience, doffing his hat, and performing tricks as if he were simply one of the acts on the evening's bill. If he hadn't ended up being a cautionary tale about the dangers of gluttony, the mosquito could have been one of American animation's first continuing characters.

A pause here for an insider's viewpoint: Between 1912 and 1914 would have been the ideal time for McCay to seek out or accept a distribution deal—Cohl's work was successful, Bray had made his first film, and distributors were looking for affordable, programmable product. *If* McCay had been interested in such a lengthy deal in which he wasn't drawing every line, and *if* he was willing to forego stage work (which he loved), and *if* he could either sweet-talk his boss or, gulp, quit the Hearst position and leap into animation with both feet, as Bray was doing— *if, if, if* . . . For McCay, the demands of commercial, industrial animation would have been ruinous.

The popular *Gertie*—"the enduring masterpiece of pre-Disney ani-mation"[44]—followed in 1914, cementing both McCay's reputation and the artistic and commercial viability of animated films.[45] Throwing him-self into this new work, McCay imbued Gertie with a playful, sensitive personality—she could be rough with a pachyderm passerby or brought to tears by a chiding word. When she lies down, her chest moves up and down like any dozing house pet; she scratches her nose with the tip of her tail, just so; her head twists coyly; and she dances. These are the little touches that will find their way into Felix's plotting, Mickey's fussiness, and Daffy's sideways glance at us. McCay introduced *personality* into ani-mation, and it felt as if it belonged there. Lessons offered weren't imme-diately or widely learned, however. Animators following McCay were more likely to borrow his techniques (especially the labor-saving ones) than his artistic ambitiousness. Bray's company, long on patent exclusivity but short on creativity, took the Gertie character and produced a knock-off in 1915, *Diplodocus*, employing some of the cost- and labor-cutting tactics of cel animation. It's not terrible—its cardinal sin is that it's almost completely unoriginal, excepting the processes employed. Bray had set out to consolidate and manage the techniques, patenting the animation process, Smith points out, which was (much) "the same that McCay had used two years earlier!"[46] McCay's assistant Fitzsimmons never seemed surprised that his boss avoided the race to industrial animation or anything that took him away from the bits he loved and valued: "He would never be bothered going into [the business of animation] like Disney," Fitzsimmons said in 1975, "he just didn't have that make-up. McCay loved to draw and if he couldn't draw he wasn't interested in it."[47]

While Blackton enjoyed dozens of firsts as he made films, McCay's firsts made animation possible. The first true animation "cycle" can be awarded to McCay—Flip's cigar moves up and down in *Little Nemo*. McCay reused original drawings for cycling purposes, as when Gertie sways back and forth; this technique is also seen in *Mosquito* and most of McCay's subsequent work. He timed movements in relation to drawings for smoothness, for lifelike-ness. He tested the accuracy and fluidity

For Gertie, McCay drew and redrew every line on this paper image (and hundreds more); his assistant helped with the backgrounds. *Gertie the Dinosaur*, Winsor McCay, 1914 (from *Animation Legend: Winsor McCay* DVD). Screenshot taken by the author.

of the drawings using a Mutoscope-like device and strove for proper registration. These attentions to detail are why McCay's work looks so much smoother than that of any other animator of the period, eerily prefiguring the look the Fleischers would achieve years later, *tracing* their filmed images using the rotoscope. McCay also developed the first "pose and in-between drawings" system, in which the initial pose and the final pose in any character movement were drawn first; then the central pose and, finally, the intermediate poses were drawn.[48] (This "in-betweening" would fade or disappear in the earliest efforts from the first animation studios, Smith notes—an unjustifiable added expense.[49]) For McCay, this practice ensured continuity and smoothness of line and figure across multiple drawings.

On his way to cinematic aesthetics, McCay used reflexivity and distancing strategies in his comics to show readers the techniques and "secrets" of the comic genre. He enjoyed having his characters break through their frames and even giving them sentience—knowing they are cartoons, understanding there are frames and images ahead (or below, on the newspaper page). McCay then brought this same sensibility to his animation, by revealing the tricks of the trade.[50] This act separates him from all other trick-film artists of the period. According to Crafton, this is how McCay achieved his "self-figuration" as an animator. And even as a comic illustrator McCay was clearly seeing cinematographic perspective and movement, admitting the "technical primacy"[51] of filmed images, according to John Fell: "At least two years before he attempted film animation McCay was employing strikingly movie-like techniques in a daily comic strip."[52]

McCay's final completed film was also his most ambitious and his most serious.[53] The world seemed to be more serious. A war had been on since 1914; in 1917, McCay had been forced to accept new terms from Hearst, surrendering his vaudeville life—Hearst simply ponied up more salary to cover stage earnings losses.[54] McCay was to be assigned editorial cartoons, period. A soothing salve, perhaps, was that vaudeville was already on the decline, thanks to the movies, and mightn't have been as homey as McCay hoped. With the trick-film phenomena wearing thin and most cartoons produced from 1915 to 1918 earning few plaudits and showing little innovation, it's no surprise that not only were audiences turning elsewhere for filmed entertainment (namely, Chaplin, live-action comedies and dramas, and the emerging serials), but its animation artists also found their own eyes wandering. Blackton turned to running Vitagraph; Bray was already transitioning into films for educational purposes; and McCay, reacting viscerally to the sinking of a British passenger ship by a German U-boat, set out to create a filmed document of the "cowardly" act. Making his own films was also his only extracurricular filmic outlet *not* controlled by Hearst. The German attack brought McCay into the war effort, and his efforts helped bring in the American people and government. McCay's finished film, *The Sinking of the Lusitania*, contained twenty-five thousand drawings and was McCay's first significant use of cel animation. Fitzsimmons was again drafted to work on the film, contributing a patentable peg system for the individual cels and arranging and photographing a set of waves drawn on celluloid sheets. Fitzsimmons remembers the project being so demanding that a second assistant was employed.[55] The German torpedo attack occurred in May 1915; just over three years later, McCay's film documenting the event was complete.[56] Given that the film was a reaction to an actual event and was designed to remind Americans of German culpability, *Lusitania* ably demonstrated the propagandistic and even jingoistic possibilities of not only film but also cartoons. Going forward, American animation would assume a direct role in times of war and times of uneasy peace (including the Depression), delivering social and political messages, public information, and even hope.

After *Lusitania*, McCay finished less and less. Fragments include bits of *Centaurs*, *Flip's Circus*, and *Gertie on Tour*, and three *Dreams of a Rarebit Fiend* cartoons he was hoping could become a continuing series. By 1921, all these had been "finished." And so was McCay. He left animation entirely around this time and publicly bemoaned the loss/lack of artistic integrity in animation in comments given at a dinner in 1927.[57] The year is significant, certainly: the year of sound film, soon birthing Disney's ascendancy, and within earshot of Technicolor—McCay might have enjoyed the artistry of Silly Symphonies as well as Max Fleischer's scientific films. McCay would die in 1934, still drawing editorial cartoons but not films. McCay would be rediscovered in the mid-1960s, leading to retrospectives of his work in museums and expos around the world and dozens of articles and books.[58] It wouldn't be until the mid-1970s that McCay's work in its entirety would be available in the United States.[59]

JOHN RANDOLPH BRAY

The third important name, Bray, will be reintroduced here, among the innovators, and then returned to in the following chapter, where the name of the game will be industry, or animation as a sustainable business. Blackton and McCay rode a winner when pioneering invention was the rocking horse; they got bucked off when an industrial turn was demanded. Third Man Bray might have been perfectly suited to benefit during this time of transition. "It was not an artistic urge that gave rise to the discovery and gradual perfection of a new technique," Erwin Panofsky wrote in 1934. "[I]t was a technical invention that gave rise to the discovery and gradual perfection of a new art."[60] McCay and, to a differing extent, Blackton had contributed directly to this art form's increase in profile, leading it from its cocooned stage to the doorsill of another level (a verge neither were to cross). McCay brought his art form to a new technology; the next step would be embracing and enhancing the technology that enlivened the art—where the balance tips toward commerce. This next man made animated films meant for the cinema screen; he saw "animated cartoons as a practical form of entertainment and business"[61]; he founded his cartoon studio on the factory floor; and he saw the profitability in continuing-character series cartoons. He was the man who went to the effort of patenting the processes of his art form and who would produce the first color animated film for commercial distribution. This was J. R. Bray.

Whereas McCay had inhabited and populated his own belle epoque, Bray has been seen as an inelegant toiler, a gifted functionary. This technically agile draftsman might be the most important name discussed in this chapter—not because he was an unmatched innovator or trailblazer, nor because his artistic skills were nonpareil. He was the artist to whom an assembly line wasn't just another iteration of "dark Satanic Mills" transplanted from New Jerusalem to New York. Bray's unwillingness or inability to see animation as just artistry was essential to saving it from a claustral fate. He wasn't the first animator whose work was seen in theaters; his wasn't the first continuing-character series; he didn't found the first cartoon studio or make the first animated film with color, and he also denied being influenced by Winsor McCay. (This last point might be as crucial as anything—McCay's fine, florid, Art Nouveau–ish work wasn't suited to industrial systemization; Bray's more familiar, less elaborate style was.) The "didn'ts" and "wasn'ts" are true but misleading, Canemaker would assert, since they don't "do justice to a career that was as important to the first wide acceptance of animation as Disney's career was to the 'second phase' of the art's development."[62] That's where we'll begin on J. R. Bray.

Born in Michigan, Bray began as a newspaper artist and cartoonist, working for the *Detroit Free News* and then the *Brooklyn Eagle* (where a young Max Fleischer would later work and they would meet), and he also contributed to popular magazines. His contributions to animation can be summarized: "[He] industrialized film cartoons," wrote Canemaker, "he streamlined all of the tasks by hiring a staff to divide the workload into . . . specialized jobs, such as animation, inbetweening, cleaning up (conforming the drawings), inking, coloring, and photography."[63] It's clear that Bray approached animation like Henry Ford approached the production of automobiles—build as many as possible as cheaply as possible. Preferred color? Any color you like, so long as it's black (and white). To accomplish this Tayloristic method, to compete with cheaper live-action short subjects for distributor dollars, animation had to expand beyond McCay's master–and–(little-used) apprentice approach. If industry was the goal, rather than one immaculate Rubens, there needed to be dozens of not-too-grubby "after Rubens" that could still sell.

The entire film industry of the 1910s was enduring the tortuous process of coalescing, of making and remaking alliances, and of competing for talent, for theaters, for regions, and for hearts and minds and pocketbooks.[64] Producers of films weren't necessarily aligned with film exchanges, where films were distributed, while theater chains were often independents simply looking for consistent product. William Fox, for example, started as an exhibitor but added production "to keep more of the money for himself."[65] Most movie moguls started as exhibitors. The era of the Hollywood studio system—in which one company owned the means of production, distribution, and exhibition—the time of monopolistic vertical integration, was still a few years off. Any semblance of order from any corner of the industry would have been welcome. This entire epoch suffers in history's gaze for these reasons, with thoughtful types like Panofsky skimming across the 1910s toward a brighter horizon, glancing at and glossing over the *"modest trick films and cartoons [which] paved the way* to Felix the Cat, Popeye the Sailor, and Felix's prodigious offspring, Mickey Mouse."[66]

Bray brought some order to the frontier of cartoons by filing for and receiving elemental patents for (often extant) animation processes.[67] In these patent applications, Bray said again and again that his processes were those that would speed up and simplify the industry—truthful statements, for the most part. One such patent application described the use of "ordinary zinc etching" to print backgrounds onto sheets of paper (so the backgrounds wouldn't have to be redrawn every frame); another, the use of "cross marks to facilitate the registration" of drawings.[68] (These crosses are visible on McCay's drawings from 1911.) "Bray was attempting to devise a system of patents that would give him control over the animation process."[69] Once those patents began to be granted, Bray (or his indefatigable wife) would visit working animation studios to let them know a new sheriff was in town. Some complained loudly (like McCay himself[70]), some had to pay up just to keep their doors open and undarkened by process servers, while for others a winnowing ensued—those smallish firms that couldn't or wouldn't pay closed their doors. (McCay would eventually pay when he wanted to license cel animation patents for *Lusitania*.[71]) This regulating also would have helped the film exchanges and distributors who could now deal with fewer short subjects salesmen, regularizing their programs and building a dependable audience. Most of these newly patented processes were already being used by most artists, and many had been achieved by McCay himself as he solved problems prepping *Nemo* and *Mosquito*. McCay had even been encouraged to file for patents himself, but he felt his "split system" was so universal that it was and should remain available: "Any idiot who wants to make a couple of thousand drawings for a hundred feet of film is welcome to join the club."[72] His blind spot makes sense. Given the way McCay had always approached his work, it likely never occurred to him that perfunctory, jerry-built animation was in any way desirable or marketable, nor that anyone would bother to patent any of its processes. McCay clearly wasn't foreseeing the advent of cheaper, faster studio animation that reduced the number of complete original drawings, streamlining the process, bringing profitability into the realm of possibility.

Bray's own animation work began in 1913, officially, when his *Artist's Dream* was distributed; it is thought to be the earliest animated film made just for theatrical distribution (as opposed to part of a vaudeville or staged performance). This simple cartoon, featuring a dog pilfering his master's food, already exhibited the economy Bray was hoping to bring to the art form (limited drawing and redrawing, simple backgrounds, still frames, cycling). The response to this cartoon landed Bray a distribution deal with Pathé—six cartoons in just six months.[73] Bray had done the work on *Artist's Dream* alone and knew that fulfilling any kind of regular production contract would demand many hands. Bray's first continuing-character cartoon, *Colonel Heeza Liar in Africa*, appeared 6 December 1913.[74] It took no time at all for Bray's cartoons to catch on: "The hunting adventures of 'Col. Heeza Liar' in South Africa raised a riot of laughter and applause," said the *New York Times*.[75] By September 1914, notices of the Colonel's antics were appearing in the "Great Films on Reel Row" column in the *Los Angeles Times*. At Clune's Broadway that same month and year, the Colonel, it was reported, "never fails to please," while *Moving Picture World* described it as "[a]nother of those irresistible funny cartoons which have taken the country by storm," complimenting Bray's "ingenious drawings" and "witty sub-titles."[76] The second title, *Colonel Heeza Liar Shipwrecked*, was greeted with equal enthusiasm. This series enjoyed a popular five-year initial run, producing more than forty cartoons; it was paused and then restarted in 1922, for an additional twenty or so titles.[77] The die seemed cast. Now armed with a distribution deal, a popular character, a functioning studio, and a few hit shorts, Bray would settle into the industry he would help shepherd for the next sixty years.

CHAPTER 2

Inking the Path to Industry

"ANIMATION STARTED OUT, WITH *GERTIE THE DINOSAUR*, AS A SIDESHOW attraction," wrote Joe Adamson, "and for twenty years worked its way steadily downward."[1] Early animator Dick Huemer remembers audience members groaning as a cartoon started.[2] This chapter is going to be about animation's fitful and uninspiring transition from infancy to industry, from more random to more uniform—an "If it moved, it was good" period.[3] It could be called the Age of the Continuing-Character Series, with characters tending to be human, not animals. Fussy grandpa types and precocious boys were everywhere at first, and then a slow transition to animal versions followed.[4] Farmer Al Falfa and Colonel Heeza Liar, Bobby Bumps and the Katzenjammers are the human prototypes; then the humanized animals Old Doc Yak and Silk Hat Harry, Ignatz, Krazy, and, finally, Felix will take us into the next phase of the industry, in which Hollywood's star system is acknowledged. This is a slow transition—by 1930, when we are presented with an almost Betty Boop, she is part dog. Continuing characters Happy Hooligan, Bobby Bumps, and Mutt and Jeff are a few more we'll meet—many shuffling out of the comic strip and into the movies and also a few created just for the screen. Familiarity mattered a great deal in the first days of animation, when finding an audience at an affordable price topped the bill: "Other cartoon characters derived from recognizable popular types drawn from popular theater, vaudeville, and folklore . . . [they] established a precedent of characters that were in circulation across a range of media."[5] The major names we'll come across will still include McCay and Bray, both carried over from the previous generation, but also an innovator who was introduced above and who both created and managed—Raoul Barré. Earl Hurd becomes an unlikely linchpin with his cel patent contributions and as the silent partner to Bray in the most powerful patent trust since the "Patent Trust."[6] We will also be introduced to some of the comic-strip artists who made the transition to film during this period, bringing their newspaper sensibilities with them. We will spend some time with three emerging studios of note in the years between Bray's first film and those of Felix and Koko, 1913 to 1919—Barré's and Bray's studios as well as Hearst's International Film Service (IFS).[7]

The first generation of American animation artists were born from comics, and they brought the comic-strip tradition with them. We've already met Blackton, McCay, and Bray, and there were many more. These early working animators and their creations were the subject of much interest, as indicated by a feature article written in 1917, listing the most noteworthy: Reuben Goldberg, Leon Searle, Frederick Opper, Wallace Carlson, Hy Mayer, Bud Fisher, and T. E. Powers.[8] Others included Sidney Smith, Frank Moser, Raoul Barré, Earl Hurd, Harry S. Palmer, Howard S. Moss, Willis O'Brien, Charles Bowers, Greg La Cava, Tony Sarg, and Herbert M. Dawley. "A large per cent of our most prominent fun-making cartoonists are either abandoning newspaper work in favor of animated pictures," a columnist wrote in 1917, "or are handling the two together."[9] The point here is there were *dozens* of comic-strip artists and animators making all kinds of films; it was likely a field day for exchanges, which could be quite picky given the excess, though the biggest names—from Carlson, Fisher, Powers, and Nolan to Barré, Hurd, Palmer, and Bowers—got the lion's share of the work.

The years 1913 and 1914 matter, given the activities of Barré (setting up the first assembly-line animation studio), McCay (creating *Gertie*), Hurd (quietly patenting the crucial cel process), and Bray, who was working through his "experimental period," seeing to the theatrical release and promotion of *Artist's Dream*, and writing up successful patent applications.[10] The new era of cartooning started in early January 1914, when Bray filed his first patent application.[11] And what a filing it was. Bray clearly wanted a portmanteau patent that could contain every aspect of animation, an "all-inclusive claim" drawing into its orbit every known (paper) animation process.[12] Just a little ironically (given Bray's intentions), by December 1914, Earl Hurd was filing his own application involving "transparent celluloid"—"probably the most basic and significant of the early animation patents."[13] Bray hadn't decided on the importance of celluloid until it was just too late. At this point, the requisite processes were in place (and in hand, for these two gentlemen) and the whistle could blow for animation as an industry. Bray was the ant to the others' grasshoppers, certainly, laying up for the future. The narrative across the years has involved Johnny-come-lately Bray sneaking hastily prepared applications 'neath the patent office door. That makes a good story, but, with seven months elapsing between Bray's first and second patent filings and then another full year passing before his third application was ready, painting him as furtive just doesn't hold up. (Hurd wasn't put off, filing his unique cel-process patent application between the times of submission of Bray's second and third applications.[14]) By the end of 1914, Bray and Hurd controlled most of the industry's processes, elevating animation from a "curiosity" to an "economically feasible" medium, and they were ready to begin licensing, yes, but also to produce their own cartoons and prove the merits of their patented processes.[15]

In 1914, Bray Studios Inc. managed to finish and release just five cartoons, including *Colonel Heeza Liar* titles; the following year, the studio produced thirty cartoons and, by 1916, forty.[16] The paper and then cel processes were the sure path to industrial success, but there were other ways to make things move. In the "one-time characters as protagonists"[17] area, ligatured-puppet animator Willis O'Brien and his *The Dinosaur and the Missing Link*, or Howard Moss's 1917 Motoy stop-motion work (and, slightly later, Sarg and Dawley's silhouette short subjects[18]) were discretely popular. O'Brien's work occupied a fascinating niche across the years; his work (with that of other special-effects colleagues) advanced animation and special effects for Hollywood feature films.[19] Just five years after a hand-drawn *Gertie* excited audiences, O'Brien's stop-motion dinosaurs in *The Ghosts of Slumber Mountain* amazed them. Bray and Hurd were striding into this new world, and we'll pause before engaging Raoul Barré and his studio saga.

In 1915, the war was going badly—zeppelin raids on England, the Gallipoli campaign, poison gas at Ypres—but for Americans the war was still "over there." Over here was cinema, the movies, transitioning from "flickering monstrosities" to effecting "the force of a whirlwind," a maelstrom in the form of Griffith's controversial epic *Birth of a Nation*.[20] Charlie Chaplin's "Little Tramp" character was also coming into full focus, 1915 being the year of his Essanay slate and rise to international fame. A young Cecil B. DeMille was experimenting with lighting for mood ("Lasky Lighting") in his boudoir-and-gavel drama *The Cheat*; not far away, Thomas Ince founded the modern Hollywood studio system in the California sunshine, making pictures as if they were factory products. The long and short of it—the movie theater was fast becoming the nexus not only of American entertainment but also of cultural and sociopolitical engagement.

The year 1915 was also a year of transition. McCay's demonstrated work (and then Bray's patents) up to but not including cel animation had set the stage. Barré's "slash" system allowed for limited layered work in paper (and sometimes glass) animation. At the next step, Bray created the background process to be separate from the layers of action, and Hurd's celluloid overlay system solved Barré's slash challenges, providing see-through layers of potential animation, and made possible the animating of only those parts that would move in a particular shot or scene, all separate from a background.[21] The process so far: Draw the least amount necessary, allow for rudimentary layers, paint one background and then reuse it, then place moving bits on layers separate from static bits, reducing workloads. Finally, add Barré and Nolan's ingenious peg system for dependable registration, and *voilà*, by January 1915, the "key elements" were in place for animation to leave the cottage and enter the factory.[22]

In 1915, Wallace Carlson started the Dreamy Dud series, as well as *Canimated Nooz*, both for Essanay; Hurd added Bobby Bumps titles for Bray Studios, distributed by Paramount. Hurd created Bobby "out of the inkwell," featuring the hand-of-the-artist image, a trope that had caught on quickly. In 1915, Max and Dave Fleischer were developing their rotoscope process (patent to be granted in 1917). When pitching the idea to Pathé, Max guessed that it would take a full year to finish even a short cartoon—he was told to come back when films could be made on a tight, production-friendly schedule.[23] Paul Terry—described in 1916 as "one of the foremost cartoonists in the motion picture industry"[24]—also accepted a position at Bray, though duress likely played a role. Mrs. Bray had visited Terry, offering a choice between an invoice or a cease-and-desist order (he was using their patented processes). Terry accepted a job, eventually producing Aesop's Fables titles for Bray. And he was good: "Paul Terry in 1916 did better quality work than Disney in 1922 (*Puss in Boots*) or 1925 (*Alice Cans the Cannibals*)," Smith attests, before admitting, "Disney later surpassed them all."[25] Never truly happy with Bray, Terry stayed less than a year. Paul Terry Productions formed in 1917 and was immediately successful before a wartime service hiatus.[26] By the end of this same year, Bray Studios had agreed to a new Paramount distribution deal and was set to deliver "a thousand feet of comedy every week."[27] The Bray and Hurd patents effectively refounded the animation industry on an industrial, assembly-line, and celluloid footing,[28] which would see it through the following decades and across both cinema and television. "Artistry-technology" had flipped to "technology-artistry."

Animation as a going concern was no certain thing in the years between Gertie and Felix the Cat—the world being in a state of war across most of the period—even though (and often because) its technology was vastly improving. Its most gifted practitioner, Winsor McCay, had faded across the years, his style not aligning with postwar modernism or gaunt Expressionism. Auschwitz would certainly change the arts forever thirty years later, but the Somme and Passchendaele were no day trips. McCay worked at a pace incompatible with anything other than his own needs. Additionally, McCay's full, rich designs and attentions to fantasy and detail were hard to draw and even harder to draw well and in repetition—most unforgivably, they didn't lend themselves to the paucity that would be industrial animation. "If it moved, it was good" wouldn't have gotten McCay out of bed in the morning by 1915. Simpler, smoother lines and rounder forms were more easily drawn by multiple hands along an assembly line of desks; depth of field and detailed backgrounds were expensive gewgaws; lateral movement meant a character could remain one size, even while walking, or, even better, could be made a *cutout* and only drawn once. Artists who took their first studio jobs in these early years, including Dick Huemer and later Shamus Culhane, weren't certain cartoons could survive such inattention, and it's likely that if the cartoons hadn't been bundled as part of a distribution program—if they'd been forced to live or die on their merits—they wouldn't have survived.[29] Exceptions might include the cartoons with benefits provided by a Canadian transplant.

RAOUL BARRÉ

In 1913, the Quebecois comic-strip artist and Paris-trained painter[30] Raoul Barré had also found himself on a cusp, much like McCay: "He was at the very source of 20th century consciousness, caught between traditional forms of expression and new means of production."[31] (Again, this also fits contemporary filmmakers like Blackton and Griffith.) Just two years after McCay's *Nemo* curiosity, Barré opened a more business-like, primarily paper-animation studio, an animation industry first.[32] Barré and William Nolan hired a staff and trained them in discrete tasks, to be able to draw like each other, and to do as little extra drawing as possible (and then photograph it two to four times). Andre Martin sums up Barré's influence on those who would come later: "Barré's early experiments prepared the way not only for the fables of Paul Terry, the Van Beuren Corporation, and the great Disney fantasy world, but also the paroxysms of Bob Clampett and Tex Avery. He spared nothing in his exploration of the world of imagination."[33] Barré is one of the animation artists whose reputation must reside on anecdotes from those who knew him and just a handful of the many cartoons he completed. Like Bray, Barré might be best remembered today for the nursery he provided to dozens of young artists.[34] Beyond Nolan, Barré's team included future live-action director Greg La Cava; also present were Frank Moser, Pat Sullivan (creator of Felix), and George "Vernon" Stallings.

The studio's maiden series, the *Animated Grouch Chasers*, didn't appear until March 1915 and was distributed by Edison.[35] The series featured animated inserts Silas Bunkum, the Kelly Kids, and Mr. Hicks within live-action frameworks, the cartoon portions very much inspired by earlier Emile Cohl cartoons.[36] And, while these films were made on the cheap and as fast as humanly possible, their creators weren't unaware of their surroundings and influences. In *Cartoons on Tour*,[37] the Silas Bunkum section featured a very Gertie-looking and Gertie-acting elephant—puckish and sensitive, swaying back and forth, leg to leg, and weeping when scolded.[38] This isn't an especially sloppy cartoon, but there is a moment on the beach when an onlooker appears for a second or so and then disappears—likely an accidental insertion (or removal) of a layer during photography. (Barré and Nolan's uninfringing "slash" paper process involved draping the background layer *on top* of the foreground drawings, holes cut strategically to allow the moving images below to be visible. Most studios used this system rather than license with Bray-Hurd, at least for a time.[39]) Moments later, when a sleeping farmer lifts an infant from his lap, the child flails his legs, each movement coinciding with the disappearance of the grass beneath him—it's there and then gone. It would have been the tracer's job (where Huemer started with Barré) to make sure those lines were redrawn on every frame: "Sometimes, an element of the background, the line of the horizon or of the floor, or of a door opening, had to be redrawn around the character at every phase of animation."[40] Or not. Neither glitch makes or breaks the cartoon—such gaffes are indications of the speed necessary to get the finished titles out the door and the complete unwillingness to reshoot anything.

Barré had made the move to New York in 1903 and eventually partnered with Nolan around 1912. Barré and Nolan improved on existing registration techniques by creating the peg system, and the studio introduced the "slash system" (sometimes called the "slash and tear system"), which saved time and energy by separating (on layered paper/cels) arms, legs, or any moving body part.[41] Their decision to animate using paper as opposed to celluloid might seem either an economic choice (wanting or needing to avoid a license fee) or just abject stubbornness about paying for what had been common practice. But it also could have been an artistic choice. Barré continued to use paper, not cels, as his medium, preferring the look: "Barré, and later on Sullivan, deliberately continued to draw on paper," Martin notes. "They wanted to preserve the qualities of contrast and graphic simplification required by this approach."[42] This lines up, artistically, with the choice made by the New York–based studios, especially Terry, Charles Bowers, the Fleischers, and Messmer, in the 1920s and 1930s to hold on to the more line-based, graphic style in the face of competitor Disney's more cinematic approach.[43]

There were identifiable speed bumps along Barré's path that afflicted many in the animation industry, including later greats like Ub Iwerks: running a business isn't for everyone, and effective storytelling is more rare than common. For Barré and Nolan, gag after gag carried the earliest cartoons, with scenes connected only by a recognized character or background; however, this approach couldn't possibly keep audience attention forever. Like many artists coming from the comics, Barré tended to prioritize gags over story and employed "riffing" in virtually every scene, a "glorious primitivism."[44] (Charlie Chaplin was also partway through his influential Essanay run by this time, and his oft-copied character riffed through scenes regularly.) Toward the end of Barré's (or Nolan's) Happy Hooligan title *The Spider and the Fly*, a character crawls from a hole (an exit from Hell) and produces, like a magician, a cartoony anarchist's bomb. He then performs all sorts of prestidigitation with the bomb, which then turns into a golf club and ball. After taking a swing (the ball plunking a passing demon), the club becomes a bomb again, which Barré leaves for Happy Hooligan to find before jumping back into Hell. It's a fun set piece that makes little sense and goes nowhere.[45]

According to Huemer, Barré began offering art classes to his animators in 1916, trying to improve the studio's output.[46] (Story improvements—storyboards or a dedicated story department—were still years away.) But this fledgling studio did bring in quite a bit of work. Barré would animate part of the Phables series, and then the high-profile Mutt and Jeff[47] work came along. Barré would partner with Charles Bowers in 1916, and, according to the scant surviving evidence of their cartoons, it seems they could have been quite a team. *Domestic Difficulties* (1916) features a typical Mutt and Jeff situation—slipping away from the wife for a tipple—but the sequence after they emerge from the bar is priceless. The boys have "collect[ed] a healthy 'bun,'"[48] as a contemporary review calls it—meaning they're drunk—and, as they stumble home, the street and world begin to swirl around them, a remarkable, novel twist on the "head spinning" trope. Nolan had worked out this background-panning process earlier, and it's put to memorable use here. The boys even bet which of the streetlights spinning around them will win the "race."

Barré, Bowers, and Nolan often provided the polished gem in what otherwise might be the tailings pile of midwar animation. A case in point from 1916, two years after *Gertie* and two years before *Lusitania*, was that of Professor Bonehead, who likely was planned to be a continuing character for Harry S. Palmer's studio. Bonehead[49] is being chased by a duck-billed version of himself, then cannibals, and then a bear. There are long moments when cutout versions of all concerned are used, rolling or flying or sliding across a still pen-and-ink background. This Palmer cartoon (that borrows liberally from existing Colonel Heeza Liar settings and events) is an amazing mess of accomplished wave-action animation, cycling to save money and drawings wherever possible, and jerky, poorly timed cutout animation. Like many of his fellows, Bonehead emerges from an inkwell—this was the time of "[t]he stars who live in inkwells"[50]—before the inexplicable mayhem begins. Still, there is an interesting shot where the cutout character, flying into the distance, clearly changes sizes, becoming smaller and smaller; this and the immaculate waves are outliers in a cartoon that looks like it was animated by several (much less experienced) hands, scene by scene.[51] What's most obvious is the segregation of the action, with scenes parsed out to individual animators with different styles and levels of expertise. (Remember, both Barré/Nolan and Bray tended to hire and train for particular tasks, at least attempting to maintain a level of continuity across individual cartoons and even series. There is no indication of such an effort here.) A section that simply features the Professor being chased by his birdlike opposite, legs spinning, left to right in front of the moving background, reads just like an animation-school exercise in which the assignment is to get the object or figure from one side to the other in the allotted seconds or frames.[52] Walter Lantz, who as a very young man worked under La Cava at Hearst's IFS, underscores this assumption: "I'd just animate a scene, and say to [Bill] Nolan . . . 'I'm taking 'em up from the left and you pick 'em up from there.' And he'd animated a scene and tell the next animator, 'I'm taking 'em out from the right and you pick up the action from there.'"[53] The work that would be done at IFS under La Cava and

Nolan was generally better realized than this *Mr. Bonehead* scene, to be sure, and often better still when Barré and Nolan had been together, but seat-of-the-pants work was widespread. Budgets and profit margins were modest. At Barré's studio, Huemer remembers having no storyboards, no character models, and scant story suggestions: "You made it up as you went along. You were given a part of the picture and you did what you wanted."[54] Any time- or labor-saving device, including stillness, was worth trying. There's a moment when Bonehead stands on the beach, having survived the waves, clutching an oversized egg. The waves are moving wildly in the background, and most other lines are also wiggling (likely a registration problem), when everything freezes—for almost three seconds, the same image has been photographed, a prolonged "hold," maybe forty frames, as Bonehead stares at the egg, wondering what to make of it. A few dollars saved before the action resumes. Some studios were trying to compete not only commercially, like Palmer's, but also artistically, like Barré and even Bray; others were simply trying to fulfill distribution contracts.

With Hearst storming the palace as he created IFS, Barré lost his animation team, including Nolan, in 1916. Charlie Bowers brought a much-needed Mutt and Jeff contract to the bereft Barré Studio, and things looked good—the Barré-Bowers Studio emerged. In a nonworking way, the famous cartoonist himself, Bud Fisher, was brought into the studio—a coup for Barré. Elsewhere, Fisher's name sold newspapers and helped get distribution and merchandising deals signed, and, as far as the public knew, he drew every bit of the cartoons featuring his characters. (He didn't. Animator Isadore Klein remembers Fisher's visits to the studio as "infrequent."[55]) But the real coup was yet to come. Fisher and Bowers would eventually force Barré out of his own studio, and fireworks ensued. After completing the shakeup, at some point Bowers rushed into the studio offices and announced, "Raoul Barré has cracked up . . . he's gone crazy this afternoon . . . he is on his way up here to wreck the studio and to shoot me dead!" Apparently, the police would get to Barré before any threat could be carried out. Things calmed, but they were never the same for Barré. The Bud Fisher Studio operated for a few more years under Bowers, and then Bowers was fired for allegedly cooking the payroll books.[56]

As cheaply made as they had to be across this 1913–1919 period, some of the cartoons still show signs of care and artistic attention. There were scores of Mutt and Jeff cartoons produced from sometimes as many as four separate studios beginning in this period.[57] Quality and creativity varied widely, but there are moments. In the 1916 title *Cramps*, Jeff wakes with a stomachache and Mutt determines to rustle up a tincture. Most of the cartoon is as simple as possible—bare rooms, black lines and white space, stillness, plenty of cycling. A few sweet bits stand out from the bland. When Mutt says he's going downstairs to the doctor's, he heads out the window, and the scene cuts to an exterior shot of the brownstone with fire escape and landings. Mutt walks across the landing and then clambers down the ladder/stairs and crawls into the window below. This additional set of drawings and frames could have justifiably been excised (i.e., Mutt exits the apartment window, cut to Mutt entering the window below—classic Hollywood cinema editing). But no—the transition from set to set is included. Second, as Mutt climbs through the lower window there is a cut to a mostly darkened scene, likely masked. The darkness disappears to reveal Mutt has tugged on an overhead light-bulb string, illuminating the space. Even more intriguing, once Mutt is finished mixing the "medicine" for Jeff, he tugs on the string and the light goes out, leaving just the silhouettes of Mutt and the rest of the room. In silhouette, Mutt grabs the medicine bottle and heads back to the window. These more-complicated-than-strictly-necessary steps are repeated when Mutt returns for another batch of elixir. To top it off, there is even a short pan when Mutt carries Jeff to a chair in their apartment. The balance of the film involves no camera movement, no resizing of characters as they approach or move farther away from the camera, and no movement on most insert shots. The animation process was now much faster, more productive, and "severely diluted," but clever turns could still be found.[58]

And then there was IFS. Since print baron Hearst was already supplementing, to a certain extent, his comic-strip artist's vaudeville and animation aspirations, and since Hearst himself was infatuated with the movies, his venture into animation mightn't have been a surprise.

A newspaper-owned cartoon studio, IFS was set up exclusively to exploit the emerging popularity of animation in relation to the properties Hearst already controlled, meaning he saw a way to sell more newspapers. *Krazy Kat, Happy Hooligan*, and *Bringing Up Father* were some of the popular strips made into animated series, many supervised by La Cava, who had been odd jobbing for Barré.[59] (Bray's studio contributed some of these cartoons to IFS as well.) Animated adaptations of *Jerry on the Job, The Katzenjammer Kids, Tad's Indoor Sports*, and *Judge Rummy* also wowed audiences for a handful of years.[60] Associated with these cartoons were some industry stalwarts: La Cava, Grim Natwick, Bill Nolan, Frank Moser, John Foster, Jack King, Leon Searle, and Walter Lantz.[61] Hype, where Hearst truly excelled, was in no short supply: "The International Film Service Animated Cartoons have broken all booking records," proclaimed one ad. "They are the most popular cartoons on the market today because 20 million people daily see them," and so forth.[62] Hearst paid well, and La Cava was able to bring in an impressive animation team. Mighty Mouse creator Isadore Klein started as a tracer at IFS, hired by La Cava; Nolan and many others came over. Not surprisingly, none of the original comic-strip artists performed any of the animation. Hundreds of (largely interchangeable) cartoons followed across the three years IFS thrived: "Like the other products of other great industries this one appears to tend more toward standardization than toward differentiation," Bragdon would write in 1934. "Animated cartoons are in their elements so much alike that they may be generalized."[63] Before being subsumed into a new Bray Pictures Corporation after Bray left Paramount in 1919, IFS was providing dozens of these films.

Hearst's own compulsions (and competition with Bray) helped sour the IFS experiment. Confusing, nasty disagreements ensued over who owned *The Katzenjammer Kids*, over Hearst's political views, and eventually over the ineffectiveness of using cartoons to sell newspapers. By June 1918, Hearst's IFS shuttered operations, and young animators like Klein were unemployed. Klein would head to Barré-Bowers, and, thanks to his experience at IFS, he was hired as an odd-job man with chances to animate on occasion.[64]

Nolan and assistants employed single-source lighting in this infernal setting, an unusual and more expensive attention to detail during an assembly-line era. *The Spider and the Fly*, Bill Nolan, 1918 (YouTube). Screenshot taken by the author.

It wasn't a completely uninfluential period, either. While at IFS, Nolan (and perhaps young Lantz) managed to create a rather thrilling scene toward the end of an otherwise unremarkable IFS Happy Hooligan title, *The Spider and the Fly*. When Happy has been thrown from Heaven for refusing to work, he plunges through the earth to Hell. His "Reception Committee" (demons with pitchforks) jabs him upward again.[65] He lands in a room unlike anything else in the cartoon—a chiaroscuro grotto with a single fiery furnace light source, presenting a scene from an El Greco, a Belasco play, or a Lasky-lit film. Hap enjoys the mesmerizing flames for a moment before a devil with a pitchfork enters and demands he start work chopping wood. He refuses, is poked for his refusal, and escapes when the devil wanders away. The cartoon doesn't make much sense (and is likely incomplete), but the Rembrandt lighting is pleasantly surprising and took much extra work, which was worthwhile. These unusual Barré and Nolan scenes are prescient: "[T]he nightmarish visits to hell . . . set the stage for all the scenes of burlesque and controlled excess which would be the hallmark of American animated film for the next fifty years."[66] It certainly prepares us for Betty, Bimbo, and Koko visiting various infernos; the nightmarish sequences in *Snow White*, *Pinocchio*, and *Dumbo*; Porky's glutton nightmares; *Fantasia*'s demons; and the many, many times Axis figures (and especially Hitler) would find themselves thrust into Hell by all cartoon makers across the next world war.

In retrospect, some of the cartoons emerging from Barré and Nolan, though clumsy and seemingly careless, still have the feeling and appearance of straight animation, where the artist draws entire scenes or routines without relying on the Tayloristic rigidity of Bray et al. Martin sees all this positively and as directly opposing what Bray and others were doing elsewhere—hewing close to their "typographical sources"—describing the Barré Studio style as offering "a caricatural tone, inventive burlesque, and carefree animation."[67] And there's more: "At that time, the drawings done by animators were filmed directly without first being traced, recopied or complemented by assistants."[68] This might be due to the freedoms allowed by the paper process, or it might have just suited these artists. Period how-to manuals insisted on reducing every unnecessary movement or line, including using as few characters as possible, and shooting on the twos and threes at the least, all "to bring down the cost of production to where it will be commercially profitable."[69] The sparse pen-and-ink style ruled the day, which is why Bobby Bumps, Dreamy Dud, *Keeping Up with the Joneses*, Mutt and Jeff, and the Phables series all resemble one another. Most look like nothing more than slightly moving comic strips, including gaze lines, thought and speech balloons, printed sound effects, sound-effect and speed lines or symbols, stars to indicate pain or a knock on the head, steam from the mouth or ears, and so on. This all was certainly familiar, and therefore recognizable to newspaper-reading audiences, and perhaps not risky in the least.

Finally, Barré was able to own and run his own studio for several years before teaming with the multitalented Bowers[70] in Barré-Bowers Studio. As the war was coming to an end, there were "at least a dozen studios operating in [New York City]."[71] Like most concerns of this period, none of these studios lasted into the sound era, though some of the characters did.[72] Barré would leave animation by the following year "to become a commercial artist," according to Klein's memory.[73] In truth, Barré did semiretire between about 1919 and 1926—to "painting and illustration" in the countryside[74]—and then returned to the city to work for Sullivan on the Felix series.

BRAY-HURD

While Barré sputtered, Bray's operation was hitting its stride, its *Colonel Heeza Liar* cartoons illustrating "a remarkable sense of both economy of drawing and promotion of the Bray studio." Further, the "promotion of the Bray cartoons through the cartoon medium shows a sense of promotion of a medium through itself equalled only by the self-congratulatory [efforts] of [modern] television networks."[75] Bray was being profiled in newspapers, magazines, and trade organs, and, by April 1916, he was still claiming that he himself was producing all background materials, writing all stories, and drawing "most of the movements." He finished by reminding the interviewer that he also invented the camera that photographs each frame.[76] Control does seem to have played a large part in Bray's success as a studio head—success that may have eluded others like Barré. Bray had an unusual ability to control (or maybe just be closely aware of) every aspect of the process, from raising capital through distribution and every bit of the cartoon making in between. Bray was also likely aware of the movie studios' working practices, especially those that dealt with serials and genre pictures, where streamlined production and hyperefficient marketing made all the difference for smaller films playing lower on the bill. Those studios, and Hollywood in general, thrived thanks to the success of "B" pictures and development of the production model required to make them affordably. Bray's cartoons don't tend to be as inventive or grotesquely watchable as those from McCay, Barré, or Nolan, but they're certainly accomplished and reliable. Solomon sums up two of these pioneers well: "Raoul Barré established the first animation studio, but John Randolph Bray organized the first animation factory."[77]

And, from the earliest days, Bray was thinking about every application of film, not just short-subject entertainments or even just animation. Seeing an opportunity during a time of war, in 1916, Bray began producing army training films for the new conscript-based ranks. (Max Fleischer was also working for Bray by this time after pitching an "Out of the Ink-well" idea and then spending some of his time in military service creating training films.[78]) The Paramount-Bray Pictographs—"The Magazine on the Screen"—brought news to life, from the war fronts to foreign vistas to human-interest stories back home. Bray was already moving from a focus on cartoons to film of all kinds, including scores of educational films meant for public schools and training programs. By 1919, Bray left distributor Paramount for Sam Goldwyn and Bray Pictures Corp., which became Goldwyn-Bray Pictograph. Bray and company were producing dozens of titles annually, for entertainment, training, and education, but profit margins were always thin. Goldwyn bought a controlling interest in Bray's studio, and, when the acquisition underperformed, Goldwyn would act on that leverage, completely reorganizing the company, stream-lining everything. Many longtime Bray artists like Hurd departed; Max Fleischer went off to start his own studio.

This reorganization was apocalyptic, but in the revelatory sense. Inklings of the next generation were appearing by 1919. Max and Dave Fleischer, who had been experimenting with their rotoscope device and clown character[79] with Bray, produced *The Clown's Pup*, starring both the unnamed clown and the fluid rotoscope process. The second and even bigger star in the still darkened firmament came from Pat Sulli-van's efforts, originally, and then Otto Messmer's talent over the long haul: Felix the Cat. Paramount Magazine's *Feline Follies* introduced the character who would become Felix. And while Sullivan's name was on every cartoon, the cat's provenance is clear: "It was Messmer who came up with the cat, devised the adventures he experiences, directed the films, and did most of the animation."[80] Messmer had been working on Hy Mayer and war-related cartoons, with Sullivan for Charlie Chaplin titles, one-offs, and Little Black Sambo knockoffs before landing Felix. The Felix animated character would carry Messmer well into the 1930s, and then beyond; he was artist for the Felix comic strip and comic books until his retirement in 1954.

We'll dip a toe into 1920 here before diving headlong in the next chapter. Bray's *The Debut of Thomas Cat*—the first color cartoon attempted for theatrical distribution and produced using the Brewster Color process—appeared. As Solomon notes, there was little reaction to this breakthrough, even in the trades.[81] In *Moving Picture Age*'s "Films and Where to Get Them," blocks of exchange films are discussed. The Bray Studios Goldwyn reel is the last item on the bill (where the cartoon often found itself) and is quietly announced as "The world's first color cartoon, *The Debut of Thomas Cat*." (On that same page, for the Bray Pictograph No. 426, first reel, the cartoon is listed as being "cut."[82] One damned by faint praise, one just damned.) In *Wid's Filmdom*, there's a bit more notice: "*The Debut of Thomas Cat*, announced as the world's first color cartoon on a caption, closes and is out of the ordinary and should go well in houses attended by youngsters. The coloring has been done fairly well and adds value."[83] The cost of this additional process couldn't be justified in relation to what distributors were willing to pay—it didn't add *that* much value. Cartoons still found themselves at the snippable end of the reel.

Color cartoons wouldn't become coin of the realm until Disney mortgaged the realm and spent the coin in 1932. By that time, the cartoon industry had blossomed to such a degree that Disney could afford to be in debt and lose money as he spent more from title to title. In 1919, that kind of security didn't exist, but a clown, a cat, a failed Kansas City studio, and dozens of fables promised a brighter future.

CHAPTER 3

A Cat, a Clown, and Some Fables

WITHOUT THE BENEFIT OF A "BLOCK" OF FILMS SENT THROUGH exchanges in the 1910s, there likely would have been no cartoon industry beyond performer McCay and tradesman Bray. Against the odds, an East Coast movement would reach and hold audiences drawn to the popular comic-strip tradition and aesthetic, "a style of black and white animation, typical of the New York School [that] always remained close to the graphic and typographic tradition which inspired it . . . pen and ink and the hand of the artisan played the major roles."[1] Again, we begin with a three-plus-one—Fleischer, Sullivan, and Terry, offering Koko, Felix, and the Fables. It was purely accidental, but, between about 1919 and 1928, these were the studios and the characters at the leading edge of animation. The plus-one was J. R. Bray, still making cartoons across the decade, though his heart and energies were elsewhere. The West Coast outlier Disney was on the rise, but fitfully, finding an Alice here and losing an Oswald there—eventually a mouse would save him. Pen and ink and the visible hand of the artists would create both Koko and Felix in these early days.

The 1920s would begin to see a demand forming for cartoons—in the early years of the decade, Terry's product was as well reviewed and well received as Fleischers' or Sullivan's—thanks primarily to two very different approaches we can call the star and the stolid. The "star" part involved two studios producing cartoons that became star vehicles for a clown and a cat. Soon, the cat was a worldwide phenomenon—"[Felix] becomes the impossible in cats, the unreal in man"[2]—while Koko more than held his own until Betty Boop could arrive a decade later (and Popeye just after that). Like Chaplin, Koko and Felix used their bodies, their wits, and the world around them—creatively, in their case surrealistically—to accomplish their ends. The "stolid" part was the reliability of Paul Terry's Fables Studio and its ever-so-adequate stream of programmable cartoons. The star and stolid approaches propelled cartoons into cinemas and audiences' hearts. Fairly cheap short subjects like these began to prove themselves—exhibitors reported positive reviews. And if you measure success by the dollar, then Terry led the way. The creators of Farmer Al Falfa and the menagerie of the Fables didn't regularly experiment, instead finishing scores of cartoons on time and on budget. The Keith-Albee theatrical circuit "agreed to underwrite the studio's expenses and guarantee bookings"—Terry's cartoons were being screened in hundreds of key theaters around the country, and Terry took a tithe on it all.[3] It's no wonder a young Disney and his colleagues—struggling to make ends meet on ad scraps in Kansas City—would look to Terry and the Fables for inspiration.[4]

The idea of a cartoon in a night's package that kept cinemagoers in their seats *through* the lights-up was a new one—the clever and attractive cartoons of the 1920s became a reason to attend the cinema in the first place, and this was before Mickey whistled a note. Once chasers, some cartoons now beckoned audiences.[5] Just four months after Felix appeared in *Feline Follies*, the die was cast: "Sullivan's cat, Felix, is one of the best known characters of the motion-picture comics, and its antics have had a record run at leading houses throughout the country."[6] This was also the period when the animators began to fade from view, naturally, as their popular characters stepped into the spotlight; Crafton sees the shift from animators appearing in their films to the characters taking center stage as the shift from the importance of the artist to the importance of the work. The animator was "retreating" as human and animal characters rose to stardom. Blackton and McCay appeared "in person" and then simply as the godlike hand and pen of the artist. "The 'hand of the artist' [then] disappears, its place now occupied by characters who become agents of his will and ideas and through which his presence is known. They are his amanuensis."[7]

In the adolescent days of animation as industry, it was Felix the Cat, Koko the Clown, and Aesop's Fables animals who starred in the most popular cartoons. Precocious little boy characters had had their day already—Felix, Koko, and the "sugar-coated-pills-of-wisdom" stampede were slowly seeing off Bobby Bumps, Dreamy Dud, and the Katzenjammers, as well as Judge Rummy, Happy Hooligan, and Mutt and Jeff. Some of the more popular silent cartoons that had emerged from the newspaper comic pages did endure across the Jazz Age and into the Sound Era; however, not many survived and not as their old selves.[8] In the early 1920s, there were no zany antics coming from Porky or Daffy, or Tom or Jerry, and a young Walt Disney was producing a handful of fairy-tale adaptations that few would see and no one would want to buy. Otto Messmer and pals drew the Felix and Charlie Chaplin cartoons, and Max and Dave Fleischer saw to Koko and then Fitz the Pup. Both Fleischer and Sullivan operations were settled comfortably in New York, at a time when the major film studios' management offices and dealmakers were also in the city.[9] Everything was working well and about to get even better.

MAX AND DAVE FLEISCHER

Max Fleischer was a man of many talents and interests. He was a gifted artist, technical illustrator, mechanical draftsman, and cartoonist—Bray had met him while they were both at the *Brooklyn Eagle*. Fleischer was also a fiction writer and an inventor (with twenty-five film and animation patents), and his science interests led him to create films about the earth's history and Darwin's and Einstein's work and theories. He brought sound to cartoons as early as 1924.[10] His studio's original characters, Koko and Betty Boop, were stars across the 1920s and 1930s; his Popeye and Superman titles were popular with audiences and exhibitors. Fleischer was at the heights of the animation and even short-subject industries from the 1920s through the early part of the 1940s. It was a nasty combination of labor unrest, a demand for costly distributor security, a removal to Miami, a need to make expensive feature films to compete with a rival, and corrosive sibling rancor that would eventually doom Fleischer Studios, but that's for another chapter.

Max had trained in the newspapers and then the bustling Bray studio, hired by technophile Bray on the promise of Max's rotoscope process. (Max would become supervising animator when, in 1916, Paul Terry left to form his own company with Amedee Van Beuren, perhaps planting a seed in Max's mind.[11]) Max and his family would spend a full year making the first clown cartoon, starring his brother Dave in the costume, and then find ways (by 1918) to streamline the laborious process so that one Out of the Inkwell cartoon per month was possible. These were clever live-action films with animated inserts and interactions (meaning they lent themselves to easier production), Dave directing the live bits and acting the clown role, Max starring as the genial animator, and Roland "Doc" Crandall assisting with the animation. The shorts demonstrated "artistic ingenuity" and were "quite original in [their] manner of presentation," and audiences immediately asked for more.[12] Part of this originality was borrowed. From the earliest iterations, the Fleischer gag men and animators were influenced by surreality, by the stuff of nightmares, with movement and metamorphosis becoming their works' constitutive elements.[13] Mark Langer identifies the two immediate benefits of the rotoscope process: "The Fleischers reveled in the freedom their invention gave them, keeping their silent cartoons in almost constant motion." Second, "[m]any things in the film change their shape and properties," not just position—"These constant transformations run throughout the Fleischer silents."[14] In this sense, they were reaching back a few years to the imported work of Cohl as well as to the work of McCay, especially his *Nemo* comic-strip world. The Fleischers' *Bubbles* (1922) offers images that resemble Cohl's Incoherent-inspired *Hasher's Delirium*, which also features a live-action opening sequence to set up the nightmarish cartoon. (In *Bubbles*, instead of a Little Hasher [a waiter], we watch the Little Clown as he is manipulated by the artist's hand.) Rather than using traditional editing (cutting and splicing to piece together a scene or film), artists who employ metamorphosis can draw their characters or worlds from frame to frame and then scene to scene, achieving "the highest degree of economy in narrative continuity" as it connects "apparently unrelated images" and disrupts "established notions of classical story-telling."[15] In *Bubbles*, the clown blows a bubble and, mimicking

Cohl's scenario, first sees his own reflection, which morphs into a devil's face, which becomes a beautiful woman's face, and, when the clown tries to kiss her, she becomes an ape. The clown then pops the bubble. In 1909–1910, Cohl had also utilized line drawing, cutouts, and extant illustrations and photos repurposed for his scenes of metamorphosis. The Fleischer operation borrowed these inspirations and more.

Going forward, the Fleischers would employ metamorphosis much, much more than Disney (see the Fleischers' version of *Snow-White* versus Disney's *Snow White and the Seven Dwarfs*). As Paul Wells reminds us, the Fleischers' use of metamorphosis for both surreal and "sinister" narrative purposes heralded a "modernity" in animation, going beyond metamorphosis for storytelling purposes and toward a way to construct "dark humor and sensual fantasy."[16] Tex Avery would employ it, as would UPA

In *Bubbles*, Koko's more realistic rotoscoped image encounters the surreal, Emile Cohl–inspired images of a demon, an ape, and here a beautiful maiden. *Bubbles*, Max and Dave Fleischer, 1921 (from *Max Fleischer's Famous Out of the Inkwell* DVD). Screenshot taken by the author.

animators, both seeking ways to define themselves against the homogenous, more cinematic Disney product of their time. Metamorphosis—allowing a constant sense of "becoming" rather than "being"—was picked up by experimental and advertising animation, non-US animators, and, to many, like the Canadian National Film Board's Norman McLaren, metamorphosis *is* the essential core of animation.[17]

After a stint in the military, making training films during the Great War, Max was a big part of the Goldwyn-controlled retrofitting of Bray's company. The Bray Pictures Corporation would, they said, "develop fully the educational and industrial fields" of film as well as films for entertainment.[18] In 1919–1920, the Fleischer name was appearing in relation to "clown" and educational pictures, including science shorts *The Mysteries of Snow*, *All Aboard for the Moon*, and *Hello Mars*. But working for Bray wasn't the Fleischers' endgame. The success of their very own Out of the Inkwell idea and character set them on a new course, and they left Bray in 1921. By October 1921, newly incorporated Out-of-the-Inkwell Films titles were being distributed around the country,[19] and Fleischer's "exceedingly clever"[20] cartoons were being lauded and programmed by Hugo Riesenfeld and Sid Grauman, two of the most important circuit names in the country. The Fleischer studio would be modeled after Bray's, not surprisingly, with intentions to make diverse cartoon and live-action products and to cater to the theatrical experience as well as to science and education. The uniqueness of their traced rotoscoped images attracted audience and exhibitor attention, setting them apart from all other studios' titles and styles, reaching back across the jerky, economy version of animation to the more fluid drawing style of McCay. Control clearly mattered, but so did artistry: "The Fleischers' silent films have a strong improvisational character, the result in part of the seemingly off-hand manner in which they were made," Harvey Deneroff writes, "with a loose gag structure—which Disney eschewed in favor of more careful plotting and acting—that allowed the animators a great deal of freedom."[21]

The new studio was initially successful[22] and quickly moved to better quarters and set up Red Seal, the film distribution company that Disney would envy. With Red Seal, the Fleischers could produce, market, and distribute their product; its structure was a balanced triangle—with production at the apex, the others anchoring—thus achieving control Disney wouldn't enjoy until the mid-1950s.[23] Out-of-the-Inkwell and Red Seal provided the one-two punch of creating *and* distributing "live-action serials, comedy shorts, scientific documentaries" and "Song Car-Tunes" (bouncing ball sing-alongs[24]), using either the De Forest Phonofilm sound system or a live orchestra.[25] It was also announced that Red Seal would focus on shorter novelty pictures alone, including mostly comedic cartoons, Song Car-Tunes, and *Animated Hair* lightning-sketch shorts from Marcus.[26] "Your Ko-Ko Song Car-Tunes and Out-of-the-Inkwell subjects have struck a responsive chord in our audiences that spells satisfaction," the Brooklyn Strand Theater director wrote to Red Seal. "They are novel and altogether entertaining."[27] Dick Huemer was hired on to Red Seal in 1923; Crandall and Burt Gillett were already there. When Red Seal began handling Fleischer titles, Disney was still having to distribute via states' rights through Winkler and her husband, Charles Mintz (see chapter 4 for more information about the states'-rights approach). This ambitious Red Seal distribution scheme included experienced distributor Edwin Fadiman,[28] De Forest as the sound-on-film process owner, and Riesenfeld.[29] And, even though these novelty packages from Red Seal were taking theaters by storm, producer Fadiman was already sounding the alarm about costs being high when compared with what exhibitors were willing to pay for short subjects. In an "editorial" piece, Fadiman bemoaned the $22.50 per week paid for a shorts package, while features might command $5,000 for the week.[30] This would be a plaintive hymn sung again and again over the years.

By 1926, the cost of doing shorts in what was largely a feature world spiraled. Fadiman and Max feuded over title credits, and Fadiman quit. In April, Red Seal sued its former president for illegally drawing funds just before his departure; Fadiman countersued, alleging misuse of funds by Max, Hugo, and others.[31] In between these filings, Max was touting Red Seal's expansion into new exchanges, and Koko merchandising and publicity stunts were everywhere. Trouble still loomed. In July, *Variety* reported that a glut of short subjects, mostly comedies, were being shopped nationwide and estimated that more than a thousand[32] would be available before 1927. By fall 1926, it came to light that Red Seal owed money to other shorts companies, to a bank, and to Max's lawyer, as well as to themselves in the form of back salaries and personal loans to the company—Red Seal was dragged into receivership proceedings. A film-processing lab was holding processed Red Seal films until all payments were brought up to date. Without those films, the Fleischers argued, no money could come into the studio.

Through all this hoopla, Koko continued to be well reviewed and a popular draw, followed by the Song Car-Tunes, which, since they employed older songs, were characterized as nostalgic, safe, and benignly popular. The Fleischers' version of Red Seal had collapsed under its own weight, and Out-of-the-Inkwell would soon follow, only to be briefly rescued by Paramount and what seemed to be an angel investor, Alfred Weiss, in November 1926. Weiss paid off the studio's debts (meaning he technically owned the unreleased prints from the processing lab), took the title of president (of Inkwell *and* Red Seal), and "hired" Max and Dave, but then he became more of an asset stripper, nudging the Fleischers out of their own company. He was eventually sued and beaten by the brothers; the Paramount relationship became even more important.[33] Koko would appear in the Weiss-named "Inkwell Imps" series in 1927, when Max and Dave signed a bright new contract with Paramount, their distributor until 1942. Their financial straits were such that they had to agree to give Paramount 51 percent control of the company and rights to all the cartoons they created, and they essentially became employees. Paramount came back into shorts in a big way in 1927, announcing two series from Fleischer and a Krazy Kat series from Winkler.[34] Fleischer Studios was created in April 1929, after months of unemployment and legal tangles. Sound was also key, Song Car-Tunes eventually giving way to Paramount's Screen Songs (using the same sing-along technology[35]) and then the Fleischers' Talkartoons, where Betty would be introduced in August 1930.

FELIX THE CAT

But before the Fleischer characters make utterance, we need to spend some time with a character who manages to have it both ways—social and alone, animal and human, domesticated and feral. (One binary escaped him, as we'll see later—he could not be mute and then talk.) He was, on day one, simply a cartoon cat surrounded by other cats in a traditional neighborhood—he even seems to have a home, which mice gleefully ruin for him when he's out trysting. The unnamed cat was also part of a largely conservative, recognizably safe pen-and-ink universe and industry, where anomalous entries tended to wither and die, and those that could do the most with the least had a chance to flourish. (This is where Otto Messmer, the good artist and great scenarist, becomes singularly important.) Ironically, this individualist cat was created for a one-off cartoon with the desired goal being a long-term distribution deal—the Cat who always walks from frame to frame and from film to film. In many cartoons, including in his debut, *Feline Follies*, Felix is "kept" by someone, attached to human care, but still manages to be his own cat. He wasn't the industry's first cat, and his success would spawn litters of lessers. But Felix was also part of the handful of role players given the approving nod by industry outsiders—A. A. Milne disliked most cinema but ranked Felix alongside Chaplin and Lloyd.[36]

Felix might have been inspired, as Sullivan and Messmer and many voices after attested, by Kipling's inscrutable Cat. (One can imagine the hoots heard in the Messmer bullpen if *that* approach was pitched.) It's more likely that Sullivan was looking for a distributable character and Messmer wanted a character that could maintain his interest. Rather than looking for a cultural metaphor, they were looking for a cat. And Messmer's pen-in-hand contributions (beyond what critics will find in upriver readings of Felix history, looking for his heart of art-ness) are encapsulated by film theorist Bela Balazs, writing of Felix, "In the world of creatures consisting only of lines the only impossible things are those which cannot be drawn."[37] Messmer could draw the needed lines: "[Messmer's] figures moved from all angles, sometimes a bit painfully, and they had the beginnings of perspective and individual character."[38] Felix arrived without name or scrip; he earned everything, he kept nothing, his personality provided by Messmer—he became the inner child personified and soon the most popular and recognized cartoon character in the world.

Felix cocreator Pat Sullivan hailed from Australia, seeing a bit of the world and life before finding his way to New York. Otto Messmer grew up near Hollywood East—Fort Lee, New Jersey—and was enamored of film from an early age. Messmer teamed with Sullivan in that magical year 1915, when the cartoons were first being made on factory floors. Sullivan borrowed from the extant Little Black Sambo character to create the "Sammie Johnsin" series—unassuming knockoff cartoons distributed by Universal. Sammie was a derivation of the "little Negro boy" or "picka-ninny" caricature popular in minstrelsy, comics, and other cartoons of the period. These include Bobby's pal in *Bobby Bumps Starts a Lodge*, as well as the entire little boys' opposing baseball team in *Felix Saves the Day*. These were popular caricatures from which audiences expected music, mime, and mischief. With the appearance of the popular Felix, these caricatures "established the link between character design and African American caricature," one historian writes. "In the 1920s blackface design was a cash cow for studios."[39] Thence Felix, Messmer would admit later.

Messmer saw Felix as the "clever trickster cat" version of the pick-aninny, though the cat spent little time in the tropes of minstrel per-formance or as an interlocutor or dimwitted straight man.[40] Felix was a thinker who got himself (and often others) out of all flavors of jams and pickles. Before that, Messmer was expending effort trying to draw the funny out of cartoon versions of the Little Tramp, which he thought was a waste, since "Chaplin and the real Keystone Kops [already] did everything possible."[41] Sullivan—more experienced in the world and more managerial than Messmer—had contracted through an intermedi-ary with Chaplin to do a short series of "Charlie" cartoons in 1916 and then another series after the war.[42] The Sammie and Charlie cartoons brought some attention to Sullivan's studio, and in 1919 they were offered a regular spot in the new Famous Players-Lasky package known as Par-amount Screen Magazine. This new Paramount program was announced in August 1919, mentioning Sullivan as scenarist, but also Terry (Farmer Al Falfa) and Moser (Bud and Susie), among others. In these announce-ments, Sullivan's name wasn't even attached to a continuing-character series; press images featured Moser's Bud and Susie characters instead. Felix was born of a fluke: Paramount had a half-reel[43] to produce and asked Sullivan for filler; Sullivan quickly passed it off to Messmer, who created the mischievous black cat, "Tom"—black because "solid black moves better" and was "easier" to draw[44] and unnamed for the moment. The vagueness of this hoped-for contract aside, Messmer "celebrated the cartoon as cartoon, as something totally removed from reality." Canemaker continues, "[Messmer] would create simple symbols of animal characters, [making] brilliant use of metamorphosis—animation's intrinsic, magical property."[45] And, even though *Feline Follies* ends with the image of Tom "taking the gas pipe" rather than accepting parenthood, it was well received, and another was requested, one that would become *Musical Mews* (1919). Paramount apparently then named the cat Felix, and a star was born.

Feline Follies appeared quietly at Grauman's in Los Angeles on 7 December 1919. Felix caught on quickly and began to be requested by exchanges and exhibitors, and Sullivan, a canny businessman and a former member of the Commonwealth, saw the value of his star overseas and made deals for distribution in Great Britain.[46] Felix may have been an even bigger phenomenon there, selling toys and sundries; appearing in parades, pantomimes, and university revues; and, unfortunately, overwhelming at least one Liverpudlian, who "was laughing at the antics of Felix the Cat on the screen at a local cinema . . . when she had a seizure and died."[47]

Messmer didn't reinvent the wheel; he made it roll much, much better. Messmer's friend and colleague Frank Moser obviously shared ideas about cats. In Moser's Bud and Susie cartoon *The Jam Makers*, the kids are accompanied by a very Felix-looking black cat; in *Down the Mississippi* (1920), the same cat's tail comes off and becomes a question mark; in another title, his tail helps him become a rocking chair; and so forth. Moser's first cartoon was released about two months before Messmer's, but it was Messmer's cat who grabbed the audience and held on. Sullivan signed a contract with Famous Players–Lasky in March 1920 to make a full slate of cartoons. Sullivan, Messmer, and their studio would then produce almost exclusively Felix cartoons from 1919 through 1929, their studio becoming, alongside Terry and Fables, the steadiest studio in the business.

Felix began with Paramount, but, by 1921, Paramount was already feeling the heat of having too many irons in the fire. Paramount owned and distributed nine short-subject programs, including Felix's Screen Magazine. The cartoon and novelty program had to give. Sullivan knew he didn't own the rights to his popular character, but he managed to convince Adolph Zukor to sign Felix over to the studio. The trades note that, by February, Felix was being distributed through Margaret Winkler (who would also distribute Fleischer and then Disney). Canemaker opines that *Felix Saves the Day* might be an in-between cartoon, one that Messmer produced after breaking from Paramount but before signing with Winkler, perhaps as proof of a better concept—he and Sullivan were trying to make a cartoon that looked as good as what Terry or Fleischer were producing. A contemporary review of *Felix Saves the Day* makes the case: "[T]he cat does some clever stunts and cuts some amusing capers"; also, "The animation is clever and will provoke a good deal of laughter."[48] There *are* clever and iconic bits. Felix catches the ball with his tail and does his "thinking walk"; actual crowd shots as well as train[49] and city street photographs are used for the game setting; a "fly cop" (an undercover police officer) is called in, and he of course *flies* up to grab the boy; Felix climbs to a jail cell window using only the question marks that appear above him as he ponders; Messmer borrows a 1916 Al Falfa gag when Felix leaps out of a moving taxi when the meter runs high; and Felix manages to have rain delay Willie's baseball game by hitting Jupiter Pluvius with a batted ball. Other characters in Messmer's world are gifted with the exclamation points and question marks above them (a cop, a street sweeper, and Pluvius), but Felix is the only one who can use them. "Felix constructs a universe using only two properties, both originating in him," Marcel Brion wrote, "material signs of the state of his own soul: the exclamation point and the question mark. Nothing more is needed for building a world."[50]

Canemaker points out that Margaret Winkler shouldered the burden of distributing Felix, selling to regions and theater chains, hyping Felix in the trades and newspapers, and spreading the Felix word.[51] She was quite good at what she did. Felix merchandise also exploded in type and popularity in many other countries. But, as early as April 1922, there were tensions between Winkler and Sullivan, a rift that would only grow as Felix grew in popularity. (There were many instances when Felix's name

Proving the world is what you make of it, in *Felix Saves the Day*, Felix wonders how he will save his friend, generating climbable comic-panel question marks. *Felix Saves the Day*, Sullivan and Messmer, 1922 (YouTube). Screenshot taken by the author.

wasn't connected to Sullivan but to Winkler, and unlicensed merchandise was everywhere.[52]) Stress notwithstanding, they signed a newer, bigger contract for a more regular film schedule in fall 1922, and Felix was riding high.

None of these backroom-meets-gossip-page antics seemed to affect Messmer and his team. The Felix cartoons were made differently from how most cartoons of this period were made. Messmer was the single, steady, guiding hand, the living model sheet for Felix and his personality, allowing for a smoothness and continuity not found in most other continuing-character series. To help, Messmer was able to hire "guest animators," including gifted artists like Barré and Bill Nolan, the latter credited with "loosening up" all animation with his "rubber hose" approach. At Sullivan's, Nolan saw to a complete redesign of Felix, making him more rounded, cuddlier, but no less himself. If nothing else, Felix was afterward easier to draw and more suitable as a stuffed toy.[53] Nolan stayed until 1924, when things got even pricklier, contract-wise. The most recent Winkler-Sullivan agreement was coming to an end. Winkler made legal notice of her intent to re-up the deal, threats went back and forth, Sullivan signed a huge new deal elsewhere (perhaps just as leverage), and Winkler fought back. Winkler's determination made sense: Felix was a star of a different magnitude—he was often "used as a bait to attract audiences to a cinema where the 'more important' feature on the same programme might be of a somewhat less viable commercial certainty."[54] Felix had become a reason for cinema attendance. (At one Boston cinema palace in 1926, a live presenter ran long, pushing the entire live-action-and-films show up against the city's early closing ordinance—the back half of the program was cut, but the Felix cartoon remained.[55])

Sullivan and Winkler came to an agreement again, entering their last contract, in May 1924. Sullivan and his attorney were looking for a home-run deal to secure more money per cartoon and more favorable terms overall. (Canemaker says the last straw involved the cutting of Felix cartoons for segmented presentations in the United Kingdom as well as the "merchandise flap," both with at least tacit approval of distributor Pathé and Winkler.[56]) Sullivan went ahead and pursued a new deal with Educational Pictures, securing much more money per film. Winkler and Mintz—the latter "a man deeply beloved by no one"[57]—sued. It all came down to an interpretive reading of the contract's renewal language. By the end of April 1926, the courts ruled against Winkler, and Sullivan was free to pursue his new deal with Educational.[58] Felix was finally free. This was to be a kind of Pyrrhic victory. "The [Felix] films had a charming inconsequence," film critic Julian Fox opined later, complimenting but perhaps damning with a single phrase. He went on, "Felix was to remain one of the purest personalities of the animated cartoon."[59] This purity was unblemished by any squeaky voice, whistling, or even synchronized ambient sound. Fascinating if there had been a carefully planned, well-wrought "Garbo Talks!" moment for Felix, but no. By fall 1927, *The Jazz Singer* was ready to change everything—everything except Pat Sullivan and Felix. This might even have been the least bumpy period in cartoon history, at least for Felix and the Sullivan studio—they were producing attractive, well-liked cartoons for a long period and faced molehills, not mountains. Things went from good to great—until Sullivan was the only major cartoon producer who didn't listen when Jakie Rabinowitz shouted over the noise of a crowded restaurant set, "You ain't heard nothin' yet!"

"3 MINUTES INTERMISSION WHILE CHANGING PICTURES"

Patent enforcement! This section is a purposeful, useful interruption—patents touched all parties discussed in this chapter. As late as 1925, Bray-Hurd was suing Paul Terry for infringement; he was one of the last major cartoon makers to refuse Mrs. Bray's invoice-type advances. Going to court has always been a good-bad coin toss: Investigation, litigation, and enforcement were expensive, as the original Trust came to learn. Discovery and deposition could and did reveal all, including closely held secrets—Edison often refused to seek patent protection outside the United States because he assumed the protection was minimal and the exposure complete. Winkler and Sullivan would advance into the courtroom only when Winkler knew she was about to lose her most valuable character and Sullivan had nothing else—everything was on the table. Bray found himself in a similar position, spending money to defend his patents against the inevitability of infringement. Terry may have held out simply to prove his point (that preexisting processes should be free to all) and to enfeeble a competitor and former boss. Terry finally agreed to settle in September 1926, by purchasing a license.[60] Beginning in 1925, Bray-Hurd was involved in suits against multiple animation studios, including Winkler Pictures and Life Cartoons. *Individuals* at tiny studios like Sherwood-Wadsworth Pictures (including Burt Gillett) were also named in spring 1927 filings, likely just to put a fine point on the suit and to rustle some feathers. By January 1930, Fables, Fleischer, Winkler, and Winsor McCay had all purchased licenses. Universal and Disney were still holding out, as was Ub Iwerks. (Iwerks took a license by August 1930, as he began a decade-long sabbatical from Disney.) A 1930 article notes that at least six of the original defendants named in the Bray suit had already gone out of business over the previous five years; in addition, neither Bray nor Hurd was leading the legal charge (rather, their expensive legal team was). Bray had "retired" by this time from the cartoon side of the business, and Hurd was writing a daily comic strip.[61] Bray and Hurd's cel-animation patents finally expired between 1932 and 1933, when it was determined they had not significantly improved on the patents—and, for the first time in years, Bray-Hurd no longer received licensing fees from the bulk of the industry.

PAUL TERRY

That other "major cartoon producer" of the 1920s is the one to whom time has been least friendly. Paul Terry was known for likening his work to products found at the five-and-dime rather than a high-end jewelry store, likely both an apology and what today we'd call a humble brag. Whichever, Terry could claim what few can. One of his characters, Farmer Al Falfa, successfully made the transition from primitive to industrial silent to sound cartoons and thence to television, all without the baggage of personality or charm. Second, Terry was able to sell his entire operation in the early 1950s to CBS and retire. Terry's studio regularly made more cartoons than any other studio, more often and more haphazardly, but also profitably. For a figure on the margins, both critically and artistically, Terry's name is mentioned often and by many. Hugh Harman would remember Terry's influence many years later: "Our only study was the Lutz book, plus Paul Terry's films."[62] Harman remembered the earliest days in Kansas City, with Disney and Iwerks—they'd get old Terry films from a friendly exchange and edit them again and again: "[T]hey needed editing anyway."[63] Terry solidified his Farmer Al Falfa working for Bray in 1915—the character "never particularly interesting or well animated"—but he was inoffensive and durable, Solomon points out, transitioning to sound and lasting fifty years.[64] Terry also set himself apart by admitting his target audience. His cartoons weren't aimed at adults or even families but were intended to elicit the "infectious" laughter of kids.[65]

Like many in the new industry, Terry had begun his drawing career working for Hearst newspapers. Inspired by McCay's *Gertie*, Terry created a Little Herman cartoon, tried to sell it, and was told by Lewis Selznick that the short film would have been worth more if he hadn't drawn on it.[66] Persisting, Terry managed to interest another distributor in his film, sold it (for slightly more than the value of the film stock), and also promised to provide another film, which became *Down on the Phoney Farm*, perhaps the first Farmer Al Falfa title. Terry tried to get Hearst to hire him at IFS, and then Bud Fisher for an animated Mutt and Jeff series, but those talks went nowhere.[67]

The solid reviews and distribution of Terry's Little Herman cartoon attracted the attention of the Brays, and, since he was using patented processes (Hurd's), Terry was given the opportunity to pay up or join up. He chose the latter.[68] The main benefit of a Bray job was the ability to make more Farmer Al Falfa cartoons to be distributed as a key part of Bray's new deal with Paramount. Terry worked with artists including Moser and Hurd while at Bray, and his 1916 Farmer Al Falfa titles were assigned to the fourth of four teams working on staggered schedules to produce weekly cartoons, a true Bray assembly-line setup.[69] Terry managed to make eleven cartoons in the year he spent there but then struck out on his own. After leaving, Terry employed cels almost exclusively and eventually created very detailed backgrounds, which was unusual for the period. These backgrounds were complex and time-consuming to make, but for a reason—they were to be used more than once. Terry created a series of burlesques (like *20,000 Feats Under the Sea*) and human-interest reels, all finding distribution and solid reviews ("[Terry] has a fine sense of the ridiculous").[70]

Terry's war service involved making training films, and, when he returned, he made more Farmer Al Falfa titles for Paramount[71] before teaming with writer Howard Estabrook and creating the Aesop's Fables cartoon series—"human foibles with animal characters . . . a perfect for-mat for cartoons," as Leonard Maltin describes them.[72] These were to be fun, innocent cartoons with often silly morals displayed at the end, setting them apart from the rest of the industry; they were produced steadily and profitably from 1921 to 1929 at Fables Studios.[73] Teaming with executive Amedee Van Beuren, the Keith-Albee theater chain, and their distributor Pathé, Terry was able to get guaranteed bookings in the United States and Canada and complete underwriting for his new endeavor.[74] The Keith-Albee circuit (which would eventually merge with Film Booking

Office and RCA Photophone to become the vertically integrated RKO) distributed the Terry cartoons into its vaudeville-cinema houses.[75] Amazingly, Terry and associates not only signed a contract that called for a finished cartoon per week but also delivered on that schedule for the next nine years.[76] Terry retained a healthy 10 percent stake in the company.

Likely a surprise to many, Terry's studio would be characterized as the most financially successful of the 1920s—outperforming Bray, the Fleischers, and Disney.[77] Terry hired well, too—Moser, Harry Bailey, Fred Anderson and John Foster, and, later, Mannie Davis and Bill Tytla, who put Farmer Al Falfa and the Fables zoo through their paces.[78] Terry used cats and mice in his "stories" ad infinitum (or ad nauseam), leading critics to paint this entire period—all cartoons from all studios—as a cats-chasing-mice whirligig without thought or form. Terry was a collector and user of gags, buying them as needed. Even though the cartoons played well and often, few critics applauded his studio's originality or unique approach; the trade journals always had good things to say, and with good reason. Like the Bray titles before them, Terry's cartoons quite dependably reached a minimum level of accomplishment, year after year, "exploiting the time- and labor-saving possibilities of the cel system" and embracing the assembly line.[79] Huemer pointed out the true value of the deal Terry enjoyed with RKO, "which guaranteed that each one of his pictures would play all their houses for a good price . . . Terry was the first one to make money in the business."[80] Everyone *wanted* to make money in the business. Terry was prepared to target the right audience (kids), employ the right process (an assembly line), and reuse as much as possible (characters, situations, gags, artwork), all keeping his product predictable, dependable, and affordable—the exhibitor's holy trinity. By 1923, when Dick Huemer joined Fleischer, he was still seeing only Terry's work as legitimate competition out in the industry.[81]

Historian Maltin's summary of Terry's studio output is hard to argue with, but it still reads harshly: "Seen today, the silent Fables have *nothing* distinctive or remarkable to recommend them. . . . There is *none* of the invention that distinguished the Felix and the Out of the Inkwell cartoons, and *none* of the personality that gave such characters as Mutt and Jeff their widespread appeal."[82] Maltin's "nothing," "none," and "none" could be upgraded to "little" in all cases without stretching the truth to snapping. In Terry's *Chemistry Lesson* (1922), for instance, some care and art go a long way: The dogs chasing after the rabbits are actually drawn and redrawn as they approach, getting bigger and bigger (meaning extra drawings); backgrounds tend to look very good; the rabbit runs like a rabbit (hopping and running) and the chasing dogs run like dogs; the farmer actually glances around before giving the hooch to the rabbit, meaning he knows it isn't exactly proper (extra drawings); having taken the elixir, the rabbit's head squashes and stretches in a nod to Cohl's Little Hasher and McCay's *Nemo*; when drinking with the featherless rooster, Farmer Al Falfa cleverly crooks his elbow and rests his boot against an invisible bar and brass rail, as if he's in a saloon; he is then blasted into space, growing larger as he approaches the camera (more extra drawings) and spinning wildly, head over heels (cycling that looks accomplished[83]); and he passes a trumpeting angel before landing on the moon, where he is confronted by a three-headed creature. These three heads, not two or one, again, required extra work in the drawing and photographing stages. A surreal chase sequence as visually involved as what the Fleischers would construct for Betty and Bimbo follows—the Farmer is chased, in nightmare-like slow motion; he tumbles back to earth and into the sea, where he meets a beautiful nymph and is surrounded by bags of money, none of which he can possess; he wakes in the embrace of the rooster. And the topper? He shares another drink with his mate.

Chemistry Lesson is no game changer, but it's easy to see how Al Falfa and Fables cartoons succeeded, their "strange, earthy charm" finding a willing younger audience, setting the stage for where animation was headed.[84] Bolder appraisals come from Conrad Smith, who applauds Terry's cartoons, seeing them as heralding the "visual style and class" of later, "better" cartoons—they simply "have more life" than earlier cartoons.[85] Carl Macek agrees and ventures further: Terry was "constantly involved with moving beyond the formal barriers and creating extravagant movements and reactions in his cartoons. It is not surprising that his films, in a sense, define what animation is all about."[86] Though lumpen and forgettable in their supposed uniformity, the Terry cartoons (1) entertained youngsters at the cinema, (2) satisfied parents (kids stayed

CHAPTER 3

in their seats), (3) satisfied theater managers, and then (4) easily transitioned to the first decade of television programming. And, in the case of *Chemistry Lesson*, there was not a mouse in sight.

As the 1920s slipped away, Terry was experiencing the wanderlust that had set him on paths years before. In this case, the spark could be heard—the cartoon industry's immediate embrace of the new sound technology. Producer Van Beuren knew the future was not a silent one and encouraged Terry to make the transition to sound cartoons.[87] Terry demurred, perhaps due to his love of the silent art form (a feeling many in the cartoon and live-action industry shared), perhaps thanks to the increased costs and workload demanded of their well-oiled machine, and perhaps just stubbornness. Worldwide star Felix wasn't going to talk, so why should Henry the Cat or Farmer Al Falfa? However, the Fleischers were making rollicking sing-along titles, and even upstart Disney was shopping for a sound system for some reason. Terry finally relented at Van Beuren's insistence, and *Dinner Time* became, arguably, the first synchronized sound cartoon. It was initially well received as a "great big hit"—"Paul Terry has done it again."[88] *Dinner Time* could treasure almost two months in the catbird seat before *Steamboat Willie* changed everything again and forever. Thanks to Disney's success, Van Beuren decided and then announced with a splash that all Aesop's Fables would have sound,[89] and Terry shepherded more synched-sound cartoons across the next year. Changes above (Pathé sold out to RKO; Van Beuren bought out Keith-Albee's interest in Fables Studio) meant that Van Beuren was able to demand anything. Terry worked himself into getting fired—whether due to the sound transition or Van Beuren's increased power and control or RKO's (alleged) profit-sharing chicanery. By summer 1929, Van Beuren Studios was born, Terry was on his own again, and Terrytoons was on the horizon.

Felix, Koko, and Farmer Al's success notwithstanding, Joe Adamson asserts flatly that "[t]he animated cartoon never really caught on in the silent days."[90] Stick figure and black-blob antics were diverting, but these short films never *topped* the bill—though Felix came close (and maybe made it in the United Kingdom). They wouldn't truly catch on until they began to sing and talk. The popularity of Mickey Mouse saw that

62

character's name at the top of the marquee, often, especially between 1928 and about 1933, by which time the Fleischer characters Betty Boop and Popeye had ascended. Sullivan refused to make the change to sound cartoons (he thought Felix would be popular forever "as is") and lost a lucrative distribution deal with Educational.[91] A change of heart (brought on by Disney's successes with Mickey and the Silly Symphonies, also by both Lantz and Terry's forays into sound cartoons and Sullivan's distributor's threats[92]) prompted Sullivan to ease into sound, often just adding sound to already completed cartoons. The results were unsatisfactory, cheaper, and sub-Disney, and these cartoons with sound added after completion never took off. To be fair, Felix in the hands of Messmer had been, like Chaplin, a pantomime performer without peer, and the jarring transition to sound just didn't fit. Maybe if Messmer and Sullivan had followed Chaplin's lead and tiptoed into sound—harumphing, acknowledging, spoofing, and finally embracing—but that was a process demanding patience from artist, distributor, and audience alike. These later Felix cartoons often lean on a piano or music maker of some sort (in a scene), and then the Mickey Mousing becomes apparent when inanimate objects start to dance—the stop-and-go pace that Messmer and Felix had created (as Felix thinks through situations) yields to relentless musical rhythms. They're not bad cartoons, but they feel much less "Felix."

A chronic alcoholic, Sullivan would die in 1933, leaving the studio in a legal and financial mess, but also leaving a legacy.[93] Crafton argues that Felix was *not* the most lucrative silent animated series, *not* part of the longest-running series, and *not* from the largest studio.[94] His "utter simplicity and freshness of design" set him apart.[95] He was also influential and trendsetting—Felix was successful because he was a *true character*, as Canemaker and Crafton so well discuss. He was universally recognizable because he was an "outsider"; he was "threatened," "starving," and "hallucinatory"; and he was at once "a good Samaritan," a "philanderer," and an "insurrectionist."[96] Like Messmer and Sullivan and all people, he was many things.

The mostly silent antics of Felix, Koko, and Terry's Fables fixed securely the short cartoon as a significant part of the movie-going experience across the 1920s. Smallish competitor Walt Disney would struggle to emulate these successes in the 1920s before co-owning the 1930s, and then the world.

But first, Disney had to struggle.

CHAPTER 4

The Rise and Rise of Disney: 1919–1932

DISNEY'S EARLY 1930S EFFORTS—AND ESPECIALLY MICKEY MOUSE—
held the salon crowd in thrall like few other popular culture figures
could. Mickey was a movie star, and Walt was a critic's darling. The truth
of it demands that, like it or not, "the Disney way," "Disneyfication,"
and "like Disney" have become measuring sticks and descriptors across
the last century, uttered by critics, oppugnants, and fans alike.[1] Disney
started just like everyone else but then became the gold standard, the
value measurement in an industry that thrived on staying competitive,
cutting corners, rationalizing, and chasing finite capital. Disney bucked
all trends, borrowing again and again; spending time, energy, and money
where others saved; and setting and exceeding benchmarks. In doing so,
he managed to survive the crush of critical praise and scorn. "He was,
first and foremost, a great popular artist," one historian wrote, "and his
unflagging need to invent new forms of entertainment drove him to take
constant risks that would have been unthinkable in a more conventional
business enterprise."[2]

The dates in the chapter heading might also need explaining. The
1919 date is an easy one: Disney first got a job in the commercial advertising industry in Kansas City and was looking to form his own small
studio. The next thirteen years would see the failure of his Kansas City
endeavors, his move to Hollywood, his marriage, the beginnings of a
studio with his brother and uncle's help, his first moderately successful
series and character, his first *successful* series and character, the loss of that
character, and the birth of the Disney empire with Mickey Mouse and

Silly Symphony sound cartoons. By mid-1932, his characters and series were feted, but he was still, in many respects, shoulder to shoulder with competitors like the Fleischers and even the prodigious Paul Terry. (And just four years earlier—ante-Mickey—Fleischer, Terry and Van Beuren, and Sullivan were *all* more successful, making and placing more cartoons, than Disney.) By 1932, Walt's exclusive, risky, and expensive deal with fledgling Technicolor would launch Disney to the front of the pack.

But it all started in 1919 in the Kansas City area, which, like today, was a center for advertising and marketing agencies. With a family farm background and after a stint working overseas in the war effort and working at odd jobs, Walter Elias Disney wanted work in the commercial advertising world. Young Disney's artistic talents were those nurtured via correspondence courses rather than innate gifts, so he tended to surround himself with better-trained, more accomplished artists throughout his life, Ub Iwerks being one of the first and most important. Walt and Ub met at one of the commercial art studios in the city, became fast friends, and, excepting the decade of the 1930s, would work together all their adult lives.

Disney's Laugh-O-gram Films produced *Newman's Laugh-O-Grams* (1921), which were assorted ads for Kansas City–area concerns and services to play at the Newman Theater and cute, *au courant* fairy-tale adaptations (*Little Red Riding Hood, Puss in Boots*). None of these efforts looked any different from those coming from dozens of individuals and agencies around the country; they were made using pen and ink and had limited backgrounds and a sparse comic-strip inventiveness, look, and quality. Disney begged and borrowed money to create the fairy-tale films, but, without a distributor, each effort was an exercise in hope and futility. Walt even tried creating educational films, agreeing to make a live-action-and-animated short film, *Tommy Tucker's Tooth*, for a local dentist. This $500 film stretched Laugh-O-gram Films to its limits, but it did prove the viability of the live-action-and-animation potential for later projects, like the Alice series. The short-lived Laugh-O-grams experiment in commercial film production was coming to an end, making Kansas City inhospitable, especially as Disney's landlord and vendors were looking to pick the desiccated corpse clean. Sunny California beckoned, as did the potential for making short-subject films.

ALICE

The Alice cartoons were a modestly clever turn on the live-action-and-animation juxtapositions made popular by McCay, by Bray in *Artist's Dream* and the Colonel Heeza Liar series, by Hurd's Bobby Bumps, and, later, by the Fleischers with their clown.[3] Disney's novel twist for *Alice's Wonderland* (1923) featured a live-action girl, Alice, in a generally friendly, animated world.[4] Alice even (very nearly) interacted with her cartoon surroundings. One contemporary writer, who was examining Disney's operation in 1934 for evidence of monetary success, noted that, though Disney was failing to make ends meet in Kansas City, the Disney product wasn't any worse than anything else in the industry, nor was it any better: "The pioneer animated cartoons, 'Little Nemo,' 'Colonel Heezaliar,' 'Krazy Kat,' 'Felix the Cat,' etc., had resembled one another pretty closely, and none of them had caused any dancing in the streets," Arthur Mann noted. "The picture people very naturally refused to buy something that had already been done. Disney had nothing worth while for them, not even a copy of something good."[5] Mann would conclude that it was Mickey Mouse alone who could keep Disney in the black. But, after seeing this single Alice title, Margaret Winkler, who had worked for Harry Warner and was already representing both Pat Sullivan and the Fleischers, agreed to distribute the modestly innovative cartoons.

And, while Kansas City could have made a good home for a small ad agency, it was not ideal for a cartoon maker and certainly not for a movie studio. The Midwest spring and summer seemed to last days, not months, while proximity to the movie industry mattered to Walt. At his brother Roy's urging, Walt sold out in Kansas City and moved to Los Angeles in summer 1923, and, by May 1924, he had convinced Ub to join him in "a real country—to work and play in—no kidding."[6] California had grown on him quickly. California was also home to precisely zero other cartoon studios, a fact not lost on Disney. Animation studios in 1924 were still on the East Coast. Most were in New York City, which Disney disliked, as he would write later to Roy: "This DAMN TOWN is enough to give anybody the HEEBIE JEEBIES. I wish I was home."[7] By late 1923, he was finally home, in southern California.

With Ub's inestimable help, the Winkler-supported Alice series gained some audience interest from 1924 onward. Disney had signed with Winkler initially (and then, by marriage, her husband, Mintz) for a states'-rights distribution deal. The states'-rights approach allowed a film producer to sell a film to a more local entity that then could sell it (and show it) within a defined region until the print fell to pieces. Most short subjects were sold this way before the larger studios began gathering them into "blocks" (a feature or two, a newsreel, a human-interest short, and a cartoon); smaller studios and shorter films used the states'-rights approach for many years, distributing to thousands of independent cinemas in smaller towns. Block booking would become foundational for the major studios, guaranteeing distribution and exhibition of the studios' product. The theater chains owned by the majors had to accept the films—they were part of the family; however, as family members, they had some say in the kinds of films going into these blocks. Independent theater owners had no such input—they had to accept a block of whatever Paramount wanted to give if they wanted to show Paramount films. To promote balance of demand in the distribution and exhibition arms of the industry, a block of good *and* bad films was generally concocted, making sure all Paramount films saw the light of neighborhood projectors. (This all-or-nothing scenario was known as "forcing."[8]) Sometimes these purchases were made sight unseen, which was known as blind booking (or blind bidding), so the contents were a mystery and often had to be purchased a year at a time.[9] It would be 1938 before the federal government took an active interest in Hollywood's monopolistic practices and a further decade before interest became action. More on that topic later.

The first deal was certainly weighted in Winkler's favor—no other distributor of note was sniffing at the unremarkable Disney Brothers product.[10] There would be more than fifty Alice cartoons produced across the following three years, during which time Walt changed the name of the company to Walt Disney Studios, with Roy's blessing.[11] When Margaret Winkler became a mother, she took a step back from the business she had founded, leaving her husband in charge. Mintz saw big things on the horizon for Winkler Pictures.

And then it all really began with a rabbit, not a mouse.

OSWALD THE LUCKY RABBIT

It was after April 1927 and with the Oswald cartoons that the Disney studio began to make some noise in the industry. The Oswald series had been the idea of people above the Disneys, including Winkler and Mintz, seeking a new series that could compete with animal-featuring series like Terry's Aesop's Fables, but also of the big-time potential distributor Universal and its president, Carl Laemmle, who had specifically requested a rabbit series and even chosen Oswald as the character's name.[12] With inhuman prescience, Walt could have seen this agreement ending badly for his studio—he didn't; he was tiring of the Alice work as well—but it did teach him a lasting lesson: ascertain and retain rights to your characters and creations at all costs. (Max and Dave Fleischer could have benefited from this dictum as well.) The setting aside of the Alice franchise and the increasing popularity of the Oswald cartoons tipped the scales of distributor-studio power back toward the Disneys, or so the brothers thought. The first cartoon (*Poor Papa*[13]) was weak, Oswald was badly designed, and both Mintz and Universal complained to Disney.[14] A redesign followed, the second title being the much more watchable *Trolley Troubles*. The pointed, negative response to the first cartoon prodded Disney to "make [Oswald's] characteristics his [entire] style and manner of doing things, rather than to give him merely a specific habit or trait," Walt wrote to Mintz. An Oswald historian writes, "Walt wanted to give Oswald a distinctive personality all his own . . . [o]ver several cartoons this persona—an emotive, fast-moving wise guy, alternately ebullient and grouchy—would come into focus."[15] Oswald was generally drawn well and moved with some grace and agility, thanks to Iwerks and Hugh Harman (and eventually Friz Freleng); the plots weren't groundbreaking but were cleverly handled and even topical. Some, like *The Mechanical Cow* and *Trolley Troubles*, were attractive enough to be well reviewed and enjoyed by audiences; their stars were merchandise friendly,[16] and they even influenced other studios' cartoon efforts. (*Trolley Troubles* was virtually remade in 1931 as *Smile, Darn Ya, Smile!* by former Disney animators Harman and Ising, becoming an early Schlesinger Merrie Melodies.) Oswald was soon being requested by local cinema owners and was quickly drawn into the comedian continuum. "If Felix's balletic movements and victimization by his environment are seen as derived from Chaplin's screen character," Crafton writes, "then Oswald may be viewed as closer to Keaton and his ability to transform the absurd mechanical environment of the modern world into something useful and humane."[17]

The real fly in the ointment seems to have been Mintz himself, and maybe Disney should have been flattered. Likely thanks to his favorable relationship with distributor Universal, Mintz's unspoken goal was the complete control of the toddler Disney studio, which was unsteady on its feet but, with a confident Oswald, showing promise. Mintz would play his hand when it came time for an Oswald contract renegotiation in early 1928, when Disney was expecting an increase in per-cartoon payment. It's possible that Mintz wasn't duplicitous but had simply been reading the trades and wanted in on the gravy. The soft hostile takeover attempt was so common as to be almost unremarkable in the film industry during this period. Cinema chains (exhibitors) and/or film exchanges (distributors) had worked backward up the supply chain before, creating or absorbing producers of film (nascent studios) to ensure vertical integration in the industry. Adolph Zukor, for example, entered the industry by investing in a theater chain, then created his Famous Players company to distribute French films, and thence began to produce important films starring noted stage actors. Formed in 1916, Famous Players–Lasky (FPL) became a heavyweight studio immediately. By 1927, when Mintz was fomenting his plans for the Disney acquisition, Zukor's FPL became Paramount Famous Lasky Corporation, a production-distribution behemoth. The live-action film industry was consolidating and merging—finger to the breeze, Mintz may have been trying to keep up with the Zukors.

It was spring 1928 when Disney realized what it meant to not actually own rights to a character that his company had been making famous—Mintz and Universal owned Oswald. In haunting coast-to-coast phone calls between Walt and Roy, they discovered the ugly truth: While Walt was in New York trying to renegotiate a better Oswald deal with Mintz, a

Winkler Pictures minion[18] was in Los Angeles quietly making job offers to Disney's key staff, including Hugh Harman, who had been with Walt and Ub since Kansas City. Mintz had decided that since Walt didn't draw anymore, he wasn't necessary—Harman was being offered Walt's job heading the studio, and he was keen to get out from under Disney's thumb.[19] (The exiting animators would continue elsewhere to work on Mintz's Oswald cartoons for about a year; Harman, Ising, and others then left Mintz in 1929 to help kick-start Schlesinger's studio at Warner Bros.) Too late, Disney faced the fact that Mintz wooed away all his creative team, excepting Ub and two others, gutting the Disney studio.[20]

Fuming and depressed, Disney would take the long train ride back to Los Angeles, along the way hatching a twofold plan to forever be his own boss *and* create a new character with Iwerks. A "product of desperation and calculation,"[21] this new character would look like most other leading characters of the day—an easy-to-draw rounded black body, curvilinear arms and legs (Nolan's much-copied "rubber hose system"), an expressive white-and-black face, buttoned shorts, and, eventually, shoes and gloves. Mickey was inspired by both Krazy Kat and Ignatz the Mouse, by the mice in Messmer's Felix cartoons but also Felix himself, by Clifton Meek's mice and those of Terry's Aesop's Fables, and by Alice's friend Julius, himself a Felix knock-off.[22] Then there are the rodents populating many of the Alice comedies, each of them an ur-Mickey, writ small. In a publicity still for the studio promoting Margie Davis as Alice, six such mice cavort around Disney, Margie, Julius, and assorted characters. One mouse is wielding a mallet, one placing a brick to trip up an unsuspecting character, one ballooning in from above, flag waving, and another dangling a fake spider to frighten Alice.[23] The impish, schoolboy characterizations that would make up Mickey are already on display. Solomon states it simply: "The artists at all the silent studios drew virtually identical rats."[24] And the rats were indistinguishable from nettlesome mice.

Faced with a lineup of such rodents, a contemporary audience mightn't have discerned the rat from the rabbit from the frog, cat, dog, or mouse (and later characters like Harman and Ising's Bosko or Foxy, the Fleischers' Fitz and Bimbo, and Iwerks's Flip made few advances). For one, it came down to a character's personality: "Disney's most important accomplishment was to take personality animation and develop it to its most eloquent degree."[25] "I want the characters to be somebody," Disney told Freleng in 1927. "I don't want them to just be a drawing." So, Mickey's personality would matter. But whose personality would Mickey have? Ub's? Walt's? Or a new spirit to match the more challenging times, where unflappable verve meets the want of the Depression head on? "No one has ever been softened after seeing (early) Mickey or has wanted to give away an extra glass of water to the poor," E. M. Forster would write. "He is never sentimental, indeed there is a scandalous element in him which I find most restful."[26] Historians would agree, giving credit to Ub: "Iwerks created a spirit of elemental anarchy that for unbridled free spirits was seldom matched in later Disney."[27] A number of leading critics also anointed Mickey as the immediate successor to Chaplin—even more academic types connected Chaplin and Mickey in their armchair analyses of the star[28]—all high praise, given the Little Tramp's popularity from 1914 onward. Those who knew Walt well, though, especially those who worked with him on the Mickey cartoons, were certain that Walt and Mickey were one and that Walt's acting as he voiced Mickey or described a scene just proved it.[29] But more on the significance of personality later.

Armed with a new character and the promise of new adventures, Disney next had to ensure that his eloping animators honored their original contracts and finished work on the Oswald cartoons, work owed to Mintz.[30] Disney and Iwerks and a handful of remaining employees (and girlfriends and spouses) worked nearly around the clock creating a few Mickey titles for potential sale, inking and painting in Disney's garage at night. They also immediately (and quite secretly, keeping all things mouse-related safe from interloper George Winkler and the soon-to-be-ex-employees) reached out to one of the few intertwined lifelines offered as he and Ub created from the shoes up not only his new star Mickey Mouse but also the expensive and unproven phenomenon of the sound cartoon. These lifelines were from Pat Powers, the Cinephone sound process, and Celebrity Pictures.

The wholesale Hollywood transition to synchronized sound wasn't a given, certainly not in 1926–1928, when initial examples of films with sound were presented and most found wanting. But Disney saw sound as the next great advance and didn't have to be cajoled into the new world: "He saw that sound was not merely an addition to the movies but a force that would fundamentally transform them."[31] Sound accompanying silent pictures had been teased for more than a decade (including with Edison's Kinetophone process), with sound-recording technology preceding filmed recordings. Two major hurdles had been consistent: reliable synchronization and adequate amplification. A third hurdle, cost, would weed out others in the production industry (and retard the adoption of sound, especially in smaller, neighborhood and rural cinemas). There had been many attempts to match either live, produced sound (like a radio broadcast) or amplified sound to moving images, all rather impractical and destined to fall by the wayside.[32]

When the sound-on-disk Vitaphone process appeared and, more pointedly, when the partly sound Warner Bros. film *The Jazz Singer* became a hit, most in the industry knew change had arrived. With profit margins already thin, however, cartoon producers like Sullivan doubled down on Felix's silence as a character-defining element and wouldn't greenlight more expensive sound cartoons (a decision he'd come to regret). Terry, in his Aesop's Fables series, wasn't so reticent. The admittedly low-end quality of his cartoons was ready to be accompanied by sounds and songs of low-end quality, confirming his own later assessment of his cartoons as Woolworth's to Disney's Tiffany.[33] Disney remembers seeing Terry's *Dinner Time*, arguably the first synched-sound cartoon, in New York, and he was not impressed: It was noisy, messy, "a lot of racket and nothing else," and he assured Roy they could do better.[34] "What Disney sensed was that it was about to become a totally new form," Schickel writes. "Disney was the first movie maker to resolve the aesthetically disruptive fight between sight and sound through the simple method of fusion, making them absolutely 'coexpressible,' with neither one dominant nor carrying more than its fair share of the film's weight."[35] Historian Neal Gabler agrees, describing the difference between Terry's *Dinner Time* and the Disney experiment as follows: "Walt had imagined [*Steamboat Willie*] as a sound cartoon in which the music and effects were inextricable from the action—truly a musical cartoon rather than a cartoon with music."[36]

But, with the sound boom rocking Hollywood, it shouldn't be a surprise that Vitaphone didn't think it needed a small cartoon company's business (not wrong, really—Disney was technically the smallest big studio in Hollywood), so Disney had to find an alternate sound process. This is where Pat A. Powers and Cinephone entered the picture. Powers had begun as a film exchange owner, an independent businessman whose natural "belligerence" had helped beat back the tentacled reach of Edison's MPPC. He grew his business into one that also produced films and would eventually merge with Carl Laemmle's company, creating Universal Pictures. After failing to take over Lee De Forest's Phonofilm company, Powers—who, putting it politely, "operated on the edges of many worlds"[37]—hired a former company employee, William Garrity (later of multiplane camera fame for Disney), to build a cloned Phonofilm device. The optical sound-on-film process[38] Cinephone came from this copying and likely could have been the target of successful infringement suits. After being pitched the benefits of multiple sound systems, Disney concluded that, for animation purposes (where the *precise* matching of sound effects, movement, and voice was crucial), the sound-on-film system was better than the sound-on-disk system,[39] though these and other early sound films were often released in both versions, since theaters were, for several years, variously sound-equipped.

Powers had lifelines to throw—he not only owned a workable sound film process but also could also act as distributor for Disney's new cartoons. Disney had already approached and been rebuffed by MGM and Universal (when the handful of Mickey cartoons were silent), and Mintz and Winkler were now the enemy, so provided no help. Paramount would say no a bit later, and other major distributors already had contracts for cartoons. Powers and his own company, Celebrity Pictures, stepped in, and—as ever—for the right fee he could make sure the Mickey sound cartoons were seen and heard by a New York audience. Disney would agree to a states'-rights distribution deal with Powers, the only one that would allow Disney to retain ownership of Mickey and the films.[40] It cost more up front, and it cost more per print, but Disney wanted no repeat of the Mintz-Oswald debacle, which is why he trademarked Mickey Mouse in May 1928 and copyrighted *Plane Crazy* just after.[41] Whenever and however his contract with Powers concluded, the characters and films would belong to Walt Disney Studios.

On 18 November 1928, *Steamboat Willie* test-premiered at the Colony Theater—it was an immediate sensation. The cartoon ran for two weeks and received universal praise before moving to the sparkling Roxy Theater.[42] Three other Mickey cartoons were being or had just been finished, and Disney was ready to deal. He was now "fielding offers" for real distribution assistance from the major studios, though each of them demanded that he sell his studio to the distributor to get the contract, which he declined to do.[43] Disney had made the deal with Powers (even though states'-rights deals put fewer immediate dollars into studio coffers) because, as Schickel notes, "[Disney] seemed to sense that it was more and better cartoons rather than large immediate returns that would ultimately establish the name of Walt Disney."[44] As often was the case, Disney was right.

For a short time, Disney enjoyed the fruits of Mickey's success. The mouse quickly became known well outside of New York and Los Angeles cinema houses, and, "by the end of 1930, [he'd] become an international celebrity."[45] Mickey was everywhere. And, rather than riding the mouse into a lather, as most cartoon producers had done with their stars (like Sullivan with Felix), Disney responded to success by bringing a new mount to bridle while expanding his studio's technical capabilities. Disney's per-cartoon costs were rising during this 1928–1931 period, from about $5,400 to $13,500, but he was spending willingly.[46] Profits were plowed back into the studio and into the new projects. Composer Carl Stalling[47] had earlier suggested a "musical novelty" cartoon (music driven as opposed to continuing-character driven) that might stretch both animators and musicians at the studio.[48] This suggestion led to the Silly Symphonies. Disney's first Symphony, *Skeleton Dance* (1929), was macabre and memorable but a tough sell. "They don't want this," Powers would cable to Disney. "MORE MICE."[49] It took a successful sneak showing at the Carthay Circle in Los Angeles, and positive audience response did the rest. It became the "first cartoon picture to be rebooked for a second showing" at a major cinema, in this case the prestigious Roxy in New York.[50] The product of other cartoon producers was often

still being treated as filler or even unwanted freebies from the distributors, left off the bill, or used as houselights-up annoyances to clear the
theater. Not so for a certain mouse and some dancing skeletons. As for
the new technology, the music needs of the emerging Silly Symphonies
prompted Disney to create a music-recording operation in Los Angeles, a
site where Disney's projects could be recorded (as opposed to New York)
and where others could rent the space and equipment for outside productions.[51] Powers was instrumental in providing equipment and training,
for which Disney paid dearly.

The relentlessly controlling Powers had helped open doors for the
Disney cartoons, in truth, but at a high cost. Powers had been holding
a percentage of every cartoon's gross as well as receiving annual fees for
the sound equipment and technologies. He'd been collecting thousands
on the nationwide success of Mickey and then *Skeleton Dance* without
providing Roy or Walt with detailed accounts. This shouldn't have been
any surprise, given Powers's résumé. But Mickey was a sensation. By
1931, there was a *Life* magazine cartoon depicting moviegoers, clad in
hat and tails, pearl and stoles, forlornly leaving a highbrow cinema with
the caption "No Mickey Mouse!"[52] By early 1932, clever cinema adverts
were using the "What! No Mickey Mouse?" headline to grab attention
and then immediately reassuring potential viewers there was indeed a
Mickey Mouse cartoon on the bill.[53] Walt had hoped for the best and
been charmed by Powers (as he was initially by Winkler and especially
Mintz), but, across the months of his association with Powers, the Powers–Disney deal wasn't providing the cash that it seemed should accompany the cartoons' acclaim and lucrative bookings. Phone calls and letters
to Powers weren't eliciting the financial brass tacks the Disney brothers
wanted, needed, and felt they deserved. A renewed contract was in the
offing, however.[54] A visit to New York by Roy brought no news except of
Powers's belligerence and Roy's certainty that they were being done dirty.
Walt then went back to New York for a face-to-face meeting.

What he found there was a smugly confident Powers. Like Mintz
before him, he held an ace up his sleeve. Powers didn't have the sword
of failed or costly cartoons to dangle over Disney; he couldn't say that
there weren't multiple distributors waiting and willing to sign the

Disneys—there were. But Powers did think he knew how the sausage was made. Powers first offered "to take over the studio" and pay Disney a staggering "$2500 per week to run it."[55] This offer indicated Powers didn't know with whom he was bargaining—Walt wanted no boss. A new tack, then. The word around the animation studios in New York had been that it was the oddly named Ubbe Iwerks who was the rara avis, without whom Mickey couldn't whistle and skeletons wouldn't dance. Walt himself had called Ub "the best animator in the world."[56] It became joltingly clear in that meeting that Powers not only agreed with Disney's assessment but also was set on hiring Ub away and installing him in his own studio, if need be, complete with a ready distributor (MGM)—and, what's more, that Ub had already agreed. It was the Mintz nightmare all over again, but worse, since Ub—the magician who had single-handedly animated *Plane Crazy*[57]—had been the stalwart from the earliest days. (Disney would forever be stunned that anyone would want to work anywhere else but on his studio's projects and that his perfectionism and bracing personality might put anyone off.)

While Walt was still in New York, Ub officially left Disney for Powers's studio[58] and what would become the Ub Iwerks Studio—and the promise of "NEW AND FUNNIER SERIES WITH SOUND"—in February 1930.[59] The ground seemed fertile for such a new planting. In April 1930, exhibitors responded to a questionnaire in *Film Daily*, ranking their short program items—cartoons came in a healthy third.[60] Composer Stalling would give notice as well, certain that, without Ub, the Disney studio was finished. Stalling would sign on with Van Beuren and Aesop's Fables but then come back to California almost immediately to work for Iwerks and, later, famously, for Schlesinger.

Not only did the Disneys not have their best animator and music man after February 1930, but they were also short a distributor *and* owed Powers a great deal of money for the pleasure of escaping existing contracts.[61] MGM was given a second shot at the bobbing apple but demurred (Louis B. Mayer allegedly wouldn't even finish screening two cartoons[62]), and a smaller major, Columbia—already known as the "Short Subjects Kings"—took the bite.[63] Some new characters followed to give Mickey both a break and a retinue; such characters included

Ub Iwerks was a gifted and speedy animator whose stories and character designs (like here in *Fiddlesticks*, starring Flip the Frog) didn't advance to match former partner Disney's. After a decade on his own, Ub would return to Disney to improve animation technology. *Fiddlesticks*, Ub Iwerks, 1930 (from *Cartoons That Time Forgot: The Ub Iwerks Collection* DVD). Screenshot taken by the author.

Clarabelle Cow and Horace Horsecollar—nice looking, but neither was terribly memorable.[64] Over the next few years, Pluto and Goofy would emerge, and Donald would first appear in 1934. But Mickey was still the face of the studio, often literally; he even "presented" Silly Symphonies. And, without other significant continuing characters to lean on (creatively, financially), the Disney artists drew Mickey into the rat race, sending him around the globe in the early 1930s, taxing the mousy Fairbanks: "[Mickey] was at various times a gaucho, teamster, explorer, swimmer, cowboy, fireman, convict, pioneer, taxi driver, castaway, fisherman, cyclist . . . carpenter, driver, trapper, whaler, tailor and Sorcerer's Apprentice."[65] This list is exhausting but not exhaustive. It doesn't include Mickey's popular comic-strip run that, beginning in 1930, would last sixty-five years and reach many more eyes and hearts than the filmed cartoons. Mickey was busy from 1929 onward.[66]

The Fleischers were in this same period putting Betty Boop into (and out of) similar exotic costumes and situations, just as Van Beuren had for his Tom and Jerry team and as Mintz had for his Scrappy cartoons. Part of Mickey's appeal included his derring-do as he rescued Minnie again and again, mimicking Keaton and Chaplin's big-screen efforts and the popular action-adventure film serials of the day. Mickey was also fast becoming a merchandise bonanza and a corporate symbol for all of Disney—his behavior would have to change with those expectations. Disney supercharged the marketing of tie-ins and merchandising, especially for Mickey, which began modestly in 1929. His quickly became "the world's most recognizable face," bringing in much-needed capital. It was Mickey's market power that kept the studio afloat—the films consistently sunk the studio into debt.[67]

With increases in quality and artistry, the Disney cartoons simply cost more, much more, than those produced at competing studios, but distribution payments were stagnant across the industry. Additional steps in the animation process improved the product but also further raised costs. For example, pencil tests became the Disney norm by 1931.[68] These were complete scenes that were pencil-drawn on paper, photographed, and screened on Moviolas for fluidity. Animators at other studios heard of Disney's improvements and either whistled appreciatively or shook their heads; they either wanted to work in such an environment or couldn't believe it remained solvent. Some of the advances—like the pencil tests, figure-drawing classes, storyboards, and color—caught on at other studios, albeit grudgingly. It was the high cost of these cartoons that helped shutter the theatrical short-cartoon industry by the 1960s, forcing the move to TV and much, much smaller budgets.

Mann points up that Disney was perennially in debt, owing money to distributors before producing a single cartoon (and eventually to the Bank of America when the studio had to expand).[69] This constant, burdensome worry, along with the workload Disney set for himself, led inevitably to health and emotional problems to which he eventually had to admit: "I cracked up."[70] On his doctor's advice, Walt and his wife took a restful, months-long vacation in 1931. When he returned the studio, output began to change—the cartoony elements and excesses began to be phased out; there was more attention to reality, to an "illusion of life"[71] verisimilitude in the character designs and the worlds around them. In 1932, a full-scale investment in color—three-strip Technicolor—was only the next bit of foolhardiness Walt pursued and Roy protested. But, if the studio was going to lead, it had to go the untraveled way. With vibrant color (a virtual guarantee the short films wouldn't make their money back in rentals), the next step became evident and possible. From 1932 onward, Disney changed from the freewheeling fantasy or cartoony world to a more idealized one in which moral lessons and cautionary tales could exist, according to historian Robert Sklar—certainly no accident, given Disney's creation of a story department as a means of controlling content and output, of cinematic body images and fully rounded characters, along with an artistic move toward verisimilitude.[72]

The Three Little Pigs and *Snow White* were on the horizon.

CHAPTER 5

The 1930s Undercard

Schlesinger, Harman-Ising, Van Beuren

As THE LATE 1920S BECAME THE 1930S, DISNEY SHED SHELLS AS IT grew, with those shells taken up by others making their way into cartoons, some trying their best to be like Disney. It was also clear by this time that cartoons had finally caught on, that hanging up a 'toon producer shingle wasn't necessarily the first draft of a long suicide note. Warner Bros. and MGM—recently reaching maturity in 1923 and 1924, respectively—fitted themselves to these cast-off shells and scuttled into the cartoon business. Early trade-offs weren't always fair:

- Leon Schlesinger convinced Warner Bros. to gather former Disney animators—and got Looney Tunes and Merrie Melodies.

- MGM wanted Disney and, instead, took up Disney's distributor (Powers) and main artist, Ub Iwerks—and got Flip the Frog.

It would be a long decade before Tom and Jerry or Bugs Bunny came of age in 1940. Warner Bros. and MGM would follow Disney—most did—but without mimicking each other. It was a competitive reef. Of the dozens of animation concerns that had set up shop in the United States since about 1912, starting with Cohl, McCay, and Barré, most had fizzled out across the lean 1910s and more expensive 1920s (thanks in both cases to Bray-Hurd). Such closures included that of McCay and Cohl's studio, which made or released its last meaningful animation work in 1921.[1] Koko and Betty, Oswald, Farmer Al Falfa, and even Henry

Cat and Milton Mouse were popular characters bursting from a popular medium. By 1929, all major cartoon producers (with the noted exception of Pat Sullivan) had at least tested the waters of sound cartoons as well, following the lead of Hollywood's studios. These same major studios were also beginning to see the value of the entertaining and dependable animated short-subject film, though by 1928 only Paramount had committed to offering a cartoon as a *regular* part of its block booking package. The rest of the majors *and* minors would soon follow.

The late 1920s must then be considered the dawn of the salad days for theatrical animation, good times that would stretch across the Great Depression and a world war. Theatrical animation even helped slay these leviathans with pluck, wit, and cartoony violence before meeting its match in the form of a tiny screen in every living room. (More on this subject later.) By the mid-1920s, the internecine and border wars in the film industry had settled considerably. Eastern concerns had moved to the West, where virtually all production was now centered. The well-known names of the Hollywood studios now existed as most people assume they'd always existed: These studios were controllers of the means of film production, distribution, and exhibition, making films large and small, while owning or controlling hundreds of cinemas across the country. And, thanks to the fact that purchasing a film performance meant buying a block of films, many of the major studios were regularly including cartoons in those packages. In mid-1930, though, about eighteen months after Mickey's "whistle heard 'round the world," not all were convinced. A May 1930 *Variety* story mentions that demand for cartoons had increased steadily and that all the major studios—Warner Bros., Fox, and United Artists excepted—had made the decision to add cartoons to their programs. (The reporter had heard the name "Looney Tunes" but didn't know what kind of short series it would be.)[2] Then a groundswell emerged: The trades reported a record run in Philadelphia for a cartoon, this one the Aesop's Fables *Romeo Robin*.[3] Earlier, Disney's critically acclaimed *Skeleton Dance* managed to sustain an initial run longer than those of most feature films and was rebooked at the Roxy.[4] Now it was difficult to justify *not* looking for a cartoon series to distribute. Distributor United Artists claimed only a handful of live-action short-subject films, while William Fox's studio had no short-subject films at all.[5] (Both United Artists and Fox would get into the cartoon game soon, United Artists working with Disney and Fox distributing Terry cartoons for Educational.[6])

For the 1930–1931 season, MGM, Paramount, RKO, and Columbia increased cartoon orders.[7] This development meant that even a marginally accomplished set of cartoons had a destination for as long as they could be produced affordably and for as long as the studios owned their own theater chains. The cartoons themselves had improved, technically. But the also-ran studios, characters, and titles were still extant; as the film studios *all* got around to setting up or securing their own cartoon sources, there was a new demand for cartoons. But maybe more wasn't better; it was just more. Complaints abounded after sound appeared, in response to trivial cartoons demonstrating "startlingly bad taste."[8] From one contemporary critic, writing in 1934, comes the following: "Most animated cartoons consist of a strung-together series of stunts or 'gags,' the more preposterous, apparently, the better, enacted by a cast of characters . . . interspersed with solo and ensemble singing and dancing, not felt as an interruption because there is so little plot or logical continuity to interrupt."[9] Bragdon was not talking about Disney here—his article was a paean to Disney's work. He was referring to the work of Mintz, Van Beuren, Terry, and Schlesinger. But, as odd as it sounds, there was a need for just the type of cartoons that Bragdon was bemoaning, and the 1930s Schlesinger studio provided them.

HARMAN AND ISING

"Harman and Ising did not so much create characters as they created studios," Barrier writes. "The Warner Bros. and MGM studios owed their existence to Harman and Ising."[10] In truth, 1930s cartoons would have been lesser if many animators hadn't tired of working under Walt's gaze (like Harman), been fired by Walt (Ising and Freleng), taken other jobs to get away from Walt (Iwerks), or been denounced by Walt as a result of a strike (Art Babbitt, et al.). Without the anti-Walt cadre, two studios representing the sheer elan of "impossibly ludicrous" cartoon-making— Warner Bros. and MGM—couldn't have emerged.[11]

Hugh Harman and Rudolf Ising had been restless since their Laugh-O-gram days in Kansas City, working fruitlessly for the slightly younger Walt Disney. The business was collapsing, and Walt went off to California to find his fortune in the movies, while Harman and Ising tried to push on with the Fables-like work they'd started—an Arabian Nights series—but found no takers. Freleng would remember Harman, whom he knew both in Kansas City and, later, in Hollywood, as both helpful and haunted, less a "creative" than an "imitator" of Walt: "[W]hen he was on his own . . . he never made it. What he did was follow Walt, whatever Walt did, he did the same kind of thing."[12] Harman, Ising, eventually Freleng, and others would join Disney in southern California, working on Alice and then Oswald titles. When Mintz undercut Disney and took Oswald, Harman and Ising followed the rabbit. More so-so Oswald cartoons were produced until Universal pushed reset, bringing in Walter Lantz to take over Oswald, and this time it was Harman and Ising being surprised.

In 1929, they approached Leon Schlesinger, owner of Pacific Title and Art, with a filmed pitch for a cartoon series aimed at Warner Bros., a studio basking in the glow of its full-scale introduction of sound to the movies. Schlesinger was not a cartoon man, but he knew the movie industry. He was also obviously shrewd; he had backed the brothers Warner in 1927 on the dicey sound film *The Jazz Singer* and had a trump to play.[13] He is often described positively not because of what he did but because of what he did not do. A "lazy" man who was "absolutely out for the money," in Chuck Jones's words,[14] he tended to leave his creative teams alone and asked only for affordable, funny, distributable product.

The young animators had made a spec film for their new company, Harman-Ising Productions, featuring a familiar setup: the animator (Ising) at the drawing board, pen in hand, sketching and chatting with his creation—in this case, a pickaninny minstrel character.[15] The inkblot "boy" could sing and dance, do typically insensitive racial impressions, and speak in an exaggerated dialect.[16] This was Bosko, "a blackface performer selling Warner Bros. films to theater audiences."[17] Like McCay with Nemo and Gertie, or Hurd with Bobby Bumps, Fleischer and Koko, or Messmer and Felix, the character is created before us and alternately obeys and ignores his creator. Schlesinger liked what he saw, or more likely he knew what he had—a chance to help Warner Bros. promote itself while becoming a known producer in an expanding industry. The pitch would be distributed as *Bosko the Talk-Ink Kid*, the first of almost forty Bosko cartoons. Warner Bros. comedy-film revue song "Singin' in the Bathtub" was repurposed for this cartoon, *Sinkin' in the Bathtub*. Brothers Warner likely weren't interested in the cartoons, frankly, but rather in the synergy. Trotting out a company-owned song and then repurposing it for use in a sound movie made possible by their Vitaphone process was good business.[18] The costs of the recently purchased music catalogs were defrayed as individual songs appeared in cartoons.

A titular example of this relationship between movie studio, music catalog, and animation is the August 1933 cartoon *We're in the Money*. The song "We're in the Money" is heard in both a Schlesinger cartoon and live-action film, reaching a larger, more diverse audience. The song had become a fist-in-the-face-of-the-Depression anthem featured in the Warner Bros. backstage musical *Gold Diggers of 1933* (May 1933), performed by Ginger Rogers. The film, the song, and the cartoon promote, without barking, FDR's Keynesian policies (i.e., increasing the country's money supply) as a means of righting the economy.[19] Disney's celebrated *Three Little Pigs* (also 1933) fits into this model. (In a more blatant example, a month earlier, Lantz and Universal had released an Oswald cartoon, *Confidence*, that featured images of a *singing* FDR; he's "the doctor" for the country offering injections of "confidence" to beat the Depression.) And, at the dime-store budgets Warner Bros. was willing to offer, cartoons seemed to be a cheap and memorable way to accomplish the cross-promotion of Warner Bros. sheet music, popular songs, and movies. The parent studio's live-action films and studio infrastructure "functioned as a trim, lean operation," according to Gomery, and "operated on the smallest budgets of any Big Five."[20] Schlesinger was merely minding the company's bottom line; frugality was a way of life. *Sinkin' in the Bathtub* featured bits from five separate recent hit songs—a smart start to the showcase; most of the first batch of cartoons (four of six) had titles that played on Warner Bros.–owned songs.[21]

Less than two years after the release of *Steamboat Willie*, Walt Disney's studio had leapfrogged the pack. (The Fleischers would be at his shoulder with their darker, more surreal and edgy cartoons and the sensual Betty Boop and the funny Popeye series, but critical and popular kudos belonged to Disney.) Disney's shadow covered everyone. Between 1931 and 1938, Disney would win *all* eight short-subjects Oscars, while Warner Bros. won none and received only one nomination. For critics and audiences alike, it was Mr. Disney's decade. But, more important for our purposes, Disney laid foundations, especially for those who would follow without following, like Tex Avery: "the 'anything-is-possible-in-these-here-cartoon-pictures' implosive bag of tricks Avery developed . . . would be inconceivable without the bedrock foundation of believability and solidity Disney brought to the sound cartoon."[22] (Harman and Ising would employ this same believability in their work, gamely trying to compete with Disney.) The laws of the cartoon world must exist and be agreed on before they can be broken. It's futile to not compare the ascending, enthroned, or descending Disney to all others—other comers (Schlesinger's, Harman-Ising, UPA) measured themselves that way, so it must be acknowledged. But it's also nice to be able to occasionally shine a light on the pesky gadfly as opposed to the prize cow. There are always other ways of doing things and doing them well. The gangs at Warner Bros. and MGM forced this view on a Disney-inclined populace.

WARNER BROS.

Even though an excited Jack Warner had supposedly ordered a full run of cartoons before he'd finished screening *Sinkin' in the Bathtub*, the public debut of Bosko and Looney Tunes was restrained.[23] By December 1930, reports from exhibitors were quite encouraging, though, with reception of Looney Tunes titles characterized as "exceptionally enthusiastic."[24] Popularity demanded another series of thirteen, this time Merrie Melodies, again using Warner Bros.–owned music, and in this case a single song (like *Smile, Darn Ya, Smile!*) and few or no recurring characters.[25] This simple 1931 order of a batch of cartoons "initiated the classic period of Warner Bros. animation."[26] The Harman and Ising Bosko cartoons looked similar to Disney's ("the same brute-simple graphic style"), were a bit less improvisational (or less sloppy) than the Fleischers' work, and were heavy on the Mickey Mousing, perhaps to the point of sending up Disney.[27] (Most of these Schlesinger animators had endured a baptism of fire over at Walt's place.[28]) These cartoons competed, yes, but, as Maltin points out, "they did not innovate or improve"; these animators wanted their work to be Disney-like but settled for Disney-lite. Maltin concludes, "One can trace the improvement in Disney's cartoons year by year in the 1930s, but there's virtually no progress during Harman and Ising's span of four years at Warners'."[29]

By 1932, both Looney Tunes and Merrie Melodies were becoming established series, programmable and popular, but competing against a crowded field: against Lantz's manic Oswald, Betty Boop's sensuality, a swarm of Terrytoons, and a few Ted Eshbaughs; against Scrappy, Ub Iwerks and Flip the Frog; and against Mickey and the Silly Symphonies. The playing field wasn't quite level, though, given Disney's hold on three-strip Technicolor, Mickey's enduring popularity, and the fact that Disney was willing to self-finance and borrow from banks to make better cartoons. In 1931, a large trade-magazine ad congratulated Disney, appropriately overwhelming a smallish, text-only announcement for the first Merrie Melodies series.[30] Months later came a salve. On the enormous Winter Garden marquee, "Merrie Melodies" was prominently displayed next to the name of the Warner Bros. features' star Joan Blondell, both obviously a calling card to passersby.[31] By 1934, it was announced that the next batch of Merrie Melodies would be released in Cinecolor, a two-strip process that proved to be popular with audiences.[32] It wouldn't take long for the new kids Clampett, Freleng, Avery, and Jones at Schlesinger's to grab attention, especially as cartoon appreciation swung from the art of Disney to the cartoony work of Warner Bros.: "The consistent quality of [Schlesinger's] short animated movies was due . . . to the gathering together of a group of talented, idiosyncratic people . . . [creating] an immediately identifiable studio style.[33]

This kind of success didn't happen overnight. Mickey had been created as an act of desperation, his acceptance entwined with the sound revolution; the artists at Schlesinger would go five years assaying continuing character types with limited success—Foxy, Goopy Geer, Bosko and Honey, and even a "Buddy" came and went without fuss or fortune. By late 1933, Harman and Ising had left for greener pastures, taking Schlesinger's only star, Bosko. Buddy was his immediate replacement. The 1930–1935 Schlesinger cartoons weren't bad (clever, good movement and music), but they weren't distinguishable from those of other second-tier studios. Industry pundits as early as 1932 complained about the lack of variety in cartoon offerings.[34] And, without Bosko, there was no longer a sellable face. Most of the other studios were offering humanized animals (Mickey, Bimbo, Oswald) or stylized humans (Betty, Popeye), while Harman-Ising kicked off with a "Bosko the what?"[35]—not an animal and not a boy. And Warner Bros.'s Buddy wasn't the answer, either. Short a lead, Schlesinger's studio became known for novelty cartoons, including Hollywood send-ups and coming-to-life titles—both attractive and fun, but neither offering continuing-character star power. This was also the period when, having lost the veterans Harman and Ising, the next Schlesinger generation emerged: Avery, Clampett, Tashlin, Freleng, and Jones. This was the group that would produce Bugs, Porky, Daffy, Elmer, and more. Harman and Ising took with them their Disney infatuation, leaving the younger Warner Bros. team to make its own way as it designed new characters and stories.

From this newer batch, in 1935, came a subdued "eureka" moment: Freleng's two-strip Technicolor cartoon *I Haven't Got a Hat* presented a handful of schoolhouse characters—two cats, a pig, an owl, and two puppies. All cute, but no shining star. For some reason, the cat, Beans, got tabbed first, appearing in his own cartoons across 1935–1936, sometimes costarring Kitty, Oliver Owl, Porky, and the puppies. But it was the stout, stuttering pig who somehow made the grade. Porky went from appearing in four cartoons in 1935 to seventeen in the following year, six of which bore his name. Hired as a director in 1935, Tex Avery was essential for some of these characters' progressions; for Porky, it was Avery directing the Beans cartoon *Gold Diggers of '49* and redesigning the pig. Porky first played the goofy sidekick but evolved into the straight man and, eventually, the corporate role, as Mickey had. Avery would help create or redesign all the major Warner Bros. characters, and he, Freleng, Clampett, Jones, and Tashlin would proceed to invent "a new visual style"—

a non-Disney style, a reaction to the Disneyfication of the short-subject cartoon.[36] By 1937, Porky was a star at Warner Bros. and taking on junior partners.

Even though Porky had cut his teeth as an Andy Devine type, the events of *Porky's Duck Hunt* (1937) would set in motion a new, beautiful relationship. Here, Porky is the straight man to a duck's insouciant nuttiness. In this Avery huntin' cartoon (where Elmer Fudd would soon make his living, also thanks to Avery), Porky is the sensible, accident-prone hero of the picture, and then there's a "crazy darnfool duck." The duck nails his first appearance as what Klein terms a "nuisance," bouncing up and down and hooting madly, yet slowing down for tsk-tsk moments, as when Porky's gun jams and the duck helpfully clears it. The duck fully embodies his character, certainly a nuisance doubling as an "over-reactor,"[37] like Donald two years earlier in *Band Concert*. Porky plays the dogged, determined, and mostly unflappable hunter just trying to make the picture and bring home dinner. These characters have personality; they are not the "characterless" Scrappy, Cubby, Flip, Willie, et al.[38] This new generation of creators at Warner Bros. was not another comic-strip generation, per se; they were raised on the fumes of vaudeville, on radio, and, especially, on the movies.

Gene Walz sees the turning point for Warner Bros. as coming in 1940, when they abandoned Disneyfication and moved on—specifically, modifying Bugs Bunny. (It likely began earlier, in 1938, when Schlesinger confirmed his studio would *not* produce a feature-length cartoon.) Bugs began as a darnfool rabbit—a nuisance in *Porky's Hare Hunt* (1938)—and then was a nameless pest in *Prest-O Change-O* (1939). Two more titles came and went before 1940, when Avery took on *A Wild Hare*, in which Bugs gets his controller personality and his line "What's up, Doc?" A new, streamlined Bugs Bunny design was ironically more like Charles Thorson's Disney character Max Hare, created in 1934. (Avery would quip later that he was surprised they weren't sued by Disney for the likeness.[39]) After 1940, Schlesinger's animators felt freer to spoof Disney and move beyond copying and homage; their efforts included Avery's *Tortoise Beats Hare* (1941), a send-up of Disney's *The Tortoise and the Hare*.[40] Bugs could be malleable and protean—a survivor. With Schlesinger at the helm, each

Warner Bros. director could approach Bugs differently, unusual for a studio that created continuing-character series. Avery can let Bugs get very full of himself and then lose, as in *Tortoise Beats Hare*. The turtles cheat, of course, taking the curse off the loss. Jones's version of Bugs takes a few punches in early rounds; then he declares war and triumphs. Jones's Bugs is also the thinker, the wry trickster, the eyebrow-raised foil to Daffy's overreactor. Clampett wasn't afraid to hurt and humiliate Bugs, gifting him a wide array of emotive responses, even pettiness. In *Falling Hare*, Bugs spars with a gremlin and gets bashed, smashed, and fooled from start to run-out-of-gas finish. Many consider Freleng's version of Bugs the pinnacle, simply because he was the most likable. There is no correct answer to which is the best Bugs; the fact that Bugs could be so many things to so many (directors, audiences, historians) and remain a popular continuing character *is* the story.

Across 1937–1940, Schlesinger's team re-created themselves, embracing the more "West Coast style" and honing characters Porky, Daffy, Bugs, and Elmer. By 1938, it's clear their bread would be buttered on the side of shorts, not features, and they were producing more shorts than any other studio, though quality fluctuated significantly.[41] In late June 1937, as the industry was awash with *Snow White* talk, Schlesinger kept his name in the news by shipping five cartoons, including "a trio of Merrie Melodies—*Sweet Sioux, Egg-Head Rides Again*, and *Plenty of Money and You*—and two Looney-Tunes, *Porky's Bad-Time Story* and *Porky's Super-Service*." The pictures vary in quality, and both Porky cartoons had been farmed out to Ub Iwerks's struggling studio.[42] In 1938, Schlesinger produced forty shorts; Fleischer followed with thirty-eight; and Disney came in third with eighteen. In 1939, Schlesinger released forty-four shorts; Fleischer, just nineteen; and Disney, only thirteen.[43] Just three years after the release of *Snow White*, the numbers were there to prove Schlesinger's commitment to the short: His studio produced forty-eight cartoons in 1940. The new directors were finding themselves as well. Avery's rule breaking, for example, was based on rules that had been in place for years, many reinforced by Disney. The first level of rule breaking becomes obvious—if Disney told his people to not impale, decapitate, or skewer their characters, those things disappeared from Disney films, and

Avery knew precisely what types of bodily damage his next film would *have to* feature. The next level is a bit more subtle. Parody or burlesque become possible when the subject or genre is fully in place, understood by all, and a concomitant weariness (or, perhaps, contemptible familiarity) with the established genre's semantic elements and syntax (and its place in culture) is acknowledged. And it wasn't just Avery: "In Clampett's best work, and in [Warner Bros.] cartoons in general, the humor is the product of a simple idea or object that invites parody taken to the absolute furthest point this side of tastelessness," Cohen writes. "Like the best black-humorists, Clampett deals with the touchiest subjects—suicide, insanity, senility—and through exaggeration makes them appropriate and hilarious comic terrain."[44]

Both Clampett and Avery took Looney Tunes and Merrie Melodies "high-octane," with more audacity, more gags, and faster pacing. Clampett's "undisciplined sproinging rubbery character-motion gave him some of the most eminently stretchable-bendable characters in Cartoon History," said *Film Comment* in 1975, "[his] anything-for-a-laugh temperament prophesized today's Sick or Black Humor."[45] Avery enjoyed "context destroying," pulling the rug out from under any semblance of sustained verisimilitude, part of the reason he would be lauded by avant-gardists and experimental film types and compared so often to filmmakers of various "new waves."[46] Clampett always wanted to make more than cartoons and would move on to television by 1949. Avery flouted suspension of disbelief, whether in his early Porky cartoons or his punny travelogues, where hummingbirds hum and mockingbirds mock.[47] If there was a laugh to be had, Avery (over)reached for it: "The restraints that other directors honored in the name of 'good taste' or 'believability' were bypassed by Avery's insane hyperboles and grotesque distortions, which knew no bounds other than those of the medium of animation."[48] In this sense, Avery was following Messmer and earlier McCay and Cohl—for whom "limitations would be the limitations of the artist, not the medium"[49]—allowing only imagination to dictate how and where and how far his characters moved; their elasticity, their fissility, or the effects of their mass; or even their relation to cinematic reality. Avery and his colleagues' style "fell somewhere between the

[cute], semi-naturalistic Disney mode and the bizarre surrealism of early Fleischer," writes Cohen. "[They are] the most consciously contemporary of cartoons, utilizing up-to-the-minute pop tunes, events and cultural references."[50] Following a spat with Schlesinger, Avery left Warner Bros.; MGM would be his next significant stop.

MEANWHILE, IN OTHER CARTOON-PRODUCING STUDIOS . . .

In 1927, Paramount signed what turned into a long-term deal with the Fleischer brothers for cartoon production; by 1931, Paramount-Famous-Lasky acquired Publix theaters to create the "largest motion-picture circuit in film history."[51] Success and expansion was a sharp two-edged sword, as we'll see. Fleischer cartoons exploded in popularity and will be discussed in the following chapter.

MGM

MGM (Loew's Inc.[52]) showed no interest in cartoons across the silent period. It wouldn't be until Disney and Mickey proved themselves that MGM took notice, first trying to secure a distribution deal with Disney. MGM wanted to deal directly with Walt, but Pat Powers threatened lawsuits if any distributor meddled.[53] MGM then helped engineer Pat Powers's coup at Disney by luring the hand behind Mickey, Ub Iwerks, with the promise of his own studio. This was MGM's first go at the brass ring. From 1930 through 1933, Ub gamely ran his studio *and* wanted to draw every frame of the frog cartoons *and* showcase emerging technologies that fascinated him, a workload he likely hadn't premeasured. One of the sore spots at Disney had been Walt's demand that Ub become a lead animator, allowing for in-betweens and the like to be done by assistants, both to give Ub more time to lead and to train younger animators.[54] Ub balked. Ub was also not much of an administrator or businessman. Some have even called out the naked emperor and said that perhaps Iwerks wasn't as brilliant an artist or as essential to Disney's success as lore continues to suggest.[55] Two-sided truths at least considered, Ub's thirty-seven Flip cartoons were well animated, pleasant, and even well received but forgettable.[56] Powers demanded a redesign of Flip after only two so-so cartoons, and he became more boy than frog. Armed with talents Grim Natwick, Shamus Culhane, Al Eugster, and even Carl Stalling, the Flip cartoons still "never caught on, probably because they weren't very good."[57]

A single sentence in Leslie Iwerks's glowing book about her grandfather underscores a fatal flaw. Discussing the tepid reception to the two-color *Fiddlesticks*, Iwerks concludes aptly, "The technology was a breakthrough, but the story felt like a retread of past successes."[58] Iwerks's cartoons never advanced in the crucial areas of character or story no matter who was the star, which technologies were employed, or which great animators assisted. Chuck Jones could acknowledge Iwerks's technical skills—Jones and Clampett had worked under Iwerks on two farmed-out Warner Bros. titles in 1937—but there were weaknesses: "Iwerks was a brilliant animator . . . [but] he didn't have any story capacity . . . he wasn't a funny man at all." (Turns out two out of three *is* bad.) Iwerks assayed Willie Whopper, a tale-telling boy, but those cartoons were no more engaging to Powers, MGM, and most exhibitors.[59] Iwerks's ComiColor shorts followed (sans MGM), twenty-five of them over the next three years, using the Cinecolor process. Though some saw these as "embarrassing" (because of their dated designs, for one thing), there are beautiful and fascinating moments across all these otherwise also-ran cartoons, including bizarre characters (the Pincushion Man) and handsome effects from an affordable multiplane process Ub built but underused. Exhibitors hated them.[60] Losing MGM, Powers and Celebrity Pictures had to distribute these, and returns diminished. Iwerks's time on his own was coming to an end; he would rejoin Disney in 1940 and remain there until his death in 1971.[61]

MGM's second grab at the elusive ring found Harman-Ising in the house, their budgets doubled, their fixation on Disney firm. They were to produce more Bosko titles as part of the Technicolor Happy Harmonies.[62] The last six of these cartoons—where Bosko is finally a little black *boy*—were regularly blasted by local exhibitors ("No good; a waste of time and money"[63]). Iwerks's ComiColor and the Fleischers' Talkartoons titles were ultimately more comparable to these than to Disney's product. Unable to stay within MGM's strict budget demands, Happy Harmonies lasted until 1937, and the Harman-Ising unit was reassigned.[64] There were exhibitors who complained about losing these colorful titles (like *Wayward Pups*) for the dusted-off, sepia-toned "Captain and the Kids," but MGM wanted better control of its product.

Attempt number three for MGM and cartoons was the charm. To better control costs, MGM created an in-house, state-of-the-art studio and hired the respected short-subjects man Fred Quimby, as well as gifted staff from Harman-Ising and Terry (including Hanna and Barbera) and even Freleng from Schlesinger's. The first series again starred the forty-year-old comic-strip characters Captain and the Kids—an odd choice. This series benefited from the money and prestige of MGM, and its films were sepia-tinted, but it never got traction and included only fifteen episodes.[65] In August 1939, a new animation unit, headed by Hanna and Barbera, opened at MGM, and musical cartoons were expected from them. In February 1940, Hanna and Barbera's *Puss Gets the Boot* appeared, featuring a certain cat and mouse, and Tex Avery's work from August 1942 marked MGM as one of the leaders for the following decade. MGM ended the decade on an upswing.

20th Century-Fox
20th Century-Fox is where we'll find Paul Terry during the later 1930s. Fox had been distributing comedies for Educational Pictures, with Terrytoons being a part of the package. Terry was producing twenty-six cartoons a year and spending one-fifth of what Disney spent.[66] Terry's crew, like many, struggled to find continuing characters (trying Puddy the Pup, Kiko the Kangaroo, even reanimating Farmer Al Falfa), and success eluded them until Gandy Goose and Mighty Mouse caught on as the war years began. Fox was still "fifth among the Big Five in cartoons," so only a relative success.[67]

RKO
RKO's decade wasn't much more scintillating until 1936, when they managed to land Disney—a coup for an eight-year-old conglomerate. Before that, since 1930, they had to settle for the talents of Amedee Van Beuren, who'd been distributing Terry's Fables since the previous decade. Van Beuren was not an animator; he entered the industry for

the investment—losing or borrowing or reinvesting money, à la Disney, weren't options. His studio was just across the street from Fleischer on Broadway, meaning there were always better (or at least trained) animators within arm's reach. Terry had left in 1929 to form Terrytoons, and Van Beuren Studios was left with many of Terry's former staff and rights to the Fables.

What they didn't have, what the business had proved was really needed, was a star continuing character, even a Bosko. By 1931, a Mutt and Jeff–like pair, Tom and Jerry, made a twenty-six-cartoon run to little fanfare. The next go was Cubby Bear, a tweaked version of Bimbo or Foxy. A Little King (Soglow's comic-strip character) adaptation and even a short Amos and Andy series followed. None of these cartoons are awful or even unaccomplished in at least some way—there were talented animators and directors at every studio. The Jim Tyer–animated Little King titles *Jolly Good Felons* and *The Fatal Note*,[68] for example, are a joy, and, if nothing else, the Little King's *On the Pan* cartoon is right up there with Lantz's *Confidence* for its FDR adulation.[69] Van Beuren lured artist Burt Gillett in 1934, at a staggering salary, and Gillett tried to bring a Disney rigor and a more professional and artistic style to the studio. Subsequent Rainbow Parade titles included a Parrotville series, *The Sunshine Makers*, and Molly Moo-Cow titles.[70] The color is vivid in these cartoons to the point of saturation, and the vapid stories and characters are overwhelmed by the oddly vibrant, overly busy, and frantic cartoon world. These cartoons, unlike the Schlesinger cartoons, didn't benefit from access to snappy popular songs; their creators settled for original songs that narrate the stories, such as they are. These songs most often play as chirpy, cartoony light opera.

The end of Van Beuren's studio was rather sudden. RKO, half owner of Van Beuren since 1930, was able to wrest Disney from United Artists by simply offering more favorable terms, including more per cartoon and a better distribution network. In 1936, Walt Disney was making the cartoons everyone wanted to program and see, so RKO saw no downside in paying a premium. By 1937, RKO was distributing a true unicorn: the first animated feature, *Snow White*, which, by 1938, was the biggest film of the year. Handling or treating a cartoon like a feature was new, and

RKO seemed to take to it. Challenges arose when the next projects, *Pinocchio* and *Fantasia*, cost more than most live-action features and underperformed, thanks to their subject matter and the darkening world. (The war would cut international distribution profits by three-quarters, impacting all Hollywood studios.) Major hurdles aside, RKO and Disney remained a couple until RKO began to fall apart and the Disneys could set up Buena Vista.

Universal

Universal was also a bit of an also during the 1930s. Charles Mintz had been handling cartoons, specifically Oswald the Lucky Rabbit, since the mid-1920s and through two of its three iterations—Disney, followed by Harman-Ising. The third go, under Walter Lantz, started in 1928 and was Universal's in-house, sound-era version that produced twenty-six Oswald titles a year.[71] Lantz created Pooch the Pup for a 1932 series and then color CarTune Classics to further borrow on Silly Symphony prestige. Walter Lantz has been described as a more "affable" Disney."[72] This moniker works better as "a more affable *Walt*," because he was clearly no Disney. He did extend Oswald's life and created Andy Panda and Woody Woodpecker. In 1930, Lantz had produced the animated segment of the Paul Whiteman film *King of Jazz*, employing two-strip Technicolor. Lantz wouldn't find a character that cast much of a shadow until 1940, when Woody Woodpecker appeared.

In one significant way, the Walts were similar—they both valued independence—and, by 1935, Lantz was out on his own. Contracting independently with Universal, in 1936 Lantz set up his own studio, brainstorming forgettable characters in the form of three monkeys, a skunk, two dogs, a family of ducks, a baby mouse, a satyr, and Andy Panda, who at least could be connected to a recent worldwide panda craze.[73] Most of this work was futile: "By 1939, Lantz had created a dozen new characters, experimented with alternatives to cel animation, dabbled in feature-film production, made commissioned films, and kept up with his contractual obligation to Universal," Adamson writes. "And his main character was still Oswald the Lucky Rabbit."[74] Lantz finally hit it big with the manic Woody Woodpecker, who appeared in 1940 and was a headline star for nearly a decade. Woody is another character who has continued to sell merchandise and even additional series and feature films well past his prime. (Woody would also be a popular figure for nose art and insignia during World War II.) Lantz kept his costs down as well, spending an average of $15,000 on each cartoon, $20,000 less than Disney's average.[75] Lantz also produced a music-based series, Swing Symphonies, tied to popular songs, and he would keep making short cartoons until 1972. As with MGM, Universal's cartoon efforts wouldn't truly blossom until the 1940s.

Columbia

Columbia had struck gold in 1929, when it signed to distribute the Silly Symphonies.[76] Columbia was one of the minor studios that was not fully integrated, meaning that it didn't own vast chains of cinemas where its films could be guaranteed a run.[77] Columbia was able to satisfy Disney's needs for Silly Symphony distributions; by March 1930, Mickey titles as well;[78] and, later, Pluto and Goofy titles. By 1932, Walt was looking to trade up to a larger distribution network for more upfront money, moving to Chaplin, Fairbanks, Griffith, and Pickford—United Artists.

What Columbia was left with for the bulk of the 1930s was Mintz (who had broken with Paramount when it took up with the Fleischers), the aging Krazy Kat, and, from 1930 onward, the new little boy character Scrappy as well as a few color cartoons from Iwerks. In 1934, Mintz began producing Color Rhapsodies, in two-strip Technicolor, the titles pleasantly indistinguishable from those of other Silly Symphony copies. Iwerks Color Rhapsodies, like *Merry Mannequins* and *Skeleton Frolic*, are beautiful but look as if they could have been designed a decade earlier. Mintz would pass away in December 1939, and Columbia's animation studio would endure instability across much of the 1940s.

The 1930s produced few cartoon classics outside of Disney's kingdom but saw to the forming, reforming, and nurturing of major talents and studios that would come to fame the following decade. The sound era was producing characters to be reckoned with, and, by 1940, Bugs and Daffy as well as Tom and Jerry were ready to elbow Disney aside in the short-subjects race. *Snow White* might have unfairly dimmed the growing lights at Warner Bros. and MGM, distracting audiences and critics alike from the short cartoon with her siren song of feature animation, but the sound and speed and sheer wit of 1940s cartoons was just around the corner. For now, the acknowledged leaders of the field across the 1930s—Disney and Fleischer—need to be properly presented.

CHAPTER 6

The 1930s Main Event

Disney versus Fleischer

As late as 1928, of the major studios, only Paramount and, of the minor studios, only Universal regularly included cartoons in their programs. The competition with live-action shorts was intense, and the novelty program was still an undividable package. Then Mickey whistled and played washboard, teeth, and teats, and the world changed.[1] By 1935, most major and minor studios had latched onto an animation producer, releasing cartoon shorts into theaters as part of a weekly package. Paramount—emerging from bankruptcy that same year—was distributing the Fleischer cartoons, and Disney, free from Pat Powers and then Columbia, supplied United Artists with cartoons. The Fleischer deal, involving a big studio name and many important cinemas, seemed to be the better one. But Disney was constantly on the hunt for better terms, trading up when he could. Going into the 1930s, Fleischer Studios was still a respected bastion of consistent, quality work; Disney was the up-and-comer. So, here's the flustering part. By late November 1928, the rest of the cartoon industry would be trying to catch up to Disney; by 1933, the race was called. As hinted at earlier, Paul Wells identifies the thing that would niggle at Max until his dying day—namely, that "all cartoon animation that follows the Disney output is a reaction to Disney, aesthetically, technically and ideologically." During and after this "usurpation" (1933–1941), animation was in line behind Disney.[2] Worse, it became clear that all animation that *preceded* the Disney output, from pigs to Bambi, was also being measured against Disney and found wanting. Such judgments were unfair, certainly, and would be tempered with the passage of time and the efforts of Tex Avery, Warner Bros., and UPA. One critic's harsh 1970s assessment of the Fleischers' product was as follows: "But the final verdict on their films must be that once you have their measure, they aren't worth a great deal of trouble trying to track down, although they are not without interest if they should actually turn up on the doorstep."[3] I disagree.

A little rehearsing here will help us catch the tune. The Fleischers had already pioneered the sound cartoon, with Song Car-Tunes and then Screen Songs, though their utilitarian approach—sound as a sing-along novelty—helped keep the technology a novelty. Other Fleischer projects across the 1920s, like the science films, weren't money-spinners, though bookings were healthy. These films were distributed by Red Seal, the Fleischer-founded company, but, without a vast cinema circuit, distribution was costly. Red Seal's own novelty program was selling across the middle part of the 1920s, as it tried to compete head-to-head with the larger film studios.[4] By October 1926, bankruptcy proceedings were underway, and the Fleischers were looking to reorganize. This is when Alfred Weiss appeared, rescued, and then ruined the studio; by 1930, Inkwell was in bankruptcy. The relationship with Paramount that Weiss had fostered was still tenable, however, and, by mid-1930, more good news emerged: Max bought back all "patents, copyrights and trade-marks" owned by Out-of-the-Inkwell.[5] The Fleischers started to get back on track with industrial films and the dependable Screen Songs and were back in the harness with distributor Paramount.

In 1929, the Song Car-Tunes gave way to Paramount's Screen Songs, which ran strongly through 1938. By late 1931, largely thanks to the popularity of Screen Songs, Fleischer Studios was banking thousands of dollars per quarter.[6] The Fleischer answer to Mickey's success, though, was the Talkartoons, first advertised in a big way in June 1929, after Paramount had signed the Fleischers to a contract whose term seemed to be a working lifetime.[7] From the beginning, it's clear these aren't Disney cartoons. The first title, *Noah's Lark*, looks like a Terry entry—animals everywhere—but there also is a Coney Island–like image, linking it to the Fleischers' urban New York milieu. "The Fleischer cartoon world is one in which everything is potentially something else," Langer writes, "with a resultingly bizarre imagery that finds its fullest expression in the cartoons of the early Thirties."[8] The proto–Betty Boop (she with the dog ears) would be introduced in the Talkartoon *Dizzy Dishes* and soon headlining.[9] Two of the finest, *Minnie the Moocher* (1932) and *Snow-White* (1933), took the sound conceit and ran with it. The Fleischers convinced popular musical acts of the day, including the Royal Samoans, Louis Armstrong, and Cab Calloway, to record versions of their hits for the animators, who would then create cartoon scenarios to accompany them. Calloway's sinewy style as bandleader and singer was perfect for the rotoscoped and then hand-drawn sequences (he is rendered as Ghost Walrus in *Minnie* and as Koko in *Snow-White*). "The effect is little short of a knockout" raved one reviewer.[10] In both *Minnie the Moocher* and *Snow-White*, the journey Betty takes is like a nightmarish Coney Island dark ride, featuring images of demons and dragons, skulls, skeletons in vice tableaux, dead-swan boat rides and speakeasies of the dead, capital punishment, gambling, and assorted spooks and ghosts. Featured songs "Minnie the Moocher" and "St. James Infirmary Blues" are funereal, certainly not Disney-like.

The first new character out of the gate would become Bimbo, meant to challenge Mickey—he sings, he dances, he plays instruments. He was another iteration of Felix, Julius, Oswald, Bosko, et al., and exhibitors reported that his early titles—*Hot Dog* and *Swing, You Sinners* (both 1930)—played well. *Swing, You Sinners* especially revealed the Fleischers' darker, metamorphic, more surreal tastes in animation, *starting* at the macabre level of Disney's *The Skeleton Dance* and venturing weirder, perhaps purposely drawing distinctions between themselves and the more cinematic Disney—"If it can be done in real life," Max would say, "it's not animation."[11] In the Fleischer world, anything that's in the frame, from a hat to a chair to Saturn, can have a life, can be threatening or helpful, can squeak or speak, and can be polite or rude. This distinction would be a boon for a few years, distinguishing the more adult cartoons from the kiddie titles—Fleischer from Disney.

With the enforcement of the Motion Picture Production Code, however, that same distinctiveness would create a ghetto effect just as

The Fleischer *Snow-White* features macabre vices of the Modern City, sung to life by a clown-ghost and ending with a satisfying dragon chase sequence. *Snow-White*, Fleischer, 1932 (from *Betty Boop: The Essential Collection* Blu-ray). Screenshot taken by the author.

obvious to exhibitors. Codes had been in place since the early 1920s, the goal being industry self-control and better PR to stave off state or federal legislation. The coming of sound kicked everything up a few notches, and, by 1930, the Motion Picture Production Code was adopted, building on a list of "don'ts" and "be carefuls" agreed to three years earlier. (It may even have been Paramount star Mae West's sexualized lines and delivery that spelled doom for Betty and her "fun morality."[12]) Even with all this, cartoons had been somewhat ignored, given their place on programs (chasers) and likely thanks to Terry's piffles of animal adventures, an acknowledgment of these films' "charming inconsequence."[13]

But by 1933–1934, *all* film was maturing, in subject matter, dialogue, and imagery, prompting "unified attacks by religious, club and parent-teacher groups" and demands that Hollywood put teeth into its

Code enforcement.[14] In May 1934, listings of "banned" films began to be released; still, no cartoons or cartoon characters were mentioned. Hollywood (over)reacted anyway. Under Joseph I. Breen, the Code began to be more rigorously and, for the benefit of complainants, more obviously enforced in 1934. Betty could probably have squeaked by with some changes (in mid-June 1934's *Betty Boop's Trial*, she shows no cleavage, for example, and still looks fetching), but Paramount was taking no chances—it needed goodwill and good (fiscal) graces. The Fleischers had to change; Disney kept on.

It's hard to conceive now, but this was a time when Disney was not the biggest fish in what was a small pond. Across the 1920s, Felix, the Fables, and the Fleischers were better known and better distributed; in the 1930s, the Fleischers had business problems, but their product was solid, respected, well reviewed, and well exhibited. Fleischer could also claim unique characters in Betty and then Popeye—there wasn't the usual host of doppelgangers trying to compete.[15] The Depression didn't hammer the animation industry the way it did most other businesses, though, with the exception of MGM, all major film studios reported losses in 1932 as box-office receipts fell and banks cut back on production loans.[16] Paul Terry kept making his animal-stocked cartoons twice a month, rain or shine. Disney suffered emotionally and personally but kept reinvesting in his cartoons and studio: "As America foundered, Walt's company flourished as never before."[17] For Warner Bros. cartoons, Schlesinger spent very little, and his cartoons lived on less. These smaller operations didn't suffer equally when attendance dropped and were likely grateful that, no matter how deep the Depression, more than sixty million people regularly went to the movies.[18] Animators were able to get jobs, quit jobs, and get other cartoon jobs when unemployment was otherwise at record levels.

Disney struggled not for lack of interest in the studio's output but thanks to Walt's insistence on regular reinvestment, better training and equipment, and better cartoons. Better always meant more expensive. The Fleischers likely didn't see Disney as a real threat for years—they had the security of a Paramount contract; until 1936, Disney was hat in hand every two years, looking for another distribution dime. "Walt Disney was an annoying pebble in my father's shoe," Max's son Richard would write years later, "a pebble that eventually grew into a rock."[19] From pebble to rock to crushing boulder—the Disney irritant increased. The industry was small, and everyone knew what everyone else was doing. Culhane notes that in the early 1930s, he and his peers would go and see every Disney release in their neighborhood theaters, "and there would be an excited discussion the next day about the fine quality of the animation."[20] They admired and envied the spendthrift Disney work. Across the decade, they were seeing plaudits—"[The] Silly Symphonies are works of both science and art"[21]—from highbrow critics fawning over Disney. If your lot is to labor making funny, affordable cartoons at Van Beuren, Lantz, or even Fleischer, such quotes might be disheartening. Max Fleischer, though, knew who he was and what he wanted his cartoons and studio to be. He valued, he would say in a later letter, "flashiness" and "delightfulness"; his artists' goal should not be to make an "animated oil painting" but a "Cartoonist's Cartoon."[22] He was clearly referencing Disney's penchant for increased realism. The Fleischers held fast to their New York upbringings and influences—in this same letter, Max hints that all of it is their "backyard," where they should stay—it's why Fleischer cartoons are rich with images of ghastly amusement parks, sweatshops, bars, gambling and assorted vices, decaying urban street life, and jazz. And, since reality isn't the goal, transformation becomes legal tender; it's all about metamorphosis—Koko from a drop of ink, Calloway's characters from Koko and a wisp of smoke, and Betty from a dog.

And what of Betty? In *Dizzy Dishes*, an unnamed, somewhat dog-like cabaret singer appears, interacting with an unnamed, dog-like waiter. Over the next few cartoons, these two would become Betty and Bimbo. *Dizzy Dishes* is a typically weird, stream-of-consciousness cartoon and recognizably Fleischerian in its night-club setting, music and dancing, swells and toughs in the crowd, ethnic accents ("I vant ham") and foods ("Where's my knishes?"), and a mincing waiter. It is also Fleischerian in that everything can be alive and can become something else. As for Betty, the singer chirps out her "Boop Boop a Doop" song, and we're done with her. Shamus Culhane admitted there wasn't anyone in the Fleischer operation who could properly apply metamorphosis to Betty, transforming her from a naive, virginal sexpot to, perhaps, an employed, self-sufficient woman of her time: "Nobody can be creative beyond the range of his imagination and his own life's experience." (Fascinating that Culhane saw none of the animators above him as being able to even *imagine* a well-crafted female character.) But the Betty Boop animators were "New York street kids," period, Culhane concluded.[23] In the few years Betty enjoyed before the Production Code came knocking, she had many adventures, she lost her clothing many times, and yet she managed to protect her virtue against "unpleasant characters with heavy hands."[24]

Paramount ran a bit scared in 1934 as the voices of reform reached strident levels. Doing business as a major studio meant ownership of large theatrical circuits, where most of the studio's money was made, and where public protest or even indifference could spell disaster, and quickly. Paramount was fresh from a buying and building spree across 1929–1930, adding hundreds of theaters to its circuits. It also underwent a painful receivership and bankruptcy (1933–1934) and a restructuring and eventual reorganization (1934–1935). In addition, RKO had defaulted into receivership, while Warner Bros. and Fox very nearly succumbed. In 1934,[25] Paramount's restructuring was still underway and not yet approved. The irony of Max depending on the solid partnership of a rock-steady Paramount should be clear. Paramount's response to the Code involved preemptive censorship, meaning making cuts before distribution and even before production. By 1935, there was still a Betty Boop, certainly, but she had sleeves and a modest skirt; disappearing were her décolletage, garter, and, most unfortunately, her narrative freedom. From mid-1934 on, her clothes stay on, we can't see through her skirt—we *can* see through her fatuous male friend, Freddy—no one's pawing at her (except a too-cute new dog, Pudgy), and the double entendres fade away.[26] Betty was now more often found at home, cleaning, cooking, and being domestic, safely away from louts and heavy breathers. She was still a merchandising star, but, without titillation, she was diminished. Story mattered, too. With Disney advancing his Silly Symphonies along more "realistic" lines every day, audiences grew accustomed to the beginning-middle-end structure of classical narrative, noting the absence in those titles of "naïve drawing and absurd dialogue,"[27] two solid legs under the Fleischer cartoon table. A third leg might be the chase-sequence scenario that closed many Fleischer cartoons, borrowed directly from Mack Sennett and his Keystone Kops, each "a majestic trajectory of pure anarchic motion."[28] Great to watch, but perhaps perceived by audiences as old-fashioned. By 1935, for example, when Disney had been "owning" three-strip color cartoons and employing that color and more cinematic technologies and structures in everything from *Flowers and Trees* to *The Band Concert*, it's easy to see how audiences could have become convinced this—meaning the Disney way—was *the* way to accomplish cartoons.

To be fair, Betty was very popular despite the Code, and, if Paramount had exhibited even a bit more spine, the change mightn't have been so debilitating. But it's also fair to remember that this transition coincided with Disney pushing onward and upward into more perfectly matched sound, double-pencil testing, first-rate animation, Technicolor, and elevated subject matter. And if audiences were making a choice among cartoon producers, exhibitors would hear of it, then distributors, and then the studio heads, and the "encouragement" from above to cartoon studios might be simple: "Start doing it the Disney way." Kind of a perfect storm, but the Fleischers had a character on board who could master those seas.

Popeye could have sustained Fleischer Studios into the 1950s; a successful series could have kept other wolves from the door, allowing Max and Dave to make artistic and financial decisions not based on want. True success with Popeye—resulting in more money being available to go around—might have soothed labor tensions; Popeye might have prevented an expensive and ultimately fatal move to Florida. (No amount of spinach could have strengthened the cracking fraternity between Max and Dave, though.) This all could have been, but for the one glaring problem—the Fleischers did not own the rights to Popeye; they were merely stewards producing Popeye cartoons. As an independent studio, Disney had remained solvent thanks to merchandising and licensing, which by the mid-1930s accounted for "one-third of [Disney's] net profit."[29] This was steady income coming between films and outside of delivery schedules—something the Fleischers knew only bits about thanks to Betty's popularity. But, of the characters and series they did own—Koko and Betty from the early days, Hunky and Spunky, the Stone Age Cartoons, and even a few Gabby and related cartoons from the end of the decade—some were out of date and the others never caught on.[30] Some of the Color Classics[31] are beautiful cartoons, but they had to compete head-to-head with Disney's best Silly Symphonies, and, after the success of *Snow White*, the feature-length animated film beckoned all. The Fleischers may have failed the moment it was decided that Disney was the horizon—always approached but never reached. Some historians have assumed that all Fleischer cartoons were of a piece, that a sampling can represent the entire batch. But, when the hundreds of gags and throwaway bits and sheer *vitalité de la vie* are considered, the more one can watch, the better. As Klein points out, the "readability of the [Fleischer] character" diminished (purposely) as the scene became "more furious," more improbable: "That gives Fleischer cartoons an extraordinary tension. The ground is never still. Gags constantly overlap . . . dozens of miniature gags pop up. . . . [they] speed along like cinematic graffiti."[32] Attempting to transition from this mayhem on a Tuesday to an outright imitation of Disney on the following Thursday—even with Paramount's support—couldn't be done, given the type and background of Fleischer artists, Maltin concludes: "Their attempts at sentiment were contrived, not sincere, and the results were some of the most treacly cartoons ever made."[33]

Just before all this came Popeye from the Segar comic strip distributed by King Features Syndicate. The Fleischers got a star when they wrangled Popeye's rights: "Far more people flocked to movie palaces in the thirties to see . . . *Popeye* cartoons . . . than ever went to watch the *Superman* or *Batman* serials."[34] King Features demanded a test cartoon before they'd give final approval; *Popeye the Sailor*, officially part of the Betty Boop series, was a hit from night one.[35] The point might be that King Features Syndicate and Popeye didn't need the Fleischers, but the Fleischers certainly needed them.[36] Popeye was popular for Fleischer Studios; he would be popular for Paramount's Famous Studios. Popeye made distribution money and was a merchandising dream—but only contractually agreed-on bits of that money came to Max and Dave. This same hiccup would appear in relation to their next very popular character and franchise: Superman. Max didn't own him, either. The hard lesson that Disney had learned from first Mintz and then Powers was that ownership was everything. The Fleischers' situation was understandable: once burned (in the Weiss fire), the Fleischers opted for the security of having a big-studio partner, a partner willing to overlook their money woes and fund even outlandish requests like a lock, stock, and barrels of ink move to Miami, but this security came at a price— *everything*. That sword wouldn't fall until 1942; we'll turn away from it for a bit.

Popeye's guest appearance signaled the beginning of Popeye and the beginning of the end of Betty. Less than a year later, everything about her was changing. Without the sexualized bits of her character, the Fleischer animators couldn't find ways to make her interesting; she became much more like characters from other studios. Between 1934 and 1936, Popeye would outpace the increasingly domesticated Betty *and* Mickey in popularity, rentals, and otherwise.[37] By August 1934, Popeye cartoons were receiving the highest praise, including best cartoon of the season, from exhibitors. Betty's cartoon dominance fell off quickly. In 1931, Chaplin requested Mickey titles to introduce the hit *City Lights*.[38] That was then. Mickey couldn't punch anyone, smoke a pipe, take a punch, or eat spinach and become a tank or battering ram. Popeye was able to remain rambunctious when those around him (meaning Mickey) had to keep their heads. At a simple level, Popeye was able to employ metamorphosis when Mickey could not. A 1935 poll asked who was more popular, Mickey or Popeye; by a slim margin, Popeye won.

Schedules were tight, and so was money, but the Fleischer Studio was successfully riding out the Depression. Max and his employees continued to innovate—if not in storytelling and character development, then in creating devices that assisted or improved the animation process. One example came to be known as the "setback process" (or "stereoptical process"), which was used to attempt to create a realistic three-dimensional effect in the animated world.[39] The "surface" image is still celluloid, featuring ink and painted characters, but the backgrounds are tiered "setbacks," built in perspective and moved incrementally. A drawback was the

Producing an uncanny but memorable image, Iwerks in *The Valiant Tailor* created a time-intensive three-dimensional process of his own that he used sparingly. *The Valiant Tailor*, Iwerks, 1934 (from *Cartoons That Time Forgot: The Ub Iwerks Collection* DVD). Screenshot taken by the author.

cost of this tedious process and a restriction to lateral-type movement, earlier seen in Iwerks's 1933 version of a similar process, and different from Disney's 1937 multiplane process that appeared to zoom *into* the layers of the created world.[40] The multiplane camera's "push in" to the cartoon world (via multiple stacked platens and cels) is equally artificial, but it better mimicked the establishing shots of classical Hollywood films and became standard. All these processes were complicated—in *Pinocchio*, shots were generally photographed at one-fifth the rate of the traditional (single platen) process[41]—meaning that using these processes was expensive and hard to justify. One of the main differences between Disney and Fleischer becomes clear in this area. Disney was willing to lose money and use the technology to its ultimate artistic effect. Fleischer

In *Little Swee'Pea*, Popeye strolls past Max Fleischer's three-dimensional "set-back" (or stereoptical) process that offers actual models built to move incrementally and in diminishing perspective. Disney's version was the multiplane camera. *Little Swee'Pea*, Fleischer, 1936 (from *Popeye the Sailor 1933–1938* DVD). Screenshot taken by the author.

could never square that with his common sense; it just wasn't the way to run a business. The result is that Fleischer's limited use of these effects looks gimmicky, and Disney's extensive usage enriches and deepens the worlds presented.[42]

Popeye cartoons were in demand but produced by rote. The Color Classics series was created to try to compete with Silly Symphonies, though, without three-strip color, they were second best at best. Even when, after 1935, the best color process was available, the cartoons remained pleasant diversions and sub-Disney. Paramount just wanted funny, black-and-white Popeyes. If the Fleischers could have gotten some traction for the Color Classics, and if their few Academy Award nominations had been more successful, they could have built beyond the

Popeye contract work and into cartoons that meant profits and, perhaps, happier employees.

There were signs of labor unrest long before any official work stoppage or strike actions at either Van Beuren or across the street at Fleischer Studios, before anyone marched and sang "I'm Popeye the Union Man."[43] The Fleischers (especially Max) seemed to ignore the "restiveness" of their own workforce.[44] The Paramount contract meant producing more than fifty cartoons per year, which meant using multiple teams and a staggered production schedule and having a less relaxed work environment and hard deadlines. Fleischer paid as well as other studios, but militant labor organization was everywhere across the mid-1930s, emboldened by a worker-friendly FDR administration after 1932. Max was a paternalistic owner who might have been surprised that anyone in his "family" could have real complaints—Disney shared this mindset, what Kanfer terms a "cloud-cuckoo land"[45]—and Fleischer pugnaciously responded to labor-related demands. The Wagner Labor Relations Act passed into law in summer 1935, giving the greenlight to worker-organizing activities. Add to this Van Beuren's shuttering in 1936, when RKO switched film providers midstream, opting for Disney, meaning Fleischer could afford to see off dissatisfied workers—a surfeit of replacements awaited, many willing "to take pay cuts and demotions" just to have a job.[46] The strike officially involved musicians, projectionists, and cameramen, but there were also sympathetic unions inside and outside the industry.[47] By 1937, Fleischer's intractability led to a National Labor Relations Board hearing and to Fleischer film showings being suspended, thanks to allied projectionists. Max would have to settle, signing a labor contract with a recognized union.

Like many workers of this period, the Fleischer employees were employees by caprice—they could be fired or demoted or have their wages reduced on a whim. They also worked more than forty hours a week and on Saturdays, and they enjoyed no paid vacations or sick leaves. Their organization and even withholding of labor makes complete sense in hindsight. It did change the familial feeling at the studio, even if that feeling was mostly in Max's head. Tensions remained on both sides, prompting Max to convince Paramount that a move to a less labor-friendly state, Florida, would solve strike problems and smooth out Paramount's production schedule.

Max had allegedly wanted to produce a feature film for several years, but Paramount was not convinced.[48] The success of *Snow White* didn't help: "Seeing that Disney is so far ahead of Fleischer in every respect—originality, colour, music, scoring, story conception, and writing, established characters and national popularity and prestige—then any attempt to follow *Snow White* would be decidedly second rate at best."[49] This was from an *internal* Paramount memo, but other voices at the studio apparently demanded production of a feature film to stay in the race with Disney. In the wake of the strike, Max resolved to move away from the labor-sympathetic Northeast, build a Disney-like studio in sunny Miami, and produce a feature film.[50] In late May 1938, Paramount agreed to bankroll the move, the new hires, and the feature film, asking only for the rights to *all* previous Fleischer films as collateral on the loan—"a monumental, tragic mistake" on Max's part, according to his son.[51] A new air-conditioned studio was quickly erected, dozens of key personnel came from New York with the Fleischers, dozens more from other studios accepted high-paying offers, and then scores (many of whom were only modestly qualified) were hired or trained in-state. The Fleischers chose Jonathan Swift's *Gulliver's Travels* as their source, a head scratcher from the start, given its complexity, mood, and sociopolitical themes. Dave Fleischer cast the characters into a light opera setting and ensured a "thickly sugar-coated" delivery.[52]

Many problems aside, the film progressed rapidly once the new studio was usable, and, as "uneven" as it is, *Gulliver's Travels* opened to strong reviews and very good audience reaction.[53] The music and visuals weren't up to Disney standards, nor did the film resemble the surreal and metamorphic best of Fleischer's Betty and Popeye titles, but there were enough memorable scenes to sell the film.[54] For many, it was seen as far more family-friendly than *Snow White*. It opened well and welcomed large crowds, finishing the year in the box-office top ten. But the domestic box office would have to do—European outlets were unwilling to acquire the film, thanks to Germany's saber rattling, which diminished potential profits.[55] The Fleischers were also now saddled with a 700-plus-employee studio that had to be fed, with the shorts continuing to be produced but not grossing nearly enough to support the studio's new appetite.

Either the lackluster run of *Gulliver's Travels* or its thrilling opening week's success prompted Paramount to quickly greenlight a follow-up feature, a feature that could either recoup its costs more quickly or continue the hot streak lit by *Gulliver's* success. Whichever, *Mr. Bug Goes to Town* became the second film approved. This project needed to work since Betty Boop was officially retired in 1939; the studio's original, wholly owned material was vanishing. Once finished, *Mr. Bug* (later known as *Hoppity Goes to Town*) was reviewed and received tepidly—some critics seeing it as weak New Deal propaganda[56]—with the usual "lacking" comparisons to Disney's work: "The picture cannot compare with *Dumbo*, in which the trials and tribulations of the little elephant interest one deeply," said one trade journal. "In *Mr. Bug Goes to Town* there is not one character strong enough to win and hold one's sympathy."[57] Oft-acerbic critic James Agee wasn't, admiring the "designed for youngsters" effort as he offered a commonly held assessment: "No menace to King Disney."[58] The Disney comparisons were expected, but *Mr. Bug* also paled in relation to other Fleischer work. And it certainly couldn't have helped that, just seven months before the film's Christmas 1941 premiere, Max had been presented with the surprise "sign or lose everything" contract from Paramount, a deal wherein Max surrendered even his personally held patents and became an employee of the studio rather than face the ultimate shame—missing payroll and declaring bankruptcy. There wasn't even time (purposefully, on Paramount's part) for Max to seek out an external loan or another distributor. He and Dave both signed. *Mr. Bug* never found an audience and lost money.

Thanks to sibling fighting, a popular but expensive *Gulliver's Travels*, the outbreak of a European war, little or no ownership of merchandising, a half-hearted follow-up feature, debt to Paramount stemming from the studio's anti-union move to Miami and creation of a new studio—because of all this, everything simply had to go perfectly for the Fleischer studio to succeed. The following commentary, though overblown, echoes the sentiment of many regarding the Fleischer legacy:

The comparison for any cartoons of the thirties has to be Disney, and in terms of technique and polish the Fleischers are simply not in the same league; they are barely in the same medium. . . . What the films do indicate though, taken as a whole, is an incredibly prolific imagination (or two imaginations).[59]

The writer was talking specifically about the Fleischer shorts and really about Betty and Popeye titles, but his remarks draw a bead on the Fleischers' entire oeuvre. The Fleischers never could escape the Disney comparison, especially once they decided to compete, film for film. But there will always be Fleischer acolytes, even if they are just those "pure" critics who equated animation with the fantastic, a relationship they saw Disney abandon. Some thoughtful critic had written this appraisal of the Disney-Fleischer dance in December 1937, just before *Snow White* could change things utterly: "Fleischer, no doubt, will never make any-thing like . . . 'The Old Mill,' but he has yet the art of working in a happy world of unreality and make-believe, and his little pictures should be given the praise they merit."[60] Even talking up Fleischer's "little pictures," the critic cannot avoid Disney, who carries the day.

And So, Disney

"Virtually every tool and technique in the animator's repertoire was dis-covered, invented or perfected at the Disney studio during this era," con-cludes one historian.[61] Imagine being an accomplished animation-industry professional working in the 1930s but *not* at the Disney studio and maybe, like a Max Fleischer, being reminded daily of the ineffable sec-ond-tierness of everything you do. Charles Solomon was writing as he looked back across the decades, his view possibly occluded by history or taste. These same sincere platitudes were being voiced within earshot of Max and the rest of the industry, too: "Within their self-imposed lim-itations the earlier Disney films, and certain sequences in some of the later ones, represent, as it were, a chemically pure distillation of cinematic possibilities."[62] In short, Disney was the bee's knees.

The first few years of the 1930s were good to Disney's films and rep-utation, if not to his studio's financial situation and his health. "There can be no comparison of this [Mickey] cartoon series. Each is as good as the last and then becomes better."[63] The Silly Symphonies premiered with the even more sensational *The Skeleton Dance* in late summer 1929. Not content to simply fulfill a distribution contract, Disney pushed forward, improving technologies, refining the process of animation and storytelling, honing his artists' skills, demanding more of "The Cartoon." Reviews of the studio's work in 1933, in the weeks following the release of *Three Little Pigs*, tried to explain: "Usually the public's approval, manifested at the box-office, is taken for granted as meaning that the picture in question is perfection. Disney isn't made that way. Like all real artists, he strives to satisfy himself and his own ideals as earnestly as any poet in a garret."[64] A "real artists'" move away from the *cartoony* at Disney's studio was apparent across this period, though it was a slow process, since the rest of the industry was still employing the "everything moves, everything has life" mode. In *Three Little Pigs*—the cartoon in which "personality animation" sparked—there are no living objects.[65] In 1934's *The Tortoise and the Hare*, the more cinematic approach means cartooniness only in the characters' sometimes exaggerated physical abilities (speed, stretchiness); *Who Killed Cock Robin?* (1935) and *Country Cousin* (1936) were similar in this way. But, even in 1935's *The Band Concert*, as a tornado approaches, wooden benches awaken and run away in alarm, following the audience.[66] These moments diminish in Disney titles, leading to the kind of cinematic and natural "reality" seen in *Three Orphan Kittens* (1935) and especially *The Old Mill*, both warm-ups for *Snow White*. From 1934 on, likely *every* Silly Symphony was in some way a proving ground for both Disney technologies and Disney animator abilities—like the ability to draw believable human characters. (And, judging by the human figures in *Goddess of Spring*, practice was needed.[67])

As early as 1931, Disney was implementing a partial conversion to the three-strip Technicolor process for the Silly Symphonies. The Depression still looming, major studios weren't eager to add "garish" color to their monochromatic feature films, leaving Technicolor without a major proving ground. Disney agreed to the added-value color process with a caveat—for cartoons, Disney's would be the sole license granted until 1935.[68] "[If cofounder] Kalmus had any other good (large studio) connections at the time," Neupert writes, "it is doubtful Technicolor would have given Disney any special treatment, but with Fox, Warner's and MGM on the run away from color, Disney Studios were better than nothing."[69] In the interim, inferior color processes (two-strip Technicolor, Cinecolor, Brewster Color) would demonstrate the primacy of the process that Disney had all to himself, and by 1935, Disney had vaulted ahead of everyone else.[70] Most important, audiences had been convinced that the look and movement and atmosphere of the Disney product was *the* way.

Similar attentions were being paid to less visible parts of the animation process. The approach to story or plot structure at most studios was quite individualized—Max Fleischer trusted the skills of his artists and depended on them to create stories, huddle for gags, and then animate that story to completion. Idea boards and maybe a setup paragraph (i.e., "Bimbo endures an initiation," "Betty is Snow-White") could be used, but no scripts were used and there were no writers, per se. The artists were gagmen, and gags came from wherever and did not have to make plot or situational sense. Disney had long wanted to get control of this process. In 1932, he set up the animation industry's first story department—initially just a group of animators who'd demonstrated agility with storytelling and plot development. Through the story department, he could control the cartoons' stories (and thus his company's output).[71]

With Technicolor on board, Walt Disney decided to repurpose *Flowers and Trees* into a full-color film—adding thousands to the budget and lines to his brother's brow. (When Walt called time-out, the film was underway; it had to be repainted with paint reinvented for the color process.[72]) Disney would then give a sneak peek to impresario Sid Grauman, who made a premiere deal immediately.[73] At Grauman's, it screened to "spontaneous reception and applause at finish."[74] *Flowers and Trees* was costly and hurried—and not even a great film (it dated quite quickly)—but it brought the Disneys their first Oscar, which was the first such award for a cartoon short-subject film. Bold claims, including this one from an industry pundit, could be heard: "Judging from today's standards it seems that it will be impossible to improve upon the beauty of these Disney cartoons colored by this process."[75] The years that Disney and Technicolor engaged in their uninterrupted dance saw the Disney product vault to the top of the otherwise black-and-white or two-strip-color cartoon peak, claiming King of the Mountain in the hearts of critics and fans alike.

And now there was really no slowing down for Disney. Versions of the pencil test had been in place since early 1931, at least, but a new layer, the "rough" pencil test, was now added, demanding more of assistants and inserting another step in the completion process.[76] This was one of many steps that gawped other studios. Asked about pencil tests at Fleischer, Max answered firmly, "If an animator doesn't know exactly what he's doing then he's no animator."[77] As late as 1938, Fleischer still frowned on (but allowed) use of such tests as his studio worked on *Gulliver's Travels* and Popeye commitments.[78] He felt his animators should be able to achieve smoothness with proper timing and talent, and his two "checkers" at the end cleaned up to his liking. Fleischer knew Paramount wouldn't pay another nickel for a pencil-tested cartoon. Disney knew this, too, and responded differently, the nickels adding up. Each color Silly Symphony title was now going to cost at least $10,000 more for just the color process. More money was moving ancillary to the actual animation, too. Animators not necessarily animating became a thing—some worked as writers, storyboard artists, conceptualizers. When Webb Smith's "storyboard" practice became known and then understood—every scene, character move, and significant camera movement and view sketched out on cards tacked up on corkboard—it was immediately adopted studio-wide, then cartoon industry–wide, and then live-action film industry–wide.[79] For Disney, this was a way of "rationalizing the chaos of cartoon creation," his focus across the 1930s.[80] And there was more to 1932 than color cartoons.

That year, one of the finest cartoons produced anywhere was produced elsewhere, at Fleischers': the Betty Boop vehicle, *Minnie the Moocher*. Flip's creator Ub Iwerks produced the risqué *Room Runners*, and a young Tex Avery's energy (along with veteran Bill Nolan's sure hand) can be appreciated in Oswald's imaginative *Carnival Capers*. And there was more than cartoons. The year 1932 saw Hoover ushered out and Roosevelt elected. By 1932–1933, the Depression had settled in, unemployment reached the double-digit millions, industrial production plummeted, and sporadic runs closed financial institutions. In early 1933, Hoover's *laissez-faire* approach would give way to the first FDR administration, and the New Deal assumed a leading role in economic regulation and stimulus. Disney also tried to take better control of his fortunes, and, turning down a sweet offer from Universal, he left Columbia for a United Artists distribution deal, significantly upping advance payments for his cartoons and keeping more of the gross.[81] His advances per film ($20,000) would have been the envy of the industry, but Walt knew he would overspend on every title.[82] He was treating his cartoon films as if they were live-action features—even though profit margins were minimal, comparatively speaking—and audiences came to appreciate the thought and attention. Disney even brought in Don Graham from Chouinard (later CalArts) to teach night classes to his crop of animators, aiming to improve their skills and deepen their art appreciation. Shamus Culhane took a job at Disney in 1933 and would stay until he'd finished work on *Pinocchio*. He reminds us that Disney's organization was raided constantly by other studios, always hoping to steal away the magic. The thought was that the pixie dust must reside not with the studio figurehead but with the gifted, unheralded, overworked animators and directors. Pat Powers tried when he lured Iwerks in 1930; it happened again when Van Beuren hired Burt Gillett to replicate the success of *Three Little Pigs*. Neither man would build the Disney-like studio and "look" being sought, and both ventures failed.[83]

In 1933, an original song "Who's Afraid of the Big Bad Wolf?" became the first musical number charted as a popular hit from a cartoon. Disney had largely been relying on songs and music in the public domain; other studios had been using songs from preexisting music catalogs, rights-free music, or music taken directly from scratchy 78-rpm records, or they commissioned sung-through light opera–type songs. "Who's Afraid?" was written for Disney by Frank Churchill, meaning all the rights and royalties stayed in-house. And royalties there were. "Walt Disney's theme song was everywhere," said one columnist. "It is one thing to be miraculously popular, and another to be murderously so."[84] The song became a cultural phenomenon, leading to sales of sheet music, recorded versions, live version rights (requested by all the big bands of the day), player piano rolls, and radio rights.[85] And it came from a cartoon, one known as "the cartoon that changed the animation industry."[86] As it was released in May 1933, during FDR's "'hundred days' campaign of legislation," many saw this film as a direct challenge to the Depression, a homily on courage and self-reliance—described alternately as Hooverian *and* Rooseveltian, it was certainly Disney, setting the tone for his studio.[87] Just a few years later, the cartoon was being discussed alongside "important" works of the time: "[Chaplin's] *Modern Times* and one other little film, only a one-reeler, Disney's *Three Little Pigs*, were *the ideological straws that presaged great social storms*."[88] This view might surprise many who know "Uncle Walt" only from TV and the theme parks; or the Disney who would treat striking employees so abrasively; or the anticommunist Disney. Writing in 1934, Bragdon called it "the best animated cartoon to date judged by any standard."[89]

The short film was being placed at the top position on marquees at neighborhood cinemas; it was held over in first-run theaters in New York for more than six months; it did well in its first run in the larger theaters and really took off once it hit the neighborhood cinemas. America's heartland embraced the film, the characters, and the song. *Three Little Pigs* cemented the importance and success of the Silly Symphonies, until then "a kind of stepsister to the enormously popular Mickey Mouse series."[90] From Barrier: "The color Silly Symphonies so dominated all other cartoon series that they won every Academy Award for animated films from 1932 . . . until 1939."[91] The Silly Symphonies had been designed to avoid the formerly essential continuing character. Disney would say more than once that not being tied to a central character freed the cartoons almost completely—his animators could do anything; stories could come from or go anywhere. The Silly Symphonies were performing well before *Three Little Pigs* but certainly much, much better after, as a late 1933 article confirmed: "For the first time in the history of motion pictures 'shorts' are being reviewed above the features on the same bill and for the first time, too, these shorts are being advertised in many instances above the full length productions."[92]

In the wake of *Three Little Pigs*, significant challenges faced the animation industry. First, the Disney way was being adopted, like it or not. It was a new corporatization that industrialized cartoons, shaving off the rough edges and often the spontaneity.[93] In many ways, it harkened back to the transitions encountered 1913–1915, as animators edged closer to an industry, thanks to Bray-Hurd and Barré. In Disney's case, the transition meant leaving behind both the comic-strip mentality and some individual flair, perhaps assigning a single lead animator to a single character across an entire film. Cartoons needed to look more movie-like, meaning the end of flatness, metamorphosis, and surrealism in most cartoons, even the end of cartooniness, except as justified by the narrative. With color and cinematic body types and human stories, cartoons became melodramas[94] requiring real emotion and depth of field. Black-and-white graphic flatness gave way to background influences from Romantic book illustrations and paintings.[95] This would include the rich, full world depicted in *The Grasshopper and the Ants* and the high drama of forbidden love and life almost lost in *Music Land*. Disney could and did easily lead the way here. The studio's "cinematic body forms" rapidly displaced the New York style, the "graphic narrative" look, even at Fleischer, Terry, and Schlesinger, but to differing degrees and effect. Audiences and distributors began to demand this "full" style of animation,[96] a style that just wasn't what the Fleischers had ever been good at or interested in. Bray had transitioned out of the entertainment cartoon industry when it sailed past his experience and interests; by 1935, Max Fleischer understood those feelings. Paul Terry lowered his head against the new wind and said he was making Terrytoons, period. The Schlesinger staff might have been least affected by this shift, as they were just getting their legs under them in the mid-1930s and were interested only in making the cartoons Disney didn't want to make. They (and Avery, Hanna, and Barbera) hoed their row and made their own way. So, between 1934 and about 1938, again, in the wake of phenomenally successful Disney cartoon releases, the industry was moving toward full animation.

A second significant challenge confronting the industry was the economic downturn affecting all. Costs to produce cartoons had risen significantly since the late 1920s, while rental rates remained stagnant, even with the success of Mickey and the Silly Symphonies. The studios distributing the cartoons weren't interested in paying more per cartoon when they knew the real return (if any) on a title went to the cartoon producer. Most cartoons did not make money during their first release; they did so only on a second release and beyond.[97] If they paid for themselves after a year or so, the studio doors could stay open. Disney always flew in the face of this practicality, spending more on each cartoon than he knew he could get in return—return not being the point. *The Band Concert* and *Music Land* demonstrate to what lengths Disney was willing to go to lead in sheer artistry, animation acumen, and personality-driven stories and characters. Animated art cost money, since animation and improving technology went hand in hand. This was Disney's arms race against the rest of the industry and Hollywood in general. The burning question became "whose economy could support such spending?" Disney's windfall during this period was his success in merchandising. Interest in licensing Mickey Mouse had started off modestly in 1929; by 1934, profits of more than $600,000 accrued. When other cartoon producers felt the bite of distributor parsimony, Disney could only smile, knowing those days were behind him.

Coincidentally, Klein sees a lull in American animation overall between 1934 and 1937, when the industry was adjusting to new mores, codes, and movie-likeness: "Animation became far more about movies and less about the printed page or vaudeville. As a result, entirely new systems emerged around what generally has been called full animation."[98] Yes, but great cartoons were still appearing. The Warner Bros. stable was beginning to form, with Daffy and Porky making strong early appearances; some of the best of the Silly Symphonies debuted in this window; the Fleischers produced memorable Color Classics, featuring the setback process; Popeye mumbled ahoy, outpacing even Mickey in some ways; and Ub Iwerks released perhaps his most (oddly) memorable work, *Balloon Land*. In just one of these areas—the Production Code demands—beloved cartoon characters like Betty Boop diminished while Popeye came into his own, but Fleischer Studios would not be the same. The expectations of the Code favored what Disney had been doing all along. By 1935, most trade journals were heralding Disney as the "look" for all cartoons, the heights to be climbed for rival studios.[99] The 1934–1937 period offered German leaders talking of lebensraum, postwar inequities, and "oppressed" Germans across Europe. Ominous mutterings from fascist types in Europe, Britain, and even the United States, coupled with the disturbing mechanical noises coming from the Nazi garage late at night, unsettled the ill-prepared "Allies." These issues were tackled in some bold cartoons. Columbia released the Krazy Kat title *Peace Conference* in April 1935, dealing with skirmishes and aggression across Europe and Asia and suggesting how popular music can help solve world problems. *Peace Conference* appeared a full five months before Disney's *Music Land* made its appearance. In this film, the countries of jazz and classical music find ways to settle differences, eventually intermarrying and building a "Bridge of Harmony."

In 1937, Disney released a Silly Symphony title, *The Old Mill*, that helped demonstrate his interest in and accomplishment of both physical and psychological realism and served as a test run for the multiplane process.[100] It cost more to be made than it could possibly make, and it won the cartoon short-subject Academy Award, the fifth year in a row that Disney won this award. In this film, only fleeting glimpses of the cartoony remain—perhaps just the frog whose eyes try to follow a firefly—as if twenty-five years of cartoon history were effectively subsumed into a "tone poem" about cooing doves, scurrying mice, and birds riding out a storm.[101] The short also features delicate special-effects animation (water reflections, ripples, raindrops, lightning, wind effects) and colors changing to reflect the passage of time from dusk to night to dawn, creating an immersive experience that is less about plot than place, time, and natural life. It's not an "animated oil painting," as Max might have groaned, but a work of fine art granted life.

On the Path to Snow White

It was "Disney's Folly" outside the studio and "The Great Experiment" within.

Well, it was as much "Walt's Folly"[102] within the studio walls as anywhere without, since the boss may have been the only employee who believed in such an undertaking. And a folly it would remain from an evening in 1934 when Walt acted out the entire film for his key staff to its debut just three years later.[103] *Snow White* premiered in December 1937 at the Carthay Circle Theatre, where six years earlier Walt had sold *The Skeleton Dance*. This time the Hollywood elite were in attendance, and response was effusive. The Golden Age of Disney feature animation had begun.

If the mid-1930s was a lull in animation, it was a deceptive one. For one, great cartoons were still being made. Additionally, it coincided with Disney being astride the mountaintop of the short cartoon and the several-years-long prelude to his industry-shaking project, *Snow White*. Thanks to the intensified application of the Code, by 1936, children became the primary target audience for animation. Paul Terry had always been making cartoons for kids; Fleischer was coming to it only after losing Betty's boop; Schlesinger's team maintained that they saw themselves as their only audience; and Disney's work seemed aimed at family viewing. Disney himself would say that he created for adults, but it has been pointed out time and again that the depicted fears and problems in his early features *Snow White*, *Pinocchio*, *Dumbo*, and *Bambi* "reflect children's deepest fears . . . honestly," writes Barrier. "They evoke profound emotions but do not cheapen them—they take them seriously. Disney's animators had proved that they could deal with strong emotions."[104] By the mid-1930s, many cinemas still put the short cartoon at the very end of the program, allowing parents time to get up for a stretch and a smoke after the feature while kids stayed in their seats.

A very big deal for 1936 and for any feature aspirations was Disney's distribution deal with RKO, a major studio. RKO had access to a larger distribution network, and the bits RKO had been allowed to see of in-production *Snow White* sealed the deal.[105] This was the second time that Disney was able to make a choice between potential distributors and on his terms.[106] The production of *Snow White* was excruciating and monumental, the studio facing entirely new benchmarks with new technologies and scores of new people; the film was released in December 1937, in fact just less than a year after the first cels had gone to ink and paint in January 1937.[107] Walt was involved at every step. He had his animators screen dozens of films, including many German Expressionist masterpieces and ballets, dances, and special features of all kinds, as they worked.[108] Members of this newest generation of animators (entering the industry in the early 1930s) were coming from art schools and film-watching backgrounds, the very depths Disney wanted to plumb. He guessed they might have to spend between a quarter and a half a million dollars to get the film he wanted. Roy was apoplectic at first and then "paralyzed," in Walt's words.[109] By the time *Snow White* was well underway, several things had changed: Disney had signed a deal with RKO for distribution, Disney had borrowed lots of money from the Bank of America, and *Snow White*'s budget had raced toward $2 million. Culhane notes there were whispers as December 1937 approached that if everything didn't go well at the premiere, a bank might control the studio.[110]

Plenty could go wrong. With a cartoon feature, there were no certainties, no built-in audience, no distribution models, no proven marketing strategies: "Predictions run all the way from assertions that it will revolutionize the animated cartoon industry to declarations that it can be nothing more than a dismal flop." In this same article Schlesinger was canvassed; he offered *Snow White* as a "1000-to-1 shot." His studio would wait and watch, and, if the experiment was a success, "I'm frank to say I will be forced to follow."[111] And then there was the film itself. As Klein so well describes, there is a balancing of inherent contradictions in Disney's "realistic" *Snow White*—the "live-action," "animated," and "shop-window" elements encounter each other in each frame to create Disney's "reality." The "live-action" characters—Snow White, the Queen, the Prince—are rotoscoped; they move and present themselves in a particularly noncartoony, almost uncanny way. The "animated" elements are the dwarfs, the crone, and, to a certain extent, the animals, all being hand-drawn and moving more like cartoons. The "shop-window" elements are the Romantic-influenced structures and backgrounds. These could be made using different paints and could occupy different layers in the process of photography, making dissonance even more possible in the fully animated film—in short, the more control and attention exerted by the animators, the more complicated and perhaps elusive an illusion of reality becomes.[112] Many hurdles—including creating rich backgrounds and layouts, working with new camera processes, making special-effects shots, and creating an "illusion of life"—had been cleared in making the Silly Symphonies leading up to creation of *Snow White*. However, creation of believable humans was still a question mark, and so was whether an audience would sit for an eighty-minute dramatic cartoon. Part of the magic of *Snow White*, Klein argues, is that Disney not only understood these contradictions but also was able to create camouflages, diminish contrasts, grade colors (including blacks), pull the backgrounds forward, and manipulate lighting to bring the contradictions together seamlessly.[113] Disney clearly subscribed to "the cult of the picturesque."[114] Snow White herself might be rendered so virginal and friendly to Nature that she is inhumanly translucent but for the animals around her. All these same elements—rotoscoped characters, animated characters, shop-window features—from the efforts of many of the same artists found their way into Fleischers' *Gulliver's Travels*, but the magic wouldn't be the same.

Like *Three Little Pigs*, *Snow White* was a musical cornucopia, with its songs released as RCA Victor hit singles and, for the first time ever, as a special collection (an eight-song "soundtrack" on three 78s). Meant to forward the plot, songs from *Snow White* appeared on soundtrack records just as they were heard in the film. After its 1937 preview, the film was test screened in New York, Los Angeles, and Miami in January 1938.[115] In the New York Music Hall test, *Snow White* performed better the second week than the first and set records.[116] Bad weather, school exams, and lack of a holiday break did not deter crowds. "Sidewalk speculators" set records, as well, getting $5 for a ticket that normally went for $1.65.[117] RKO was making sure *Snow White* was the single feature at theaters it owned and was set on convincing other circuits to do the same. RKO was expecting a $5 million gross; *Snow White* made $8.5 million in its first run.

Snow White was by far the biggest box-office success of 1938, doubling grosses of its nearest competitors. The film primed the pump for animated films to be treated like live-action features, at least for a short time, and was a proving ground: "[U]ntil *Snow White*, animation's vocabulary was incomplete, after *Snow White*, it was possible for animation [to] make audiences laugh or cry."[118] Perhaps the bridge too far was that

Disney wanted his next two features to make audiences laugh, cry, and even think.

PINOCCHIO AND *FANTASIA*

The follow-up films to *Snow White* had been in the pipeline for several years. *Pinocchio*, what would become *Fantasia*, *Bambi*, and a return to the *Alice in Wonderland* world were slated.[119] *Alice* was still too recently visited a project for Disney (and *Alice* adaptations were elsewhere in Hollywood), so *Alice* slipped down the list. *Bambi* would be delayed, as it proved to be a treble challenge—narratively, cinematically, and physically, given the strike actions that the studio would endure. The more cartoon-like characters and designs of *Pinocchio* and what started as *The Sorcerer's Apprentice* beckoned; new characters would populate the first film, and Mickey[120] would star in the latter, with music orchestrated by Leopold Stokowski. Mickey was Walt's choice, even though the Mouse had fallen off in popularity, giving way to Donald, specifically, but also to Goofy and even Pluto. As *Snow White* was nearing completion, the trade journals could mention two feature-length Disney animated projects already underway, without knowing titles. Disney didn't even know for sure; in preproduction, projects advanced fitfully. In August 1935, Disney had mentioned that *Snow White* was in progress, that his studio was planning to release a feature animation every eighteen months, and that *Bambi* was *perhaps* his next feature.[121] *Bambi* was thought to be coming in 1938; it wouldn't be ready until 1942, its release slowed by new technologies, "illusion of life" concerns, the outbreak of war, and a nasty strike. In addition to all this, Disney had been building an air-conditioned studio (which Feild called both "dignified" and a "factory" in the same sentence[122]) in Burbank; Disney had far outgrown the cramped Hyperion Avenue facility—and moving began in August 1939.

Never too far away, by April 1940, the "Phoney War" had been underway for at least seven months. Germany had raced across Poland, Russia had invaded Finland, Britain was trying to defend Scandinavia, British rationing had begun, the Japanese invasion of China continued apace, and German planes had attacked Scapa Flow. Before the end of April, Roosevelt would reiterate American neutrality. In this same month in Burbank, Disney had millions tied up in sixteen ongoing projects without a set distribution schedule for any of them.[123] Hybrid films that would be released before *Alice in Wonderland*—including *Reluctant Dragon, Dumbo, Song of the South, Melody Time*, and *Fun and Fancy Free*—didn't exist when the war began. The war and strike changed things at Disney. *Bambi* wouldn't debut until 1942, *Alice in Wonderland* in 1951, and *Peter Pan* two years after that. In 1940, Disney was in the red to the tune of several million dollars, and, without a new RKO deal, the skies grew even darker.[124] In May, film distribution in most of Europe and Scandinavia ceased, while France and Britain held on.[125] Paris would fall the following month. German propaganda included crowing about the losses Hollywood studios were made to endure.[126] This was the distribution barrier that *Fantasia* and *Pinocchio* smacked headlong into, a wall that would have crushed even a *Snow White*, and there was no talk of *Fantasia* merchandise and, thus, none of the easy money from merchandising, which the studio had come to rely on. The prewar chill led to layoffs and retrenchment, tasks Disney did not relish.

Pinocchio

Pinocchio was a harder nut to crack than *Snow White*. Production of the film was started and stopped more than once; months of design and story work were produced and discarded; animators were assigned and reassigned; the character of Pinocchio was changed from a "grotesque"[127] to something much closer to a real boy made of wood. "*Snow White* may have provided Disney with his finest moment," Finch asserts, "but *Pinocchio* is probably his greatest film."[128] *Pinocchio* is a better film than *Snow White*, technologically speaking, featuring more widespread use of the improved multiplane process, a broader color palette, more and better effects animation, new painting and airbrushing techniques that achieved the "realer"[129] look Walt was hoping for, a more mature story with consequences, and a thrilling whale sequence. "Walt wanted his second full-length movie to be purely and simply a work of Art."[130] But it is also scarier and less kid friendly: "Pinocchio is the darkest in hue of all Disney's pictures and the one which, despite its humor, is the most consistently terrifying."[131] Contemporary reviewers noted this quality immediately, wondering whether the film could overcome its dire moments and bleak world and reach the broad audience that *Snow White* found, an audience that *Pinocchio* would need, given its cost. It would have been even more grim if the Jiminy Cricket character hadn't been introduced well into the production process to soften Pinocchio's unpleasantness, even cruelty, drawn from the source material.[132] (Critics might have been more impressed if this nastiness had stayed; audiences would have hated it.) The script was rewritten to centralize Jiminy with Pinocchio, and it was suggested that songs for Jiminy would seal the deal.[133] Both "When You Wish Upon a Star" and "Give a Little Whistle" became hits. Adding the cricket was inspired—Jiminy's "direct spiritual descendants" have been seen in Disney's films ever since (and now in competitors' films as well).[134] Critics were almost universal in praising the film—again, often based on its formal elements—"[Disney] has wrought a second full length cartoon of consummate artistry" and "Technically *Pinocchio* far surpasses its predecessor."[135] The $2.6 million spent on the film certainly appears on the screen.[136] If the reviewers hedged at all, it wasn't about the scariness of the film; it tended to be in relation to *Snow White*, interestingly, an admittedly less accomplished film that perhaps provided a more satisfying experience with broader appeal. Most reviews were raves. But, with at least 45 percent of *Pinocchio*'s potential box office unavailable, thanks to the active war overseas, domestic rentals and attendance would have to rival *Snow White*'s phenomenal success two years earlier. Those hoped-for returns didn't materialize.

Barrier helps lay out the bad news for 1940. *Pinocchio* did well but not *Snow White*–level well. Foreign-language dubs were little required, and returns from the larger New York theaters were unimpressive, but Disney still had a new studio and films underway to pay for as well as a bank to calm. Selling preferred stock, Disney went public, raising funds, but all of it earmarked for retiring debt, finishing *Fantasia*, and paying for a new studio that employed at least a thousand at this point. The bankers set a credit limit and even "insisted, too, on a cut in salaries."[137] After the smashing success of *Snow White*, this retreat into penny-pinching fueled bad feelings, especially among newer, younger staff, leading directly to labor unrest in 1941. When Roy had to write off a million-dollar loss against *Pinocchio*, the studio was faced with the possibility that "*Snow White*'s box-office success could thus have been a tremendous fluke" and that *Pinocchio*'s numbers were more realistic and what could be expected with *Fantasia* and *Bambi*.[138] Other flukes? Disney and RKO had set the *Pinocchio* release date not long after *Gone With the Wind* appeared, and competition from *Gone With the Wind* clearly impacted *Pinocchio*'s numbers.[139] Second, *Gulliver's Travels* finished its first major New York run less than a month before *Pinocchio* debuted. Third, some neighborhood theaters were showing *Pinocchio* on a double bill, something RKO had avoided for *Snow White*. *Pinocchio* made dozens of critics' and film circle "Top Ten" lists for 1940 but was missing from similar lists compiled by theater owners. One bit of good news for 1940: Ub Iwerks returned to the studio, first as a lowly checker. Over lunch with Walt, it was decided that Ub should take up a more generalized technical role; if films like *Fantasia* were going to work at all, it would be thanks to technical craftsmen like Iwerks. Walt assigned Ub the development of an optical printer for special-effects work.[140] Old Kansas City pals Walt and Ub were back in the yoke, meaning 1940 wasn't all bad. But thanks to many mitigating factors, *Pinocchio* didn't enjoy the plain sailing that *Snow White* had, and Disney had every reason to begin worrying about *Fantasia*.

"The Concert Feature"

"He wasn't aiming at anything highbrow. Nor was he trying to bring classical music to the mass audience," Bob Thomas would write of Walt and *Fantasia*. "He was simply trying to use serious music as another tool for animation."[141] *Fantasia*, or "The Concert Feature"—"a bold attempt to do something that had not been done before"[142]—was likely doomed from the start. Both Disneys eventually agreed it would be a hit; it looked great and sounded amazing, the latter thanks to the new multitrack, multispeaker Fantasound system. But it wasn't a Mickey feature, it wasn't a colorful but brief Silly Symphony title, and it certainly wasn't *Snow White* or even *Pinocchio*—which left audiences and critics wondering just what it might be: "*Fantasia* is most interesting as a catalog of what the Disney artists could do at the time . . . the techniques themselves rather than the uses to which they are put command our attention."[143] Audiences in the millions had fallen for the dwarfs, for the cute animals, for Snow White; they'd pressed deep into cinema seats when the evil Queen and Crone appeared; they'd whistled with Jiminy and cringed when Stromboli or Monstro was on screen. Parents had then gone home and purchased Disney books and records to relive the memories. Much of this was missing in relation to *Fantasia*. As a "concert feature," with its focus on existing music as opposed to character—or even music *as* a character—*Fantasia* clearly missed most audiences. Mickey's appearance in *The Sorcerer's Apprentice* could have become a memorable late Mickey short title, a throwback, given that he isn't talking, relying on his pantomime skills.[144] This nine-minute Silly Symphony title metamorphosed, thanks to Stokowski's influence and Disney's amenability, into a collection of proposed short cartoons attached to classical pieces. It all sounded more manageable as a series of mouthfuls rather than an entire meal, but multiple sequences meant multiple separate teams (along with interstitial bits), employing new effects animation in wildly different mise en scènes—from cartoony to realistic to pastoral to abstract.[145]

Encumbrances being acknowledged, some of the finest animation produced by Disney artists can be found in *Fantasia*. For special-effects animation, "The Nutcracker Suite" section amazes; it includes nothing bombastic or explosive but, instead, rather delicate, flowing motions, yielding glistening, glittering points of light, gradual illumination of flowers, fairies flitting and sparking to life everything they touch. The enlivening droplets cascade down and across the spiderweb, applied carefully by proto–Tinker Bells, until the spider's art is a new canvas, made more lovely by "extensive use of stipple, translucent inks, dry brush and airbrush techniques" and the multiplane process.[146] Many of these cels *each* took five hours to ink and paint; creating some of the images required using up to twelve exposures and involving the entire multiplane camera team.[147] "The Dance of the Hours" portion is an animator's exercise in how to give the appearance of mass and balletic agility to ridiculously ungraceful characters. Finally, a mixing of special-effects animation and masterful figure work comprises the "Night on Bald Mountain" scenes. The waking-of-the-dead sequence prefigures the spare, suggestive UPA studio work by a few years; the muscled Chernabog and the

Trying to conflate art and commerce, Disney employed expensive special-effects animation in *Three Orphan Kittens*, *The Old Mill*, and, spectacularly, *Fantasia*. *Fantasia*, Disney, 1940 (from *Fantasia* Blu-ray). Screenshot taken by the author.

sinewy smoke, clouds, and lighting designs provide the film's climax. The close-in work on the demon's massive, caressing hands is worth the price of admission.

Audiences and distributors had wanted more mice, then more pigs, then more dwarfs, but Disney wasn't keen on repeating himself, even though he had built a following on recurring characters and series. Maybe he really hoped they just wanted more Disney. With a budget reaching about $2.28 million, *Fantasia* couldn't find an audience during the early part of the war. The missing payout led to a forced 20 percent reduction in overall studio operations; it ended the Silly Symphonies, and two smaller films—*Dumbo* and *The Reluctant Dragon*—were hustled to the front of the production queue.[148] Given that so few films were produced before or have been produced since to compare with *Fantasia*, as Finch points out, "*Fantasia* is truly a phenomenon."[149] And, like the dancing mushrooms and the visualized soundtrack, there are segments of *Fantasia* that will live forever. Critics were apportioned as well, with opinions ranging from "masterpiece" to "promising monstrosity" to "remarkable nightmare."[150] If *Fantasia* was, indeed, Disney's "last moment of risk and experimentation until the late 1980s,"[151] he went out in a blaze of unmatched special-effects animation glory. Considering both *Pinocchio* and *Fantasia*, it's fun to wonder (as Disney probably did) whether things would have been different had European audiences been exploitable in the early war years.

It is generally the case that the beginning of something means the end of something else. For the Hollywood movie industry, a coal-seam fire smoldered from 1938 on until flaming up in 1948. In the following chapter, we will see how the cartoon industry helped fight the war, taking advantage of the very monopolistic tools—including block booking and ownership of vast cinema circuits—that the US Justice Department sought to end. In 1938, the government sued the vertically integrated major studios. Unaligned theaters had been forced to play by cartelized rules agreed on by the major (and minor) studios, the major studios owning nearly all the most lucrative theaters in the country. These studios had agreed to not compete among themselves, where possible, acting as a monopoly. Independent theaters had to agree to almost any demand, including accepting block and blind booking, if they wanted access to the major studios' stars and films. By 1940, as the Depression was ending but war in parts of the world was ramping up, a consent decree was signed. It was meant to be a kind of binding gentlemen's agreement—if the major studios wanted the Justice Department to stay away, they'd fulfill the agreement. The decree provisions "included establishing trade shows in lieu of blind bidding and limiting block booking to packages of five films. Unable to force exhibitors to purchase an entire yearly program of A's and B's, the major studios phased out B-level production in the late 1930s and early 1940s."[152] The short-term results were good for the smaller studios in particular and those interested in producing genre pictures. The increase in cinema attendance during the war—requiring increases in production at all studios, large and small—distracted from the legal action. The fact that the suit eventually reached the Supreme Court indicates Hollywood was unwilling or unable to sufficiently live up to its side of the decree, and the Justice Department moved ahead with the goal of severing the major studios from their theatrical circuits.

The consent decree was a beginning; an end was less than a decade away. But, as with most smoldering fires, it's hard to take seriously a slow-burning disaster that is well out of sight. Just a few years after the war, this little conflagration would erupt and change the studio system entirely.

CHAPTER 7

World War II

Cartoons—An Essential Industry

THE WAR YEARS WERE DIFFICULT FOR THE LARGE CARTOON STUDIOS
Disney and Fleischer/Famous. Both had new facilities to pay for and new
employees to keep busy, and then the war happened. World War II "was
at once Disney's salvation and the final blow to any hopes that the bright
promise of the early Disney features would be fulfilled."[1] Production of
a first-rate cartoon feature every eighteen months wasn't supportable
without worldwide distribution, and the box-office surplus from *Snow
White* wouldn't reappear with later, technically superior Disney films. The
film needs of the government, the military, and the war effort in general
saved Disney; Schlesinger's studio was *made* by the war, as were, in many
respects, Avery and Hanna-Barbera at MGM. Cartoon stars reminded,
convinced, sold, and warned as they supported the Allied effort. Dumbo
was scheduled to be on the cover of *Time* magazine on 8 December 1941,
but events of the war intervened. Disney's sparkling new studio was supposed to be making colorful cartoons but immediately became a military
maintenance and storage facility. For a time, Walt Disney Studios was a
secure, quasi-military facility where cartoons also happened to be produced. Disney survived the war, slimmed down but largely intact, able to
produce short and even feature films; the Fleischers lost their studio and
were vestigial to the industry from that point.

And what was the measure of success in the animation industry as
war descended? In the 1940s, it was manifold—first, managing to make

cartoons at all, and then making cartoons to assist the war effort, cartoons that were faster, more violent, more suggestive, and more entertaining than ever before. It was also surviving as a cartoon producer with limited materials, personnel, and distribution outlets; it was working with characters who were fast becoming national treasures. And, while Schlesinger's studio was busy creating a stable of beloved, enduring characters, Terry was content to regularly produce versions of the cartoons he'd been offering since the 1920s. Columbia guttered across the war years, flaring occasionally. Fleischer and then Famous also seemed to be marking time and meeting deadlines. At MGM, Hanna and Barbera created and then produced one series of cartoons featuring two beloved characters, bringing home five Academy Awards across the decade. Avery was Avery wherever he went. And all this is not even what most people remember from this amazing decade of American cartoons.

Disney's 1940s had started badly, as we've seen; Tex Avery's decade began much better. Both at least reached and survived the 1940s. Charles Mintz died on 30 December 1939, setting off years-long unsettledness at Screen Gems. Without Mintz, Columbia's cartoon-producing entity would be functional, but certainly at the back marker, and unsettled—"seven different regimes" headed Screen Gems across the same period that saw MGM win five Oscars.[2] First Avery, then Disney.

Still at Schlesinger's, Avery hit his stride immediately. In March 1940, an "ace of a cartoon" *Cross Country Detours*, one of Avery's travelogues, appeared.[3] We are guided through the vistas and introduced to the inhabitants of picturesque America in these cartoons, the narrator employing an "overly patient, overly 'bright' tone, generally reserved for madmen, morons, children, and documentary film audiences."[4] Blackouts take us from scene to scene, and every tranquil moment, sublime expanse, and noble animal is a setup. A "Do Not Feed the Animals" rule is enforced *by* the animals; a "shy little deer" becomes a "dear" and va-vooms her way off camera; a lizard shedding her skin becomes a rotoscoped burlesque routine; and a "natural bridge" in Bryce Canyon is a gold-toothed dental bridge. Avery gave other animators and studios permission to undercut the all-powerful narrational voice. Hoary jokes were a favorite of both Terry and Avery (Terry even kept a card catalog of jokes, gags, and situations[5]), but Avery presented them with such aplomb and cheese, almost daring the audience to not laugh, even flashing hand-held signs to that effect, that they continued to work. Avery understood the media he lampooned: first, radio and feature films; then the short film subject; and, later, television. If Disney focused on a child's experience, as Rosenbaum argues, that focus "is neatly balanced by Avery's preoccupa-tion with peculiarly adult problems and concerns (mainly sex, status, and procuring food.)"[6] Avery also liked "toying" with the grammar of film and film technology and even with film viewing. In *Who Killed Who?* a man in the front row of a movie theater (projecting *Who Killed Who?*) stands and moves along the seats toward the aisle. The on-screen charac-ter waits, watches, and eventually hits the man with a truncheon. Avery assumed a movie-literate, spectator-aware, and even cartoon-fluent audience, poking fun at clichés, using those same clichés, and parodying film genres.[7] Disney had "don'ts," and upstarts like Avery could and did take up that gauntlet. He fashioned for himself a neat anti-Disney exis-tence, a "modernism focus[ed] on the specifics of his [cartoon] medium" in which he could parody other animators' cartoons.[8] Avery's puns are elegant and corny, his violence fast and faster, his reflexiveness drawing attention to the cartoon, the animator, the audience, and the conven-tions of projection and viewing. And, even though he wasn't much older, Avery trained Clampett, Jones, and Bob Cannon, among others. Between 1936 and 1942, under Avery, Schlesinger's is characterized as "short on bombast and budget, but high on energy, speed, inner-city urbanity, and sheer wit."[9] The first four articles (half the magazine's pages) of the special 1975 *Film Comment* issue are devoted to Schlesinger's cartoons, celebrating their "gem-like condensation[s] of wit and multilevel signifi-cation."[10] More later on Avery and his blossoming at MGM. Close iris.

On the Disney lot, it wasn't as much about shorts as coming up short. Both *Pinocchio* and *Fantasia* cost too much and made too little. In total, Disney lost about $1 million across 1941 and 1942.[11] Disney had already reported a seven-figure loss for the fiscal year ending 28 September 1940.[12] So, the decade started awash in red. *Bambi* was underway and making new demands of both animators and technology and would be further delayed thanks to the war and strike. Disney had borrowed too much and built a costly new studio that now had to be staffed and maintained. The glitter of riches after *Snow White*—the highest-grossing film of 1938—had simply whetted appetites, fostering unrealistic expectations for future projects, the privations of war and rising costs not considered. The scores of newer artists and personnel hadn't struggled with the studio across the 1930s. Couple that with a capricious bonus system—"Walt's favor was the sole criterion for promotions, raises, and bonuses"[13]—and organization of a restive labor force got much easier. The structure of the efficient and compartmentalized new studio discouraged party feeling— gone were the days of easy access to Walt and the camaraderie of the more intimate old studio.[14] Max Fleischer had been certain his employees could come to him with any concerns—he was the kindhearted paterfamilias; Disney felt similarly and knew his "boys" appreciated and respected him. In other words, they felt there was no need for outsiders defiling the temple. Cutbacks, which might have been related to the bottom line, were now jaundiced with anti-union coloring, and organized labor saw its opportunity to make inroads at non-union holdout Disney. Other cartoon studios had already fallen into line with the unions or, in the Fleischers' case, lost the battle but prolonged the war by quick marching to sunny Miami. During flush times, the absence of a union wasn't a concern, but when the studio entered straitened circumstances, and Disney began to lash out at "ungratefuls," a union became attractive to chastened employees. Parts of 1941 would be the ugliest in the company's history, even before the end of the fiscal year showed a deficit.[15]

The Disney studio had attempted to quell unrest by allowing the organization of an in-studio union group, but firebrands like Art Babbitt joined the Screen Cartoonist's Guild instead. Disney and Babbitt had reportedly always bristled around each other, so it was not a surprise when Disney fired the agitating animator responsible for the Wicked Queen, Geppetto, and Goofy. This development wouldn't have been much of anything if Babbitt had been fired for poor performance, but since it was known the dismissal was union-related, picketers were on the street the next day, 29 May 1941, and grievances were filed.[16] Many of those who would form into UPA during and just after the war were on that picket line, as were many newer, mid- and lower-level employees.

The strike featured well-designed signs and lots of acrimony across three and a half months, orchestrated by union official Herb Sorrell. Disney blamed ungrateful employees and active communist agitation. At the studio there was likely at least one former communist, Dave Hilberman, a handful of Coca-Cola socialists, and then dozens of young employees working right at the poverty line. Organizers of the strike were able to increase pressure on Disney by convincing unionized affiliated groups—Technicolor employees, cinema projectionists—to refuse Disney service. Production at the studio continued at a reduced pace.

Disney was tossed a lifeline in the form of a State Department–supported goodwill tour of South America, which provided an opportunity to meet fans, spread American goodwill, discourage Nazification, and gather inspiration for future projects set in the other hemisphere. It was also an opportunity to get away from the strike. The strike was settled by October, with Disney having to rehire Babbitt and agree that the studio would in the future lay off, when needed, both striking *and* nonstriking personnel equally. Walt would eventually downsize the staff—1941 and 1942 saw the entire industry struggle—and most of those who had been involved in the strike, including Babbitt, were gone.

During the war, studios continued producing straight-ahead entertainment cartoons for weekly distribution, making allowances for missing (drafted/enlisted) employees, reduced material, reduced salaries—and the cartoons kept coming. In addition to producing films, several studios produced insignia for Allied military units, with Donald Duck themes being the most popular. Disney did all these jobs without profit.[17] Images of Popeye, Bugs, Daffy, Woody Woodpecker, Andy Panda, and many new characters invented on demand graced patches and served as fuselage art. By 1943 and beyond, the all-out war effort was underway. Between 1941 and 1945, Disney released seventy-seven short-subject titles, one more than in the previous five-year period, and the same as would be produced between 1946 and 1950.[18] Some of the best Hollywood cartoons ever produced emerged during the war. Lantz offered his best Woody titles; Avery hit the ground sprinting at MGM with *Dumb-Hounded* and *Red Hot Riding Hood*; Hanna and Barbera churned out award-winning Tom and Jerry titles; Frank Tashlin and his proto-UPA staff at Columbia produced scattered gems; Terrytoons managed to entertain with Mighty Mouse cartoons;[19] Schlesinger's crew made the seven-minute cartoon their very own, offering classics *The Dover Boys*, *Pigs in a Polka*, and *A Corny Concerto* from Jones, Freleng, and Clampett, respectively, while Disney finished and released the studio-saving *Dumbo* as well as the beautifully naturalistic *Bambi*, all in the depressing first years of the war. But the war and rationed life at home did intrude into cartoon worlds. Warner Bros. tended to revel in the topicalities of the war years, while Disney avoided such dating references, as would MGM in some of its product, like Tom and Jerry titles: "World War II hardly existed in their world."[20] MGM's Avery unit helped pick up the slack on that front. In *Jerky Turkey* (1945), war references include gasoline ration-card stickers, a navy gun crew on the *Mayflower*, an "Okie" working at Lockheed—he's "4F" (unfit for military duty)—and a vulture operating a black-market storefront. Rather than demonstrating a lack of patriotism, producers who avoided overt topicalities were likely trying to ensure the cartoons' reissue appeal—the knockabout Tom and Jerry cartoons never did go out of style.

There were *many* types of war-related animated films produced from 1941 to 1945:

- Instructional films for or from the defense industry (*Four Methods of Flush Riveting*; *Ice Formation on Aircraft*), which were designed to explain specific procedures, machines, or industrial processes and weren't broadly screened outside of defense plants

- Instructional films for the fighting services (*Position Firing*; *Stop That Tank!*; *Enemy Bacteria*), which were more sober and demonstrative without being bland

- Educational/reminder films for the fighting services (*Private Snafu*; *Flat Hatting*; *A Few Quick Facts*), which were often more humorous while delivering a serious message

- Educational/incentive films for the home front (*Scrap Happy Daffy*; *Point Rationing*; *Why We Fight*), which could feature significant propaganda moments and used emotion and persuasion to lead to action

- Entertaining cartoons with a war-related message or subject matter (*Falling Hare*, *The New Spirit*)
- Entertaining "[h]ard propaganda" cartoons that lampoon the enemy directly (*The Ducktators*, *Blitz Wolf*, *Cap'n Cub*, *Tokio Jokio*) and therefore have since been censored more than any others, thanks to cartoonists' freedom to ridicule the enemy, often via racial stereotyping[21]
- Bond-drive cartoons (*Any Bonds Today?*, *Doing Their Bit*, *The Thrifty Pig*)

Using cartoons as effective teaching and learning tools, even for adults, came to be understood early, and lessons were learned across the war years: "The cartoon is more effective than the photograph and whenever certain facts must he learned by the student, the introduction of a little humor in the cartoon is an aid to memory."[22] Donald Duck encouraged Americans to pay taxes early; Private Snafu reminded soldiers of their rote-but-life-and-death duties; careful diagrams taught about tank rifles, best riveting procedures, and disease control. One serving officer noted the value of these films "converting a civilian into a soldier."[23] This was the endgame for many of these wartime propaganda films—convincing all Americans, those serving and those at home, that they were an active part of the war effort and that each had a crucial role to perform. Disney would set its own pedagogical categories by 1942, announcing that, for the duration of the war, the studio would focus on "Entertainment, for Disney feels morale at home is as important as food and guns for our boys at the front," and "Training," "Educational," and "Psychological" films.[24] Disney would carry on making these films after the war. Similar films were being produced at most studios: Culhane remembers working on *Enemy Bacteria* for Lantz and the navy, Capra's *Two Down, One to Go* (on the defeat of the Axis Powers), and *Lend Lease*.[25]

Disney feature films were still in play, but they also most often lined up with the war effort—*Victory Through Air Power* would lead home-front propaganda, while *Saludos Amigos* and *The Three Caballeros* trumpeted America's "Good Neighbor" policy. Work on Disney entertainment feature films like *Bambi* and especially *Peter Pan* and *Alice in Wonderland* continued but on backburners. Instructional films tended to be light on humor and silliness and heavy on demonstration. (The *Rules of the Nautical Road* series was noteworthy—the navy consistently "vetoed" *all* Disney attempts at even hints of humor.[26]) Educational or entertaining films (for the soldier and the home front) often mixed humor and patriotism, as in Donald's *The New Spirit* and *The Spirit of '43*. There's plenty of crossover between these categories, of course. In Warner Bros.'s *Ducktators*, the Axis leaders are caricatured and finally beaten up by a reformed dove of appeasement, and the cartoon ends with a reminder to buy bonds. Disney's *The New Spirit* short film was seen by thirty million people, the result being Donald convincing more Americans to pay their taxes early—a minor miracle. In *The Spirit of '43*, saving money (and lending it to the war effort) was the message.[27] These shorts were successful: "[I]n eight minutes, *The New Spirit* presents its case in a manner that no freedom-loving American will be able to resist."[28] *The New Spirit* was commissioned and (partly) paid for by the Treasury Department and was released to exhibitors for free. Disney tended to spend more on the cartoons than the various government entities were able to pay, his way of contributing to the war effort.

This new spirit rang in before the United States entered the war. In March 1941, with overseas distribution on hiatus and feature-film prospects bleak, Disney was sizing up work potential for his studio and the war effort. He contacted his neighbor Lockheed and, in consultation with Lockheed, created *Four Methods of Flush Riveting*, on spec, and purposely without humor or Disney characters. The result is a straight-ahead how-to guide for a riveting process, depicted step-by-step; the film is easily understandable and rewatchable—a training film. With the finished film spooled up, in April 1941, Disney invited military and defense guests for a visit and showed them what his films could do.[29] The film was made available as an example to others in affiliated industries as well. The National Film Board's John Grierson was impressed and immediately secured Canadian rights to *Four Methods*; he also signed a contract

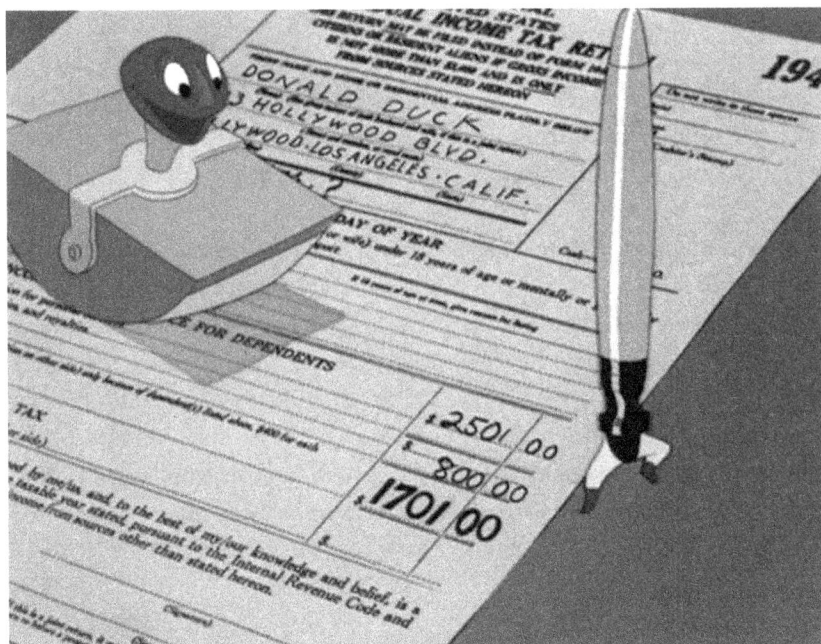

In *The New Spirit*, Walt Disney offered the services of his star Donald Duck to the war effort to playfully encourage Americans to pay their taxes early; almost 40 percent did just that. *The New Spirit*, Disney, 1942 (*Walt Disney On the Front Lines* DVD). Screenshot taken by the author.

for *Stop That Tank!* (a Disney anti–tank rifle training film directed by Iwerks). Grierson likewise contracted for entertaining bond-raising films *The Seven Wise Dwarfs*, *The Thrifty Pig*, *Donald's Decision*, and *All Together*.[30] For these war-certificate titles, Disney would repurpose footage and characters from *Snow White*, *Pinocchio*, *Three Little Pigs*, and Mickey and Donald color cartoons. This way, the films were finished faster and more cheaply and provided recognizable characters, incentivizing Canadian audiences to purchase bonds. Bits of the popular songs "Who's Afraid of the Big Bad Wolf?" and "Heigh-Ho"—with slightly altered lyrics—were also deployed in two of the shorts. The last eighty seconds or so of these cartoons feature the on-the-nose propaganda bits, where animated military images, sounds, and graphics are used to highlight the importance of every purchased bond: "To Win This War Spend Less and Lend Your Savings."

Just after the attack on Pearl Harbor, the US Navy ordered twenty "aircraft and warship identification" films from Disney—all on low, fixed budgets and short turnarounds.[31] It wasn't glamorous or even terribly appealing, but, with this multifilm contract, Disney knew he'd found a way to keep his studio going through the war while contributing to the war effort. He would later say that up to 75 percent of his wartime output was war and government related; in 1943 alone, 94 percent of everything Disney produced was under government contract in some way.[32] Gomery puts a finer point on it: "Disney came to rely on the government."[33] In November 1942 alone, Disney shipped 30,000 feet of finished footage, mostly for naval contracts, an amount equaling everything Disney had produced the previous year.[34] "[By 1942,] the studio became quite literally a defense plant, and the people who worked on these films could rightly claim a share in each American victory."[35]

The production of entertainment films did continue, with caveats. Disney's *The Reluctant Dragon* (June 1941) was an advertisement for the studio, frankly, and a "quickie," in Disney's words, designed to cost little and make lots.[36] It was also a cheeky behind-the-scenes look at the studio, animation *and* live-action, and was released just days after the beginning of the strike action. This film would be plagued by the perfect storm of both the strike and the war. The film had to do well domestically; instead, *Reluctant Dragon* became a handy target of onsite picketing at domestic movie theaters. Perhaps because it was neither fish nor fowl, *Reluctant Dragon* struggled. The film managed to recoup some of its cost at the box office but still lost about $100,000.[37]

As the war was beginning, animator Frank Tashlin moved around the industry, from Warner Bros. to Disney to Columbia (Screen Gems) and back to Warner Bros., before eventually settling into a successful career in film directing. While at Columbia, Tashlin would use the Disney strike casualties to beef up his operation, providing work for Zack Schwartz, John Hubley, Dave Hilberman, Ted Parmalee, and Bob Wickersham.[38] The films Columbia produced usually had forgettable storylines, and their sound designs were equally uninspiring. However, they were often fun and moved like Disney and Schlesinger cartoons, sometimes boldly, making for an oddly watchable concoction. Titles like Tashlin's first (*The Great Cheese Mystery*) and the Fox and Crow series, kicking off with *Fox and the Grapes* in 1941, employed the black-out gag motif used for years in Warner Bros. titles.[39] With the violent, failure-rich blackout gags propelling Tashlin's cartoon, *Fox and the Grapes* would be an obvious primer for Jones and Maltese and their later Coyote–Road Runner series. Tashlin's *Cinderella Goes to a Party* (1942) shows influence from the war but also from *Snow White*, *Dumbo*, and Disney generally; most of the crew had been working months earlier at Disney. In it, a clumsy fairy godmother appears to the voluptuous Cinderella, who is working in a scullery. The fairy flashes her AFL union card and preps Cinderella, but not for the "royal jam session." Using scarce aluminum, Fairy Godmother concocts a B-19½[40] bomber for Cinderella's ride to a lavish United Services Organization party. With Prince Charming, she dances the samba until the clock tolls midnight and then races home. Her plane reverts to pots and pans—"After all, these pots are on the priorities list!"—but Fairy Godmother saves Cinderella. A montage of spinning newspapers and magazine pages follow, detailing the Prince's search (a reward in war bonds is offered), until the next headline trumpets, "EXTRA! CINDY FOUND: Riveting Tail Assembly at Lockheed." Not just a damsel to be saved, Cinderella was working for the war effort. Budgetary considerations aside, the quick wit and visual agility of this cartoon points to the talented crew behind it.

Tashlin surrounded himself with young animators ready to try anything, and his work at Columbia tended to be more fun, inventive, and cinematic than the studio's usual fare. Just a year or so after arriving, Tashlin would be replaced at Screen Gems by industry veteran Dave Fleischer, fresh from losing his own studio. Fleischer's sensibilities were worlds away from where Tashlin and his young hires had been heading, so the war and other jobs scattered the staff.[41] Hubley and several others left to join the Army Air Force's First Motion Picture Unit (FMPU), led by Frank Thomas. Columbia would spin lazily until the later part of the decade when UPA was brought on board.

The war didn't kill the feature cartoon but certainly changed it. The smallish *Dumbo*, released in October 1941, steadied Disney. Made for about one-third the cost of either *Pinocchio* or *Fantasia* and half of what *Snow White* cost, "straight cartoon" *Dumbo* was an immediate hit, a pick-me-up for both audiences and the studio in the darkest days of the war. *Time* magazine was effusive, hugging the phenomenon deep into the bosom of current events: "Among all the . . . forbidding visages of . . . 1941, his guileless, homely face is the face of a true man of good will."[42] It was also one of the rare mixings at the Disney studio of the cults of the line and the picturesque, of East Coast and West Coast styles, juxtaposing graphic flatness against the Technicolor-cinematic in one film. The "Pink Elephants" sequence offers metamorphosis and surreality the Disney way—the characters accidentally drink alcohol and begin to hallucinate. It's a narratively justified trip. This scene acknowledges without apology the cartoony nature of the characters, settings, and movements, acknowledges squash and stretch, and points up the almost xerographic creation, copying, and deployment of moving images. In this, the film reaches back across Disney's recent history to the Wild, Wild East of earlier cartoons, to the elastic, straight-ahead-drawn figures from New York animators like Messmer and Jim Tyer, and to the early 1930s work of Fleischer.[43] The film even touches avant-garde boundaries, as it acknowledges the frame between us, the audience, and the characters Dumbo and Timothy. Tiny pink elephants march across the bottom of the frame, then up one side, across the top, and down the other, all followed by the droopy gaze of Tim and Dumbo (and us). "It is at this moment, I think," writes one critic, "that *Dumbo* stops being merely a very affecting and accomplished film, and becomes a great one . . . the 'Pink Elephant Dance' is magnificently unexpected and it is one of the Disney Studio's great individual set pieces."[44] This atavistic section recalls the freedoms of early Fleischer as well as the styles of Nolan and Barré and even McCay and Cohl. From this shot's vantage point, the audience is now in the world of the illusion, of the pink elephants, and we'll stay there until the hallucination wears off, and the narrative can resume at dawn.

To many critics, *Dumbo* was a welcome return to where Disney had been in the Mickey and the Silly Symphony days, lauding the film's

WORLD WAR II

"freedom from the puppeteering of *Snow White*, the savage satire of *Pinocchio*, the artiness of *Fantasia*, and the woolgathering of *The Reluctant Dragon*."[45] *Dumbo* was probably more of a Roy Disney kind of film; it had a smaller budget, a shorter window of production, and "less emphasis on the kind of bravura animation and visual design" than did *Pinocchio*, *Fantasia*, or *Bambi*.[46] And it was a much-needed financial success.

A different kind of success in 1941 was the Fleischer Superman series, bankrolled by Paramount and released just in time to help America fight the Axis. The series was also *commissioned* by Paramount—the Fleischers thought that producing these cartoons would be prohibitively expensive and wouldn't benefit their studio. They were right on both counts. The cartoons were cinematic versions of the comics, made in color and with special-effects animation, including modeling, rotoscoping, chiaroscuro lighting, live-action camera angles and camera movement, and a heightened "cartoons noir" sensibility.[47] Several of these, including *Japoteurs*, *Jungle Drums*, *Destruction, Inc.*, and *The Eleventh Hour*, referenced the war effort directly. The Superman series emerged to a marketing blitz and strong public and critical reception, but all that cooled quickly. Critical and exhibitor reception swung from "for the kiddies" to "only for comic readers"—insults both—though kids always seemed to be pleased. The films were also so expensive that Paramount could afford only two batches—nine titles from Fleischer and eight more from Famous. Viewers seemed to tire of them first, as exhibitor and audience feedback indicated. Commenting on *The Magnetic Telescope*, *Variety* snarked, "Follows the usual formula. Annoying array of implausibilities except for juveniles."[48] By the seventh cartoon, *Electric Earthquake*, reviews settled into the "Fair" category—not the response wanted when costs approached $100,000 per episode. Also interesting were the reviews that equated Superman cartoons with kids' entertainment. A generational bias against comic books might have helped doom this ambitious series.

The end of 1941 was shaping up to be a challenging time for the cartoon industry, even with the war far away. Lack of foreign distribution hurt studios offering expensive feature films, meaning Disney and the Fleischers. The much-anticipated release of the Fleischer studio's second feature, *Mr. Bug Goes to Town*, was set for 5 December. The events

147

of 7 December cast a pall on everything. *Mr. Bug Goes to Town* opened to fair reviews and disappointing box-office receipts, making less than $250,000. It was also too often compared unfavorably to *Dumbo*.[49] This outcome was all Paramount needed to pull the trigger, given the running score for the industry: two successful cartoon feature films (*Snow White* and *Gulliver's Travels*), three flops (*Pinocchio, Fantasia, Mr. Bug*), and one pleasant success (*Dumbo*). Paramount took the studio from the brothers, rebranded it as Famous, and began the move back to New York. Before the third *Superman* cartoon was even released, Max Fleischer's presigned resignation was accepted, and Max was out of the studio he'd founded. Dave had already quit. By May 1942, Disney's only real competitor was no more.

December 1941 was also key for the immediate future of the animation industry. With a war on, it would have been easy to justify the cessation of any activity that required war-related materials—film stock, chemicals, equipment, and personnel. There was much to be done to put the country on a war footing, and cartoons were likely at the bottom of almost anyone's list. The film industry would need to justify its existence, especially if it wanted to keep its draftable employees. A War Production Board oversaw the consumer-goods industries' transition to war-materiél production across the country. For example, the production of personal automobiles ceased for the duration; military vehicles rolled off these assembly lines instead, Ford building B-24s rather than Business Coupes. The same Lionel Corporation that had been saved by affixing a Mickey Mouse image to its products years earlier now produced warship compasses. This transition was folded into the animation industry, by necessity but also patriotism. Disney had set the ball rolling with *Four Methods of Flush Riveting*. The usual number of entertaining short-subject films were already in the pipeline on and after 7 December 1941, but it wouldn't take long for the faraway war to come home. Between January 1939 and September 1945, of the nearly five hundred commercial cartoons produced, almost half of them mentioned or depicted the war effort.[50]

The seven major cartoon producers strove to maintain a business-as-usual attitude during the war. Parent studios still made live-action fiction films for theatrical distribution, and newsreels and novelties continued to be produced. Blocks of films were still going out to exchanges and thence to theaters, so cartoons were needed. Other cartoons, those not destined for theatrical distribution but specifically for civilian, defense and military training, information, and education purposes were coming from Army Signal Corps studios and the FMPU.[51] Animation-industry staff could be drafted into these units but could also enlist and be assigned. Cartoons may have been just what Uncle Sam needed in this early war period. Into mid-1942, the war was not going well for the Allies—there were headline-grabbing setbacks across the Pacific and tonnage losses due to marauding U-boats, and shortages had already begun to bite at home.[52] In 1942, cartoons from the major studios referencing the war focused on the military, home-front shortages and sacrifices, the "V for Victory" theme, war bonds and stamps sales, and "vilification" of the enemy.[53] In some cartoons, there were simply visible scrap- or bond-drive or rationing posters—in backgrounds, not highlighted—or jokes about whitewall tires (made of prioritized rubber), unnecessary travel (gas rationing), prime cuts of meat (rationed), and "4F" designations. Other cartoons more directly sold the war effort, scorched the enemy, and reminded Americans of the need for sacrifice.

A bit late to the game, the MGM studio headed by Fred Quimby quickly became the best in the industry behind Disney when it came to equipment and working conditions. The animation studio was situated on the fabled MGM lot and produced fewer pictures per year, enjoyed better conditions, and could afford more polish than its competitors. This polish allowed Tom and Jerry to get away with the violence and body mutilation they engaged in regularly—"brutality and sentimentality" were the two extremes in these cartoons.[54] Motion picture exhibitors had voted Disney's short-subject films as the best in the industry 1938–1942, when Merrie Melodies rose to second place; Bugs Bunny was so popular he came in fifth in this same 1942 poll.[55] MGM's cartoons didn't make the cut. MGM's Technicolor offerings had hovered outside the top ten for several years, but Tom and Jerry and Avery's cartoons vaulted them into the top five. By the mid-1940s, the "slick" look of the cartoons and the "self-confidence" of Hanna and Barbera as producers made Tom and Jerry an industry juggernaut.[56] These cartoons are beautifully brutal or brutally beautiful—either way, their popularity can't be denied. Increased brutality also meant increased sentimentality (overly cute character modeling, syrupy story lines, etc.). Regarding character creation, even at its peak, MGM lagged well behind Warner Bros., apparently content to produce new and profitable Tom and Jerry cartoons from the Hanna-Barbera unit, stand-alone single titles that tried for the Disney "look" from the Harman-Ising unit, and scattershot characters (excepting Droopy and perhaps Screwy Squirrel) from the Avery unit.[57] The fifth cartoon produced by the Hanna-Barbera unit as a partnership was *The Midnight Snack*, another cat-and-mouse (now Jasper and Jerry) cartoon, and, by the time of the film's release in July 1941, enough positive feedback had arrived about *Puss Gets the Boot* that Tom and Jerry could truly be born.[58] It would be after the war, really, when the redesigns for Tom, especially, ceased and Hanna and Barbera were working on little else that the cartoon duo took off. Tom and Jerry won five Oscars during the 1940s and were at least nominated every year from 1943 on.

And there was a war on, too. The 11 June 1942 victory at the Battle of Midway was a much-needed boost for the US war effort. The studio with the highest regular operating expenses began to see fortunes improving as well. For the fiscal year ending 3 October 1942, Walt Disney Productions reported a loss of *only* $191,000—four times less than in the previous fiscal year.[59] Coincidentally, the number, speed, and vigor of war-related cartoons increased in late 1942 and across 1943. In 1942, 44 percent of the cartoons released from the major studios featured war-related content; in 1943, that figure would rise to 65 percent.[60] By 1943, the predominant war-related bits in cartoons involved not the serving military but the home front, with themes including rationing, shortages, and the black market, followed by inclusion of "armed forces references . . . and Hitler caricatures."[61]

Almost four years after it was supposed to be finished, the animated feature *Bambi* was released in August 1942. *Bambi* cost about $1.7 million and made just less than that in its initial release.[62] It was the final film from Disney's Golden Age—or the first film of its Gilded Age—a masterwork of *cinematic* animation. It was also the last fictional animated feature Disney would make until 1950 and *Cinderella* as well as the official debarkation point for most *haute culture* critics who couldn't leap off the Disney bandwagon fast enough. "*Bambi* is full of . . . passages the brilliant and the banal cheek by jowl," concluded one of the more reasonable voices, "which reflect the confusion of artists in transition, not the mechanical dullness of cynical entertainers."[63] It was the point where, according to critic Panofsky, Disney "lost his stride and regained it" only scatteredly thereafter.[64] *Bambi* was the film in which, Manny Farber said, "Mickey wouldn't be caught dead."[65] But, with the premiere of *Bambi*, Disney was also "the undisputed master of the animated cartoon," this proclamation from an exhibitor-leaning critic, one who knew a distributable film when he saw it.[66] For another reviewer, *Bambi* looked more beautiful than any previous Disney title, yet offered no "whimsical plot"—a tiny regret—and then he lamented, "The great change is that Disney has quit making animated cartoons."[67] Disney's continuing reach for naturalistic images and movement undercut the fantastical in his work, the cartoony completely eschewed—to many, a cardinal sin. Most highbrow voices turned away from Disney films thereafter—dismissing chimeras *Saludos Amigos*, *The Three Caballeros*, *Make Mine Music*, and *Song of the South*—eventually embracing the anti-Disney UPA aesthetic. Disney trundled on, of course, making short films for the war effort and international relations and finding solace in the rereleasability of the Golden Age titles for the last twenty years of Walt's life. The release of the "cute and pretty" *Bambi* was a turning point.[68]

"Cute" had helped Disney rise to the top in the first place, of course. The sequence in which Bambi learns to walk is a case in point—he is ungainly and clumsy but adorably "cute," a fixation that has been characterized as an "infantilizing celebration."[69] This descriptor had affixed itself to Disney's product early—"we were talking about cute things: cute poses, cute this, cute that"—and would become one of the critical blackjacks used against the studio as well as a way for UPA to define itself in opposition.[70] The events of July 1942 alone might explain *Bambi*'s unsteady footing in the world—it was the time of El Alamein, Guadalcanal, and Stalingrad. It mightn't have mattered what critics had said at all, frankly. A film enduring such a lengthy gestation had consequences: "By [August 1942, *Bambi*] was already a relic of another time:

a film about gentle animals, released in the midst of war . . . an expensive, elaborate film, from a studio that could no longer afford to make such things."⁷¹ By fall 1942, *Bambi* was playing as the top picture on double bills with forgotten war pictures like *The War against Mrs. Hadley* and *Manila Calling*. Better, by 1945, *Bambi* was with *Dumbo* as part of a twin bill in some cinemas, the profitable and likable *Dumbo* helping his forest friend a great deal.

But *Bambi's* reception might also have been tempered by the wartime entertainment other cartoon studios were delivering, and audiences were clearly responding to, notably shorts from Schlesinger and MGM (and, occasionally, Columbia). After clashing with Schlesinger and leaving Warner Bros., Avery found his way to MGM, where he also found his voice. Avery's first supervised production at MGM, *Blitz Wolf*, became one of the studio's key marketing tools—it was immediately hailed as "the best industry-produced war short of the past year in a nationwide poll of exhibitors." Four of these ten were MGM short subjects.⁷² (*Blitz Wolf* was the only cartoon on the top ten list.) *Blitz Wolf* is a model Avery film—it makes fun of a beloved Disney cartoon (*Three Little Pigs*), retelling the story that had been told by most cartoon studios since 1933; it features corny puns, cornier sight gags, and signs for the audience; it stars a mustachioed Adolf Wolf; it reuses hackneyed gags; it acknowledges its cartoon-ness and is cartoony; it is irreverent and risqué; it employs Goldbergian mechanized gadgetry; it even manages to sell war bonds. Oh, and Avery blows Adolf Wolf to Hell.

Less than a month after *Blitz Wolf* appeared came a Chuck Jones title from Warner Bros., *The Dover Boys*. Not a war-related cartoon, *The Dover Boys at Pimento University* was instead a faux-nostalgic throwback to a book series that had been popular more than two decades earlier. Narrated by the sonorous John McLeish, the story follows a planned outing of "dainty Dora Standpipe" and the three Dover Boys, their day nearly despoiled by the devious designs of archenemy Dan Backslide, "coward, bully, cad, and thief." The characters often move in blurred streaks, coming to precise stops and holding stiff photographic poses— they "pop from pose to pose, with a few frames of 'smear' action between each position—resulting in a new cartoon 'logic' . . . making them faster

Tex Avery enjoyed context destroying, Disney bashing, and Hitler send-ups; in the *Three Little Pigs* takeoff *Blitz Wolf*, he was able to revel in all three. *Blitz Wolf*, Tex Avery, 1942 (*The Compleat Tex Avery* LD). Screenshot taken by the author.

and funnier."[73] It's a nineteenth-century sampler come to life, and, in a defiantly non-Disney approach, "Jones calls attention to the poses."[74] This same paring away of the frame's clutter would happen in wartime FMPU work, paving the way for Hubley, Cannon, and Schwartz to present a cleaner, stylized look for full animation when UPA would begin producing cartoons after the war. Finally, the backgrounds in *Dover Boys* are like impressionistic, airbrushed watercolors as opposed to oil paintings, and there's clearly a move away from even Warner Bros.'s version of verisimilitude in almost every way. The reactions to Disney and the effects of wartime budgets and materials were having an impact across the industry. At Schlesinger's, in Norman McCabe's *The Impatient Patient* (1942), former Disney artist and soon-to-be UPA man Dave Hilberman offered similarly spare layouts and backgrounds; Gene Fleury's clever, sparse backgrounds are seen in the otherwise excruciating *The Unbearable Bear*

(1943), one of Jones's "Sniffles" cartoons. This cartoon is a plot-heavy mess (with four separate story lines), and Sniffles is cloying.[75]

At MGM, Hugh Harman continued to labor on Disneyish cartoons that owed much to the defunct Silly Symphonies. These were often beautiful, full-color, and fully animated shorts featuring naturalistic animals, layouts, and background designs. These were unironically stuck in the previous decade, too, *The Field Mouse* offering sweet mice who learned lessons about family and hard work. In February 1942, Harman produced *The Hungry Wolf*, a sincere tale of a wolf *not* eating a rabbit because it's the right thing to do. The syrupy-sweet young rabbit, lost in a snowstorm, not seeing the wolf as a threat and weeping for the wolf to be his father, convinces the starving predator to choose death instead. The rabbit's family takes the wolf in and feeds him a Christmas dinner (meaning some poor turkey wasn't so persuasive). There is some very nice effects animation depicting snow, wind, and fire, and the sound design and music are top shelf. It's also very much in the vein of the treacly cartoons being made in the 1930s. Exhibitor reviews for the cartoon were a funny mix. One theater owner in Canada called *The Hungry Wolf* "Very poor." Another reviewer from Florida rated it "Very good." The latter review was from a state prison.[76] In this same year, Disney would release a feature, *Bambi*, that did everything Harman aimed for but better. Also, the slam-bang cartoons from the other units at MGM and everything coming from Warner Bros. in 1942 made Harman's work seem quaint. Harman would leave MGM and try to set up his own studio again, always pining for his own Disneyfication.

A new Disney effect appeared in August 1942. Disney's "feature" *Saludos Amigos*, a kind of Latin American travelogue, drew together several short subjects begun during Walt's South American excursion. Donald and Goofy both appeared in individual short-subject components, and new characters, like the Brazilian parrot Joe Carioca, made *Saludos Amigos* memorable. *Saludos Amigos* was well animated and even well received, for the most part—one critic calling it "singularly beautiful and diverting" propaganda—and it premiered across Latin America before opening in the United States.[77] Several countries *not* depicted in the film registered complaints with the State Department and Disney, demanding that they be included in future films.[78]

Hundreds of straight-ahead informational or training films, like *Four Methods of Flush Riveting*, were produced in the 1940s by dozens of studios, from Disney to Jam Handy, but also the FMPU, with think tanks, universities, industrial and transportation concerns, trade unions, and even states looking to communicate some vital message. Most of these aren't clever or terribly watchable—just narrowly informative. But there were several animated series contracted by the military and government just for serving soldiers; these light-hearted training films with recurring characters were inspired by the past twenty years of personality animation, with characters including Private Snafu, McGillicuddy, Mr. Hook, and Grampaw Pettibone. Aside from the wise old aviation teacher Pettibone, the characters were typically lazy, selfish, and thinking only of home or pursuit of easy pleasure; hard lessons followed when shortcuts were taken or rules not strictly followed.

Part of the Army-Navy Screen Magazine, the most popular of these were those produced by Schlesinger's crew starring Private Snafu. "They have been called the Army's safety valve," wrote an industry veteran: "*Pvt. Snafu* expresses the average serviceman's gripes and kids them. *Snafu* somehow always manages to do everything wrong, but much can be learned from his humorous plights."[79] Voiced by Mel Blanc, Snafu's messages were serious, with topics ranging from army discipline and attention to duty and disease prevention to inflation, fearmongering, the dangers of loose lips, and the challenges of transitioning back to civilian life. They were designed for the active soldier who might have been in harm's way just hours before a screening.[80] In *Spies*, Snafu has information about his unit's orders and is sure he can keep the secret, the "chain and pad-a-lock" on his brain secure. There are Axis stooges, including Göring and Mussolini, listening everywhere, of course, and Snafu's alcohol-plied hints result in a U-boat wolfpack waiting for his convoy. In *Booby Traps*, "If you are a boob, you will be trapped," warns the narrator. Snafu tells him to go to Hell and then encounters multiple booby traps (in a desert seraglio, the women are dolls with bombs in the place of buttocks and breasts)—and he is eventually blown up. In *Gripes*, Snafu is promoted by the "Technical Fairy: First Class" (certainly a Disney swipe), and he runs the army into the ground; in *Fighting Tools*, Snafu learns that only well-maintained weapons can defeat the enemy; and in *Home Front*, Snafu gets to see what's really happening at home—tank and ship building, victory gardens, and win-the-war volunteerism. Snafu would also learn about the dangers of rumors, tropical disease, and food waste; the importance of camouflage, gas masks and gas drills, necessary censorship, fighting the war to the end, and investing in savings bonds; and the value of far-flung assignments late in the war. Snafu became "a Pacific favorite," according to brass returning from war-theater inspections; film showings where a thousand or more servicemen watched weren't uncommon.[81]

Schlesinger's Snafu was talked about in the trade journals. Other characters like him, created by other studios, didn't rate as much publicity.

The sweary, slightly risqué Private Snafu shorts were made for the armed forces. In *Spies*, soldiers are reminded that the penalty for loose lips is a quick trip to Hell. *Spies*, Warner Bros., 1943 (*Looney Tunes Golden Collection* DVD). Screenshot taken by the author.

Titles in the Harman-produced McGillicuddy series, "Commandments for Health," were made late in the war after Germany was defeated and the focus had fallen squarely on challenges in the South Pacific. "Thou shalt not use any spots except chosen ones for the deposition of your excrement" was a typical commandment addressed in the series (character voice also provided by Blanc). Other common topics were how and why to keep yourself and your gear clean, what water to drink and what foods to avoid, and so forth. These titles were designed to protect health and save lives behind battle lines. Harman and his team avoided even a hint of full animation, which would rely on poses, fewer in-betweens, and select movements, and instead relied on strong key drawings. Mr. Hook was a hapless sailor, often aboard a ship, while Grampaw Pettibone was the voice of wisdom, reminding "hot shot pilots" that death awaited if they couldn't keep an eye on their altimeters or fuel gauges. And since the first (and assumed only) audience were serving military members, all these cartoons were more risqué than usual, including minor nudity and cursing. The goal for all these titles had been the same—to educate often battle-weary servicemen without boring them, demonstrating *and* entertaining where possible.

The home-front cartoon was also a place where much-needed humor could help bitter medicines go down. Going without was a challenge; rationing took good planning and creativity; patience wasn't a virtue but a requirement; saving and buying bonds rather than spending also had to be encouraged—the cartoons aimed right at the American public came to be crucial and memorable. Here Paul Terry was able to stand shoulder to shoulder with the rest of the studios, at least as a conveyor of the government's message, and especially if those messages were aimed at younger audiences. *All Out for V* (1942) is a recognizable Terrytoon that manages to help fight the war at home with chirpy good humor. A Terry studio historian calls it "a masterwork of animated filmmaking," which is potable if one adds "for a Terrytoon title."[82] It is certainly more memorable than most of Terry's catalog, which was all, admittedly, memorable enough to be popular in cinemas for many years. In *All Out for V*, the forest animals hear explosions and see a newspaper headline about the war. Without waiting for instructions, they get to work. As Terry was wont to do, he used recycled and repurposed footage from earlier cartoons: The beavers chew into trees, sending logs flying, those logs forming into log cabins, using footage borrowed from *Landing of the Pilgrims* and reused in *Winning the West*. These cabins become a War Production Office, orders go out over the radio, and, for some reason, there is a receiver set in a forest clearing. A forgettable patriotic song begins, and the animals become or create tractor treads (caterpillars), sawmills (termites), harvesters (ants), gun-barrel cutters (parrots), uniform makers (mosquitos), metal cutters (fireflies), and helmet presses (turtles). Not everything makes sense, even in a make-believe world of sentient animals. The tiny tractor already existed, but it was without treads until caterpillars pitched in. Woodpeckers hammer premade nails into logs. With their feet, chicks stamp "V" on freshly laid eggs, goats milk each other (an odd sight), and a cat forces a hen to lay egg after egg. Some of these moments are mildly creative; other scenes just depict the animals pitching in and doing human activities (a rabbit collects for the Red Cross). An explosion has broken the peaceful morning in nature, but fighting isn't depicted, raising the issue of whether this is the home front or the battlefield. Maybe it's both. It's a mixed bag but delivered with spirit—as a closer, the characters even fight Japanese beetles, forcing them to flee. It's not clear whether the beetles are Japanese soldiers or unfortunate Americans who happen to be Japanese and live near a coastal area (if this is a reference to internment camps, it's more disturbing). *All Out for V* is an enjoyable Terrytoon and was even nominated for an Academy Award.

In the Disney version of the home-front cartoon, the "hope of American agriculture" fought the war with its own "Panzer forces" and "battalions of combines," supported by "regiments of trucks, divisions of corn pickers, potato diggers, planting machines" alongside "columns of milking machines." Disney's *Food Will Win the War* (1942) preached the Good Word of food as a weapon, bringing necessary war-production responsibilities right to America's doorstep. Educational but also humorous was Disney's *Out of the Frying Pan and Into the Firing Line* (1942), a reminder to housewives of the importance of leavings in the war effort: "Fats make glycerine, and glycerine makes explosives." Minnie appears as the subject and object of this lesson, while Pluto is the miffed pet who is denied his snack of leftover bacon grease. The statement that "[m]eat drippings sink Axis warships," accompanied by a well-drawn image of a torpedoed enemy battleship, is a memorable cinematic moment. Even Pluto is convinced when he sees that it is soldier Mickey who will benefit from the extra ammunition.

The entertaining but educational Warner Bros. cartoon *Scrap Happy Daffy* (1943) was directed by Tashlin and drawn by soon-to-be UPA employees Phil Eastman and Dave Hilberman. It is a clear primer for how to influence audiences without overt propaganda, a display of director Tashlin's cinematic influences as well as of the limited animation style that will be favored after the war. Tashlin brought a live-action awareness to Schlesinger's output, introducing montage effects, dissolves, and oblique camera angles, all from the "real" movies. Much of this work had to be back-seated for the educational wartime cartoon, but Tashlin's cinematic-ness shines through. The camera angles in *Scrap Happy Daffy* are varied and creative, what Tashlin would later explain as his attempt at "a poor man's Ufa."[83] Many of these scrap films were aimed at kids who could go home and start rummaging around the house and neighborhood for donatable materials. Rather than provide a printed or even spoken laundry list of qualifying items, Civil Defense Warden Daffy leads us along a fence with chalked images of all these sundries—an effective teaching technique. Daffy then must battle Hitler's secret weapon sent to destroy the scrap heap—a junk-eating Nazi goat.

Another Warner Bros. effort early in the war was also meant to educate the population and was clearly molasses-coated propaganda (sugar being rationed): *Point Rationing of Foods* (1943). Directed by Chuck Jones and brought to life by Cannon, Hilberman, and Ken Harris, *Point Rationing* reminds Americans that food production must serve the needs of the men in combat first and the needs of the war effort in general as well as the needs of our allies, where possible. It informs viewers that food in dried form and in cans is best suited for the war effort and that anything connected to those foods and forms will necessarily be subject to rationing. Boldly offered—"The United States Government Presents"—the film is meant to educate as soberly as possible the American consumer, consumers accustomed to walking into a grocery store to

Looney Tunes characters like Daffy Duck pitched in to support the war effort. *Scrap Happy Daffy* encourages Americans to gather and donate everything from pots and pans to electric fans. *Scrap Happy Daffy*, Warner Bros., 1943 (*Looney Tunes Golden Collection* DVD). Screenshot taken by the author.

purchase canned goods at any time and in any amount. The film is meant to educate, not convince. Rationing is carefully explained as the only way to ensure that a "fair share" of precious foodstuffs is constantly available and that hoarding is avoided. The film also makes clear what items will *not* be subject to rationing, where to find and how to best use ration booklets, and which items cost more "points" than others, so housewives can plan weekly menus. The film uses both full and limited animation effectively, rationing its own efforts to get the most from a meager budget. The housewife character is fully animated; the secondary characters, actions, and backgrounds are limited, typically just posed drawings. Production of these cartoons kept quite a few animation personnel out of active military assignments and behind a desk or at a camera, still serving the war effort by educating Americans.

One cartoon that sits somewhere between outright government propaganda and entertaining custard is Warner Bros.'s *Foney Fables* (1942), directed by Freleng and written by Michael Maltese. The title is quite topical, given talk over the previous two and more years of the "phoney war" being waged somewhere over in Europe, a war that mightn't exist and that certainly shouldn't involve American forces.[84] The cartoon is presented like a fairy-tale book, a series of narrated chapters with "pages" turned by hand, and the familiar tales are humorously tweaked. In some, the twists are Avery-like, as in the initial "Sleeping Beauty" scene, in which the Prince—moving in for a gentle kiss to awaken the sleeper—instead shouts and shakes her awake. Similarly, the Boy Who Cried Wolf is eventually eaten by the Wolf, and the "This Little Piggy Went to Market" baby complains of a corn.[85] Other sequences lean quite topical, dating the cartoon to the war years. The lazy Grasshopper sits around watching the Ant work, even cautioned by the industrious Ant, but the Grasshopper flashes the war bonds he has purchased—and relaxes anew. Also, a Goose doesn't lay golden eggs, but rather aluminum eggs labeled "For National Defense"; a lamp is rubbed in an Aladdin sequence, but a strike picket sign pops out instead; and, when Old Mother Hubbard's dog reveals she has a fully stocked cupboard, the dog calls out, "She's a food hoarder!" *Foney Fables* ends up as an entertaining reminder of the value of maintaining good health and participating equitably in the food-for-the-fight cause, and it even evokes the charged home-front political climate. And, by the time this cartoon was entertaining American audiences, a phony war had become very real.

In 1942–1943, Disney created several films that straddled both the requests of the Office of the Coordinator of Inter-American Affairs (CIAA) and the Disney studio's desire to produce entertaining and patriotic cartoons. Studio schedules were packed even without these special films. By May 1943, Disney had a logjam of entertainment shorts (intended for theatrical distribution) of seventeen cartoons; in their way were the orders for "army and navy training films and other governmental product" that Disney had accepted, all of which had an automatic "green light."[86] Four of these were Disney's "psychological" cartoons. "These films—*Der Fuehrer's Face, Reason and Emotion, Chicken*

Little, and *Education For Death*—were as pointedly anti-Nazi as anything the studio ever made."[87] These titles were indicative of "Disney's all-out war effort"; they also kept films in the pipeline.[88] Disney gauged the winds and acted early: "Of all the producers, Disney threw his company most whole-heartedly into the war effort."[89] These films were distributed across Central and South America, but success in US theaters was also accomplished, especially with one of the films, *Der Fuehrer's Face*. The title song, covered by Spike Jones, became a nationwide hit even before the film was released. It was known as "the great psychological song of the war," and the cartoon visually lampoons Hitler and Nazism, with the help of Donald Duck.[90] Local and regional advertisements for theaters lucky enough to be playing *Der Fuehrer's Face* screamed out the good news, often much more visibly than the titles of whatever features were playing. *Der Fuehrer's Face* would win the Oscar for best animated short subject.

Education for Death: The Making of a Nazi was one of the "psychological productions" (a "purely propaganda short"[91]) that entertained but also chilled, adapting a story about Hitler's cradle-to-grave plan for indoctrinating German children. Reviews suggested that even the colorful Disney cartoon approach couldn't dull the "aspect of horror" in Hitler's scheme, but it was well received by exhibitors and audiences (always hungry for war-related information). *Reason and Emotion* and *Chicken Little* rounded out the CIAA contract obligations. In the trade journals, all these films were quite well received for just what they were—entertaining propaganda. In addition to these war-related films (and the in-progress *Victory Through Air Power*), the studio was also managing to create eight Donald Duck, four Pluto, and two Goofy cartoons. Also continuing in the background was work, in various stages, for the South American titles and proposed features like *The Gremlins*, *Peter Pan*, *The Wind in the Willows*, and *Alice in Wonderland*.

Disney mightn't have benefited overly from the war—the studio was unable to produce the elaborate feature cartoons on which Walt had earlier set his sights. Disney had to settle for lesser animation-and-live-action projects and dozens of war-related shorts not only to demonstrate the Disney magic but also to keep the lights on. The future would be fewer cartoon features, much more live-action filmmaking, and theme parks. Other studios experienced the war a bit differently. As for the Schlesinger crew, they made their bones during the war. It was during this magical Clampett-Jones-Avery-Freleng era that the Warner Bros. studio came into its own, its offerings characterized by "lightweight satire of the topical, the trendy . . . the mildly proletarian impulse . . . the break-neck pacing and tightly gagged structure; an attitude that would be called anything from irreverent to tasteless."[92] By 1941, Steve Schneider argues, the artistic prowess of animators at Warner Bros. had finally caught up with their vision—they could animate the world they imagined, the gags as they'd envisioned.[93] The national zeitgeist helped: "The anxieties and tragedies of the war fostered a more ferocious national mood which, ironically, favored the philosophical direction of Warner Bros. cartoons in general."[94] This wasn't the mood of the Depression and the early Mickey Mouse era. It wasn't even the voiceless violence of Tom and Jerry's species-justified chases. By 1942, Schneider continues, the Schlesinger crew reached their "watershed year"—everything was in place so that, for the next sixteen years, Warner Bros. would be producing the most popular shorts in the industry. Jones shrugged off Disney sentimental-ity, and others came into their own and out of Avery's shadow.[95] And 1943 was the biggest year of wartime production of all sorts—and when 50 percent of all American cartoons were war related. The cartoons were made to cater to both the GIs and their anxious families at home. "Many of these cartoons give the impression that the directors had caught the mood of the public," Weinman notes, "and its mixed feelings about the war: patriotism, fear, xenophobia, and slightly forced good feelings about their allies."[96] This view likely describes not only the mood of the public but also that of the fighters.

And the accelerating, high-octane wartime shorts coming from Schlesinger's gang were finally doing regularly what had before happened only occasionally—besting Disney where Disney had been best. The short-subject cartoon laurels swung to Warner Bros. and to MGM and never swung back. Facing few expectations beyond delivering watchable cartoons under budget and on time meant the young animators could do almost anything in almost any way. Their workplace patina was flak-ing, but Warner Bros. had infrastructural solidity, a foundation of funny cartoons that put them ahead of Terry's lot at Fox and most of what came from Columbia; Warner Bros. animators were producing unforgettable characters, racing past MGM's roster; they were likely not even considering whatever Famous was producing. But there was competition—competing stresses engendered by the war, wrenching Americans from fear to duty, from isolationism to globalism, from jingoism to patriotism to superpower status. Throughout the 1940s, these were the polarities with which Warner Bros. animators played, their "elements of craziness clashing with elements of full control."[97] This shouldn't be a surprise. Deadly V-rockets flew like sparks from the German hearth even when Hitler was losing the war, and, by 1945, Japan was promising self-destruction rather than surrender, so there were contradictions in everyday life. At Schlesinger's, there was also room for personality behind the personality animation, and there was not just a singular, signature studio style. In addition to the gifted "layout and background artists, effects and character animators," one critic concluded, "there are five directors . . . five different styles, five different approaches, five who set the standard we have come to expect from a Warner cartoon."[98] Freleng, Clampett, Avery, Jones, and Tashlin couldn't have drawn a deep breath at Disney's; in fact, all of these five had spent some time at "the" studio, learned a thing or two, and come away gasping. This clutch of personalities needed a mostly indifferent rubber-stamp leader who could clench purse strings, shout and swear, and then relax as deadlines were met and "the cartoons did well at the box office."[99] Schlesinger had avoided the kind of strike that so roiled Disney by rolling over and agreeing to a union labor contract. This yacht-owning boss wasn't a fan of unionization but understood how the winds were blowing. This surrender kept Warner Bros. artists from the barricades and at their light tables.

The war also demanded a few changes at Schlesinger's and allowed for a few more. In the announcement of the 1943–1944 release schedule, Schlesinger admitted that, due to the increased demands of war contracts, "only" thirteen Merrie Melodies and thirteen Looney Tunes would be produced. Twenty-six Merrie Melodies had been expected to complement the thirteen Looney Tunes, continuing the studio's lead over all other studios. Fewer cartoons meant one other change, though—all these cartoons would now appear in Technicolor, so there were no longer differences between them.[100] Finally, the amazing success of Warner Bros. cartoons at the distribution and exhibition points made the next innovation seem obvious—rerelease of the best titles back into theatrical distribution. In 1943, it was decided that, as Disney had discovered with the rereleases of *Snow White*, there was still money to be made from yesterday's product. Schlesinger had agreed to create a new "Hall of Fame" title card—replete with the image of a small trophy and a "Blue Ribbon"—for each of these revisited cartoons. The first of the reissues was the 1938 Avery cartoon *A Feud There Was*, released 11 September 1943. These reissues were an immediate success.[101]

Following his freshman hit with *Blitz Wolf*—for which MGM was taking out full-page ads in trade magazines—Avery enjoyed a steady run of memorable cartoons. His move to MGM coincided with an explosion of vitality in his work, and Avery joined "Buñuel, Rossellini, Fuller and Godard in the elaboration of a modernist film vocabulary . . . piling up the excesses of multilayered contradiction, de-normalizing the whole process of linkage articulating the absurdities of Our Daily Lives."[102] With *Dumb-Hounded* (1943), Avery presented the refined and accelerated narratives he preferred, his pop and smear techniques given free reign as the war moved on. More than five years before the spareness of the first Road Runner–Coyote cartoon, Avery was already hyper-focused on the "character wants objective but obstacle" paradigm: for example, Droopy wants to catch Wolf, who wants to avoid capture. He permitted no narrative fat—no subplots or unnecessary secondary characters. It's decidedly *not* the Disney model of deep, rich character motivation and illusion of life; it's context destroying and acknowledgment of the medium's tricks. "[Avery's] effects—more distancing than endearing—come off more like Godard's or Eisenstein's than like Disney's," wrote Adamson. "He enjoys telling us it's a cartoon we're watching—*his* cartoon."[103] *Dumb-Hounded* stars one of Avery's few original characters, Droopy, a saggy, laconic hound. The convict Wolf doesn't merely run from Droopy; he streaks from city to city, flashes of color and speed lines. At one point, he runs right past the edge of the film, and we get to see the sprocket holes zipping by, destroying any illusion of the sanctity of diegetic space. In a later

Droopy cartoon, *Northwest Hounded Police* (1946), the Wolf convict runs off the film strip again, and then he takes cover in a movie theater, where he sits to watch an MGM cartoon starring Droopy, who greets him from the screen.

Avery's most ambitious work "explicitly signals its cartoon-ness" and an awareness of its production, in critical theory terms.[104] His animated films are reflexive, as they comment on filmmaking and the film industry and uncover the nuts and bolts of the animation process. Avery's cartoons can speak directly to audiences, acting as discourse, Lindvall and Melton continue. In *Who Killed Who?* Avery's detective character interacts with an audience member watching the cartoon, and Avery employs a live-action narrator not only to introduce the film but also eventually to be outed as the one who "dood it." These cartoons can also reflect their creators, as the animators can appear as themselves in the cartoon (McCay, Cohl, Messmer, Fleischer, and Lantz did so), but following Disney's example more likely and lastingly the animator's personality becomes apparent.[105] Avery cartoons don't often feature Avery, but his rule-breaking and context-betraying personality reigns across his many films. By the time the wolf is flattened by a house-sized rock in *Dumb-Hounded*, it was clear that nothing would be the same in cartoons—the new generation had arrived.

Back at the Disney lot, if *The Reluctant Dragon* had been a public-relations piece for Disney, then *Victory Through Air Power* (1943) was a feature-length ad for the person and theories of Alexander De Seversky—it is propaganda and advertising, full throttle. Alternately bold and boring, pedantic and persuasive—arguing that long-range aircraft tactics would shorten the war—this film lost money as a feature but certainly changed modern tactics. The film was reviewed well, but, at sixty-five minutes and without much Disney humor, it wasn't programmable. The film ended up grossing just a few dollars more than it cost to make: "Given the unique nature of this picture, though, its success would be measured in terms of influence rather than box office receipts."[106] Churchill saw the film and was a fan; he convinced Roosevelt to see it, likely affecting strategy for the D-Day invasion. And even though the film didn't cause lines at the box office, with its earnings, revenues from *Saludos Amigos* and the constant contracted work going on

In the Droopy-starrer *Dumb-Hounded*, Tex Avery assumes a film- and cartoon-literate audience will enjoy a peak behind the medium's artifice. *Dumb-Hounded*, Tex Avery, 1943 (*The Compleat Tex Avery* LD). Screenshot taken by the author.

at the studio, and profits from rereleases and merchandising, Disney was able to finally announce a profit at the end of 1943.[107]

Other studios were not worrying at all about costly feature films or even about costly shorts—just deadlines. Aside from the well-received *All Out for V*, Paul Terry tended to produce forgettable, programmable cartoons across the war. Terry's elaborate and patriotic *Shipyard Symphony* (1943)—where animals build a battleship—owes a debt to Freleng's *Rhapsody in Rivets* (1941). Some sequences are nearly duplicated.[108] It's set in a wartime shipyard and manages to be watchable without doing anything new or clever. Other modest exceptions include the Mighty Mouse titles and some of the Sourpuss and Gandy cartoons, mostly due to their consistent energy. Terry's wartime contributions tended to be earnest rather than accomplished. A review for the "Terrytoon Special,"

167

Camouflage, from a projectionist at Fort Bragg displays the qualitative differences in cartoons of the day: "We held a stopwatch on this one to discover the period between laughs. We didn't find out. Not even a smile cracked."[109] Soldiers mightn't have been Terry's preferred audience. His most popular character, Mighty Mouse, first appeared as "Supermouse" in *The Mouse of Tomorrow* (1943), complete with blue-and-red costume and Superman-like powers. It wouldn't be long before he became Mighty Mouse to avoid litigation. Most of Mighty's cartoons weren't really his— he would simply appear well into the story, when some situation seemed bleakest, and save the day.[110] The Mighty Mouse cartoons, compared side by side to the Superman cartoons, may have fared better with both critics and exhibitors, interestingly—and they outlasted the Man of Steel series. In the films, the goose Gandy and the cat Sourpuss (the latter often Sergeant Cat during the war) visit the various theaters of operation. In Europe, they attack Hitler and Mussolini at Hitler's mountain retreat (*The Last Roundup*); in Africa, they survive Egypt and Rommel (*Somewhere in Egypt*); in Asia, they are with the Flying Tigers (*Aladdin's Lamp*); and in the South Pacific, they report for duty (*Somewhere in the Pacific*). There's no need for a military setup, generally; Gandy and Sourpuss are already in military kit, and then the adventures start.

These films would have been more affordable than first-run Disney, Warner Bros., or MGM cartoons, and they enjoyed solid exhibitor reviews, especially from small-town cinemas. Historians Michael Shull and David Wilt describe this series well: "Imaginative and well-animated, the biggest flaw in the Gandy Goose/Sourpuss cartoons is that they are simply not funny."[111] "Funny" is a value judgment, of course; however, while they have amusing moments, these cartoons are almost never clever or wry—they have vigor without wit. In *The Mouse of Tomorrow*, for example, Mighty Mouse's debut, dozens of cats are waiting at mouse holes on the main street as the narrator introduces the setting: "Now in this little village there lives a large population of cats." The camera moves in on these cats as they peer into the holes, tails waving. Dissolve to a tracking shot along one row of these cats, and the narration continues, "Big cats and little cats, fat cats and thin cats, white cats and black cats, alley cats and house cats." We see all these cats (in a nonanimated shot, mind you, a painting), and the cats are *precisely* as the narrator describes. This is not a setup and payoff, as we'd see in most cartoons from most other studios; we don't see two normal cats and then a strange one or any punning or plays on words (maybe the fat cat looks like Hardy and the thin cat like Laurel), and so forth. Avery, Clampett, or any Fleischer animator would lose his mind trying to go this long without a gag. The mice, by the way, are almost identical in their designs. "The humor, such as it was in these cartoons, resulted from mild sight gags or knockabout humor," Shull and Wilt continue. "Even the physical comedy in the Terrytoons is conventional: Practically nothing goes on in these shorts that couldn't occur in live action."[112] Barbs acknowledged, these cartoons were made and purchased and viewed for almost twenty-five years before Terry sold out to CBS—when they were repackaged and watched all over again.

Terry was done no favors by way of gifted competitors. *Red Hot Riding Hood* (1943) has all the elements of an Avery classic—bait-and-switch plots, an over-the-top central character, corny gags and handheld signs, and an object of desire; sometimes the object is food or a conquest, but here it's sex in the form of the nightclub entertainer Red—and there is another Red, this one a Grandma set on out-wolfing Wolf. The film starts as a typical Hollywood retelling of the classic tale but is recast into a ritzy nightclub world of liquor, girlie revues, and rationed whitewall tires. There are two very memorable sequences in this film: Red's song and dance for Wolfie and then Grandma Red's pursuit of the Wolf, turning the lusty tables on him. The Wolf's clapping and table banging and full-body erections for Red are memorable, but the Wolf having to endure a dose of his own medicine is the transgressive part that lasts. This very handsy grandma-wolf character returns as Cinderella's Fairy Grandmother in *Swing Shift Cinderella* (1945), where, if Cinderella is late, she'll miss her midnight shift at the "Lockweed" plant. Both Red and the Wolf would find their way onto military insignia—Red was inspired by nose-art models (like Betty Grable) as Preston Blair and Avery created her. There would eventually be five of these Wolf and Red cartoons; MGM would say that these films were the most popular shorts they ever distributed.[113]

In 1943, noted entertainment columnists Ed Sullivan and Jimmy Starr had called *Red Hot Riding Hood* the best and funniest short of the year, blurbs that MGM pulled into full-page advertisements for exhibitors.[114] The cartoon was repeated several times on its first night in many cinemas, always due to audience demand; it was booked more times than any MGM short subject; and the success of *Red Hot Riding Hood* spawned immediate new cartoons starring Red.[115] Servicemen were able to see this one uncut; home-front audiences had to settle for a slightly edited version. A showing to servicemen at Fort Bragg was typical: "One of the best cartoons of the year—pleased everybody. The howling wolf brought on a craze that had the barracks howling for nights after."[116] Avery even admitted they were "thinking of the army" when they were creating Red and her admiring Wolf.[117] The film also survived a changed ending. An ending in which Grandma has caught the Wolf and they are being married was original, to be followed by images of the Wolf and their children at the club howling at Red's performance. Too much. The *less* offensive ending had the Wolf swearing off "dames" or accepting death—Red emerges into the spotlight and the Wolf shoots himself dead with two pistols. His ghost picks up where his whooping body left off.

Less entertaining but equally important to wartime efforts were the millions of feet of training films being produced across 1944–1945. A film like *Position Firing* became crucial by 1944. In that year, heavy bombers made by American factories rolled off the assembly line with regularity—those bombers needed protection from enemy fighters, so trained gunners were in high demand. *Position Firing* taught the waist gunners how to aim properly. Hubley, Frank Thomas, and Rudy Larriva created this controlled but not humorless film—it starred a Snafu-like character, Trigger Joe, whose first actions always taught new gunners what *not* to do. By the end of the short film, Trigger Joe is using the tools he's been taught and successfully shooting down the enemy. Bill Scott, later of *Rocky and Bullwinkle*, spent his Air Force time at FMPU as a gofer, a cel washer, a painter, a model maker, and an occasional in-betweener for more seasoned animators. He remembers working in three areas—"general instructional films," "specific training films," and "maps and topographical . . . for fighter pilots." In the first, he helped out on *Camouflage*, directed by Thomas and starring a chameleon; in the second, he chipped in on *Position Firing* to familiarize recruits with "gun sights"; and in the third area, he helped build and paint the enormous, soundstage-sized, three-dimensional topographical models (of enemy port cities) for pilot and bombardier training.[118] At MGM, newly commissioned *Major* Rudy Ising was assigned to shepherd Hanna-Barbera's efforts, resulting in many navy tactical and training films, including films looking at "sanitation, submarine camouflage operations, and destroyer attack procedures."[119]

PUPPETOONS

Occupying an unusual wartime niche was puppet animator George Pal. His "Puppetoons"—carved wooden figures with movable, replaceable body parts[120]—appeared in Paramount's Madcap Models series. Pal was Hungarian by birth, and his work stemmed from the European tradition of puppeteer Ladislaw Starewicz, abstract artist Oskar Fischinger, and the longstanding artisanal traditions of European animation. The memorable *Tulips Shall Grow* ("loveliness on the screen," said one exhibitor[121]) came in mid-1942 and was both enchanting and mournful. In a painstakingly rendered three-dimensional setting, young love blossoms among the tulips in prewar Holland. The Nazis had overrun Holland in May 1940 and brutally occupied the country for most of the war. In the film, the arrival of a clattering mechanical army—goosestepping "Screwballs"—brings destruction on the ground and from the air. The lovers are separated in the melee. The boy prays in a bombed-out church, and, as an answer, a fierce storm downs the enemy's translucent planes and rusts the metallic, mechanized army. A lone, final tank sinks into a waterlogged shell hole and disappears. Happily, the girl has survived in the ruins of a windmill, and she and the boy are reunited. Spring returns, small clouds form the "V for Victory" in the blue sky, and an amended title promises *"Tulips Shall Always Grow."* This would have been a very bold, optimistic statement at this point in Holland's occupation, as Nazi reprisals against continuing Dutch resistance meant concentration camps and death. Critics were impressed: "[I]t succeeds in making the war a fairy-tale fantasy without making it silly," said one. "Even Disney might learn something from the smooth blending of animation and music in this short."[122] By the following year, Pal had upped his studio to two eight-hour shifts a day to fulfill army and navy training-film contracts and to make entertainment shorts for cinemas starring a young boy, Jasper.

Pal's Jasper series featured a black boy, and, like many cartoons from this period, the depictions haven't aged well. In *Jasper and the Haunted House* (1942), Jasper is tasked with delivering a pie, but he is sidetracked through a haunted house by a ne'er-do-well scarecrow, he turns white when scared, and his pie is eaten. As the cartoon closes, Jasper and the scarecrow have been flung out of the house and through a billboard advertising a brand of gooseberry pie, "Spooks." Conveniently for the writer Webb Smith, "spook" not only meant the spectral figures in the haunted house but also had become across the war a slur for blacks. Jasper whacks the scarecrow with the empty pie tin, but this cartoon, like most of Pal's work, slipped into the shadows of history. These Pal films looked quite different from everything else being produced in Hollywood at the time, a refreshing break for exhibitors.

Also effective as propaganda but with more blister than bloom was Lou Bunin's *Bury the Axis* (1943), in which Hitler, Mussolini, and Hirohito are mercilessly lampooned. Their individual puppets are grotesquely caricatured—shrunken bodies, large heads, bulging eyes, sallow cheeks, and pronounced brows. Hitler is a goosestepping megalomaniac marching in a line of geese across France, Holland, and Norway, only to come scurrying back, wounded, from Russia. Mussolini is a dog (whistled up by Hitler) who comes out of his doghouse to bark and strut before he scurries back inside, a frightened cur singing, "I'm only a boarder in Hitler's New Order." And Hirohito is a slithering snake, announcing his godlike status ("I am the Son of the Sun") as he performs a *Great Dictator*–like routine with an explosive. The cartoon promotes China, Great Britain, Russia, and the United States (and the United Nations) working together to "bury the Axis." Using carved wooden puppets, these craftsman-like ways meant that it took twenty-two weeks to finish a seven-minute cartoon, and yearly production was six titles. Pal would transition to live-action filmmaking by 1950 and produce classics *Destination Moon* and *The War of the Worlds*.

Hitler, Mussolini, and Hirohito are lampooned and then slaughtered, in puppet form, in Lou Bunin's contribution to the war effort, *Bury the Axis*. *Bury the Axis*, Lou Bunin, 1943 (YouTube). Screenshot taken by the author.

And there was still some off-the-books work. Cartoons for the military and defense training, cartoons for the home front, and traditional cartoons for theatrical distribution were made regularly during the war and occupied most animators' time and energies. In the run-up to the 1944 presidential election, Roosevelt was popular and the war was going well, but the country was clearly tiring of the war, the tom-tom of self-sacrifice, and the "stay the course" rhetoric. Roosevelt was also terminally ill. Many of the Hollywood leadership, including Walt and Roy Disney and Leon Schlesinger, were in the Thomas Dewey camp (or at least they wanted "Big Government" and FDR out of office).[123] The left-leaning *Hell-Bent for Election*, produced by the nascent Industrial Films (later UPA), was a reelection-campaign propaganda film for FDR. The production was a cartoonists' union class project, directed by Chuck Jones, produced by Stephen Bosustow and John Hubley, designed by Zack

Schwartz, and drawn by Bob Cannon, Shamus Culhane, Ben Washam, and many others, all volunteering their time and energies. Like the later *Brotherhood of Man*, this film was financed by the United Auto Workers, at that time quite powerful and politically active. *Hell-Bent for Election* was designed to be shown in trade-union halls and community centers, or anywhere that laborers could see it and be convinced to give FDR a fourth term. It was reported that the film was being made available for showings (with an accompanying projector) for $25 and for only $10 if one already had a projector.[124] *Hell-Bent* was clearly a one-off—a "useless" artifact beyond its first and only intended purpose. But it was well made and watchable—"out-spokenly pro-Roosevelt . . . [and] funny enough to amuse Republicans"[125]—and therefore a popular film beyond its intended audience. In rural areas, a kind of agitprop mobile-unit arrangement roadshowed the film from town to town.

Directors like Tex Avery didn't seem to have been as impacted by the war as their studios or the industry. *Village Voice* film critic J. Hoberman

Hell-Bent for Election is an after-hours effort from many hands, made to encourage a vote for FDR in 1944. *Hell-Bent for Election*, Chuck Jones, 1943 (*Saved from the Flames*, season 7, Kanopy). Screenshot taken by the author.

would later write of what he termed "vulgar modernism," and the first medium and artist he gets to will suit us fine. Hoberman thumbnails his terms: "Conscious of its position in the history of (mass) culture, the sensibility [of vulgar modernism] developed between 1940 and 1960 in such peripheral corners of the 'culture industry' as animated cartoons, comic books, early morning TV, and certain Dean Martin/Jerry Lewis comedies." And the clincher: "The Manet of vulgar modernism is the animation director Tex Avery." Avery's craft is almost entirely the "popular, ironic, somewhat dehumanized mode" that looks at itself, navel-gazing into "the specific properties of its medium or the conditions of its making."[126] He shares this reflexive space with earlier artists like Cohl and McCay, with the least sense-making bits of the Fleischer cartoons of the 1920s and 1930s and rare out-there Hollywood films like *Hellzapoppin'* and influencing the surrealities of *The Goon Show*, *MAD*, and Monty Python. The images Hoberman has chosen for the article relating to Avery are from a 1945 Screwy Squirrel title, *The Screwy Truant*. In this cartoon—aware of its cartoon-ness and the industry that created it—characters from another well-known series, Little Red Riding Hood and a Wolf, run into the picture, and Screwy takes the Wolf to the title card, pointing out who headlines the cartoon. The Wolf assumes it must be "one of those corny 'B' pictures," insulting Screwy. After challenging the Wolf to a fight, Screwy runs to Grandmother's house, and the intruding cartoon characters disappear.

At that time, months-long intervals between releases of Avery cartoons gave audiences a much-needed break—today, binging on Avery cartoons can be a strain. Part of this issue was his penchant for repetition, for putting in his thumb and pulling out the same plum, again and again. Original audiences might have just started to forget sequences like a doors scene in *Screwy Truant*, where doors appear in walls and floors, characters chasing through all. It's funny and clever. But it would reappear (likely the precise cel layers with new characters laid in) in a subsequent cartoon, *Little Rural Riding Hood*. And so on.

Screwy Squirrel was a five-title character—a short run, 1944–1946—but the length of his run was just about right, given the character's role as embodied anarchy, destroyer of contexts. *Screwball Squirrel* (1944) is almost a parody of the seven-minute cartoon, and it's certainly a deconstruction of "The Hollywood Cartoon." Screwy introduces himself in juxtaposition to little Sammy Squirrel, a treacly-cute Thumper-like Disney animal in a Disney forest caught in an Avery world. Avery knew that this all works better if the audience brings their expectations of what a "proper" cartoon should look, move, and sound like, and Avery's team creates a recognizable setting, allowing Screwy to decontextualize, pleasurably working against what the audience expects. If one definition of what elicits laughter is a "sudden, pleasant psychological shift," then Avery provides that, fortified, to a generation weaned on Disney formula.[127] Screwy leads Sammy behind a tree and pounds him, taking control of "his" cartoon. (Sammy obviously hadn't seen the title card—his face wasn't on it.) Screwy then cues the first event, a ringing phone, and the cartoon begins.

Screwy can move tree knot holes; he can step out of a frozen frame and move the needle on a phonograph to start things anew. The ink-and-paint (not flesh-and-blood) of Meathead's face can come off completely, thanks to flypaper—leaving a pure white blank—and, when the squirrel registers surprise, he grows six separate heads, one of the many distancing strategies that keeps us from truly identifying with the character. Screwy will then wonder what's happening next, lifting the edge of the frame to see what's coming. He sees where he's supposed to be and goes there, waiting in a hollowed-out tree base to hit Meathead with a bat. The squirrel and the dog will jump into a barrel and roll dangerously down a hill, a typical drumroll soundtrack element accompanying. At the bottom of the hill, we see it is Screwy on the snare drum, and he also plays the crash sound effects with the very instruments (bass drum, cymbal, slide and bird whistles) used to create the cartoon's soundtrack. The dog tries to surrender and end the picture, and the iris begins to close, but Screwy can force it open again and keep the picture going, promising the dog a fair chance at him. To paraphrase Richard Schickel's comments about the unique "critical language" of the cinema, thinking here of the cartoon, instead, "A cartoon by Avery owes nothing to anything but the history of the cartoon."[128] Avery is often making cartoons about the making of cartoons, and he is keenly aware of the history of the medium. Again and again, the illusion of an immutable diegetic reality is undercut, and the nuts and bolts of cartoon construction are acknowledged—just the way Avery liked it. Lastly, the still-sweet Sammy Squirrel reappears to tell us *his* cartoon would have been "cuter." He is beaten up again.

In the same year that Sammy Squirrel got his, Disney's "breathtaking novelty"[129] *The Three Caballeros* appeared as a "feature" pieced together from 1941 travel footage captured while Disney was in South America; it also included material from visits to Mexico in 1942–1943. These were meant to be wartime "Good Neighbor" propaganda films, not brilliant stand-alone works—each was a fulfillment of a much-needed contract. These were also key in that Walt could keep the studio running and people working during difficult times, while reemploying a process little used since the Alice days: the combination of live action and animation, now in color.[130] This kind of advancement and experimentation characterized most Disney films across even the fraught 1940s.

Reviewers and exhibitors mention again and again the pleasing novelty of mixing live-action and animated sequences, in films ranging from *Reluctant Dragon* to *Caballeros*; they also appreciated the exotic Southern Hemisphere settings, characters, and songs of the latter. These Good Neighbor films, as a batch, have always been considered lesser-thans, but many viewers at the time were quite thrilled with the *variety* of high-quality work Disney was offering.[131] (Most of the films they were seeing during the war were traditional black-and-white genre pictures.) Critics like Wolcott Gibbs blasted *Three Caballeros*, though, seeing an absence of Disney artistry and in its place a "monstrous," "perverse," and "achingly empty" farrago of experiments.[132] Critic Barbara Deming sideways praised where Walt was going, arguing that what he'd wrought was nothing less than "a nightmare of our times"[133]—pretty strong stuff for a film starring three cartoon birds. Deming saw Disney's "artless" work not as monstrous but as barefacedly honest; in good times, he could produce Mickey Mouse, but if times were dire? "If the time is one of crisis, and [society's] values will no longer serve but are in conflict and in question, if the prevailing state of mind is a deep bewilderment, he will improvise with equal lack of inhibition."[134] And *Reluctant Dragon*, *Dumbo*, *Bambi*, *Victory Through Air Power*, *Saludos Amigos*, and *Three Caballeros*—all made with a war on and with the mindset of business-as-usual-as-possible—give new meaning to Disney's belief in "plausible impossibilities." By this definition, these fractious agglomerations of "atrocious taste" (Gibbs again) in which things are in a constant state of "falling asunder" (Deming) describe the world as constituted in 1945—winding down from an enervating, destructive world war, with no hint of a particularly rosy world peace on the morrow. In his "honesty," Walt may have been setting the table for Kurosawa (*Rashomon*), Buñuel (*Los Olvidados*), Ray (*Pather Panchali*), and the various "New Waves" that were waiting to crest just after the war. And to add fuel to this reckless fire I've started, Disney was creating these "new" films not primarily via the commercial market but with the help of funds from the government, from the state, just the way many New Waves would be supported and allowed their experimental, anti-traditional freedoms in the 1950s and especially the 1960s.

Whatever the critical frippery, *Three Caballeros* was better received than both *Bambi* and *Victory Through Air Power*, "reaching $900,000 in billings in just 11 weeks, compared to 31 weeks for *Bambi* and 48 for *Dumbo*." The film was also a major hit in its target region, South America.[135] In the end, the hybrids *Saludos Amigos* and *Three Caballeros* turned a profit for the studio—good news after *Pinocchio*, *Fantasia*, *Reluctant Dragon*, *Bambi*, and *Victory Through Air Power* had lost money.[136]

In retrospect, it's nothing short of amazing that, even as a war raged and the animation industry had to pitch in and fight, Walt Disney was able to produce six feature-film cartoons, while the combined six other major cartoon studios managed to produce just one. Also amazing was the fact that an all-out war couldn't derail the cartoon industry; it just shunted it onto a stay-in-business sidetrack for a time. Hundreds of cartoons continued to be made, about half of which had something to do with the war effort. Warner Bros. and MGM might have accomplished their best work during the war. Tom and Jerry emerged from the mid-1940s in fine form, clutching three Oscars. Tex Avery dabbled with forever greatness, and the former Schlesinger crew took the lead in high-quality shorts production and kept it into the 1960s. There would be more great cartoons emerging from all these studios over the next decade, but, as the Cold War period set in, there were new threats. One was the once-spurned "consent decree," revivified in the postwar era; another was a new style in animation to be led by a new studio, UPA; a third was television, the destroyer of cinematic short-subject worlds.

Each would transform the animation industry.

CHAPTER 8

Postwar or Pre-TV?

IN 1946, ONLY ABOUT ONE HALF OF 1 PERCENT OF US HOUSEHOLDS owned a television set.

That number would change.

The war was over, and yet the war had just begun. Audiences had been tiring of "war pictures" for some time, so the transition to entertainment was welcomed.[1] Disney and RKO were planning for the postwar period with new, lighthearted films like *Make Mine Music*, and Disney helped his bottom line by rereleasing *Snow White*, *Pinocchio*, *Bambi*, and *Dumbo* in 1945.[2] Profitable reissues could now pay the studio's bills and pay down debt when new projects underperformed. Reissues or "revivals" became popular during the war and across the studio system, when original productions dipped but audiences increased. The revival of *Pinocchio* would run five months, outgrossing *Snow White*'s original run in some cinemas. But these were transitional benefits. Some exhibitors wanted a quick business-as-usual approach, getting back to normal as quietly as possible. Studio advertising tended to connect the previous few seasons of high-quality film work with what was to come in 1945–1946, building not on the war victory but on the titles created by each studio. Audiences and exhibitors were assured that "color and music" would continue, that popular films hadn't been popular simply due to the paucity of competition during an overseas conflict.[3] The industry had enjoyed elevated viewership across the war and wanted to see that trend continue. Repeat bookings were reported for "Disney shorts, Paramount's color musicals [Puppetoons], and MGM's *Red Hot Riding Hood*" as of August 1945, as

Japan finally capitulated.[4] There was no looming sense of an audience drop-off, but rather an expectation of a return to blessed normalcy.

The sage may have been Leon Schlesinger. In June 1944, as the far end of the war was just being glimpsed, Schlesinger responded to questions about the future of his business and of animation in general. His artists may have scoffed at him (he was never accused of knowing much about cartoons or humor), but Schlesinger answered by saying that the world was finally discovering animation, stumbling onto it during the war, and its future would include education, public health, and especially advertising—he saw cartoons selling products and progress, citing the success of "his" Snafu films.[5] Schlesinger would retire just days later, to his yacht and an ancillary role at the new Warner Bros. animation studio.[6] Over the following fifteen years, cartoons were going to be extremely active in advertising, in persuading, in educating, and in entertaining. Cartoons would also slink out of theaters and onto television, pausing for a while on prime-time TV before staking a lasting claim to Saturday mornings. But, in June 1944, Bugs was everyone's favorite star, cartoons were the most popular short subjects, and that pesky war was still on.

The end of the war meant the end of rationing, war footing, and "stay-the-course" propaganda; it also meant the end of many government contracts and a return to straight-up competition with other studios and, soon, with television. The war years were a high point, creatively and economically, for much of the industry producing shorts. The studios had made dozens of war-related films, helped raise awareness of home-front needs in relation to rationing and economizing, facilitated the training of soldiers and factory workers, and entertained across dark days. Disney was awarded a Distinguished Service Certificate from the government's Savings Bond Division. There were congratulations when looking back, but there was uncertainty when moving forward. The final form of a Justice Department consent decree, which took a decade to produce and would address just what would be done about Hollywood's monopolistic distribution and exhibition practices, was an axe waiting to fall. Was television a threat or a passing fad? With the film industry in a forced holding pattern during the war, all bets were off as to what would happen in the industry as consumer spending (often on cars, houses, and household gadgetry, including televisions) and the birthrate exploded after the war. The labor and material costs of doing business in Hollywood were also on the way north after years of moderation. A Cold War and an Age of Anxiety[7] were on the horizon.

There were three animated films released in 1946 that contrast well across the short period between the end of the war and the beginning of television. All three dealt in some way with race: *Brotherhood of Man, John Henry and the Inky-Poo*, and *Song of the South*. The first is a didactic, limited-animation short; the second offers Black folklore in frame-by-frame puppetry; and the third is a now-notorious live-action-and-animated feature. All three represent high points for their creators, and yet all live in relative obscurity today. UPA's *Brotherhood of Man* discusses the essential sameness of all men beneath the skin. Using clever, spare animation, the film aims to take the wind out of the sails of prejudice and racism. It was to be screened for the United Nations Security Council and purchased by the War Department for "re-orientation" work in post-Nazi Austria and Germany.[8] The educational *Brotherhood of Man* was screened for unions and school, charitable, and religious groups across the country. Disney's *Song of the South* premiered in Atlanta to warm reviews and strong box-office performance, garnering special consideration for its technical wizardry and star, James Baskett, and yielding the hit song "Zip-a-Dee-Doo-Dah."[9] Pal's Puppetoon treatment of the American folklore hero John Henry drew positive responses from both critics and exhibitors—it was "different—plenty different," but also "excellent."[10] Pal had even hired a Black actor, Rex Ingram, to narrate and voice the characters. Alternately, at the time of its release, *Song of the South* was "lambasted" by the National Association for the Advancement of Colored People for offering "a dangerously glorified picture of slavery."[11] Surprised, the Disney studio countered, defending the film's postslavery setting and strong, positive central Black character.[12] Quite unusually for the studio, Disney had vetted the film, the characters, and even the script not only with white members of the Left but also with representatives of Black communities, apparently knowing the subject matter was fraught. Disney wasn't a dim rube who didn't know better; he was simply hoping for better. As for Pal's work, *Ebony* magazine in 1947 was of two minds, lamenting the "Negro" tropes still present in Pal's Jasper cartoons but praising *John Henry* as "the first film that deals with Negro folklore that has a Negro as its hero . . . no Negro stereotypes, [and] treats the Negro with dignity, imagination, poetry and love."[13] There were other Black reviewers and critics who also saw and appreciated what Disney was trying to do in *Song of the South*—"depict American folklore" and "put the Uncle Remus stories into pictures."[14]

Audiences liked *Song of the South*, and it made some money over its high production budget. One exhibitor spoke for many: "A very fine picture especially suited for small towns."[15] Disney, taking advantage of heated headlines as the House Un-American Activities Committee (HUAC) tried to root out "Reds" in Hollywood, would quickly rerelease *Song of the South* in Atlanta and beyond in mid-1947, reselling American folklore to proud Americans.[16] The animated sequences were heralded and accomplished, and the wedding of live action and animation is still impressive. It was generally agreed that if there had been much more cartoon and less of anything else, the film could have soared, but Disney was purposefully trying to move into new areas of complexity and art—thus the hybrid. Reviews were polarized, and *Time* magazine's entry spoke for one camp: "Technically, the blending of two movie mediums is pure Disney wizardry. Ideologically, the picture is certain to land its maker in hot water."[17] Similarly, Bosley Crowther titled his 1946 review "Spanking Disney," admitting Disney needed to be taken behind the woodshed. On the other side, *Film Daily* was perplexed by critical response to the film: "Whyinhell aren't film critics content to be entertained (or even bored, if they must) by pix instead of attempting to read into 'em social significance or its lack?"[18] "Could have played it a week," wrote a small theater operator in Indiana. "It is the best of the Disney's and the old colored man stole the show . . . he was great."[19] Another small town exhibitor appreciated what Paramount, Pal, and *John Henry* were offering: "Many of Paramount's cartoons seem to be telling pleasant little stories, and it is a welcome change from some of the silly and pointless cartoons being made these days."[20] The controversy surrounding *Song of the South* has grown over time. The film was withdrawn from release in the 1960s and then rereleased in the 1970s.

But it wasn't plain sailing for the "progressive" *Brotherhood of Man*, either. By 1947, *Brotherhood* was being mentioned in testimony before the HUAC—having been contributed to by blacklisted screenwriter Ring Lardner Jr.[21] Official mentions of *Brotherhood* in the trade journals diminished considerably after this tainted publicity, and governmental overseas distribution was quietly scrapped. In 1951, the film would be mentioned again in HUAC proceedings, proving there *is* such a thing as bad publicity. While *Song of the South* is now considered dated and embarrassing but perhaps harmless, the film continued to see the light of rerelease for many years, including in 1986, the year of its fortieth anniversary and its "final" release. A 1986 review was supportive, provocative: "*Song of the South* succeeds as an experiment in moviemaking technique, as a plea for interracial understanding, and as a perceptive psychological portrait of a confused child."[22] The film is now available only in bootleg versions and is one of many cartoons wearing the infamous "banned and censored" badge. *All* of Pal's Jasper cartoons are also on these informal lists.[23] Ultimately, *John Henry and the Inky-Poo* was added to the National Film Registry in 2015, while *Brotherhood* was selected for saving by the National Film Preservation Foundation. None of these three differently impressive 1946 films are much viewed today.

All three of these films mattered, as did the filmmakers. The changes that would affect the industry across the following few years touched them all. Peak film viewing in 1946 coincided with peaks in production, and the falloff in attendance after 1946 had a ripple effect. Fully half the cinema-viewing audience disappeared between 1946 and 1953.[24] With fewer people attending regularly, fewer pictures were needed (and fewer employees were needed to make the films, fewer to distribute and then show those pictures, etc.). The studios were still vertically integrated, and these effects were vertical as well: job losses from the stars in front of the cameras all the way down to teens shoveling popcorn into buckets. Unemployment increased after the war, as did marriage and childbearing, meaning there was less discretionary income. With costs rising dramatically, the industry's trifle—the animated short destined for theatrical distribution—became unaffordable caviar. Disney had always spent more on his titles, but RKO wasn't finding exhibitors willing to pay more for the privilege of showing Disney cartoons. Pal announced that his costs, already high thanks to the labor-intensive nature of puppet animation, were increasing (up 164 percent, he said) across the late 1940s.

Let's take a quick sidetrack to two other endeavors that struggled in the postwar climate. In February 1946, the Harman-Ising studio resurfaced, promising to make high-quality animated *features* for United Artists for about $1 million each. They announced two of the three films: a King Arthur story and an adaptation of *The Little Prince*.[25] These features did not materialize. Studios and banks were in a wait-and-watch mode, especially in relation to features. Other Pal-like work from this period, including Morey and Sutherland's April 1946 short *The Lady Said No*, flashed brightly but couldn't catch on. This Puppetoon-type animation, directed by Tashlin and distributed by United Artists, was part of the Daffy Ditty series. It is beautifully rendered and, given its complexity and cost, was destined to be a rarity.[26] Five years earlier, the Daffy Ditty series might have succeeded. The minor studio Republic Pictures was even trying to get into the animation business at this challenging time, hiring Clampett, employing the proprietary Trucolor process, and planning to produce six color cartoons. The only Clampett title was *It's a Grand Old Nag*, which came and went without much fanfare. Leonard Levinson and Impossible Pictures would pick up the baton and produce four more in the Jerky Journeys series, including *The 3 Minnies*, a cute, insensitive story of how Minnetonka, Minnesota, and Minnehaha came to be. Not terrible; not terribly memorable. Traditional entertainment cartoons were a dicey proposition in 1946.

And solutions? Disney slowly transitioned from producing animated short subjects to making live-action nature films, live-action features, and carefully spaced feature animation projects. Disney pursued diversification in ways other animation studios never imagined. He looked to television and theme parks not as competitors for leisure hours and dollars but as new, dependable sources of revenue. George Pal would move away from making short subjects to contributing special effects for films, creating industrial projects, and directing live-action science-fiction films. He did well in all these areas. UPA would enjoy an influential but brief run as cartoon aesthetics doyen and will be discussed in the next chapter. Warner Bros., Famous, Terrytoons, and MGM all continued to make traditional cartoons into the 1950s, and some did so well beyond. Television would beckon all of them—well, all their back catalogs.

The winding up of a patriotic war turned pent-up attentions elsewhere. Red scares and strike actions erupted in 1945–1946 across the country, directly affecting the animation industry. In May 1945, Congressman Richard Nixon and his subcommittee began looking into previous and current strike actions and were especially interested in potential communist influence in those actions. By May 1945, a widespread film-industry strike was entering its ninth week. In August 1946, more than two dozen unions picketed Disney following a Disney layoff wave that crested at 450 employees—about 40 percent of the studio's staff.[27] Since the unions' successful strike in 1941, any wage advancement the unions achieved at Disney had been met with a reduction in operating expenses; Disney (and other studios) weren't operating at prewar profit levels and couldn't afford a 25 percent wage increase without cutting somewhere. (These were the same cost increases that Lantz, Pal, and others bemoaned, pleading for an increase in rental rates, which sat snugly at 1940 levels.) Union wage victories were often followed by industry-wide layoffs. This one-step-forward-two-steps-back gait pushed many animators out of the larger studios and into boutique, educational, and television-related production.

For Disney, the late 1940s was a time of rethinking, retrenchment, and reappraisal of just where the "Disney effect" would be most effective. The answer for Disney was making fewer, better feature-length animated films; a move away from the hybrid and "anthology" films that Disney had thought might be the ticket during the war; and an increase in live-action films. Short-subject cartoons were on the way out—they just couldn't pay for themselves in a reasonable time, some taking up to five years to break even; they were to be supplanted by nature films.[28] Disney made a little money in 1946, and, by mid-1947, the bottom line was improving, gradually, and share dividends increased. The studio was also able to report, for the first time since the start of the war, a full feature production schedule into the future, a sign that business might be returning to a kind of normal. Disney wouldn't experience a box-office hit, however, until 1949's *Seal Island*, followed by 1950's *Cinderella*.[29]

By 1945, Bugs Bunny was the most popular Hollywood cartoon character, according to an exhibitors' poll. Disney's shorts came second. Bugs is at his most endearing when, as he's living his own life and minding his own business, he is set on or challenged—when someone else's status quo tries to forcibly supplant his. His best cartoons are those that lean on his personality, his slow-burn character, as opposed to relying on speed or violence. Bugs is a "controller," Klein points out, well beyond the "nuisance" or "over-reactor," where Daffy, Woody, and Donald reside.[30] There's a reason Bugs Bunny Specials became a much-desired series, separate from all other Warner Bros. output by early 1944—they were *his* cartoons. Some of Bugs Bunny's best cartoons, including *Rabbit Fire*, *The Rabbit of Seville*, and *What's Opera, Doc?*, would appear five and ten years later. In the late 1940s, Tex Avery, whose *Blitz Wolf* was released in 1942 and who had been making violently speedy cartoons at MGM since 1942, was producing arguably his best cartoons, the personality employed his own, and featuring many new characters. MGM was taking out full-page ads to promote Avery characters like Red, the Wolf, and Droopy—Wolf and Red's *The Shooting of Dan McGoo* particularly heralded in March 1945—Avery's name wasn't above the titles, but his cartoons were often at the top of the bill and much anticipated.

Avery's approach in *King-Size Canary* is always above and beyond, his characters less important than the effects of the elixir they drink to best one another. Avery's cartoons often employ escalation. In *Screwball Squirrel*, it's the violence and rapidity of the attacks on the dog; in *Bad Luck Blackie*, it is the size and deadliness of machines and vessels falling from the sky; and in *Dumb-Hounded*, it's the type of getaway transportation the Wolf uses. In *King-Size*, Avery gags and characters set the stage: A starving cat seeks a meal, first dealing with a bulldog with sleeping pills and then raiding the "Coldernell" fridge, where there is a "For Rent" sign in the "Furnished" but otherwise empty freezer; a sardine can is opened to reveal a "Kilroy Was Here" sign but no sardines. A found bottle of Jumbo Gro fuels the rest of the picture, starring a cat, bird, bulldog and mouse. The cat chases the bird across the screen, yes, but also across different interior backgrounds that are purposely dissimilar—Avery has these characters running from animated frame to frame, across different backgrounds where baseboard and ceiling lines don't match up. This is the kind of seam between painted scenes that is generally cropped just out of camera sight in the cartoon studio—here they are highlighted for one of Avery's favorite pastimes: not forwarding a brilliant character, like a Bugs, but destroying a context, acknowledging an artifice. He is laying bare the foundations of the animated cartoon. The building-size bulldog is soon chasing the equally large cat through a cityscape, before the much larger mouse becomes the cat's protector. The cat drinks more so he can grow and eat the mouse, chasing him through the southwestern United States before the mouse drinks again and grows. Both look like enormous, bottom-heavy eggplants with undersized heads, arms, and legs. (Avery was reveling in elements of "body horror" long before any manga or anime title.) Soon the inflated cat and mouse are the same gargantuan size, the bottle is empty, and, in an Avery moment, the mouse tells us the picture must end—they've run out of "the stuff." This is one payoff, but a more visual one awaits. The camera pulls back to reveal they are standing on the Earth, now seemingly the size of a large beach ball compared to each of them. They wave to us as the cartoon ends, having employed topical references, brash characterizations, silliness, and surreality. Avery was well past making Disneyfied cartoons.

While Bugs was chomping through carrots and in peak form, and Avery was busy being everything Disney wasn't or couldn't be, Disney's stylus was stuck in a groove, even after the shakeup of the war. *Make Mine Music* (1946), *Fun and Fancy Free* (1947), and *Melody Time* (1948) were cobbled-together cartoon segments linked to musical subjects or themes. There were positives. Together, they added up to a shorter, programmable Disney feature, which exhibitors wanted. Each "feature" was cheaper to produce than *Bambi*, less experimental than *Fantasia*, and more chipper than *Pinocchio*. They seemed to be perfectly safe bets. Live-action bits were often a smaller part of these concatenations, but the animated sequences greatly outnumbered anything else. These also tended to be reviewed as "less pretentious" Disney cartoon offerings by exhibitors, especially those in neighborhood theaters. But there were also negatives. These packages were generally dismissed by critics as "blue plate specials"—they'd liked Disney before he became a vox populi. Agee called them "tacky"; Crowther thought they appealed to "the lower taste of the mass audience"; for Farber, Disney had been "entirely unpleasant" since 1942.[31] In this unsettled postwar period, Disney floundered uncharacteristically, starting and then stopping a series of government films, considering and then deciding against a series of educational films, and casting around for a "something completely different" that didn't involve cartoons or live-action-and-cartoon hybrids. Fascinated by the wilds of Alaska, Walt greenlit the gathering of seal and Eskimo documentary footage.[32] From this, both *Seal Island* and "True-Life Adventures" were born in late 1948. *Seal Island* won an Academy Award in 1949, and the nature films made money and cost relatively little.[33] Reviewers and audiences were enthusiastic. Out of the red and into the black.

Disney's ventures into the wilds of the deserts, into the rivers and mountains, would carry the studio into the television era and beyond.[34] With those successful live-action distractions underway, work on the animated "musical mélanges" (or "package" films), films that would pay handsomely in parts rather than sums, could continue.[35] Reviewing one of these three package films suffices for all three, one critic saying he felt "that these . . . items were lying around the studio and someone got the idea to paste them together in a manner recalling *Fantasia* . . . 'a poor man's *Fantasia*.'"[36] But there were rave reviews, too. For one, *Melody Time* offered "breathtaking beauty, infectious merriment, and haunting music"; this critic was certain Disney had a hit.[37] *Melody Time* for others was Disney's best, most, and worst all in one: "The things that used to be best about the best Disney movies are now so emphatically good that they verge on mere blatancy; the old weaknesses have grown a hundred times their old size."[38] This critic still managed praise for Disney's artistry, praise missing from the *Time* review for the "off-balance and inconsequential" *Fun and Fancy Free* a year earlier, juxtaposed with the backhanded compliments ("naïve charm") for *Make Mine Music* from the year before.[39] Admittedly, by producing such similar films, Disney was making critics' jobs much easier. Some of the musical featurettes drawn into these packages had been on the shelves since 1940, leading one animator to joke that these features were all part of "Walt's remnant sale."[40] They might be a Poor Walt version of his cartoon monasticism, but these segmentable features would eventually pay off in ways *Fantasia* could not. As early as 1955, parts of *Make Mine Music* were reissued as *Musicland*, and, in 1957, *Pecos Bill, Casey at the Bat, Blame It on the Samba, Once Upon a Wintertime*, and *Two for the Record* were all being distributed theatrically as individual short subjects.[41] Many of these animated sequences were repackaged not once but several times in the ensuing decades. In the early to mid-1950s, most existing cartoon collections were in the process of being repackaged and reframed for TV. One of the main differences between Disney's cartoons treated this way and those of other studios was that Disney retained ownership and therefore control of his cartoons and characters. It continues to benefit to this day from that ownership. Youngsters, since the advent of Disney home-video releases, likely know titles like *Johnny Appleseed, Peter and the Wolf,* and *Willie the Whale* as stand-alone shorts as opposed to as segments of any feature. Scoffed at as a clumsy clutch, the package films' individual sections not only have paid for themselves but also have become classics.

Critic Richard Schickel spewed the "fall" of Disney best, though, through the megaphone of late 1960s cynicism and know-better-ness—post-Watts but intra-Vietnam and intra-Nixon: "Between [Disney] and his past he had erected a screen on which were projected only his own old movies, the moods and styles of which he mindlessly sought to recapture in the bastard cinematic form of the half-animated, half-live-action film."[42] This comment was markedly unfair (Schickel's *Disney Version* often showing his own favorite "old movies" as he denounces) but certainly *en pointe* for the time (c. 1968) when Disney could be officially declared passé. Still, there was money to be made, even from the brittle-boned films on offer from Disney. *Melody Time* opened at the Astor on Broadway and had tie-in deals with the "Carnation Contented Hour" on NBC radio as well as with the US apple-marketing bureau (for *Johnny Appleseed*). Disney also advertised the film in all the major magazines of the day, from *Life* to *Farm Journal* to *Country Gentleman*.

In April 1947, Paramount announced that it would up its cartoon output, bucking a recent trend across the industry.[43] Paramount also announced that both "Little Lulu" and George Pal's popular but expensive "Puppetoons" were going away. The rising expense and long-term backlog at Technicolor hampered cartoon production—unlike other short subjects, *all* cartoons from the majors had to be produced in color (black and white was no longer acceptable to exhibitors or audiences). Even more convenient color processes, like Trucolor, Magnacolor, Polacolor, and Cinecolor, were tough sells and often were used only as a last resort. Short of adopting the Disney model and borrowing against a feature film's potential success, it was hard to justify continuing the production of a labor-intensive color series like Pal's—exhibitors weren't offering higher rental rates, and regular deadlines favored more traditional cartoons. (This "facility trumps quality" mode is why Terry glided across these challenging years, churning out and selling his cartoons with dependable regularity.) By May 1947, it was reported that the shorts market in general was being squeezed.

This was just the beginning of animation's challenges in the postwar environment—things would get harder as television got up to speed. Longer feature films meant double-feature bills didn't need filler material like short subjects, and fewer orders were coming in, meaning reduced returns. Over the first half of the 1947 schedule, Disney reported earning more than $1.8 million from feature-film rentals; shorts brought in about $547,000; and government films, more than $97,000. Other income (from commercial films, comic strips, merchandise licensing) totaled almost $525,000. Disney's nontheatrical income had slightly outpaced its income from theatrical sources; more money was coming in from sources outside the theaters.[44] By the middle of 1948, though, Disney was reporting a significant drop in profits, with Roy blaming the currency control situation in Europe.[45] The studio could access that "frozen" overseas money (profits earned in Britain, for example) only if they spent it overseas as well, leading to films like *Treasure Island* (1950).

A 28 May 1947 *Variety* headline said it all: "Cartoon-Making Kicked Around." These were parlous times: Little Lulu and Puppetoons were booted at Paramount; Columbia shut down in-house Screen Gems; and

Disney winnowed the ranks to stay ahead of union-won salary increases. Paramount was defending its choices by sharing that cartoon labor costs had risen 41 percent over the past year and Technicolor charges had increased (and such increases were retroactive back to the first of the year!), raising the *average* completion cost of a cartoon to $25,000 (from $17,000 just two years earlier). Unionized artists and affiliated industries had become quite active after the war. Industry veteran John Sutherland had recently gotten out of the cartoons-for-entertainment business in favor of commercial and industrial work; Lantz had even switched distributors, from Universal to United Artists, trying to compete in the age of all costs escalating while rentals lagged.[46]

The year 1947 was also a challenge for Hollywood in the political arena, another sign that nothing would be the same in the postwar period. HUAC convened for hearings after Congressman John McDowell returned from a "fact finding" visit to Hollywood. There had been talk about Hollywood's politics and power during the war, especially in relation to the studios' agreement with Roosevelt's support of then-ally Stalin and Soviet Russia (via films produced, like *Mission to Moscow*, and even the Bugs cartoon *Herr Meets Hare*). But there was also concern about many in the industry who seemed more pacifistic than jingoistic, embracing "peace at any cost," and there were even those who had felt at some point that communism *might* be the answer, as had been promised across three decades of Soviet Russia. McDowell had met primarily with producers and come away with two revelations: (1) Hollywood producers were *not* Red wolves in sheep's clothing (they had assured him); and (2) "[t]here are Communists in all branches of the industry—artists, directors, soundmen, photographers, and, most importantly, writers."[47] Studio heads tended to be more conservative, even right wing, and were glad to help; Disney, for example, saw an opportunity to justly wreak revenge on the Sorrells, Hilbermans, and Babbitts of his recent strike-wounded past. Disney would name both Hilberman and organizer Sorrell when asked whether he knew of or suspected any communists of influencing his employees. As McDowell suggested, it would be writers who paid the ultimate price, screenwriters constituting most of the ill-famed Hollywood Ten.

On a lighter note, the budget-conscious Terrytoons got it right the few times they weren't actively fending off creativity. Some of Terry's postwar Mighty Mouse cartoons were inspired by the cliffhanger excitement of radio and film serials (and their own "Fanny Zilch" starrers from the early 1930s), where "In our last episode" presaged a nail-biting adventure. *A Fight to the Finish* (1947) features Mighty Mouse saving Pearl Pureheart from the evil Oil Can Harry. What stands out in this Terrytoon are the clever bits, morsels most often absent from Terry titles. First, there's the whole setup—adeptly mimicking a fast-paced "Perils of Pauline" or Republic cliffhanger or even a noir-ish Fleischer Superman cartoon. Then, the second image after the Mighty Mouse song is a freeze frame of our hero and villain, locked in a fistfight, waiting for us to enter the picture, along with the Narrator: "As you remember folks, he was locked in a desperate struggle with the villain. But on with the story— they're off!" The frame unfreezes, and they fight. In full mellerdrammer mode, the "cat" villain sports a long mustache and coat, and the heroine is tied up in another room, "awaiting the outcome." The short acknowledges the audience, the potboiler genre, and its conventions. "As far as Oil Can Harry is concerned," the Narrator intones, "this is a fight to the finish." The villain then turns to the camera and says, "As far as I'm concerned, this is a fight to the finish." Mighty Mouse doesn't freeze when this aside happens; he waits, hands on hips, for the line to be delivered and the action to resume. Everyone is in on the joke.

The first image of the film is a high-angle shot of "old Beaver River Station" perched on a cliff next to a rickety trestle, rain lashing, lightning flashing; the next view of the station is from well below, down in the gorge, looking up, storm still raging. These are angles borrowed from Gregg Toland, from Murnau and UFA; they're special-effect shots worthy of some Silly Symphonies, the better Happy Harmonies, or the Superman series. Moments later, when the station is ablaze, the lighting effects take the flames and darkness into account—unusual for a penny-pinching studio like Terry's. When the Narrator tells us "Mighty Mouse and Oil Can Harry are still at it, hammer and tong!" we cut to the duo fighting with, yes, hammer and tong. Cut to a struggling Pearl, who will "never give up hope." She talks to us as well, promising to "never give up Hope—he's my favorite radio comedian." This is Avery-level cornball humor, as is the situation, as are the character designs and the tempo—the Warner Bros. effect was clearly in place in this title.[48] Oil Can Harry is about to be finished off by Mighty Mouse when he sees a sprayer of DDT—he uses it offscreen—and, when we see Mighty Mouse again, he's not only tied to a railroad track but also has a bomb, fuse burning, perched on his nose. The villain flees to a faraway Victorian house; Mighty Mouse finally makes it there, crashing through several doors (a recurring Terry gag). Harry has locked each of the three doors and then swallowed the keys; the third key provides a mini payoff: he salts it before swallowing. They then fight with pistols (within arm's reach of each other), followed by swords, leading to a ranging, Fairbanks-style fight through and atop the house. Pearl is dropped into a river and surfaces on a convenient log—convenient for a sawmill, of course, a serial cliff-hanger scene in film since the 1910s. While the boys sword fight in and around the house, Pearl sings, "I'm floating down the Swanee River"—then we cut back to the boys, still crossing swords, and then back to Pearl, who sings, "*Still* floating down the Swanee River."[49] She's commenting on her acted-on place—and perhaps all Rebel Maids before her—in these here adventure cartoons. (This is certainly an Avery-influenced cartoon, but our Pearl is no Red.[50]) The direct address, the "salted" key, and this little verbal gag—one that manages to acknowledge the character's place in this artificial construct—and the crosscutting editing techniques germane to these types of films are worth the price of admission. This is not the kind of cleverness generally found in Terrytoons. And just as Pearl is about to be halved and with Mighty Mouse on the way, an interposing Narrator brings the cartoon iris to a close for the week—only to have it reopened and the action finished on request by the original Narrator. Mighty Mouse saves Pearl, and they dance and sing in a lovely garden. Not consistently above average but always fun, these fourteen Terry titles impress in surprising ways.

For 1948–1949, MGM announced only fourteen new cartoons, nine of which were Tom and Jerry titles, and Warner Bros. announced thirty-eight. Increasing costs, stagnant returns, and even the popularity (and affordability) of reissues were significant factors in production by

Mighty Mouse appears in *A Fight to the Finish*, a much-better-than-average Paul Terry release that borrows from both Expressionism and the adventure serials of yesteryear. *A Fight to the Finish*, Terrytoons, 1947 (YouTube). Screenshot taken by the author.

this point. In February, Walter Lantz was asking for the equivalent of two paid admissions—no more than 75¢ in 1948—to be added to the flat rate paid for a cartoon. Six bits would be the difference between profit and loss, he argued. The cost of a Lantz cartoon (never a premium product, but always serviceable) was $12,500 in 1941 and, by 1948, ranged from $26,000 to $35,000. Rental rates from 1941 through 1948 had risen only 15 percent. Lantz also noted that the numbers of cartoons had dropped, too, from about 185 in 1941 to fewer than 100 (many of these reissues) in 1948.[51] Reissues had become de rigueur across the entire motion-picture industry by fall 1947. This somewhat new revenue stream encouraged producers to avoid topicalities in their films, where possible, enhancing rerelease potential. Lantz would hold on longer than any, making cartoons until 1972.

Also arriving in May 1948, the long-simmering disagreement between the independent theater owners and the major studios began to boil. Rehearsing momentarily: The American motion-picture industry had begun as a jumble of film *exhibitors* (using converted storefronts, outdoor venues, vaudeville stages), *exchanges* that would gather, catalog, and distribute titles, and eventually *studios* (in converted office spaces and warehouses) where films were produced. Initially, production was the least-considered aspect of the nascent entertainment—anyone with a rented, purchased, or knocked-off camera and some space could make a distributable film. Mergers and alliances over the years often concentrated two of the three areas, before merging all three into mega-companies that became Paramount, Loew's (MGM), RKO, et al. These large studios tended to own not necessarily the most but certainly the most profitable theaters in all regions (or "zones") and could control precisely where and for how much their own films would play. This situation upset independent theater owners, who found themselves dealing with a kind of cartel. "Clearing" and "run-zone" issues sat atop the list of grievances for many independent theater owners. An entity like Paramount would make its latest five-star picture available first to its large, wholly owned city theaters and then, after a profitable run, would make deals for neighborhood theaters. The neighborhood theaters—separated geographically into zones—had to wait for the film to run its course at the first theater(s) before they could book the film. Large integrated studios were discouraging any kind of competition around that first run. Larger theater circuits not affiliated with studios could (and did) do the same thing, protecting their biggest and most profitable houses. Independent cinema circuits and neighborhood houses had to toe the big studios' line if they wanted the biggest films. "Clearance" issues would continue to be a problem going into the next decade and even linger today.

Lawsuits were filed in 1938 and then paused as the war got underway. Hollywood's monopoly was finally acknowledged, leading to a consent decree, meaning remedies had to be explored. The big studios offered grudging remedies across the years (involving percentages and clearance finagling), but all fell short of what the government would accept—a relinquishment of the monopoly created by the existence of vertically integrated studios. Implementation of the decision reached in *United States v. Paramount Pictures, Inc.* (as applied by lower courts) in 1948 was landmark: "Arguably, no U.S. antitrust action of the postwar period has had a more profound effect on an industry than the Paramount case, which brought the famous Hollywood studio era to an end."[52] The largest studios would have to spin off their theater chains (almost 1,500 theaters for Paramount, for example).[53] For the first time in many years, the majors would have to consider whether the films they were producing could compete with other studios' films—without a wholly controlled chain of theaters, there was no certain end point for every film. Theater owners could now dicker with the studios, playing one against another for the best deal, making reasonable or even unreasonable demands, and so on. This was good news for many in the industry, but not for all. The first victims were the intended ones—the major studios would feel the pinch of divestiture and competition. Collateral fire fragged any film product that hadn't been paying for itself. Block booking had meant theater chains accepting a batch of features and short subjects. From this point on, theater chains could say "no" to all or parts of the block. Cartoons had been a part of those blocks for many years. Disney's distributor RKO was the first to act in the "divorcement" case, signing a consent decree to that effect on 1 November 1948. RKO was agreeing to split into two separate companies. Paramount followed; after a bit more courtroom wrangling, Warner Bros., 20th Century-Fox, and MGM also signed. The days of the vertically integrated Hollywood studio were coming to an end (as the process of divestiture played out), and the modern era was beginning.

That new era dawned with television as a distraction and wouldn't end until Hollywood was TV's handmaiden. Television and animation weren't an "eight o'clock day one" kind of tandem, either, likely due to the ease with which a camera could be pointed at a live actor and a posed, live product—with no wait time for an animated commercial to be produced. Also, it would be a few years before the valuable backlogs of the animation studios were recognized as affordable, convenient programming material for television, and Hollywood could compete with itself all over again. From about 1941, there were scattered bits of animation (whether drawn, manipulated mouths on "talking" animals, or stop motion), but the first made-for-television animated show wouldn't appear until 1949's *Crusader Rabbit*. By 1949, all major film studios were exploring the new competitor and potential bedfellow, TV.

There were other relationships in play during and just after the war. Propaganda and education held hands as battles raged in Europe and the Pacific. Disney's *Education for Death* and *Reason and Emotion* had taken the American audience inside the Third Reich's dangerously *un*reasonable mind. Schlesinger's *Point Rationing* informed and reassured; it helped the government, keeping angry Americans from storming their local grocery stores for canned peas. The "Is it education or propaganda?" question came up much more noticeably after the war had been fought and won. The emergence of powerful and leftish unions and workers, waves of strike actions, and demands to completely reform the capitalist system (upending the labor-management relationship) were new battles as the Cold War got underway. The hearts and minds of Americans were now in jeopardy, it seemed, and needed (re)education. *Brotherhood of Man* had been a leftish response; the HUAC hearings had been a more rightish one; Hollywood's own blacklisting had even been a response. (In an important way, UPA itself was a response.) Industry veteran John Sutherland's response was Fun and Facts about America, a short film series funded and shepherded by a conservative foundation and college and distributed by MGM. These "economic education" titles included *Make Mine Freedom* (1948); *Meet King Joe, Going Places,* and *Why Play Leap Frog?* (1949); *Albert in Blunderland* (1950); *Fresh Laid Plans* and *Inside Cackle Corners* (1951); and *Dear Uncle* (1953). After theatrical runs, these cartoons were to be made available in high school and college classrooms and to civic-minded organizations. The films set about explaining and defending free-market capitalism; the American worker's place in the capitalist economy; the importance of taxes and of profit reinvestment; the dangers of inflation, of too much governmental planning, and of "-isms" (meaning socialism and communism, not capitalism); and so forth. These were unapologetically patriotic and promised to present "what has made America the finest place in the world to live."

The cartoons are all watchable, and one or two are even entertaining. *Albert in Blunderland*, an alternate reality wherein the all-for-all colony mind of the ant world—work as assigned, all freedoms "donated" to the state—is a not-too-veiled reference to life in the Soviet Union and its in-thrall satellite states. It's unsettling and well drawn, employs strong voice work, and even looks a bit like an Avery cartoon.[54] "Is it entertainment or propaganda?" reviewers asked, likely right along with audiences.[55] (It was having to compete out of the MGM gate with one of the best Tom and Jerry titles, *The Hollywood Bowl*.) The theatrical run for *Make Mine Freedom*, as distributed by MGM, benefited from full-page ads (as traditional cartoons did) and was co-promoted by the American Legion.[56] That expensive level of marketing doesn't seem to have been deployed with most of the later titles. Reviews of these films identified them as American and capitalist (and anticommunist) propaganda from the start—these weren't opaque fables. *Make Mine Freedom* was both "over simplified" and a "star-spangled reaffirmation" of the American way as well as "[a] good little cartoon that shows up Communism."[57] In the cartoon, a shady huckster is trying to sell the cure-all "-ism" to average Americans; there is an "-ism" for laborers, for management, for farmers, for businessmen, and so forth. "John Q. Public" reads the contract's fine print and refuses, sensing his freedom is the price. One review of *Meet King Joe* (about the American worker) poked a bit of fun: "Communists won't like it at all."[58] Nor did students, apparently, as hisses and boos were reported at a university showing in North Carolina.[59] In *Dear Uncle*, the "billions" of postwar dollars sent to Europe are justified, but "hidden" taxes are booed, and the Soviets are depicted as the menace, just waiting to overrun a lackadaisical United States. As the series progressed, the trade journals paid less and less attention.

This chapter should end on an uptick or with a flourish; for theatrical cartoons, the postwar period was scattershot and hesitant, but there were positives. Disney had been reaching for that next brass ring since 1938 and *Snow White*. He'd made technically impressive films (*Pinocchio*, *Fantasia*, *Song of the South*) and sweet films (*Dumbo*, *Bambi*) and time-marking films (*Make Mine Music* and its cousins) as well as many shorts that were classics or at least could account for themselves respectably. What he didn't have was a certified hit. That lukewarm streak ended in 1950, the year that Roy Disney would simply call "our *Cinderella* year."[60] *Cinderella* was the film, according to Ward Kimball, that audiences "wanted" after shorts and the war: "Walt would meet people outside, critics and so on, and people said: 'why don't you do something like *Snow White*?'"[61] The character and story had been with Disney since before there was a Disney studio—in Kansas City, there'd been a Laugh-O-gram version; there was talk of making a Silly Symphony title from the story; and the first script for a *Cinderella* project was produced in 1940.[62] *Cinderella* does owe a great debt to *Snow White*, as many critics pointed out, Disney (and his audience) finding comfort in the familiar, the recognizable. With *Cinderella*, Disney hit a just-over-the-wall home run, pleasing nearly everyone with his first true feature animated film since *Bambi*. One *Cinderella* reviewer said it quite simply: "Ye olde Disney magic."[63] Bosley Crowther, only four years on from "spanking" Disney over *Song of the South*, spared the rod, saluting *Cinderella* for its "rippling laughter, pictorial fascination and youthful joy." Crowther concludes, obviously happy to be presented with a film he could fete, "Mr. Disney has wanded his usual miracles."[64] As Schickel points out, 1950 was a watershed year for the studio. Disney money held overseas (in the United Kingdom) was being spent, finally, for live-action films *Treasure Island* and then *Rob Roy*; the "potential of the nature series" had become evident at the box office; and *Cinderella* "untapped the greatest flow of coin into the box offices since *Snow White*."[65] *Cinderella* would make almost $8 million in its first run.[66] By the end of the fiscal year, Roy Disney was reporting a gross of almost $7.3 million, the studio's biggest year to date.[67] The music rights for the songs and soundtrack stayed with Disney, selling sheet music and thousands of records. *Cinderella*'s profits helped reduce the studio's debt load, reassured audiences (and Disney) that feature animation could still top a bill, and allowed Disney the luxury of making the deals and short-term alliances necessary for TV and theme-park pursuits.[68]

Disney animator Ken Anderson could feel the changing winds as the 1940s gave way to the 1950s. It was a time of transition, when he and many others were weighing career moves, staying in the business, or getting out completely: "I think—even in 1949—while the guys were leaving the Studio because of the time after the War, and there was a big transformation going on, everybody was deciding what they wanted to do."[69] If 1950 was indeed Disney's Cinderella year, several *former* Disney artists were about to grab the new decade for themselves, making off with the magical coach and maybe the pumpkin, too.

The glass slipper now fit UPA.

CHAPTER 9

UPA and/against Disney

"WHAT CAN WE GET RID OF?" ASKED MANY ARTISTS DURING AND AFTER the war, referring specifically to the fully animated frames they'd created for all major cartoon producers.[1] What "stuff" was necessary? What could or should be peeled away? Could the inherent limitations of the medium be acknowledged, embraced, transcended? From about 1919 through the early war years, each studio had its own version of full animation, but all leaned toward cinematic body forms, realistic or naturalistic movements and designs, synchronized sound, and hints of roundness, three-dimensional depth, and perspective. Terry and the Fleischers' work might have been more cartoony; Disney certainly pushed ever closer to live-action cinema; others moved back and forth across this spectrum. What, of all that, a few artists were asking, can we do without and still muster a recognizable cartoon? Quite a lot of doing without, was the answer.

The United Productions of America (UPA) qualifies for its own chapter, given its humble beginnings, meteoric rise, aesthetic-advancing designs, and Icarus-like fall in the space of just twelve or so years. But, in the spirit of the rest of this book, it'll have to be sharesies. Disney could claim twenty straight years of artistic success and industry leadership by the time UPA released in 1948 its first theatrical entertainment cartoon, *Robin Hoodlum*, a new twist on Columbia's Fox and Crow tandem. Disney and Mickey and sound had careered animation into new directions twenty years earlier; everyone else followed. The industry was yawing once again in the wake of UPA's spare, thrusting line-and-color approach, unknowingly prepping the industry for the doomsday advent of TV cartoons—and once again everyone followed. The fact that UPA grew out of Disney-fertilized soil and was consistently measured against Walt's way, work, and worldview means we need to keep both within reach. Without the straits of Disney, a strike, and the war, there would have been no UPA.

We can start a bit out of order since a typically dull work action looms large in the genesis of UPA. A major plot twist came during the production of *Fantasia* and fulminated across a work action that grew into a bitter, personal strike in 1941. Labor unrest had swept across the cartoon industry, cresting in 1937, as unions made headway into studios. The Fleischers were targeted, and, since Disney had a well-earned reputation for intractability (and for rewarding/punishing on a whim), West Coast work stoppages seemed inevitable. Many eventual UPA employees (including Jules Engel, Babbitt, and Hubley) worked in controlling positions on *Fantasia*, and almost none of these returned to Disney after winning the contentious strike, thanks in part to Disney's blacklisting. Disney finally left the country for a Southern Hemisphere trip, and the strike was settled in his absence. One of the men Disney had fired because of his unionizing activities (and his vitriol directed at Walt), Art Babbitt, won a place back at the studio but was a pariah, and, after his war service, Babbitt didn't stay at Disney long. UPA was forming by that time.

To be fair, Disney's run as the *unquestioned* leader of the animation industry might have spanned only from the mid-1930s through the release of *Bambi* in 1942. The sometimes dark and often creative Fleischer cartoons—including Betty Boop and Popeye titles—provided healthy competition for audience attention in the early 1930s. Mickey's short-subject hijinks earned fans high and low, and Color Classics and Comicolor crept across the gunwales by 1935, but the thrilling feature *Snow White* cleared the decks from 1937. Many critics who had been celebrating Disney's advances since Mickey's heyday popped their monocles when confronted by *Bambi*'s cinematic reality, its slavish devotion to natural details and movement. Some, like Panofsky, famously heard the bell's toll even earlier: "[I]t was, in my opinion, a fall from grace when *Snow White* introduced the human figure and when *Fantasia* attempted to picturalize The World's Great Music."[2] And Bragdon comments,

"Indeed, realism is the thing which the animated cartoon should run away from: the nearer it approaches purely naturalistic effects the more it ceases to be itself."[3] For many, Disney alone was forcing animation along the path toward photo-real live-action cinema and nothing more, abandoning art for art-like, leaving the cartoony to other studios. Artists not at Disney believed strongly in the cartoony *and* their own versions of full animation. Not long after the release of *Bambi*—what venerable critic Manny Farber had called Disney's "Saccharine Symphony"—those who would form UPA were plotting their eventual *coup esthétique*. Critics were ready to join the assault.

Writing in 1951, when both anti-Disney and pro-almost-anything-else sentiment was at its peak, Isobel Sagar could already discern UPA's attractiveness, but also, without putting too fine a point on it, its evanescence: "Their color, line, and design, derive from modern art—Matisse, Dufy, Klee, Mondrian—each beholder will think of a different artist," Sagar notes. "The styles of the *New Yorker* and other magazines are also visible." The absence of a unified message or look is touted as the essential marrow, but that freedom carries a cost. Sagar continues, "UPA cartoons have different directors, and the happy result of this is that each cartoon has a quality of its own . . . [t]here is never any rigidity of style or subject matter."[4] Myriad directors, individualist cartoons, no common cause excepting a break from the norm. This leftish, alt-Disney movement was then dependent on (1) critical underpinning, (2) a right-trending government fixated on a Cold War and a hot economy, and (3) exhibitors who could sell the unicorn of UPA's *The Unicorn in the Garden* to a Speedy Gonzalez audience. This all jibed for a short spell, but Mr. Magoo would soon have to carry the studio's water. If UPA blossomed from the erudite *New Yorker* panel cartoons, then Disney, Fleischer, and most others count the "vulgar stereotypes" and "base pleasures"—both "earthy and raucous"—of the newspaper comic strip as their compost.[5] Sagar accurately notes that these UPA cartoons exist as an answer or reaction to the predominant style, the Hollywood cartoon as evoked by especially Disney, but also Warner Bros. and MGM, and that they rely on an audience steeped in or willing to be exposed (or aspire) to high culture. Perhaps most tellingly, these are one-offs in a business of popular continuing-character series, the skeletal "rigidity" that built the Hollywood cartoon empire, and on which different flesh has been draped and redraped, from Heeza Liar through Magoo and a donkey named Donkey.[6] In a similar vein, the cousinly comic strips "derived their value from their freshness, like produce and journalism (and, to a degree, works of modernism)," whereas UPA's higher art demonstrated higher class intentions.[7] There is no denying UPA's influence and freshness of style, but there's also no denying that Mickey, Bugs, and even Tom and Jerry were feted as cultural icons in the twenty-first century, while Gerald McBoing Boing was not.

But to UPA. Established first as a kind of co-op-cum-studio by Stephen Bosustow, Dave Hilberman, and Zack Schwartz in 1943, first called Industrial Film and Poster Service, then called United Film Productions,[8] and eventually called United Productions of America by 1945, UPA came into its own in 1948 when the war was over and commercial contracts and theatrical distribution became available. Experimentation with sparser styles and less populated, less busy frames—a full animation different from Disney's—reached back to lessons learned on *Fantasia* but also to Jones's *The Dover Boys*, animated by eventual UPA artist Bob Cannon. *Dover Boys* offers stylized backgrounds, non-naturalistic movement, a reflexive narrator, and elaborate character squashing, stretching, and smearing. One contemporary critic saw UPA's approach as employing an "economy of means" and mentioned by name the windmill at which they tilted. "In conscious revolt against the increasing naturalism of the cartoons of Disney and Disney's imitators," Arthur Knight exults, "the UPA people have shied away from 'multi-plane' cameras and live-action techniques. Wisely, they concentrate on their drawing."[9] Some of this same addition by subtraction is found in the indie cartoon *Hell-Bent for Election*, also directed by Jones, produced by Bosustow, designed by Schwartz, supported by the UAW, and produced with other pre-UPA personnel. Volunteer efforts and a limited budget meant the cartoon is a mix of recognizably Jonesian characters set against a stylized world, but the success of the cartoon certainly propelled its independent-minded creators down the track toward UPA as a new aesthetic and even a new studio.[10] Precursors to UPA's style can be seen in Columbia's *Professor*

Small and Mr. Tall, *Vitamin G-Man*, and *Willoughby's Magic Hat* (all 1943), the latter an odd mashup of a Superman-inspired villain and damsel, a Dopey-like protagonist, and a suggested, freehand design, background, and layout.[11]

Writer and animator Bill Scott would describe UPA aesthetic leader Hubley: "He was the guy way out on the end of the string, pulling animation as a medium after him, as far as its expanse and what it could do."[12] More designer than animator, Hubley would lead out on UPA films' looks. Military animation experience contributed to UPA's new aesthetic as well, presaging UPA's "cult of the line," its artists' fascination with "simplified lines, flat fields of color, and collage."[13] UPA animators would eventually employ a stylized animation, crafting a looser, refined International Style of their own. Inspirations were drawn from the Bauhaus; from Gropius and Le Corbusier; from Weimar animators Richter, Eggeling, and Reiniger; and from film stock scribes Len Lye and McLaren and German expat Fischinger, who worked many years in Hollywood. The Weimar animators had made clever and creative ads for tires and cigarettes, learning their animation and film craft as they unified the artistic disciplines of design, architecture, theater, and film, ultimately wedding this signature style to commercials.[14] Like the UPA folks two decades later, these Weimar animators also created sequences for live-action feature films. Most of this advertising and interstitial work was necessary "bread and butter" of the interwar German film world, paying the bills and allowing more artistic work to be done on the side.[15] UPA animators would find they had to strike this same balance in their postwar world.

Beyond Weimar, the influence of modern art in the 1930s and 1940s began to be seen in popular American culture—this modernism was cleaner, more efficient, and especially apparent in layout space changes. The movement and ethos echoed the architectural move away from blighted cities to sparkling suburbs, indoor malls, and even strip malls—Klein calls it the animators' "hygienic fantasy."[16] Experiencing *Gerald McBoing Boing*'s uncluttered space for the first time underscores this description. At FMPU, the seconded former Disney and Warner Bros. artists had been given a fraction of a normal budget but a bounty of control over project look and personality, as long as the message was conveyed and the objective met.[17] Hubley and Schwartz said they wanted these so-called "nuts and bolts" films made to be as entertaining and energetic as any typical studio short; they had to have "humor," "personalized or intensified image[s]," "emotional impact," and "imaginative association[s] of ideas" so that they became memorable.[18] These films included training films for the military, like the *Flight Safety* series; films for the GIs and the home front meant to educate, remind, or demonstrate; and even more usual short cartoons with war-related messages or themes, like the Hitler-bashing *He Can't Make It Stick* (1943).

And, while we're on about bashing, it might be that Disney as the Chernabog of dark-hearted, simple-minded animation, raised-in-the-barnyard-but-never-far-from-it, isn't the whole truth or even most of it. For Dan Bashara, UPA's purposeful reordering of the animated frame and the hoped-for reordering of animation's audience points us away from Disney and Fleischer and more toward the key time between various artists' work at one of the major studios and the end of the war.[19] Walt's ego, ethos, and edicts have been blamed across time for the discontent, the striking, and the quitting of Disney. And then the rock is tapped and out flows UPA. But is there more in the artists' work during the war that helps explain the proto-UPA seeking for order, for precision, as Bashara discusses? The Hubleys and Schwartzes, Cannons and Bosustows all worked for Disney and then for the military—that seems to be a bottleneck canyon that narrows and constricts, only expanding again when, back from the locust-and-honey wilderness, UPA is formed, and then only for a brief spell. In the military, they experienced more restrictions as they were assigned maps, diagrams, and educational and training film subjects. The fanning out to freedom is the UPA time. It's unprovable, but perhaps the military time has as much to do with the creation of UPA and these artists' reorienting as Disney. The pointing finger might be better directed across the entire cartoon industry of the 1930s and into the 1940s (these men also worked at other studios), not just fixed on a tyrannical Walt. Their stints in the military's prop wash forced the reordering, and they embraced these strictures.

According to Schwartz, this limited version of full animation came about naturally, thanks to very low budgets for various pre-UPA 1943–1944 films, the need to get ideas across as quickly and efficiently as possible, and the poster work background Hilberman provided.[20] By the end of the war, UPA was thriving, making training films for the military as well as socially conscious films like *Brotherhood of Man*. This latter type of project would diminish in appeal just a year later, when the HUAC convened and Hollywood's past and present (real or imagined) communist sympathies made headlines. The rapidly chilling Cold War years were paranoiac. Films made during the war to support Soviet allies became, to some, evidence of Hollywood's active Fifth Column. Not surprisingly, government and military contracts to studios like UPA dried up quickly and formerly leftist labor cadres in big industry (where UAW lived) were purged, reducing to a trickle any funding for sympathetic projects. Even commercial work (including the work of post-UPA studio Tempo Films[21]) fell prey to a soft blacklist wielded like a cudgel. Before that hammering, however, a few films were managed.

In 1948, Columbia Pictures would hire UPA to make cartoons.[22] To some, this was Bosustow selling out (ideologically, artistically), not an economic necessity, and the short-lived *Robin Hoodlum* series began. UPA's significant titles are few but memorable and include *The Magic Fluke* and *Ragtime Bear* (both 1949), the latter of which starred a new character—the bald, myopic Mr. Magoo. It was Magoo that brought financial success to the UPA/Columbia association, which was ironic, since one of UPA's earliest hopes had been to avoid continuing-character cartoons like those produced by other studios. Reputationally important were the Academy Award–winning *Gerald McBoing Boing* (Cannon; 1950), Hubley's *Rooty Toot Toot* and Cannon's *Madeline* (1952), and the odd but beautiful 3D cartoon *Tell-Tale Heart* (1953), directed by Ted Parmelee. These were the cartoons that critics fawned over, cartoons they saw as ushering in a new, post-Disney epoch in animation aesthetics and polity.

Of these, *Gerald McBoing Boing* and the Magoo cartoons are the most renowned titles from the maverick studio, with Mr. Magoo becoming a lasting star, but they are also quite different in both style and effect.

Gerald set the tone for UPA—high art, a whimsical *New Yorker* gravitas, presenting ideas via the cult of bold lines and flat colors and acknowledging the significance of the daring graphic designs appearing in contemporary magazines and on television as well as the poster-art style found in many children's books of the 1940s and 1950s.[23] Poses are often held for extra frames (Klein calls them "starkly elegant pauses"), and the design of both characters and backgrounds is forwarded—animation now taking a back seat. Movement is often mechanical, coloring outside the lines is permitted, and the middle ground space so craved by "full" animators nearly disappears or is simply flattened out along a plane.[24] In *Gerald McBoing Boing*, the layouts tend to be a single color and the characters and sets/props are drawn using noticeable, self-conscious lines and precise poses and even movements—such as when Gerald's father dials the phone, his fingers nowhere near the rotary. "[T]he form frees itself entirely from the object it represents," noted a contemporary critic. "Not only does this leave the clarity of the action unimpaired but it even heightens it, permitting of swift transformations and startling points."[25]

Disney had become known for the synchronized mickey-mousing of sound to movement from 1928 onward (first *any* movement, and then *realistic* movement). UPA set about unlinking; in UPA films, lines can't contain colored forms, sound effects come when they come, music underscores, often detached from visual beats—while rendering characters and backgrounds as more visually aligned ("[t]he character was always *in* the background," artist Jules Engel would say[26]). Gerald's sounds-instead-of-words approach is the ne plus ultra of contra-Disney and was read that way by contemporary critics and fans; Schwartz's goal was to move "away from the influence of live-action motion pictures."[27] They strove to undo what Disney had done, in many respects. "UPA was a brilliant look at repression, consumer normalcy, and the new topology of the fifties, a world that promised freeways, housing projects, and a mechanistic normalcy, but was stricken by anxiety, like those little UPA characters."[28] It was likely the "stricken by anxiety" bit that pushed UPA's cartoons beyond Disney's anthropomorphic Goofy, who could wrestle with driving or gym equipment without requiring a therapist visit just after; or Wile E. Coyote's unsuccessful but never permanently anxious

The spare look and clutter-free space of *Gerald McBoing Boing* careered the cartoon industry away from Disney and, for better and worse, toward the paucity of television animation. *Gerald McBoing Boing*, UPA, 1950 (*Jolly Frolics* DVD). Screenshot taken by the author.

exploits; or even Donald Duck's apoplexies that never did last past the end of the cartoon. UPA put the cartoon on the couch.

And, while Gerald and his one-off friends might settle comfortably on that modish divan, Magoo would mistake it for something else entirely and turn it to a different purpose. It may be that the narrative demands of a continuing character by nature prevented or reduced this strickening potential, since the blackout gag transition within some cartoons or the blackness between one week's Daffy Duck cartoon and the next allowed any unspent anxiety to dissipate—for Daffy *and* the audience. The next scene or the next week represented a fresh start for the winless Coyote or Ralph Wolf or the frustrated Elmer Fudd—no such break becalmed the single-appearance character cartoons, the cartoons UPA artists *wanted* to produce. With costs rising and rentals stagnant,

Columbia would encourage (and then require) Bosustow and UPA to create more McBoing Boing cartoons, with modest success, and, by 1956, *only* Magoo titles, but their hearts clearly weren't in the forced continuity.

Gerald McBoing Boing had won UPA's first short-subject Academy Award and critical plaudits galore in March 1951, though this simply raised the expectations of critics and distributors alike. It can be argued that the other studios regularly nominated for such awards were merely choosing from myriad titles out of their regular yearly schedule, the cream rising to the top. UPA was *trying* to produce a memorable, awardable film on each go. In 1949, when Warner Bros. won the Oscar for Jones's *For Scent-imental Reasons*, the studio released a total of thirty-four cartoons. That same year, UPA completed and released just two. The following year, UPA managed to release eight shorts, two of which were nominated for Academy Awards, while Warner Bros. released thirty-one titles, none of which received nominations. For UPA, the award-to-numbers-of-titles ratio was impressive, though the studio never released more than ten cartoons in any year across the 1950s, winning two additional Oscars.[29]

At first, it likely seemed to be a perfect launch—a small studio makes a handful of "event" films that woo critics and audiences alike and produce box-office receipts as well. Critics herald a new era in animation, one based on the sparkling designs of the Modern Age, relegating the breakneck buffoonery of Depression-era and wartime cartoons to relic status. They seemed to have fully embraced what many thought animation should be, always: "The very virtue of the animated cartoon is to animate, that is to say endow lifeless things with life, or living things with a different kind of life."[30] As UPA was welcomed fully into the cartoon-producer club, Columbia's expectations grew. Across much of the industry, quality mattered less than a continuous, affordable flow, especially as production prices increased and distributor fees held steady or even dropped.[31] (The industry decamp to television and advertising was on the horizon, certainly.) Though petted as "relaxed and iconoclastic" in one of myriad fawning profiles of the day, UPA also had to deal with the hard realities of the marketplace: meeting deadlines, fulfilling Columbia's need for consistent production of new and lucrative material, and creating likable continuing characters.[32] UPA had flirted with but matured "beyond" animal stars, eschewing what Hubley termed "the vaudeville world of pigs and bunnies," refusing to budge, while other studios offered a ragbag of characters, but mostly animals.[33] It is telling that those retrograde animal cartoons starring Bugs and Daffy, Tweety and Sylvester, and Tom and Jerry remain fixtures on TV today and are also still appearing on merchandise and even in feature films.

UPA didn't have the luxury afforded most cartoon studios in which repetition, rote, and reuse could fulfill a distribution contract. Paul Terry didn't blink at reusing entire set pieces in multiple cartoons, recycling and being certain most young viewers wouldn't know or care. At UPA, until Magoo, each next drawing was a new drawing; each next background, a new vista; each next character (mostly), a new character; and so on. Hubley wouldn't last long, leaving UPA and moving into TV ad production, setting up a cenobium that quickly attracted clients and Oscars. Hilberman and Schwartz had moved into TV commercials as early as 1946. The fact that most of UPA's personnel (studio head Bosustow excepted) had never wanted to rejoin the industrial version of cartoon making, preferring the craftsmen-friendly, artists' studio model, quickly began to work against the studio's bottom line. Challenges appeared: disagreements about studio leadership, about credits for awards, about the continuing contract with Columbia, about the studio's decidedly left political leaning when the country was hewing right, and more. These troubles would boil up long before the end of UPA's first distribution contract with Columbia in 1953.[34]

And, at just about the same time, UPA-like limited animation (in the form of *Crusader Rabbit*[35]) appeared on some of the nation's TV screens, and the second round of HUAC hearings began, signaling the beginning of the beginning of the end for UPA. But the halcyon days were still being enjoyed, for the most part—effects of blacklisting wouldn't bite for a few months, but they were coming. Before the celebration of its maiden Oscar win for *Gerald McBoing Boing* could die down, the dual stress of success and expectation drew a bead on UPA. The studio was not only making erudite but watchable and sellable cartoons but also now doing so in the spotlight that had been yanked away from other studios but especially that of Disney, who had testified as a friendly

HUAC witness in 1947. Various testimony had named UPA employees Hilberman, William Pomerance, Hubley, and Philip Eastman as at least Communist "sympathizers."[36] In 1951–1952, thanks to HUAC pressure on—and sometimes complicit with—studio heads, actions were taken to demonstrate the industry's commitment to rooting out "persons of questionable loyalty."[37] Most studios began to shed their higher-profile fellow travelers to appease congressional committees and audiences alike.[38] UPA was compelled (by Columbia, it was alleged) to offer its own altar lambs, especially those with well-known progressive leanings like Hubley, who would leave UPA in 1952. Columbia felt it had to force the issue to keep its public image clean, preserving a right-to-not-hire clause for anyone it deemed dangerous.[39]

Despite these challenges, by 1953, the UPA look had become the industry standard, replacing Disney and the Disney version of full animation, of cinematic bodies, of realistic movement. Critics and audiences were seeing that UPA animators looked at space differently, led by the layout and background gifts of Hubley and the poster mindset of Hilberman, leading to very different takes on animated space and movement. In the projects UPA accepted, from its earliest iterations, Klein sees a melding of Modern Art with Modern Consumerism (and space); this changing sensibility, for Klein, was in play as early as the late 1930s.[40] The Bauhaus family influence was significant across graphic and architectural arts in the United States, especially in Gyorgy Kepes's book *Language of Vision* (1944), which animator-soldiers absorbed during their time at FMPU.[41] Modern art, even abstract art, became marketable on a mass scale, which almost seems like a contradiction, Klein notes. But UPA's "limited style" would be quickly co-opted by the marketplace and other studios, and this new radicalism was then mass produced, less personal, and less unusual. It would soon be further devitalized for the small TV screen, where budgets plummeted while demand for minutes increased.

This was all true up to a point for UPA and the short subject. Competing with Disney in the feature market was the step not taken. UPA never could convince either itself or a distributor to finance the spare, esoteric[42] UPA approach at the feature level and, on that battlefield, tussle with Disney. The UPA *look* had become the industry standard and was based on the long-gestating transition in art, architecture, and advertising that Disney himself never openly embraced but that many of his artists were influenced by and borrowed from. *Dumbo* wouldn't have happened without these influences, nor *One Hundred and One Dalmatians*, nor, frankly, some of the aesthetic chances taken well back in *Fantasia*, on which many future UPA artists cut their teeth. But these last are all feature animations, which Disney had consciously bought into twenty years earlier, nearly bankrupting the studio more than once. No other studio matched Disney's success with or dedication to the feature animated film—the Fleischers' studio tried and failed, becoming Famous; Leon Schlesinger said no to features and focused on short subjects, becoming rich; others (Lantz, MGM, Terry) batted the idea around, but none wanted the debt load or studio size such an undertaking required. In 1952, UPA was certain it could raise the $750,000 it would take to make a feature, but from where was the great unspoken question.[43] (The vigor with which Bosustow talked about a UPA feature made it seem as if he could speak it into existence.) The success of Magoo might have obviated the need for a feature at UPA, at least for a time—they couldn't pique Columbia's interest in more original projects or a cool *New Yorker*–style feature film, so a much-liked and critically praised series and character had to suffice, at least for studio management. Critical plaudits are fulfilling, not necessarily filling. *Gerald* and *Rooty Toot Toot* earned the studio its laurels, but Mr. Magoo paid the rent and fed the bulldog.[44] Critic David Fisher, writing in 1953, offers a typical assessment: "Whereas Disney is the exponent of the comic strip technique and the 'funnies' mentality, [UPA] inherits the tradition of the sophisticated magazine cartoon with its visual and verbal criticism of manner and morals."[45] A version of this line appeared in virtually every article on UPA or the state of the modern cartoon across the 1950s, likely because the writers were interviewing Bosustow and he was using the same answers for columnists like Fisher, Sagar, Crowther, Stocker, et al.[46]

But such individualism is difficult to maintain—as both Disneys had discovered when deep in hock to the Bank of America—especially in a commercial industry like Hollywood moviemaking. UPA was swimming in the same waters. By 1952, *Variety* reported, UPA *might* have been just breaking even, given the distributor-friendly deal it had signed with Columbia. And, by 1956, Disney had a popular theme park to lean on, financially—no other animation studio had such a deep back pocket.

Fisher continues, admitting to the secret of UPA's success: "[I]t is not an interest in the technique or artistic forebears of the U.P.A. group that brings audiences . . . it is Mr. Magoo himself."[47] UPA had created a great character, and, after laboring through a series of smart but discrete cartoons, a likable, watchable, appointment-viewing-type character was gold. The Magoo cartoons were, in fact, entertaining bagatelles featuring an approachable, appealing character going at his own speed through the modern world. They may have employed Auden's "age of anxiety" wanderer Magoo, but these situational titles and plots of the everyday had starred Goofy a few years earlier. These Magoos relied on the familiar gag structure of classic Hollywood animation, plots built around comic misunderstandings, and encounters riffing on Magoo's nearsightedness again and again and again—endless variations on a single theme. (Hubley quickly came to dislike these cartoons for this last reason.[48]) "Mr. Magoo represents for us the man who would be responsible and serious in a world that seems insane," Fisher continues, "he is a creation of the 1950s . . . his situation reflects our own."[49] Without saying it, Fisher is juxtaposing UPA's noble modern hero to Disney's heroes, the latter not terribly changed from the 1930s or even earlier. (Interesting, then, how Disney's characters have remained popular and in the public eye, while UPA's, excepting Magoo, have all but disappeared. Magoo has also been severed from any popular connection with UPA, like Popeye from the Fleischers.) Julian Fox notes that the postwar era of cartoons (and design) enacted by UPA was itself an atavistic reaching back to the "utter simplicity and freshness of design" that graced the early Felix cartoons.[50] Magoo himself is the 1950s version of the Old Man type—echoing Doc Yak, Colonel Heeza Liar, and Farmer Al Falfa—nothing new here.[51] But it is familiarity that accounts for part of his appeal. Like Harry Langdon's baby-faced character in Capra comedies, or Harpo Marx, Goofy on his clock-cleaning stroll, or the infant Swee'Pea, Magoo can wander in and through and out of dangerous situations, the hands of an unseen god protecting him, suffering no harm or heed. The upstart studio's only successful continuing character demonstrated where audience demands met commercial realities, where Mammon met Mondrian (and neither blushed), and it wasn't at the coalface of High Art. It was Magoo.

UPA's influence waned in part because it was a reactionary movement, configured almost entirely against the Disney aesthetic, and—over its first ten years or so—offering a completely identifiable difference to what had become the cartoon norm. UPA fell victim to the demands of the very market it harumphed at—continuing characters and even feature animated films had become rules, not exceptions. As hinted at earlier, just a few years into UPA's life, the trade journals were abuzz with talk of esoteric and winsome possible UPA features based on James Thurber's work, breezy adaptations of Gilbert and Sullivan operettas, and even a version of Ben Jonson's play *Volpone*.⁵² None of those came to be, nor anything close to a feature during UPA's time of strength and creativity. Throwing all caution to the wind (and after most of the studio's original talent had gone), UPA in 1959 finally produced a feature starring Magoo, *1001 Arabian Nights*, which performed poorly. (One review was kind but honest: "Pretty good Magoo . . . is better than no Magoo at all."⁵³) Magoo's schtick becomes tiresome across its seventy-four minutes, and the film devolves into a slapstick farce, which isn't surprising except it had seemed evitable: In the end, it must drink from the same stream as all other animated features and compete in the same arenas. None of these UPA projects could have reached the audience that *Bambi*, *Sleeping Beauty*, or even the Fleischers' *Mr. Bug Goes to Town* entertained. In the end, the formulaic and more gag-friendly Magoo was UPA's feature offering, a slightly tarnished egg from their golden goose, and then UPA began to all but disappear.

Disney's lavish budgets and willingness to add fine quality-control steps into the already chock-full animation process discouraged most competitors from trying to compete, at least blow for blow. Harman and Ising tried to do it at MGM, opting for budgeted treacle, occasionally managing a comer; the Fleischers also tried to throw money at two features in the hopes of achieving that Disney look—and lost their studio instead. Thanks to its reactionary genesis, UPA struggled once it reached the top of the hill. UPA's vulnerability was its métier—its gleaming look of the future could be quickly and rather easily co-opted by other studios (including Disney, on the sly[54]), for keeping-up-with-the-McBoing-Boing reasons, for cost-cutting and animation-saving reasons, for reasons monetary or mercenary. Television producers aped the strip-mall bowd-lerization of the International Style—they produced cartoons, including the Mel-O-Toons series from United Artists, for mass entertainment and to sell products, making quick use of a diminished UPA look, tai-lored to match the drastically reduced TV budgets. Gerald himself even had an animal doppelganger in the Mel-O-Toons world: Panchito, the donkey who couldn't bray. It's not really a coincidence that *Little Hawk, Christopher Columbus, Panchito,* and the other Mel-O-Toons titles and early Hanna-Barbera and Jay Ward series made for television appeared in 1959, just when UPA was ceasing to be an innovative producer of interesting cartoons (and Disney was swooning in the excesses of *Sleeping Beauty*). Simply, Irene Kotlarz reminds us, UPA had "introduced a differ-ent aesthetic which was partly determined by economic considerations, but it was also partly conceived as an alternative to Disney and it was a style more suited to television."[55] UPA's artists and defenders would go to their graves arguing that the "economic considerations" were in the back seat (if they were along for the ride at all), that Art and Discovery propelled the new aesthetic, and that its suitability for television was regrettable serendipity. After celebrating UPA's unique mission, Kotlarz would also admit that the studio "was still essentially popular entertain-ment, embracing an idea of 'Art.'"[56]

With the benefit of hindsight, it's easy to discern UPA's fatal flaws. The c-word that comes to mind is "continuity." Cartoon distributors and exhibitors had come to depend on the recognizable recurring characters from most major studios; titles with continuing characters were easily programmable into movie houses across the country for audiences ready to enjoy them. A continuing-character emphasis would allow for War-ner Bros. teams to seamlessly work on Bugs, Sylvester, or Yosemite Sam cartoons, or these same characters could be passed from teams led by Clampett or Jones or Freleng. These streamlining processes worked well at multiple studios, allowing for reuse of artists' skill sets and even of cels or backgrounds if needed, reducing some costs as other expenses rose.

By 1960, after several years of "debacle and retreat," having released its unsuccessful feature film and lost its Columbia distribution deal, UPA could no longer claim to be either a haven for iconoclasts or a for-profit studio. Bosustow sold UPA to Henry G. Saperstein, who jettisoned all High Art notions in favor of many more Magoo cartoons.

In the end, a bit of architecture might have been key to UPA's disappearance or remembrance. The Fleischers had gone to great expense to build a state-of-the-art studio in Florida, finishing their feature films there and making Superman fly; Disney's new studio had opened in 1940 and looked every bit the easy-going, junior college campus version of a Hollywood studio; Warner Bros. enjoyed the ill repute of Termite Terrace and thereafter, like MGM, proximity to the parent studio's vast and glamorous movie lot. UPA's purpose-built studio on Lakeside Drive, completed in 1949, was a John Lautner–designed masterpiece that, had it survived, would likely have preserved at least steel, wood, and glass memories of the fleeting UPA experiment, providing a pilgrimage destination. The Fleischers' studios became a well-known albatross to Paramount; Disney's studio could double as a hospital and did duty as a military base—these are at least memorable moments connected to actual studio buildings. The spare and elegant UPA studio remained in the family, as it were, into at least the 1970s, when UPA was more a name for distribution than production. The most ironic of ironies came in 1983, when Walt Disney's nephew Roy Jr. bought the former UPA Pictures studio next to the Smoke House Restaurant and tore it down, replacing it with a forgettable office building to house his family holdings company.

UPA had dethroned Disney, especially in the eyes of the cognoscenti, in the creation of theatrical shorts just when, coincidentally, Disney was moving away from theatrical shorts to animated features, live-action films, television interests, and a successful theme park. UPA's "highbrow," educational influence couldn't carry over to feature animated films—appropriate funding never materialized—while its aesthetic was cribbed away by lesser artists for the lesser medium, television. UPA was left as a kind of lacuna, for most, its influence and history often found accidentally.

Like Magoo, memory can be a bit myopic, too.

Magnavox Destiny

"The story book closes"

As the war ended and the Television Age, the Consumer Age, and the Space Age began, "cartoons at the movies" entered a death spiral. To get some perspective, let's start with the live-action Hollywood film industry across this postwar period. About 354 feature (nonanimated) films were released in the United States in 1945; by 1955, that number dropped to 247; by 1965, only 147 feature films; and, by 1975, 137. And, as the feature went, so went short subjects. Labor costs were skyrocketing across the film industry, pushing studio overheads higher and higher. As early as 1952, Darryl Zanuck at 20th Century-Fox was looking to slash costs. He considered asking directors to helm one *free* film per year, reduce footage shot, and limit camera setups and angles; the studio could greenlight only "surefire" pictures, and all could work longer days to reduce shooting schedules.[1] (Reducing or stopping payment for cartoons fit here quite naturally.) Television rightly gets much of the blame: "In 1946, only about one-half of one percent of US households owned a television set." By 1949, almost 250,000 sets were being installed monthly in the United States; three years later, there were nearly twenty million in place. By 1954, more than half of US households owned at least one set, and, in 1960, that figure rose to almost 90 percent.[2] And, by the time Hanna-Barbera and Filmation were ruling Saturday mornings in 1978, it was 98 percent. Walt Disney knew television was the future long before most—for him, paradoxically, it was a way to reach potential film audiences and advertise for Disneyland. But cinema viewership had never reached TV's level of saturation and never would.[3] Theatrical animation had risen from humble beginnings across three and a half decades, severally adapting and improving and profiting; after summiting, the theatrical-animation industry saw steady challenges, declines, and transitions over the next thirty-five years.

The 1950s became a crucible, separating Disney from UPA from almost everyone else, seeing to the removal of cartoons from cinemas, and divesting many longtime industry employees of their jobs. Before the decade's end, Hanna and Barbera had been fired from MGM; Terry had sold his catalog and studio to CBS; Warner Bros. had closed, reopened, and burned brightly for a final stretch before closing again, leasing the studio space to DePatie-Freleng; Columbia and UPA felt their way along with Mr. Magoo; Lantz produced a seemingly endless supply of forgettable, colorful diversions (highlighted by an Avery and Maltese tenancy); and Paramount dissolved Famous Studios in 1956, with the productive but bloodless Paramount Cartoon Studios carrying on into the 1960s.[4] Cartoon producers appreciated the immediate problem of their own back catalogs appearing on TV *and* competing with newer, more expensive theatrical titles, but cash infusions from catalog sales were welcomed. Excellent short cartoons did appear; these included some of Jones's best work (Bugs outwitting Daffy and Elmer, classics like *One Froggy Evening* and *What's Opera, Doc?*). The spare brilliance of the Road Runner outpacing the Coyote excited audiences and aesthetes alike. "Time is not an issue; only logical sequence," writes Richard Thompson. "Plot has been superseded. Road Runner films rank among the most austerely pared-down works of modern art."[5] Thompson identifies later critical classics, like *Last Year at Marienbad*, as direct descendants of these short films: "As in New Wave theory, situation and character fill the vacuum left by plot."[6] Another critical darling, Tex Avery, offered brilliant cartoons at MGM and Lantz before making the leap to TV. UPA held serve for the first half of the decade before economics demanded that Magoo supplant Magritte—it had to be *ars pecuniam*, art for coin's sake. The 1946–1965 period saw the entire Hollywood film industry move away from production and toward distribution and marketing, sharing risk factors with coproductions and independents, risks brought on by rising costs and attendance drops.[7]

It was no surprise that, as production fell off at the studios proper, their ability to subsidize cartoons also decreased. By late 1960, it was necessary to offer proof of life for the short subject. Said one exhibitor, "Unfortunately, the shorts now available add no allure to a theatre's ads. A cartoon is only a cartoon, a travelogue only a travelogue. Except for Disney product, none have any identity."[8] Motion-picture showings transitioned from packages to stand-alone films (or low-rent double features), and there was no time or need for filler material. It may be that short subjects only survived thanks to the postwar rise of film festivals in the United States and abroad and the Academy's continuing issuance of awards for the short film.[9] After Warner Bros.'s *Knighty Knight Bugs* took the statuette in 1959, there was a gap during which no traditional Hollywood studio cartoon won an Oscar. Instead, in 1960–1964, it was *Moonbird* (Hubley), *Munro* (Deitch), *Ersatz* (Dušan Vukotić), *The Hole* (Hubley), and *The Critic* (Ernest Pintoff). DePatie-Freleng[10] and *The Pink Phink* would break this streak, winning in 1965, to diminished fanfare. In a profit-driven business, there was no fortune made on either a bargain-basement Terrytoon or a Disney masterpiece—reputations, yes, but not much money. The material that had supported the short subject for decades—knockabout and verbal comedy, serial stories, news of the day, human oddities—transitioned easily and affordably to smaller screens at home.[11] The phrase on the lobby placard—"Also Selected Short Subjects"—was fading away. Popular Saturday cartoon-only showings at neighborhood theaters dropped off significantly by late 1955, thanks to Terry and Disney's move toward TV.[12] Kids could stay home and watch cartoons; local theater managers lodged futile complaints.

Across the 1950s, the theatrical cartoon landscape would change dramatically. By the middle of the decade, virtually all mentions in the trade journals of Hollywood animation (Disney excepted) were in relation to television, including mentions of catalog sales, cartoon commercials, and new TV programming. Theatrical animation hadn't ceased, but eyes turned elsewhere. The influential International Style in art and architecture had taken hold in animation, lifting UPA to the top of the pile and marking other cartoons as old-fashioned; the decade saw "consumer desire" catered to in animation, and the art form would have to turn to business for survival.[13] Anarchy—at least in terms of a raging Donald, an obsessed Wile E. Coyote, or Tex Avery—was effectively controlled, contained, and packaged, leading to destinations like Disneyland and anthologized television collections.[14] We can give Hanna and Barbera blame for the for-profit approach to TV animation, certainly, but also credit for mainstreaming animation, the lowly cartoon, as just another part of a media viewing menu. This situation paved the way years later not only for the rebirth of theatrical animation (whose creators were raised on TV cartoons[15])—from *Who Framed Roger Rabbit* through *Toy Story 5* and beyond—but also for the audience's eventual acceptance of the cinematic animated film as being no different from the live-action film, which is where we are today.[16]

As mentioned earlier, *Cinderella* (released in February 1950) started the decade off right, as a solid hit borrowing on Disney's beloved past, and it reduced the studio's debt load. By the end of the decade, the cool, affected *Sleeping Beauty* (January 1959) cost almost three times as much as *Cinderella* and chilled critics. As the decade ran out, UPA's *1001 Arabian Nights* and Disney's *One Hundred and One Dalmatians* signaled an end of an animation age. Walt grumbled about the looser, freehand style of *Dalmatians*, and, for critics, the Magoo feature was "pleasing, if too talky."[17] Feature animation was faltering just when TV cartoons hit their stride. The siege engine television—in the deceptively innocent form of *Crusader Rabbit*—had breached the walls in January 1949, providing ultra-cheap cartoons for the new medium to premiere in 1950. These were interstitial cartoons, five minutes apiece, with "continuing story" serial-style episodes promised. The distributor charged $75 to $150 per week for the five-day cartoon packages.[18] Demand for affordable interstitial segments increased as programmed TV hours expanded. For theaters, fewer and fewer short cartoons were created—fewer were ordered, fewer were needed. The demand for anything that was not a feature film decreased as the studios not only competed for theatrical bookings but also did so against a drop in cinema attendance. From about 1943, motion-picture attendance declined; during the period from 1947 to

1954, it plummeted—from about fifty-eight million down to twenty-six million weekly. The mid-1950s saw a slight rise to thirty million, before enduring a steady drop of another twenty million from 1958 through 1965. Advertising to cinema owners during this period used terms like "reviving" and provided helpful tips, giveaways, and new best practices meant to lure audiences back into theaters. Average attendance then hovered in the ten million range between 1965 and 2002, stagnant even as the total population increased.[19]

Columbia and UPA began the decade in typical fashion, planning and then producing three Magoo titles, three Jolly Frolics, and twelve Color Favorites—a healthy eighteen-cartoon run. Warner Bros. units were expected to produce ten cartoons at six minutes each; at MGM, Hanna and Barbera were creating about eight per year.[20] Disney was frequently doing that, reissuing older cartoons, shooting live-action True-Life Adventures and international features, and producing his next several animated features as well. In 1951, that feature was *Alice in Wonderland*. The studio anticipated that a healthy follow-up to *Cinderella* could further push the studio into the black and solidify a five-or-so-per-decade feature animation schedule. A frosty reception to Disney's version of *Alice* brought the studio back down to earth. It cost $3,000,000 to produce and made less, initially, struggling against both the source material and those who reverenced Louis Carroll and John Tenniel. The Disney version was no longer *the* version.

Putting the industry on tenterhooks, the HUAC reconvened in 1951 for another round of testimony and hand-wringing, and UPA cartoons became *all that*, changing the look of what had been understood to be popular animation. The Disney hegemony was in question: "Regarding cartoons: it is apparent that the limited number of Disney productions are still superior to those made at other studios," one critic wrote in 1951, "although a mechanical slickness appears to be replacing the kindness and warmth which once infused Disney's creations."[21] For some, the Disney atelier had become a factory. UPA was the only studio coming into its own in the 1950s, enjoying center stage as the industry looked away from Disney and celebrated the newcomer. Yearly exhibitor polls and overall box-office receipts continued to favor Disney (and, to a lesser extent, Warner Bros.); while UPA took the kudos, Disney counted the money coming in from reissues, merchandising, and, soon, a theme park. In 1951 and 1952, respectively, while Disney was wincing to critical raspberries aimed at *Alice*, UPA's *Gerald McBoing Boing* and *Rooty Toot Toot* were feted with spreads in *Life* magazine. But turning laurels into liquidity proved to be alchemic. In February 1952—when UPA couldn't have been hotter—it had to give up its option on author Thurber's work. They couldn't raise money for the feature(s) they planned; Columbia had already said no, though was *perhaps* interested if it could have more control of UPA (Columbia was considering buying 40 percent of UPA's stock in April 1952). Bosustow wanted to do a version of *Finian's Rainbow* but could find no financing, and Hubley was becoming persona non grata thanks to blacklisting.[22] The hot new UPA cooled a bit—partly thanks to HUAC rumblings about communists hiding under the platen—and old hat Disney proved he could do some things better than the upstart. When Hubley left UPA in 1952, the fires of modernistic creativity went with him. UPA soldiered on with rehashed Magoo and Gerald series, and Shamus Culhane was inviting disaffected UPA folk to New York City to join his TV ad firm by late 1953. Many in the industry left for Madison Avenue or to set up their own studios or pursue other careers in the arts. The hauntingly beautiful but murderous *Tell-Tale Heart* in 3D[23] helped scuttle the UPA ship. Though it is remarkably evocative, *Tell-Tale Heart* is ironically too artful and *uncartoony* for its own good, still being a cartoon, after all, to its beating heart. By 1954, UPA was relying on Magoo to pay its bills, and experimentation was set aside. This period saw other studios attempt UPA-influenced cartoons, including Warner Bros.'s *Goo-Goo Goliath* and *From A to Z-z-z-z* (both 1954[24]), among others. Neither of these is bad, but the studio's continuing-character cartoons are better remembered. Disney's *Pigs Is Pigs*, in the UPA style, is a slightly more stylish Disney short, but more like a one-off.

In 1953, Disney also cut a cord that had long held the studio back, Walt believed; he left the faltering RKO for the greener pastures of self-distribution and Buena Vista. If nothing else, the Disney studio could now claim complete control over film production and distribution, becoming more of a major studio in Hollywood. The first feature animated film distributed by Buena Vista was *Peter Pan*. Yet another beloved English property, *Peter Pan* was a certified hit that still managed to upset many. Himself a fan of the emerging UPA, British critic David Fisher bemoaned the Disneyfication of Peter and Neverland, seeing Disney's "comic strip mind and sentimental vulgarity" in every character and setting.[25] Clearly, the war years had turned many minds against Disney— or just turned them elsewhere. In this case (and in Fisher's article), it was the simultaneous premiere of Magoo that thrilled this "disappointed" Disney critic—could the UPA product signal "a new development . . . in public taste"?[26] It would for a very short while; change was everywhere.

The year 1953 also saw the Warner Bros. cartoon operation shut down for the first time, overreacting to 3D-related uncertainty and a significant decline in revenue, contracts, and rentals, as that money moved to television. Warner Bros. still managed to release fifteen cartoons, including the last Merrie Melodies short, in 1953; MGM accepted fifteen films from Hanna and Barbera and Avery (and then terminated the Avery team); Columbia also announced fifteen Color Favorites; Paramount offered eight Popeyes, six Caspers, and sixteen other cartoons; Fox released thirty Terrytoons; Lantz offered a full slate of Woody Woodpeckers; many Looney Tunes and twelve UPA titles also appeared; and all were released to cinemas. More than one hundred theatrical cartoons in all were released (or rereleased) in 1953. Pollsters pointed out that, even in 1954 (several years into UPA's run of human-foible cartoons), "the four top winners are all animal cartoons."[27] UPA had the critics' attention, but audiences still chose for themselves. For 1953–1954, MGM cartoons were rated most popular by exhibitors and were followed in popularity by Bugs Specials, then Looney Tunes and Merrie Melodies, and then Disney, Lantz, Popeye, and Terrytoons. Eight of the ten most-liked short subjects were cartoons.[28] Live-action short subjects that weren't from Disney almost disappeared from the list. A live-action Disney True-Life Adventure won as best short subject of the year, another sign of changing times.

In 1954, Disney signed a momentous deal with the fledgling ABC television network, becoming "the first leading Hollywood producer to enter into formal alliance with television."[29] The three-year agreement was meant to facilitate a *Disneyland* television show, promote the planned "Disneyland," showcase nature films, and open the Disney back catalog to millions of TV viewers. Disney embraced television from the outset and with much success. ABC funded a portion of the proposed Disneyland as part of this deal—Disney using the fledgling network to his own ends—and, by mid-1960, the deal was wholly bought out by Disney.[30] By its first full year of operation (1956), Disneyland had become a family destination, a cash cow. Disney and his studio were financially secure, finally, and not dependent on the next box-office hit.

The Cinemascope[31] release *Lady and the Tramp* (1955) did well, but not as well as *Peter Pan*, and would be the last animated feature of the 1950s before *Sleeping Beauty*. Simply put, television was stealing the spotlight, so it takes our attention for a moment. In 1955–1956, there were three big sales, two involving animation, and all "film for TV" deals. First, Paul Terry sold Terrytoons to CBS for $5 million. There were 1,100 cartoons in the deal as well as all merchandising-licensing rights[32] to Terrytoons characters. Many of these earliest Terrytoons had already been popularly appearing on *Barker Bill's Cartoon Show* and, later, *Captain Kangaroo*. (CBS would continue to run Terrytoons until 1973 under Gene Deitch and then Ralph Bakshi.) Second, Paramount sold most of its shorts catalog to a TV corporation, UM&M. This did not include the Popeye shorts, since King Features Syndicate still owned half of that property. The Popeye catalog would be purchased by Associated Artists Productions, Inc. (AAP), which immediately made money in regional television syndication fees.[33] For $21 million, AAP also acquired the pre-1948 Warner Bros. library; AAP was announcing a two- to three-year "profit threshold"—all gravy after that. For AAP, Popeye was put to work, licensed to sell Flav-R-Straws, Bosco, Kellogg's, 7-Up, Schwinn bikes, and Post cereals; Bugs shilled in a similar manner.[34] By 1957, *The Popeye and Bugs Bunny Cartoon Hour* was leading the after-school ratings in dozens of markets. (By the early 1980s, MGM would purchase the entire AAP catalog in an MGM/UA deal.) Virtually all studios that had been producing cartoons since the 1920s either licensed, like Disney, or sold their back catalogs to television entities during the 1950s. The earlier cartoon sales were said to be spurred by Disney's successful move into television as well as CBS's deal with UPA for an all-cartoon TV show.[35] By early 1956, more than 3,100 shorts were already sold, with another 1,800 ready to change hands. CBS had made $600,000 syndicating Terry's catalog in just three weeks, and the die was cast.[36] *Variety* even created a scoreboard to keep track of the deals, as major studios cashed out of the animated cinema shorts business.[37]

In 1958, only fifty new cartoons were released to cinemas. The six- or seven-minute cartoon now cost upward of $70,000, even for non-Disney studios, a doubling from 1948. Rental charges paid by distributors hadn't increased much at all.[38] Lantz wrote a pleading op-ed piece in 1951 (and then again in 1956) bemoaning these facts and prophesying the end of the industry if things didn't change.[39] He wasn't wrong. New Mickey Mouse cartoons stopped being made in 1953,[40] the same year in which Warner Bros. closed its doors for the first time. Jones's Coyote and Roadrunner and Bugs and Elmer were at their best, though, with *Zoom and Bored* appearing in September 1957, two months after *What's Opera, Doc?*—oases in a desert of cartoon time fillers. It would be 1964 when the last theatrical Bugs cartoon, *False Hare*, limped across the finish line, made without Jones, Maltese, or Noble. Relying on talk rather than action or character, the short is inferior and even speaks its own disinterested epitaph. Says Bugs of the setup and caricatures, "So I'll go along with it. Things are kinda dull around here anyway," and, "This'll set rabbits back a thousand years."[41] The Pink Panther moved into Bugs's home and thrived for a short while, but Warner Bros. animation was done.[42] When MGM's Fred Quimby retired in 1956, Hanna and Barbera began cutting corners, approaching what would become their "cheaper" look very quickly. Technically, they'd come to this earlier, creating rough versions of their expensive Tom and Jerry shorts, using hundreds of drawings to map out the cartoon rather than the thousands required to create a polished version. The last Tom and Jerry cartoon of this period, *Tot Watchers*, appeared in late summer 1958 and had the hallmarks of a "planned animation" short—lateral movement, cycling, no resizing, sound effects, and music replacing movement, and so forth. Hanna and Barbera had already been let go in May 1957, when MGM shuttered its shop, the duo's multiple Oscars notwithstanding. They landed on their feet, even

In Hanna and Barbera's *Tot Watchers*, the limitations of "planned animation" are already apparent. As the child scoots laterally across the bottom of the frame, Tom and Jerry's eyes follow without really following. The cartoon is colorful, stylized, and thrifty—hallmarks of Hanna and Barbera's imminent television work. *Tot Watchers*, Hanna-Barbera, 1957. Screenshot taken by the author.

in reduced (TV) circumstances. For NBC's *Ruff and Ready*, new distributor Screen Gems would offer H-B Enterprises an anemic $2,700 for a finished five-minute cartoon. By December 1957, the cartoons were airing. Two years later, H-B Enterprises premiered Huckleberry Hound and friends, for television and with Kellogg's money, truly the shape of things to come.[43]

SLEEPING BEAUTY

For Walt, *Sleeping Beauty* was to be his crowning achievement, a work of high art that would enchant and entertain families. At $6 million, it was the most expensive Disney film ever, released in 1959 to lukewarm reviews and lackluster box office, performing like its more affordable predecessor *Lady and the Tramp*. The *Times* thought it "sentimental" and too cousinly to *Snow White*, but "it all comes out nicely."[44] It was also about four years late, thanks to Disney's inattention to story and the distractions of Disneyland, television production, live-action films, and so on. One critic—after raving about the film's bold designs and use of color, movement, and "gloriously present" metamorphosis—writes of the climactic battle scene that droops to a listless denouement: "Here we have a harmless vision. The story book closes."[45] The film was also released first in 70-mm Technirama and six-track stereo format. Disney wanted to recoup costs in the upscale cinemas so outfitted. Neighbor-hood theater owners and those who ran drive-ins—calling themselves "the loyal friends' theatres"—complained that Disney had abandoned them.[46] The "moving illustration" *Sleeping Beauty* was almost eight years in actual production, its "decorative abstraction" meant to "demonstrate conclusively the superiority of the Disney style [and] also constitute a major assault on everything UPA represented."[47] It managed to be both things without truly being successful. The latter half of the decade saw employee downsizing across the major studios, at home and abroad, the closing of several thousand movie theaters, and a 23 percent drop in film rentals.[48] The entire film industry was struggling.

In 1962, Hollywood released only 102 features, down from 362 in 1936.[49] A steep reduction in the number of produced and distribut-able films meant fewer short subjects, too. This was also the year that saw the talent agency MCA take over Universal, with the goal being a "mega-conglomerate."[50] By the beginning of the 1960s, the produc-tion and distribution changes for Hollywood cartoons were evident. As mentioned, Disney had already moved on from shorts as a fixture, embracing feature cartoons, live-action shorter subjects and features, and Disneyland. Other studios didn't have the luxury of having myriad irons in the fire and were forced to lay off workers and eventually close or sell out. As early as 1950, Disney had realized that a single television view-ing experience (like the Disney–Coca Cola Christmas Day broadcast, *One Hour in Wonderland*) could draw as many viewers (twenty million) as bought tickets for most Hollywood films. That math was easy. This snapshot of announced releases from all theatrical-animation studios in 1960–1961 proves the diminishing point:

- Columbia—newer character Loopy de Loop and some one-off cartoons; also, reissues of Magoos and Color Favorites

- MGM—*no new short subjects*; sixteen Gold Medal reissues, mostly Tom and Jerry

- Disney/Buena Vista—twelve reissues, one new Goofy and two new Donald titles, and two new two-reel cartoons (*Goliath*

II,[51] *The Saga of Windwagon Smith*)—with the Goofy and Donalds meant to be the end of those character series

- Paramount—twenty color cartoons, eight reissues; Paramount surveyed exhibitors and was encouraged to create *more* cartoons

- 20th Century-Fox—Terrytoons offered eighteen new cartoons and six reissues; also, new stars Hashimoto-San, Hector Heathcote, and Silly Sidney, all during Ralph Bakshi's tenure (these would all end up on TV soon); distributors said these characters were created to appeal to "all races, sexes, and ages"[52]

- Universal—also went against the grain and announced nineteen new cartoons from Lantz and six Woody Woodpecker reissues

- Warner Bros.—announced only that there would be twenty Merrie Melodies and Looney Tune titles as well as Bugs Bunny Specials; also, some Blue Ribbon reissues, which continued to be very popular

None of the debuting characters gained any audience traction; after a run of a few to a few dozen cartoons, they were gone. The days of fifty-two or even twenty-six annual cartoons issuing from any of the major studios had clearly passed and wouldn't return—except on drastically reduced budgets—when almost all new animation was being created directly for television.

By the beginning of the 1963–1964 season, Warner Bros. (via DePatie-Freleng) offered a full run of forgettable new cartoons and thirteen Blue Ribbon reissues; the Warner Bros. spokesman wouldn't (or couldn't) commit to a similar shorts program for the following year.[53] Just after Warner Bros. closed its doors,[54] Freleng and DePatie leased Warner Bros.'s former space and equipment, producing the *Pink Panther* series, among others. Not long after (July 1964), Warner Bros. had a change of heart and contracted this new company to make cartoons under the "WB" moniker and employing Warner Bros. characters. Forty shorts were generated, all suffering from reduced budgets, reduced creativity, thrifty sound and movement, etc., but cinematic animation continued. Perhaps as a sign of diminishing respect and returns, when DePatie-Freleng was formally announced in June 1963, *Variety* printed Friz Freleng as "Frib Frelend."

LATER DISNEY TITLES

The 1960s offer a list of Disney feature films that have become staples largely thanks to the emergence of home video, a handful of hummable songs, and appealing characters. Most of these films, when premiered, were not runaway hits; these were rather safe, amiable, family films, released when most Hollywood (and international) films grew darker and more pessimistic. *One Hundred and One Dalmatians* (1961) is remembered not only for its freer look and over-the-top villain but also for Disney's admitted dislike of the ubiquitous lines on every level of animation, from character to deep background. The new Xerox process used to copy pencil drawings to cels without an inker saved hours but also forced a UPA-like line cult into a Disney feature, a look Disney had spent years erasing from his animators' efforts. Disney complained without demanding changes, proving he'd turned his deepest, dearest attentions to his theme-park fascinations—Disneyland, Disney World, and EPCOT—once and for all.[55] If anything truly aligns the films after *Sleeping Beauty*, it's Disney's distance from most of them, his never-before dependence on directors like Woolie Reitherman, his allowance for inept story structures, also-ran music, and just un-Disney-like faults. In addition to thinking about new attractions, Disney was shepherding a dozen live-action films across 1960 and 1961, films ranging from *Toby Tyler* to *Babes in Toyland*. Adding *Dalmatians* meant a baker's dozen. *Dalmatians* performed well enough at the box office, but the following decade saw a decline in feature animated film quality as other parts of the Disney portfolio—television, the parks, and live-action films—went to the head of the line.

Disney's *The Sword in the Stone* (1963) underperformed at the box office, though it was generally well reviewed (it was "agreeable") as a welcome Christmastime film for "the young and young at heart."[56] The energetic *Mary Poppins* (1964) was an outlier, given its combination of live-action and animation, but was a certified hit, successful critically, at the box office, and as a licensing cornucopia (records, sugar ads, chocolates, cereals, dolls). One noted caveat is the fact that Disney's most successful film of the decade was mostly live action with animated scenes—not a straight-ahead animated feature. Disney had also come to rely on more, smaller live-action films (like *Son of Flubber*) to keep work going at the studio and balance out the expensive, few-and-far-between animated features.

Lasting change was everywhere in the movie industry. In mid-October 1966, Paramount Pictures—the Fleischers' former distributor—became a subsidiary of the conglomerate Gulf + Western. The next year would see Warner Bros. merge with Seven Arts. RKO was already just a memory. At Disney, a different kind of change was occurring. Almost no one at the Disney studio knew the boss was ailing. His cough had been legendary— warning employees from afar when he approached: "Man is in the forest!"—but not worrisome. Disney's short illness and death in December 1966 cast a pall on every part of the empire; the Disney magic might have been Disney himself, after all. Just weeks after his passing, one wag asked, only half-jokingly, whether Disney after Walt would become "Christianity without Christ."[57] *The Jungle Book* premiered ten months after Walt's passing and was the final animated film on which he'd worked closely; it was also a financial success, Disney's passing perhaps bringing more audiences to cinemas (they certainly flocked to the theme park). But if the 1960s were troubling, the next decade would be a waking nightmare for the industry as "animation limped into the seventies."[58]

AND SO THE 1970S

From Peter Biskind came, "Everything old was bad, everything new was good. Nothing was sacred; everything was up for grabs."[59] Leonard Maltin describes this period's animated Disney films tellingly—*Sword in the Stone* wasn't bad but "has left no traces," *Jungle Book* is likable but completely "forgettable," *The Aristocats* "unmemorable," and *Robin Hood* "undistinguished."[60] He's being kind. Charles Solomon calls *Aristocats* and *Robin Hood* "the worst animated films in the studio's canon," and the "late Sixties . . . the nadir of American animation."[61] By the early 1970s, old-guard animation personnel were dead or near retirement, many having spent their silver years making cereal and beer commercials or in the limited animation of "the American tragedy . . . Saturday morning

TV,"[62] a far cry from idyllic days at Disney, Fleischer, or Warner Bros. (By the end of the 1970s, when brand-new animators like John Lasseter arrived, Disney was in its "dormancy," having produced only three animated features: *The Aristocats*, *Robin Hood*, and *The Rescuers*.[63] No flops—*Robin Hood* made good money, and *Rescuers* fared even better.)

The generational gulf had widened, too. Tex Avery's final days were spent on rehashed characters like Cavemouse and Kwicky Koala for forgettable H-B projects—he was head down on "the hopelessly Sisyphean task of creating anything of quality or value" and died in August 1980.[64] Even in death, as the figurehead of his industry, Disney took the most abuse. In 1968, novelist James Michener was blaming "the optimistic pablum of Mickey Mouse" for fostering a "bland attitude" that led to Vietnam;[65] that same year, artist Ernest Trova would claim that "the swastika, the Coca-Cola bottle, and Mickey Mouse are the most powerful graphic images of this century";[66] by 1974, Disney was being mentioned in relation to Nixon, his influence blamed in part for creating the unscrupulous "young aides" capable of Watergate and the administration's cover-ups;[67] and, in 1975, film critic Jonathan Rosenbaum was comparing Disney to Leni Riefenstahl.[68] This last wasn't intended as a slur, but wow.

The decade was an odd, troubled time for feature animation and Hollywood film in general. By 1971, weekly attendance had dropped to less than sixteen million, while TV viewership grew.[69] As if uncertain about any tomorrows, the Disney studio hired very few new artists between 1970 and 1977, meaning no one was being trained by the venerable animators who had been hired by Disney himself.[70] Longtime animator Eric Larson admits no one at the studio much thought about the future "until around 1970," when mortality loomed larger, nudging them into a training mindset.[71] By 1977, after the completion of *Rescuers*, Disney studio veterans Ollie Johnston, Milt Kahl, and Frank Thomas retired, Reitherman retired from directing, and John Lounsbery had passed about a year earlier, widening the studio's generational gap.

Beyond the paucity of new talent, most animated fare from all studios was now being made for or ultimately released to television, not to movie theaters, including projects lengthy enough to be considered features, like the Rankin/Bass *The Hobbit*.[72] Second, to ensure immediate profitability, a significant number of "features," like *Superstar Goofy* and *Bugs Bunny Superstar*, were just bits of extant short cartoons stitched together with newly animated linking material. This was how Warner Bros. animation kept itself in the feature-animation game without having to risk making a feature.[73] Third, "adult" theatrical animation was an undiscovered country—maybe the generation nursed on Disney wanted cartoons to grow up with them? Disney alum John David Wilson pulled together the 1970 animated feature *Shinbone Alley*, based on old comics, a play, and a musical—it was well reviewed, but audiences didn't show up. Inspired by Bakshi's unexpected hit *Fritz the Cat*, an extremely cheap (*Cheap!* was its working title) and crude film from Charles Swenson, *Dirty Duck*, appeared in 1974 to little response. Also inspired by *Fritz* was its sequel, *Nine Lives of Felix the Cat*, also 1974, made without Bakshi and selected to Cannes, oddly. It didn't cost much, and it made less. Don Jurwich and a raft of underemployed H-B animators contributed to the grindhouse fairy-tale spoof *Once Upon a Girl* (1976), making an undistributable feature of what many animators had illicitly doodled from the beginnings of the industry. Mainstream films on offer included the lackluster Hal Sutherland and Filmation offering *Journey Back to Oz* (1974);[74] the Disney hybrid *Pete's Dragon* (1977); the earnest, Disneyish *Raggedy Ann & Andy* from Richard Williams and a handful of former Disney animators; Ralph Bakshi's *Coonskin* (1975); the dark, postapocalyptic fantasia *Wizards*; and, with producer Saul Zaentz, even a fascinating, rotoscoped *The Lord of the Rings* (both 1978).[75]

Bakshi's controversial race-relations film *Coonskin* was intended as a satire of both *Song of the South* and contemporary Blaxploitation films, a condemnation of racism and racist imagery, but the finer points were lost on most. The film generated protests and reduced the number of screenings well after his *Fritz the Cat* had started the decade off with a coveted "X" rating and a tumescent box office. Given the multimillion-dollar response to Bakshi's $700,000 *Fritz*, it's fair to assume that 1970s audiences *seemed* to want something more than Disney could offer and that American animation was about to change forever. *New York Times* critic Vincent Canby complimented *Fritz* as a "low, bawdy cartoon feature" that's "almost drab," like a "spectacular Terrytoon."[76] In all, it's "a far cry from Disney."[77] Within a year after *Fritz*, more traditional titles—including Hal Sutherland and Filmation's *Treasure Island*, Disney's partly recycled *Robin Hood*, and Hanna-Barbera's *Charlotte's Web*—appeared. (The Filmation title sank without trace; *Charlotte's Web* underperformed, becoming a cult classic on VHS.) Bakshi's follow-up films (*Heavy Traffic*, *American Pop*) cost more and made less, much less, and the wholesale adult animation revolution sputtered.

Just off-screen, most of the big studios were also transitioning from family to corporate ownership and management in the 1960s—Universal bought by MCA; Paramount, by Gulf + Western; Warner Bros., by Seven Arts and then Kinney; MGM taken over by Seagram and then Kirk Kerkorian, which merged MGM with United Artists, which had been a Transamerica Company. Film catalogs became commodities, and studios, like any other investment, needed to turn a profit. Not surprisingly, the darker, conspiratorial, more pessimistic, and generically unstable films emerging from the turmoil of the late 1960s were uneasy double bills with *Jungle Book* or *Raggedy Ann*. The emerging "blockbuster" films and mindset didn't help, either. Populist films that could sell tickets and merchandise and spawn sequels—*The Godfather*, *The Sting*, *Jaws*, and especially *Star Wars*—filled movie theaters and studio coffers. No animated film could compete head-to-head with these kinds of films . . . yet.

At Disney, the two decades following Walt's death were challenging at best. It's not too rabid to say that short-subject theatrical animation died with Walt and that feature animation survived, but just. Paramount Studios closed one year after Walt's passing; Lantz finished in 1972 (admitting he hadn't recouped the costs of his cartoons from a decade earlier); and Terrytoons shuttered in 1973. In 1969, the WB-Seven Arts version of Warner Bros. folded after producing the unprogrammable *Injun Trouble*, an insensitive cartoon at least three decades out of its time. (At the Warner Bros. studio, DePatie and Freleng gamely limped along, producing theatrical "Dogfather" cartoons until 1976—these had not much of a pulse.) Disney[78] had been the only one willing to sacrifice for the art form; the rest of the industry pared back for meager theatrical budgets, turned entirely to television (as Hanna-Barbera and Terrytoons did), or closed their doors (as MGM, Paramount, and Warner Bros. did). In 1967, Roy Disney had assumed command at the studio, and the "What would Walt do?" refrain touched almost every decision, project, and investment.

With the state of the industry just a few years after Walt's passing, the refrain might have quickly changed to "What *could* Walt do?" Roy would survive his younger brother by only a few years, dying in 1971, just weeks after opening the financially invigorating Disney World. Donn Tatum and then Card Walker succeeded Roy before Walt's son-in-law and studio producer Ron Miller took the reins in 1980, though he seemed ill suited for the responsibility (except that he was married to a Disney).[79] Miller remained nominally in command until it was clear that an active, hostile takeover meant to strip assets from Disney forced the Disney family and parts of the board to make changes, bringing in (as president) businessman Frank Wells in 1984. Michael Eisner (chairman and CEO) was hired as the creative force, and Jeffrey Katzenberg came along with Eisner. Out the door that year went tens of millions of dollars (called "greenmail") to buy out the interested raiding parties, along with market confidence and, with the founding of the more "adult" distribution arm Touchstone, perhaps the public's goodwill. No one could have known Disney animation was four long years away from its new beginning.

CHAPTER 11

From Retrograde to Renaissance

TO BE FAIR, MANY HAVE BEEN CALLED THE NEXT WALT. STEVEN SPIEL-berg has been labeled as the "modern-day Walt Disney"; John Lasseter has been thus rechristened more than once; and so with Jim Henson, Don Bluth, Andrew Lloyd Webber, John Updike, Steve Jobs, Rich-ard Williams, Hiyao Miyazaki, and scores of obscure local cranks and geniuses dreaming of unmade cartoons, animated movies, or theme parks.[1] In 1994, a *Wall Street Journal* writer called Katzenberg a kind of "re-incarnation of Walt Disney" in a story that angered Walt's nephew Roy, alienated Eisner, and even fuddled Katzenberg.[2]

But a couple of major caveats should accompany us through this chapter.

One: Hollywood feature animation *survived* after the 1970s, because other cooks, including Disney graduate Bluth, DreamWorks SKG, Pixar, Fox Animation, Blue Sky, Warner Bros., Amblimation and Universal, Sony Pictures Animation, Illumination, and other artists, studios, and distributors, most capable of producing Disney-like (and better) ani-mated films, elbowed into the kitchen and provided that oh-so-necessary c-word: *competition*.

And two: In order to *thrive* after the 1980s, the feature animated film had to move out of special event, boutique status and achieve feature-film stature—the animated feature had to be treated like and then perform like a typical Hollywood film.[3]

There was also to be a key third element, and it feeds or starves the first two: Could any studio in Hollywood *other than Disney* make money or, even more, oxygenate the studio organism with just feature animation? This question was being asked as late as 1997, after the tidal wave of new Disney hits drowned Bluth's five-in-a-row disappointments on the eve of the release of the anticipated and expensive Fox and Bluth feature *Anastasia*.[4] The answer will be a qualified "yes," but that wouldn't be certain for several bruising years.

The expense of marketing and theatrical distribution for animated features has put off many: "Getting fifteen hundred prints of films into theaters is one thing; getting fifteen million people to see it is another."[5] Hanna-Barbera, Warner Bros., Mattel (the Barbie franchise), Hasbro (G.I. Joe, Transformers, and My Little Pony), and dozens of smaller firms opted instead for television or direct-to-video avenues and those potential millions of viewers for most or all feature distribution. Hundreds of titles and millions of dollars were represented in this quietly gigantic nontheatrical category. The venerable cartoonery Warner Bros. had been active for years, cobbling together old titles into reduced-risk "features" and distributing those to television and VHS (occasionally to cinemas). Warner Bros. ventured into deeper waters with originals like *Space Jam*, *Iron Giant*, and *Osmosis Jones*—the first an unexpected hit, the other two crushing flops—before scuttling back to the safety of videos featuring Scooby Doo, Tom and Jerry, or the Justice League.[6] Getting an animated film into hundreds or thousands of theaters raises the break-even threshold above what most projects can reasonably expect to reach.[7] And, by the 1980s, big-studio feature animation was on shaky ground. One of the first items of business on the Wells-Eisner agenda after the 1984 soft coup was the cessation of Disney animation: "It's not making any money," Frank Wells is quoted as saying.[8] This is a curious comment when considering the recent Disney animation titles. Though expensive and troubled, *The Fox and the Hound* made money in its initial release in 1981, *Pete's Dragon* likely broke even, *Rescuers* was a hit, and earlier *Robin Hood* and *Bedknobs and Broomsticks* did well. None was a runaway sensation, but all seemed to have paid for themselves.[9] Wells might have been saying, "It's not making *enough* money" (perhaps compared to Disney theme parks, television, and merchandising), or maybe they expected *all* film-production units of Disney to improve, to reverse the market-share slide *all* Disney films had experienced across the late 1970s.[10] Wells and Eisner were there to balance the books and produce only profitable films (à la Eisner, Katzenberg, and Barry Diller's successful Paramount model—to "run [it] like a real business"[11])—and modern Disney animation clearly hadn't proved itself to at least Wells as being worth saving. It seems only Walt's nephew Roy E. Disney's willingness to helm the animation division from 1984 stayed the execution, and later Katzenberg caught the cartoon spirit, too—credit should be given where it's due.

DISNEY, CIRCA 1984

This section will start where many mountain assaults begin—at the lowest point, where everything else is up. This was Disney animation in 1984—producing lackluster features and struggling with a changing marketplace, talent pool, and audience. It didn't help that takeover elements—"swashbuckling corporate raiders"[12]—were circling the parent ship, ready to board and plunder (and then carry off booty, such as the Disney films back catalog, the theme parks, the real-estate holdings, and the merchandising rights). In 1982, the full studio had endured a net income drop of almost 20 percent; by 1983, profits fell and the live-action film division could manage to produce only three new films.[13] There were also international cartoon competitors. The biggest adult animated feature of the early 1980s, *Heavy Metal*, was a Canadian cult title distributed by Columbia. Most feature animation in the 1980s was coming from Japan—nineteen Japanese features released theatrically in 1984. Such releases included Topcraft's *Nausicaä*, the beginning of what would become Studio Ghibli's amazing catalog. There was just a single forgettable American feature[14] from a minor American studio (Marvel) that year—a year, ironically, when animation was celebrated in association with the Los Angeles Olympics. Before 1984 came the cut-out animation *Twice Upon a Time* as well as Ralph Bakshi's *Fire and Ice*, both 1983 (and both box-office failures), and, in 1982, there was H-B's *Heidi's Song* and Bluth's *The Secret of NIMH*. *NIMH*—"the seed that began the animation boom of the 1990s"[15]—managed to make almost $15 million against a $7 million budget,[16] while the H-B film lost money in its theatrical release.

Just one month before the release of the R-rated, teen-pleasing *Heavy Metal* came Disney's *Fox and the Hound*, significant for different reasons. Optioned as a novel and then adapted into unrecognizability, the film became a flashpoint for a power struggle at Disney between factions young and old, corporate and artistic. Well into production, many creative personnel quit the studio entirely. It was Walt acolyte Bluth who led the large group of leavers in September 1979, setting up his own studio and producing passably competitive, Disney-like, and often accomplished films.[17] Bluth, Richard Rich, Tim Burton, Bill Kroyer, and Henry Selick were all disaffected Disney artists who would go on to establish direct competition with Disney in the feature animation industry, Burton and Selick in the stop-motion area (*The Nightmare Before Christmas*) and Bluth and Rich in more traditional hand-drawn animation. Kroyer (*FernGully; Tron*) worked in both traditional hand drawn and computer-generated (or CG) animation. Bluth (*An American Tail; Thumbelina*) and Rich (*Swan Princess; Trumpet of the Swan*) considered themselves the torchbearers for Disney-type family animation.

Disney's newest and most expensive animated project, *The Black Cauldron*, was supposed to have premiered in 1984, but it was postponed due to script challenges and disagreements between new boss Katzenberg and the film's production team over its scarier scenes.[18] The 1985 film was released to a first-ever (for Disney animation) PG rating, mixed reviews, and a weak box-office performance, failing to outearn both a rerelease of *Dalmatians* and a much, much cheaper *The Care Bears Movie*.[19] The soured icing on the cake for 1984 was Disney very nearly falling prey to that outside takeover, the result of which would have been asset stripping, fragmented divestiture, and the end of the Disney corporate empire. The tug-of-war pitted Disney son-in-law Ron Miller against nephew Roy E. Disney—both against outside bidder Saul Steinberg—with family and factions choosing (and even switching) sides. There was still a takeover, albeit a velvet one involving Wells, Eisner, and Katzenberg. Disney remained intact and wouldn't be so threatened for another twenty years. Eventually, the Disney family, friendly outside stockholders, the board, and some executives managed the crisis, but at great expense.[20] More on that outcome and the next attack later.

The near end of Disney, however, signaled the beginning of the brightest years for all theatrical animation, salad days still being enjoyed forty and more years later. Newest arrival *Super Mario Bros.*, of Nintendo Pictures and the emerging "Nintendo Cinematic Universe," crashed the feature animation party and yielded box-office billions.[21] Considering box-office returns and marketing successes, many of the later animated features from each active studio outperformed even the live-action blockbuster films around which studios organized their release schedules. The animated feature was moving away from "special event" status and into studios' regular rotation of tentpole films, one of the critical caveats mentioned earlier. By 2001, when Pixar's *Monsters, Inc.* was being prepared for distribution, a lawsuit appeared, claiming Pixar had lifted the story and characters without attribution. In testimony, Disney's Dick Cook called the film a "tent pole" film for Pixar/Disney, as significant as *Harry Potter and the Sorcerer's Stone* for Warner Bros. and, for Disney, the summer blockbuster *Pearl Harbor*.[22] (The judge would allow the film to be released on time and eventually ruled in Pixar's favor, finding no copyright infringement.) But there was Disney itself calling one of its co-owned films a tentpole—and *Monsters, Inc.* easily outpaced the live-action tentpole *Pearl Harbor* at the box office.[23] Ten of these films, from *Frozen* to *Minions* to *Super Mario Bros.*, have made more than $1 billion, and, of these ten, six are sequels or branch-offs from an original title. In relation to *Frozen*, reaching more than $1.28 billion to become the highest-grossing film of 2013, this success was Disney closing a loop. In 1937–1938, *Snow White* had been the most successful film in Hollywood, easily outpacing all traditional films at the box office. In 2013, *Frozen* had beaten not only *Iron Man 3* but also franchise entries from *The Hobbit*, *Hunger Games*, and *Fast and Furious*. That same year, other blossoms appeared—four of the top eleven films in the worldwide box office were animated.

These seeds had been planted as Disney painfully reorganized under Eisner, Wells, and Katzenberg almost thirty years earlier. From the nadir of 1984, Disney's release pipeline was soon cleared of *Black Cauldron*,

The Great Mouse Detective, and *Oliver & Company*—their modest grosses reaching about $21, $25, and $53 million, respectively[24]—before the 1988–1990 releases of the groundbreaking live-action-and-animated *Who Framed Roger Rabbit*,[25] the Broadway musical–influenced *The Little Mermaid*, and the "well-animated piece of nostalgia"[26] (and Disney animation's first sequel) *Rescuers Down Under*.

While 1984 was a harrowing year, and 1985 little better, thanks to the uncertainty of the expensive *Black Cauldron*, the beginnings of the videotape wave emerged in these two years as Disney released *Robin Hood* and *Pinocchio* for sale (not just for rental), and sales exploded. This cash injection likely muted the sting of the so-so performance of the theatrical animated films, proving the after-theater value of even *Robin Hood*, "hardly one of the great triumphs of Disney storytelling."[27] Prior to this time, theatrical rereleases were seen as the surest way to reprofit on a Disney film. By 1978, before the home-video revolution, the value of the classics was understood: "The Disney animated films are not so much movies as they are annuities."[28] The films were already generational by the late 1970s. Selling millions of videocassettes at $25 to $45 each was a stunning windfall, and, at first, when video rental stores were the target customers, even titles like *Robin Hood* sold for $79.95.[29]

However, 1988 was a year of animated classics—Otomo's *Akira*, Švankmajer's *Alice*, Takahata's *Grave of the Fireflies*, and Miyazaki's *My Neighbor Totoro*. This was the same year that Wells and Katzenberg worked out the latter's incentivized contract, one that seemed so safe for Disney—before the release of *Roger Rabbit*, *Little Mermaid*, *Beauty and the Beast*, or *Aladdin*, and before the sales of tens of millions of video cassettes. But, for us, the year 1988 was significant for three other films, two already mentioned. Two very different Disney animated features were released—*Oliver & Company* and *Who Framed Roger Rabbit*—as well as Bluth's *The Land Before Time*. The first film was what might be called a "typical" Disney animation, adapting a well-known story and characters with restless energy and chirpy songs, some contributed to by Billy Joel, Bette Midler, and newcomer Howard Ashman (of Ashman and Menken fame). The Katzenberg-shepherded[30] *Oliver* brought in a respectable $50 million in its initial run;[31] it was smart and fun, and, except to true fans, it has been largely forgotten. The second film is the reason *Oliver* gets short shrift. *Roger Rabbit* was a blockbuster of a film, produced by Touchstone (not Disney, thanks to the Junoesque Jessica Rabbit[32]) and Spielberg's Amblin Entertainment, adroitly combining animation and live action and, perhaps most important, bringing to thrilling life beloved animated characters, some not glimpsed since the 1920s. *Roger Rabbit* made a staggering $330 million in its original release—second at the 1988 domestic box office and in the world[33]—and must be credited for reanimating old cartoons and the animated film in general. Suddenly, there was gold in them thar 'toons. *Roger Rabbit* was risky, costing more to produce ($50 million) than most animated films could expect to gross in preceding years. With *Roger Rabbit*'s financial bona fides in mind, it became increasingly defensible in Hollywood to spend money on quality animation features, and studios and financiers took notice.[34]

Disney had nearly enjoyed the pool to itself until 1986, when the upstart Don Bluth's first hit, *An American Tail*, emerged. It's a meticulous, beautiful film, helped a great deal by animation fan Steven Spielberg and Universal backing the project, and it made almost ten times what it cost, beating out Disney's *Great Mouse Detective* by a wide margin. The 1987–1988 span saw some real, budding competition, where *American Tail* was able to outearn a rerelease of *Cinderella*, followed by *Land Before Time* and *Oliver & Company* going neck and neck. Up against the animation juggernaut Disney, an almost-win smells like a stunning achievement. This success set a high bar; unfortunately, for every *American Tail*, there was a *Thumbelina*, *Rock-a-Doodle*, *Troll in Central Park*, or *Pebble and the Penguin* for Bluth—ambitious money losers. (*Troll* would open to less than $72,000 at the box office.) But Bluth's next project, *The Land Before Time*, might also be called a "typical" Disney animation—an orphan-and-journey story, endearing characters, more chirpy songs—as Bluth was keen to keep classic Disney alive. The film cost much less to make, had a passable Disney look and feel, and, for Disney, represented real competition, making almost $85 million and spawning thirteen direct-to-video sequels as well as video games and a television series, and so forth.[35] (Spielberg's Amblin also helped this film find its way.) But the threat faded quickly. Thanks to disagreements between Bluth and

Amblin, as well as a cost-cutting move to Ireland, Bluth's *All Dogs Go to Heaven* (1989) did not benefit from the Spielberg name or tempering, and, with Bluth left to his own creative and storytelling devices and what Jerry Beck terms his odd, "erratic tone shifts," the film underperformed.[36] (*All Dogs* also had to compete directly against *The Little Mermaid*, released just days earlier.[37]) Later, in 1997, just after Disney and Pixar agreed to a new and more equitable distribution contract, Pixar owner Steve Jobs would write to shareholders, reminding them of the "only two significant brands" in the animated film industry—"Disney" and "Steven Spielberg." Two years after the release of *Toy Story*, Jobs was set to offer Pixar as the third brand.[38] If Bluth followed the trade journals from afar, this would have been a crestfalling moment—he was not "significant," over the years he had rejected both Disney and Spielberg, and computer animation wasn't his bag.

After the disappointing *All Dogs*, Bluth's next four films cost more than they made, often much more, while Disney and Pixar films soared at the box office. But a salve appeared as Bluth's *Anastasia* broke the streak, introducing Fox Animation Studios to the world, earning $140 million and briefly vaulting Bluth back to significance. His very next feature film, *Titan A.E.*, sank both his reputation and Fox Animation, as it grossed about half or less of what it cost to make, crushed by also-rans *Dinosaur*, *Chicken Run*, *Emperor's New Groove*, *Rugrats in Paris*, *The Tigger Movie*, and even *Road to El Dorado*. Outside the Bluth-Disney cage match, more adult animation had also appeared, including *Bébé's Kids*, Bakshi's *Cool World*, and Bill Plympton's *The Tune*, all in 1992, none drawing much audience attention. This same year, the lackluster *Tom and Jerry: The Movie* appeared from Phil Roman and Warner Bros., not Hanna-Barbera, earning back its production budget but no profit.

The floodgates hadn't opened yet; perhaps lessons had been learned from Bluth's experiences as he poked at Disney. Since Disney had been releasing high-quality and profitable animated films regularly since 1988 (e.g., *Aladdin* grossed more than $500 million in 1992) and Bluth could manage a streak of only two hits against the (Disney) house, there may have been reticence across the industry to try to compete. So, what would it take to compete regularly? Quite a bit, apparently. On the heels of

Aladdin's success, even as live-action films and television at Disney were floundering, thanks to a robust animation slate and an even more bountiful home-video season, Disney was enjoying record earnings.[39] The year 1993 saw the release of five different animated features from five separate sources:[40] *Batman: Mask of the Phantasm, Once Upon a Forest, We're Back! A Dinosaur's Story*, the long-gestating Richard Williams film *The Thief and the Cobbler*,[41] and *The Nightmare Before Christmas*. Five was not an unusually low number for that time, and with good reason—producing animated features was still quite risky. (In fact, a rerelease of *Snow White* to theaters in 1993 outpaced *all* Walt Disney films at the box office.[42]) The first four titles all lost money, some a considerable amount. Only Tim Burton's *Nightmare*—a Touchstone film—succeeded, reaching more than $91 million and rightly becoming a classic of stop-motion figure animation. None of the others could even manage to break even. What would it take? It would take a wannabe Walt.

A willing and motivated industry scrapper like Jeffrey Katzenberg had to leave Disney, like Bluth before him; he had to ally himself with established industry titans Spielberg and David Geffen, forming DreamWorks SKG—a modern-day United Artists—a troika able to convince (*unlike* Bluth) major studios and investors to regularly join with them to exploit a potentially lucrative feature-film, animation, and TV market. Katzenberg left Disney in 1994 when he wasn't offered a significant promotion after Frank Wells's death, but momentum gathered slowly.[43] The new DreamWorks studio suffered through mediocre film and TV offerings before completing an animated feature. In summer 1998, Spielberg's *Saving Private Ryan* brought in money and critical kudos, and more risky DreamWorks ventures could move forward. Suggested by Spielberg, *The Prince of Egypt* was the first DreamWorks animation project, a traditional-and-CG mix. The computer-animated *Antz* would premier earlier that fall, however. The swap likely came to be thanks to Katzenberg's realization that *Prince of Egypt*, though award-friendly, could not be the merchandising milk cow *Antz* promised and thus was a much better sophomore.[44] *Prince of Egypt* was gifted a Christmas 1998 release and was critically well received, though the scads of ancillary revenue Disney enjoyed were absent. Its opening watch party—described by one guest as "that long dark Friday night of the soul"—proved *"Prince of Egypt* was no *Lion King.*"[45] It had been September 1998 when *Antz,* the "first" Dream-Works (via Pacific Data Images, or PDI[46]) animated film, appeared, and the comparisons to Pixar's in-progress *A Bug's Life* would resound through the industry, though they are very different films. (A miffed Lasseter once called *Antz* the "schlock version" of *Bug's Life.*[47]) *Antz* cost upward of $100 million, made about $172 million, and was aimed at a slightly more mature audience; released two months after *Antz, A Bug's Life* made more than $360 million, three times its production budget, reaching the family audience.

This same year, Warner Bros. Animation, missing out on the big toon dollars, rushed back into the feature animation waters, nearly drowned, and almost took another studio down with it. Warner Bros.'s "schizoid movie" *Quest for Camelot* was an unholy mess that lost money, saw to the shutdown of several projects in the innocent bystander Fox Animation pipeline, and forced Bluth (at Fox) to turn to a direct-to-video Bartok project to try to justify saving *Titan, A.E.*[48] At Warner Bros. Animation, the *Quest* flop was followed by the releases of *Iron Giant, Osmosis Jones,* and *Looney Tunes Back in Action,* each of which cost more than they made. Bluth's beautiful "ice in space" film would also fail to thrive, and Fox disappeared.

From the fruitful period from 1988 to 1990, armed with the one-two punch of Roger and Ariel (and, to a lesser extent, Bianca and Bernard), the American cartoon industry at large had been slow to follow Disney's lead. Across twelve years after the release of *Roger Rabbit,* the number of American-produced (or even -coproduced) animated features never reached double digits, hovering safely in the four-to-eight-per-year range, even as, before the end of the century, Disney offered up bargain-priced megahits *Beauty and the Beast, Aladdin,* and *The Lion King,*[49] followed by the more dear and less boffo *Pocahontas, The Hunchback of Notre Dame,* and *Hercules,* and the hits *Mulan* and *Tarzan,* and Pixar (conjoined to Disney[50]) rendered *Toy Story, A Bug's Life,* and *Toy Story 2.*[51] The goal of releasing a hit animated feature every eighteen months or even more often had been realized, but costs spiraled with success. Labor got more expensive as Disney tried to keep its animation talent in house. Other studios not rich in feature-animation genealogy may have bridled, though, at the soaring costs involved in making feature cartoons—and traditional ones at that—preferring to spend that money on more live-action films with much quicker turnaround times and easier paths to profitability. Disney's cartoon pedigree made any move away from animation a tough sell, even as costs per cartoon rose toward and then well past $100 million for each, while worldwide grosses settled into a "disappointing" $250–$450 million range.[52]

Perhaps not surprisingly, there was a lull after the release of *Toy Story*—not unlike the quiet shock in Hollywood after *Snow White* debuted in 1937. Many of these cartoon blockbusters regularly saw off other well-made and potentially watchable films, like, in the case of *Toy Story* in 1995, the meritable (and traditionally animated) *Balto* from Spielberg and Amblimation. In addition, the "staying power" success of a completely CG film, like *Toy Story*, surprised most, digital houses included. It would be mid-1996 before PDI[53] and DreamWorks went to work on *Antz*, and the race to be the second such animated film was on, "and it didn't matter if it was all that good or not."[54] It was 2001 when DreamWorks released *Shrek* and 2002 when *Ice Age* emerged from Fox's Blue Sky. At that point, Disney faced fully capable (CG) competition in the world of feature animation. (Pixar was technically also a box-office competitor for Disney, though their distribution relationship meant this was nearly in-house. Disney would fully acquire Pixar in 2006 in a deal worth $7.4 billion.) Coming from Katzenberg and DreamWorks, *Shrek* was on its face anti-Disney, and its "hip, unearnest storytelling" was the new baton the makers of *Ice Age* and their followers ran with.[55] In 1939, that competition had been the appealing (to contemporary audiences) *Gulliver's Travels* from the respected Fleischer studio, and for a very short while it had seemed an arms race was underway and a vying feature animation industry was about to emerge. That contest would have to wait more than sixty years.

Part of the "whole new world" in the Disney versus DreamWorks dance involved people. Now at DreamWorks Animation, Katzenberg, observing the (mostly) hand-drawn beauties of *Pocahontas*, *Hunchback*, and *Hercules*, set poacher's traps for key Disney personnel, including

Andreas Deja (*Lion King*), Glen Keane (*Little Mermaid*), and Ron Clements and John Musker (directors of *Aladdin*), traps baited with traditional animation support and lots more salary. New Disney president Michael Ovitz managed to fend off Eisner's former protégé and hold on to most of these targeted talents,[56] though Eisner had to agree to raises, longer contracts, and the greenlighting of *Treasure Planet*, a cherished and expensive write-down-in-waiting.[57]

It turned out that Disney's unquestioned success with a streak of films, from *Beauty and the Beast* uninterrupted through *Tarzan*, was front-loaded, at best. The first three were certified blockbusters, with *Lion King*, for example, making almost $1 billion by 1997, when worldwide box-office receipts, merchandise sales, and home-video revenues were totted up. *Lion King* had cost less than $75 million, including approximately $30 million in overhead charges. But, as the studio tried to compete with the rest of Hollywood, overhead soared at Disney for all films across the 1990s. *Pocahontas*'s gross came to a respectable $350 million, while the $180 million *Hercules* (including overhead; its production budget was announced as $85 million) could bring in only $253 million. If they spent $180 million to make, market, and distribute *Hercules*, Disney lost money on what seemed like a guaranteed hit.[58] At Disney, the long-gone Katzenberg was being blamed for these subpar performances;[59] ironically, these were the same films that Katzenberg was gazing at fondly as he formed an animation identity at DreamWorks. Many were being fooled, apparently, by good press and enviable grosses, ignoring the charges against the films before any profit could be made.[60]

As early as 2000, the grip of traditional animation seemed to be slipping—the artistic and financial fiasco of DreamWorks's "make or break" *Road to El Dorado* chilling everyone[61]—and CG animation had arrived. (By 2006, ten computer-animated films from eight different distributors reached movie screens.) But old habits die hard. Even after the success of the CG *Shrek*—including the film's drowning of Disney's *Atlantis: The Lost Empire* released weeks later and a sneak attack on the overwrought Disney summer blockbuster *Pearl Harbor*—Katzenberg still wanted to match Disney by hand, meaning mastering traditional animation. Katzenberg's "fractured fairy tale"[62] *Shrek*, the CG cartoon that saved DreamWorks, was then followed by two ambitious, tradition-ally animated[63] features, *Spirit: Stallion of Cimarron* and *Sinbad: Legend of the Seven Seas*. Neither film was able to cover its costs—*Sinbad* lost so much money that the studio nearly sank—and the bloom was off the traditional animation rose at DreamWorks and almost everywhere else. Multiple box-office hit sequels have followed *Shrek* and *Ice Age*, all CG. Less than a decade later, Illumination and Universal anted up with the beginnings of the uber-successful *Despicable Me* franchise, which includes the tot-friendly *Minions* and has generated almost $4.7 billion in international box-office revenue and countless merchandising profits. From that time until now, computer-animated films (hits and also-rans) have become a regular part of the large studios' yearly programs. After *Sinbad* sank, the following film from DreamWorks was *Shrek 2*, which made nearly a billion dollars and was the highest-grossing film of 2004, emphatically burying traditional animation.[64] The decision to spin off (and take public) animation from the rest of DreamWorks came in the wake of *Shrek 2*'s success. At around that same time, and even before the sluggish performance of *Home on the Range*, Disney was also officially phasing out traditional animation.

At the time, there was talk[65] that this decision wasn't only based on film performance (*Lilo and Stitch* had done very well) but also directly inspired by the souring Pixar-Disney relationship, and *Shrek 2*'s[66] run-away receipts underscored the point. Essentially, Disney was doomsday prepping for a Pixar bugout. The success of Pixar films had convinced other studios that CG didn't have to be reserved just for effects moments alongside traditional animation—moose antlers in Disney's *Brother Bear*, creatures and environments in DreamWorks's *Sinbad*, or the giant in Warner Bros.'s *Iron Giant*. DreamWorks, Illumination, and Blue Sky embraced animation by computer, while Disney dithered—traditional animation had made Disney, so that's understandable, and Walt's nephew was nominally in charge—and they tried to have it both ways. Disney products varied: one year, *Home on the Range* (traditional), and the next, *Chicken Little* (CG); *Meet the Robinsons* and *Bolt* were both CG, then *The Princess and the Frog* was a hand-drawn film, and so on.

A potential interregnum gaped in February 2004, and it wasn't the split of Katzenberg and DreamWorks Animation from DreamWorks. At Disney, the events of 1984—an attempted hostile takeover—reappeared but in hulking form. Disney's market value in 1984 had stood at about $2 billion; by 2003, it was almost $50 billion—an attractive content plum—and its stock prices in early 2004 were down about twelve dollars from just 2002. There were pirate activities inside the Disney ship as well. Eisner and his minions were in the process that year of cleaning house, forcing the retirement from Disney's board of older members including Roy E. Disney, who had been instrumental in bringing Eisner to the company nineteen years earlier and in saving Disney animation. Roy's resistance to Eisner's strong arm earned him a walk off the plank. However, the Disney family, still major stockholders, weren't going to leave company management quietly. Both Roy and staunch ally Stanley Gold strategically resigned, writing (and posting) informative letters laying out their grievances and belief that it was Eisner who must leave. Eisner's headaches included the collapse of negotiations with Pixar, the studio that had just produced the Oscar-winning, billion-dollar-earning *Finding Nemo*. Steve Jobs wanted to stay in the Disney family but only with a more favorable deal and only if Eisner was gone.[67] In between animated hits in 2004—after *Nemo* but before *Incredibles*, both from attractive in-law Pixar (and while Disney was offering up *Brother Bear* and *Home on the Range*[68])—the mega-company Comcast was the sea monster come to eat them all up.

Comcast was the largest cable operator in the United States and keen to now own a batch of valuable content it could deliver to households, and Disney—undervalued and attractive—fit the bill. What began as a friendly merger escalated into a hostile offer when Eisner and the board dug in, Roy and allies lobbied for a complete board shake-up from without, and Comcast apparently assumed a lowball offer could woo unhappy Disney stockholders looking for more efficient corporate management. All this drama played out in newspapers and financial journals, many seeing positives in the potential alliance, including establishing better competition in an industry of predatory conglomerates like Time Warner and Rupert Murdoch's Fox. Those at the ground level either hoped that

Comcast could invigorate the theme parks and even the Disney media product or were concerned a new, non-Disney corporate culture could ruin the magic.[69] Others, like Diane Disney Miller, railed against Disney losing its uniqueness—and certainly the independence her father had reverenced—if ever the Comcast byline appeared beneath the Disney logo.[70] Several months of great uncertainty at Disney and Comcast followed as the $49–$66 billion tender (fluctuating with stock values) was in play, with Disney's stock rising (thanks to *Nemo* and *Pirates of the Caribbean*) and Comcast's stock slipping. By late April, the Comcast offer was withdrawn, but days later (after a no-confidence vote from shareholders) Eisner was removed as chairman but remained CEO.[71]

THE CG STUDIOS

And now, DreamWorks, Blue Sky, and Illumination. These and others democratized top-shelf computer animation, aiming to entertain audiences from toddler to grandparent, a refined kind of four-quadrant audience in which billions of untapped admissions awaited. At the beginning of *Close Encounters of the Third Kind* (1977), Roy Neary (Richard Dreyfuss) pitches a family outing to see *Pinocchio*, and his oldest boy, Brad, complains, "Who wants to see some dumb cartoon rated 'G' for kids."[72] By 1977, who indeed? Coincidentally, this was ten years after Disney's death, and supposedly the end of what brother Roy had promised in 1967 was "the most beautiful ten-year plan we could ask for."[73] That decade would be hard. When Richard Schickel was researching and writing the pleasantly caustic *The Disney Version* in the later 1960s, that's the environment he was informed by—in the era of Vietnam and civil-rights unrest, Disney was old and kiddie and capitalist. More recent computer-animated films have managed a minor miracle—bridging the audience gap, filling seats with entire families because there's something for all of them. Nintendo and Illumination's *The Super Mario Bros. Movie* (2023) welcomed more than forty years (and several generations) of Mario fans to his cinematic coming-out party. In 2022, *Minions: The Rise of Gru* tapped into a teen TikTok audience who dressed to the nines and attended screenings of the film in large groups or projected the film and staged raves beneath it, an unintended throwback to the small playgrounds that used to sit beneath many drive-in movie screens. (This *Despicable Me* franchise off-shoot made $940 million.) It's no coincidence that the noticeable jump from single- to double-digit animated films released per year occurred between 2000, when there were seven, and 2001, when twelve appeared, just when DreamWorks and Blue Sky were getting up to speed and Illumination was on the horizon.

DreamWorks has released more than forty animated features[74] since 1998. Many are one-offs, including *Road to El Dorado*, *Sinbad*, *Flushed Away*, *The Bee Movie*, and *Megamind*. Some of these struggled (*Bee Movie*) or failed outright (*El Dorado*, *Sinbad*, *Flushed Away*[75]), generating no theatrical sequel traction, or simply suffered in relation to proximity, like *Megamind*. In summer 2010, the unheralded Illumination title *Despicable Me* appeared and, on a $69 million budget, raked in more than half a billion dollars. Three months later, DreamWorks's *Megamind* appeared and, on a $130 million budget, managed to earn *only* $321 million. The era of relative success for blockbuster animation had arrived. Less than three weeks later, Disney released its newest princess movie *Tangled*, which made almost $600 million. Two other franchise titles from this same year—*Toy Story 3* ($1.07 billion) and *Shrek Forever After* ($756 million)—bashed all other titles. But here's what matters: In 2010, six blockbuster-type animated films were released between March and November, competing for similar audiences, seemingly, and they still managed to amass almost $3.8 billion at the box office. Nonetheless, *Megamind*'s performance, as compared that that of the tepidly reviewed but oft-watched *Shrek 4*, prompted pundits to see DreamWorks as being forced to wait out dry stretches—enduring the aftermaths of *Turbo* and *Mr. Peabody and Sherman*—before the next franchise entry (like *How to Train Your Dragon 2*) would be ready for distribution. More important, in 2010, DreamWorks could claim three of the top six animated films of the year, one more than Disney, and take home almost $1.6 billion from those films.

There was plenty of good news, though the value of franchise films, when compared with the value of singular titles, means that, to this day, DreamWorks moves forward in fits and starts.[76] Immediate box-office success mattered and could eventually pay regular dividends, but a film library *really* mattered, especially when Eisner first surveyed his new fiefdom in 1984, exulting, "You could finance a new Disney World by the unused value of our film and television library."[77] Across the following years, Disney relied on its classics for home-video sales and to raise capital when movies and television were struggling and the parks needed major attention; DreamWorks wasn't so blessed yet, and the "lean times" felt particularly skint.[78] Even with many very lucrative films, DreamWorks Animation had to go its own way in 2004, spun off to raise outside capital and service debt, the kind of separation no one at Disney wanted to imagine.[79] (The following year, Paramount bought DreamWorks completely.) The lasting, bill-paying success for Dream-Works has been franchise films that generate theatrical sequels, starting with *Shrek* and including *Madagascar*, *Kung Fu Panda*, and *How to Train Your Dragon*. Of these to date, the *lowest* achiever at the box office was the Cannes-nominated *Shrek*, reaching $484 million (earning eight times its cost); the highest, *Shrek 2* at $928 million (a little more than six times its cost). Most of these films and their sequels (when traditionally distributed) averaged between $500 and $750 million at the box office and have also generated millions in merchandising; they are blockbuster films that spawn sequels, lucrative television series, and video games. The second emerging tier would include *Puss in Boots*, *The Croods*, *Trolls*, and *Boss Baby*. These films have also done well, but sequels have been released during or adjacent to a pandemic, to reduced distribution, no theatrical distribution, or simultaneous theatrical and streaming distribution, meaning revenue estimates fluctuate wildly.

One of the twelve animated films released in 2002, *Ice Age*, was from a short-lived newcomer. Dollar for dollar, the most successful animated franchise does not boast a Disney or DreamWorks lineage; rather, it's an East Coast anomaly called Blue Sky. Emerging from a digital-effects company founded in the aftermath of *Tron*, Blue Sky had a deal with 20th Century-Fox but no blank check. Fox Animation head Chris Meledandri shepherded the beautiful disaster *Titan A.E.*, with CG from Blue Sky, and a string of clever, well-crafted hit films followed. Recipe? Low budgets, vibrant animation offering new worlds, the familiar "incredible journey" scenario, strong character design and voice casting, and clever scripts. The four films of the *Ice Age* franchise were budgeted $60–$95 million and averaged just more than $700 million in returns on each film. The two *Rio* films (brightly colored birds in a lush tropical setting) earned four and five times their production budgets, and Blue Sky produced successful one-offs including *Robots*, *Horton Hears a Who*, *The Peanuts Movie*, and *Ferdinand*. *Spies in Disguise*—their first film to star "humans" in a modern world—was the last film released and fared less well. The studio came into Disney's crosshairs after Disney's acquisition of Blue Sky parent 20th Century Studios in 2021. Blue Sky was closed, partly due to economic conditions brought on by the pandemic, but mostly thanks to redundancy. Of the thirteen films produced by Blue Sky, only one (its last) failed to perform commercially, an enviable track record.

Elsewhere, created in the wake of DreamWorks's *Shrek* success was Sony Pictures Animation (with Columbia and from Sony Pictures Imageworks), another entrant in the digital animation race. *Open Season* (a hit) appeared in 2006, followed by the so-so *Surf's Up* and *Cloudy with a Chance of Meatballs*, but also *Smurfs*, a franchise-spawning hit that quintupled its production budget. Other successful Sony franchises began with *Hotel Transylvania*, followed by *Angry Birds*, *Peter Rabbit*, and the acclaimed *Spider-Man: Into the Spider-Verse* and *Spider-Man: Across the Spider-Verse* (2018 and 2023).[80] Even Sony's critically reviled *Emoji Movie* (2017) managed to quadruple its $50 million production budget, meaning a sequel is likely. Another smaller, almost start-up studio is Skydance Animation, founded in 2017 and creatively led by John Lasseter. To date, Skydance has offered *Luck*, *Spellbound*, and (soon) *Ray Gunn*, the latter written and directed by Pixar alum Brad Bird.[81]

By 2007, Meledandri had left Blue Sky to join Universal and found (and partly own) the most recent Disney contender, Illumination, setting the stage for another remarkably successful run of animated films, with most of the animation work performed overseas. To date, the studio has released or announced Seuss adaptations (*The Grinch* and *The Lorax*), multiple *Despicable Me* franchise films and offshoot *Minions* titles, multiple *Secret Life of Pets* and *Sing* films, and the first Nintendo Cinematic Universe title *Super Mario Bros.* Most of these films rely on low budgets (around $80 million), whipsmart writing and performances, and catchy music and movement. The one bad egg in the Easter basket, *Hop* (2011), still managed to treble its production budget. On average, Illumination films have cost only $75.2 million and brought in an average of nearly $700 million each, with *Minions, Despicable Me 3*, and *Super Mario* each passing $1 billion. When NBCUniversal bought DreamWorks Animation in 2016, Meledandri assumed nominal control of DreamWorks Animation *and* Illumination, though the DreamWorks arm continues to operate with some autonomy. Bringing the *Shrek* franchise back to life was announced soon thereafter, and the successful sequel to *Puss in Boots—The Last Wish* (2022)—was the first film from those efforts.

Additional perspective comes from the Disney side of the battlefield, with some specific numbers to hold up against DreamWorks, Blue Sky, and others. While DreamWorks and Blue Sky in the early 2000s flowered with hit after hit, Disney countered with this salvo between 2000 and 2009: *Fantasia 2000, Dinosaur, The Emperor's New Groove, Atlantis: The Lost Empire, Lilo and Stitch, Treasure Planet, Brother Bear, Home on the Range, Chicken Little, Meet the Robinsons, Bolt*, and *The Princess and the Frog.* These were a mixture of traditional, CG, and traditional-CG films, and most lost money or just broke even. A sequel or addendum to *Fantasia* had been Walt's dream since the early 1940s, so *Fantasia 2000* was Roy E. Disney's fever dream (and Eisner's nightmare). If the threshold for profitability for films like these is about two and a half times the production budget, then most of these films barely treaded water. The new *Fantasia* lost money. Those that made money tended to (1) make less than the DreamWorks and Blue Sky titles while (2) costing more, often nearly twice as much. Of this list, only three films (*Dinosaur, Lilo*, and *Brother Bear*) certainly crept into the black; two films may have broken even (*Chicken Little* and *Bolt*); the other *seven* lost money—some, like *Treasure Planet*, spectacularly so. Directors Musker and Clements's "target audience of preteen and teenage boys apparently still associated hand-drawn, 2-D animation with children's fare and wanted no part of it."[82] Another "dumb cartoon . . . for kids," this one rated PG, young Brad Neary might have pouted. Only three of the Disney films crossed the $300 million mark; only two of them were budgeted at less than $100 million.

Michael Eisner had been fond of saying he'd always look for the "single and doubles"[83] of film, meaning not "event" films with expensive talent and high overhead but smallish films that could safely perform well enough to pay for themselves and justify the next project. Those films became harder to find across 1990–2004 at Disney. In his annual letter to shareholders, penned as 1999 closed, Eisner touted the upcoming "remarkable" films *Fantasia 2000, Dinosaur, Kingdom of the Sun,* and *Atlantis.* Three of these four flopped or underperformed; these included *Kingdom of the Sun* (which became *The Emperor's New Groove*—"built on the wreckage of a completely different film"[84]). *Dinosaur* kept its long neck above water, but only just. *Dinosaur* sold on home video but sparked no franchise energy and briefly cooled Disney's CG fires. Single, double, or was it a "hit by pitch"? Whatever, Disney was taking a thrashing from the smaller, more streamlined animation studios.

The dam finally broke for Disney with *Tangled* in 2010, a computer-animated release that made almost $600 million,[85] likely saved the "Disney princess" franchise, and was followed by a blockbuster hot streak: *Wreck-It Ralph, Frozen, Big Hero 6, Zootopia, Moana, Ralph Breaks the Internet,* and *Frozen II.*[86] The water gets muddy after that, when streaming services like Disney+ emerged and films could be released there, or there *and* in limited distribution simultaneously (as with Pixar's *Turning Red* and Disney's *Raya and the Last Dragon*), or during a shortened theatrical release window and then onto a streaming platform, and so on. "Revenues" become much harder to track; films that "make money" are much harder to identify.

What the efforts and successes of DreamWorks, Blue Sky, Sony, and Illumination might finally demonstrate is the promise of animated film as part of a movie industry. To differing extents and with obvious hiccups acknowledged for at least two of these (Blue Sky and Illumination), these outcomes proved that a studio can exist and support itself creating and distributing *only* animated films. Disney's (and formerly Fox's) Joe Roth asserted as early as 1994 that such focus was not only possible but might be essential, that "making a successful animated film 'has to be the will of the entire corporation—not a side business.'"[87] Walt had known this truth during his studio's Golden Age, though he drifted away from it in subsequent decades, and now a reinvigorated Disney was finding its way back, with hard-learned lessons for others dipping into the same feature-animation waters. Blue Sky disappeared, thanks to a merger in which there were unfortunate redundancies, not because of business failure. Illumination is at the top of the film-by-film financial heap as of this writing. Sony might be just coming into its own. DreamWorks has gone through multiple iterations over the years, producing and distributing live-action films as well as animated features and television; its distributing entities have come and gone like mixer dance partners, but it continues to produce saleable, popular films. The most recent animated films produced by DreamWorks—*Captain Underpants* (2017), *Abominable* (a Chinese coproduction, 2019), *Bad Guys* (2022), and the second *Puss in Boots* film—have all paid for themselves and then some. Sequels for *Trolls*, *Kung Fu Panda*, and even *Shrek* are all on the DreamWorks calendar.

Dollars and Sense

Some additional numbers might be illuminating here. Between and including 1989–2022, there have been sixty-one animated features reaching the top ten in worldwide box-office performance (a nearly two-per-year average). In only two of those years have there been no animated films in the year-end top ten; fourteen years saw one top-ten animated film; eight years boasted two; eight years claimed three; one year offered four; and one other year (2010) produced five separate top-ten films that were animated.[88] Overall, five of these animated features have reached number one since 1988, when *Who Framed Roger Rabbit* reached the number-two spot. These films are now fulfilling the second caveat proposed earlier—they are being treated like and performing like normal live-action feature films. There is no sign of a slowing, either, beyond factors external to the industry (like a pandemic). If anything, like Disney of old, Hollywood is beginning to rely on its animated fare to support the rest of the studios' output. Universal/DreamWorks announced films include a fourth *Trolls* and a fourth *Kung Fu Panda*, and a fifth *Shrek* film is coming. A sixth in the *Ice Age* franchise series has been announced. Paramount and Nickelodeon continue to produce popular movies starring Spongebob SquarePants, and a new *Teenage Mutant Ninja Turtles* feature franchise bowed in 2023. From Disney, sequels to *Toy Story*, *Zootopia*, and *Frozen* were announced in a clump, all in response to the unexpected drag on corporate profits inflicted by the high costs of streaming. Clearly, current Disney leaders see cartoons as the studio's only sure bet. At Universal (DreamWorks and Illumination), *Sing*, *Madagascar*, *Despicable Me*, *Minions*, and several other franchises are simply waiting in line for their inevitable sequels to be greenlit, answering Disney's bell, proving there's truly safety in numbers (3s, 4s, 5s, even 6s). Even more tantalizing is the runaway success of video-game stalwart Nintendo's first franchise film, *Super Mario Bros.*—already in the billion dollar club—and the certainty that Sega (home of the emerging *Sonic the Hedgehog* franchise) has other characters lining up for their own films.

So, it's to be cartoons.

Hollywood's future is an animated one.

NOTES

INTRODUCTION

1. Pointer, *The Art and Inventions of Max Fleischer*, 146. Max was thinking of his own future feature at the time.

2. Susanin, *Walt Before Mickey*, 46–47.

3. See Bak's *Playful Visions* for more; see also Bendazzi, Furniss, and Crafton.

4. *MAD* artist-of-the-margins Sergio Aragonés.

5. Canemaker, "Winsor McCay," *Film Comment* (1975): 45.

6. Stephenson hints at Disney's domination of the industry; see *The Animated Film* (1973), 35.

7. *MPH* (3 April 1937): 26.

8. "Mr. Terry and the Animal Kingdom," *New York Times* (7 July 1940).

CHAPTER 1

1. O'Sullivan, "In Search of Winsor McCay," 7.

2. Crafton, "Animation Iconography," 414.

3. Cofounded with Albert E. Smith; they purchased Edison's thirteenth Projecting Kinetoscope (Dewey, "Man of a Thousand Firsts," 47).

4. Smith, "The Early History of Animation," 26.

5. McCay admitted to being "one of the first men in the world to make animated cartoons" (Canemaker, "Winsor McCay," *Film Comment*, 44).

6. Bray, "Development of Animated Cartoons," 395.

7. Bragdon, "Mickey Mouse and What He Means," 40.

8. Canemaker, "Pioneers of American Animation," 38.

9. Couperie, *A History of the Comic Strip*, 9.

10. Ramsaye, *A Million and One Nights*, 654.

11. Seldes, *The Seven Lively Arts*, 231.

12. Smith, "Early History of Animation," 23.

13. *Variety* reviews of McCay's "Seven Ages" show from 1906 mention chalkboard and paper.

14. McCay's version, according to period reviewers, involved less talk—even complete silence—and elaborate drawing (*WMLA*, 109).

15. Smith's "Early History of Animation," 24–25.

16. Crafton, *Before Mickey*, 46.

17. Dewey, "Man of a Thousand Firsts," 45.

18. Dewey, *Buccaneer*, 170–71.

19. "Kalem," *Variety* (30 October 1909): 10.

20. Crafton, "Tricks and Animation," in Nowell-Smith, 73.

21. "Flickers" had been used in vaudeville houses to clear the house between shows; "chaser" didn't necessarily mean a cartoon—rather, it was the last scheduled item. *MPW* (January 1908): 21.

22. Solomon, *Enchanted Drawings*, 13.

23. Macek, "From *Little Nemo* to *Little Nemo*," 10.

24. Macek, "From *Little Nemo* to *Little Nemo*," 10.

25. Quoted in Adamson's "Joe Adamson Talks with Richard Huemer," 13.

26. Canemaker, *Winsor McCay: His Life and Art*, 131; see also Solomon, *ED*, 17.

27. O'Sullivan, "In Search of Winsor McCay," 3.

28. Chute, "Keeping Up with the Jones," 14.

29. O'Sullivan, 6; Canemaker, *WMLA*, 109.

30. "Grand's Excellent Bill," *Indianapolis Sun* (19 March 1907): 10.

31. "Winsor McCay," *Variety* (16 June 1906): 8.

32. "People of the Stage," *Cincinnati Commercial Tribune* (28 November 1909).

33. Apocrypha, maybe, as related by McCay, but also from his assistant, John Fitzsimmons (see Canemaker's "Winsor McCay" and "The Birth of Animation"). McManus created the *The Newlyweds* and *Bringing Up Father* strips; both were adapted into cartoons.

34. McCay's out-of-town trips to play vaudeville houses would end around 1917 at Hearst's demand, though New York–area shows likely continued (Hoffer, "From Comic Strips to Animation," 31n27).

35. Cohl had beat all to the punch with drawn animated efforts in 1908 (*Fantasmagorie*); by 1912, he was in the United States, working on projects for Eclair. Cohl's films began to appear in the United States by 1909.

36. Films from Méliès and Cohl were in broad circulation in the United States in 1909; dozens of smaller newspapers exulted in these traveling, hand-colored "trick-films."

37. He and director Griffith might have run in similar circles; their breakthrough film releases (*Gertie* and *Birth of a Nation*) were just a year apart. McCay, like Griffith, would struggle with the direction and change in art and the film industry—and eventually be left behind.

38. The mechanical and technical processes would be patented beginning in 1914 and enforced until 1932 by Bray and Hurd, who became a Trust-like concern with the willingness and ability to enforce patent observance.

39. Crafton, *BM*, 134–35.

40. Canemaker, "Winsor McCay," 45.

41. Canemaker, "Winsor McCay," 45.

42. Canemaker, "Winsor McCay's *Little Nemo* . . ." 31.

43. Hoffer, "From Comic Strips to Animation," 25.

44. Crafton, *BM*, 110.

45. Hoffer, "From Comic Strips to Animation," 25. McCay had also adapted this setting and character from a *Dream of a Rarebit Fiend* episode, dated 25 May 1913.
46. Smith, "Early History of Animation," 25.
47. Quoted in Canemaker's "The Birth of Animation," 14–15.
48. Canemaker, "Winsor McCay," 44. McCay called this the "McCay Split System" (Canemaker, *WMLA*, 141).
49. Smith, "Early History of Animation," 29.
50. Fitzsimmons remembers a "reporter" visiting McCay for a story on his process, and McCay willingly revealed all. It's thought that this may have been Bray (O'Sullivan, 9).
51. Wylie Sypher, *Rococo to Cubism in Art and Literature* (New York: Vintage, 1960), 296.
52. Fell is discussing *Nemo* in "Mr. Griffith, Meet Winsor McCay," 77.
53. McCay had talked about his interests in "serious and educational work" in film as early as 1912 (Canemaker, *WMLA*, 137).
54. Canemaker, *WMLA*, 151–52.
55. Canemaker, "The Birth of Animation," 15.
56. The film took twenty-two months to complete; other studios were producing five- to eight-minute cartoons every one to two weeks.
57. Klein, "How I Came to Know the Fabulous Winsor McCay," 51.
58. Hearn, "The Animated Art of Winsor McCay," 28.
59. Canemaker, "Pioneers of American Animation," 38.
60. Panofsky, "Style and Medium in the Moving Pictures," in *Film: An Anthology* (1969), 15–32.
61. Canemaker, "Profile of a Living Animation Legend," 28.
62. Canemaker, "Profile of a Living Animation Legend," 28–29.
63. Canemaker, *WMLA*, 142.
64. See Ramsaye and Hampton, as well as Gomery's *The Hollywood Studio System* (1986).
65. Eyman, *20th Century-Fox*, 3.
66. Panofsky, "Style and Medium," 23 (italics added).
67. See "Bray-Hurd: The Key Animation Patents" in *Film History* 2.3 (1988): 229–66.
68. Solomon, *ED*, 24; Canemaker, *WMLA*, 142.
69. Solomon, *ED*, 24.
70. Bray would unsuccessfully sue McCay for refusal to pay licensing fees on processes he'd employed prior to Bray submitting patent applications. Using *Nemo* as his ironclad example of preexistence, McCay prevailed. Bray would have to pay McCay's court costs, and he, quietly, even paid McCay over the years a small share of licensing profits (Canemaker, *WMLA*, 143).
71. Canemaker, *WMLA*, 152.
72. Canemaker, *WMLA*, 142.
73. Callahan, "Cel Animation," 224.
74. *MPW* (October–December 1913): 1354.
75. "Society in Whirl," *New York Times* (29 January 1914): 9.
76. "Dramatic Review," *Los Angeles Times* (30 September 1914): II6; see also *MPW* (October 1913–January 1914): 42.

77. Canemaker, "Pioneers of American Animation," 38.

CHAPTER 2

1. Adamson, *Tex Avery: King of Cartoons*, 18.
2. Adamson, "Joe Adamson Talks with Richard Huemer," 12.
3. Adamson, "Joe Adamson Talks with Richard Huemer," 12.
4. See Crafton, *BM*, 271–99, for more on these character types.
5. Sartin, *Drawing on Hollywood*, 182.
6. Just when Edison's Motion Picture Patents Company was being dissected in the courts, Bray-Hurd was legally tightening its grip on animation's technology (Koszarski, *An Evening's Entertainment*, 171).
7. Solomon, *ED*, 22.
8. This list, to this point, is drawn from Martin Jameson's "Cartoonists in Filmland" in *Cartoons* 11.1 (1917): 116–24.
9. Jameson, "Cartoonists in Filmland," 117.
10. Canemaker, "Profile of a Living Animation Legend," 28.
11. Bray would next file on 29 July 1914 and then again on 30 July 1915. His later partner Earl Hurd would file his first application on 19 December 1914, another on 30 October 1919, and another on 9 March 1926. "Bray-Hurd: Key Animation Patents," in *Film History* 2.3: 229–66.
12. Crafton, *BM*, 145. Bray even tried to patent *all* hand-drawn animation, but the patent examiner had seen McCay's work and balked (Cabarga, 16).
13. Smith, "Early History of Animation," 26.
14. Hurd's cel patent would be granted in June 1915 (Crafton, *BM*, 153).
15. Koszarski, *An Evening's Entertainment*, 170.
16. Martin, "In Search of Raoul Barré," 11.
17. See Crafton's "Automated Art" chapter in *Before Mickey* for more information.
18. Bray was even considering a five-reel silhouette *feature* with C. Allan Gilbert in 1916 (Lenburg, 46).
19. Shay, "Willis O'Brien," 23–24.
20. The "whirlwind" quote comes from the film's review in the *New York American* (4 March 1915): 10. Winsor McCay was employed at this same Hearst newspaper, and Walter Lantz was an office boy there.
21. The individual sheets of celluloid could also be washed and reused.
22. See Richard Koszarski's "Animation" section in *An Evening's Entertainment*, 170.
23. Cabarga, *The Fleischer Story*, 22.
24. "*Farmer Alfalfa Invents a New Kite*," *MPW* (18 March 1916): 1857.
25. Smith, "Early History of Animation," 30.
26. Terry made films for the war and, by August 1919, had signed to make Farmer Al Falfa cartoons for Paramount; Moser and Sullivan were also signed. *MPW* (2 August 1919): 722.
27. Denig, "Cartoonist Bray with Paramount," in *MPW* (11 December 1915): 1988.

28. Many continued to use paper animation, avoiding Hurd's cel process and fees. In years to come, some studios would balk at the inclusion of sound or, later, color in their cartoons. Those holdouts generally ended with the sad end of the holdout.

29. "A Talk with Dick Huemer" in Peary, 29–36.

30. Perhaps the second such after Cohl, an established artist who discovered cinema at the age of fifty.

31. Martin, "In Search of Raoul Barré," 15.

32. In these earliest studio settings, paper *and* cel systems were used. The strengths and preferences (and ages and experience) of animators also mattered.

33. Martin, "In Search of Raoul Barré," 12.

34. Crafton, *Emile Cohl*, 179; see also Martin, "In Search of Raoul Barré," 12.

35. "Calendar of Licensed Releases," in *MPW* (20 March 1915): 1804.

36. Crafton, *Emile Cohl*, 177–78.

37. Premiering in August 1915 and pitched as "Raoul Barré's Clever Cartoons" in *MPW* (14 August 1915): 1199.

38. Bray's own *Gertie* knock-off, *Diplodocus*, also emerged in 1915.

39. Crafton, "Tricks and Animation," 74.

40. Martin, "In Search of Raoul Barré," 11.

41. Martin, "In Search of Raoul Barré," 11; Crafton, *BM*, 194–96.

42. Martin, "In Search of Raoul Barré," 11.

43. See Langer's article "Regionalism in Disney Animation" in *Film History* for more.

44. Thompson, "Meep Meep," 128.

45. In this same cartoon, Nolan's "rubber hose" style of animation is apparent from the first scenes—rubbery, fluid limbs were easier to draw and redraw. This approach would carry over to the thin, pipe cleaner–like limbs of the Mickey-type characters appearing toward the end of the decade. As Disney moved toward cinematic body images, the "rubber hose" look faded (Solomon, *ED*, 29).

46. From Adamson's "Joe Adamson Talks with Richard Huemer," 15.

47. As in the case of Little Nemo, live-action adaptations, sheet music and songs, merchandising, and a stage play preceded the animated version of Mutt and Jeff.

48. "Domestic Difficulties," in *MPN* 14.18 (4 November 1916): 2864.

49. The cartoon might have circulated in January 1917 as *Mr. Bonehead Gets Wrecked*. *MPW* (6 January 1917): 102.

50. Fox, "Felix Remembered," 44.

51. And it does *not* resemble Palmer's fine pen work in the *Keeping Up with the Joneses* cartoons from the previous year or even his work in *Curfew Shall Not Ring* from 1916.

52. In Professor Driskel's animation classes at UC Santa Barbara in the early 1990s, the object was a red ball.

53. Peary, *AAC*, 193.

54. Adamson, "Joe Adamson Talks with Richard Huemer," 12.

55. Klein, "Pioneer Animated Cartoon Producer," 54; Solomon, *ED*, 23. Klein would eventually work for Van Beuren, Famous, and Disney, among others.

56. Klein, "Pioneer Animated Cartoon Producer," 57–58.

57. Solomon, *ED*, 21.

58. Koszarski, *An Evening's Entertainment*, 172.
59. Crafton, *BM*, 179–81.
60. Theisen, "The History of the Animated Cartoon," 246.
61. Canemaker, *WMLA*, 149. McCay's name was part of the 1916 announcement for the new IFS, but he never supplied any cartoons.
62. IFS advertisement, *MPW* (8 July 1916): 198.
63. Bragdon, "Mickey Mouse and What He Means," 41.
64. Klein, "Pioneer Animated Cartoon Producer," 53–54.
65. This scene would be revisited in Osamu Tezuka's *Jumping* (1984).
66. Martin, "In Search of Raoul Barré," 11.
67. Martin, "In Search of Raoul Barré," 11.
68. Martin, "In Search of Raoul Barré," 11.
69. Quoted in Koszarski, *An Evening's Entertainment*, 172.
70. Bowers made live-action-and-animated films, including *Egged On* (1926).
71. Solomon, *ED*, 22.
72. As Martin's invaluable "Origin and Golden Age of the American Cartoon Film" chart reminds us, others (including McManus and Cohl, Wallace Carlson, Colman, Hugh and Shields, Pat Sullivan, Hy Mayer, Pat Powers, F. M. Follett, Harry Palmer, and Paul Felton) at this same time were trying to make a go in this nascent industry. Most came and went quickly, and there were certainly many more who left no trace.
73. Klein, "Pioneer Animated Cartoon Producer," 55.
74. Martin, "In Search of Raoul Barré," 12.
75. Smith, "Early History of Animation," 28.
76. "Movie Cartoonist Is a Very Busy Funmaker," *The Sun* (2 April 1916): 2A.
77. Solomon, *ED*, 26.
78. Dave Fleischer was serving the war effort as a film editor.
79. "Koko" wouldn't be named until 1923–1924. Reviews and advertisements for his cartoons called him "The Little Clown," which was likely a Chaplin association. "Out of the Inkwell," *Motion Picture News* (30 August 1919): 1779.
80. Canemaker, "Pioneers of Animation," 38.
81. Solomon, *ED*, 26.
82. "Bray Pictograph No. 426," *Moving Picture Age* (April 1920): 39.
83. Listed as "Bray Pictograph, 423, Goldwyn," in *Wid's Filmdom* (February 1920): 28.

CHAPTER 3

1. Martin, "In Search of Raoul Barré," 11.
2. Marcel Brion, quoted in Canemaker's "Otto Messmer and Felix the Cat," 34.
3. Hamonic, *Terrytoons*, 100.
4. See Gabler, *Walt Disney*, 60, 87.
5. Terry would say later that an exhibitor had told him Terrytoons were ideal for clearing the house at the end of a program (Maltin, *Of Mice and Magic*, 126).
6. "Cartoon Creator Signs Up," *Motion Picture News* (27 March 1920): 2938.
7. Crafton, *BM*, 298.

8. Their lives in comic strips, comic books, and stage plays were more successful than any attempt at sound versions or TV adaptations. In 1938, MGM Studios would try to inaugurate its studio with a new run of *The Captain and the Kids* cartoons—audiences didn't respond.

9. Terry's offices were in New Rochelle, about twenty-five miles from New York City.

10. The "first" sound cartoon may have been a sing-along, *Oh Mabel*, that was made in 1924; the Song Car-Tunes would appear regularly until 1926, when Red Seal closed shop (Langer, "Max and Dave," 49).

11. Hamonic, *Terrytoons*, 80.

12. "Progress in Animated Drawing," *MPW* (22 June 1918): 1707; "Short Stuff," *Wid's Daily* (7 September 1919): 24.

13. See Paul Wells's terrific discussion of metamorphosis and animation in *Understanding Animation*, specifically chapter 3.

14. Langer, "Max and Dave," 48.

15. Wells, *Understanding Animation*, 69.

16. Wells, *Understanding Animation*, 73.

17. In addition to Wells's discussions, see Klein's discussion of Fleischer work in *Seven Minutes*, 64–67.

18. "Goldwyn and Bray in Alliance," *Motion Picture News* (7 February 1920): 1457.

19. Langer, "Max and Dave," 48.

20. *ETR* (5 November 1921): 1583.

21. Deneroff, "The Thin Black Line," 22.

22. In 1924, the studio was visited by the Mountbattens, fans from the royal family.

23. Dick, *Engulfed*, 150.

24. Of which there were thirty-six produced, with twenty-one using synched sound (Bradley, 94).

25. Crafton, *BM*, 175.

26. *Variety* (20 August 1924): 21.

27. *Exhibitors Herald* (28 November 1925): 54; the sing-alongs were credited by local managers with bringing older audiences back to the theaters.

28. This name is spelled in the trade journals and newspapers as "Fadman" and "Fadiman."

29. The Disneys had to wait until the 1950s to set up their distribution firm, Buena Vista.

30. *ETR* (5 September 1925): 33.

31. "Fadman Sued by Seal," *Variety* (14 April 1926): 24.

32. *Variety* reported there would be 850 feature films, to be distributed from 1925 to 1926.

33. This was a stay of execution; Max and Dave would endure this removal again in 1942. Ray Pointer and Richard Fleischer discuss these events.

34. *EH* (7 May 1927): 64. Both contracts—for twenty-six cartoons each—were renewed the following year.

35. Paramount's Screen Songs continued to be requested by exhibitors and were even translated for overseas distribution, beginning in November 1930.

36. "Four Famous Writers," *Motion Picture Classic* (June 1926): 24–25.
37. Quoted in Canemaker's "Otto Messmer and Felix the Cat," 34.
38. David Low, quoted in Canemaker's "Otto Messmer and Felix the Cat," 33.
39. Lehman, *The Colored Cartoon*, 12–13.
40. See Sartin's *Drawing on Hollywood*, 44; see also Lehman and Sammond for minstrelsy discussions.
41. Quoted in Canemaker's *Felix: The Twisted Tale*, 38.
42. Messmer was drafted and served in the military; Sullivan did not—he served time in prison for rape and was released in 1918.
43. These novelties were often divided by the half-reel, with a live-action something as the lead and the cartoon as the chaser.
44. Canemaker, "Otto Messmer and Felix the Cat," 36, 58.
45. Canemaker, *Felix: The Twisted Tale*, 39.
46. Felix merchandise sales *were* huge in the United Kingdom, though, on one of his visits, Sullivan noticed dozens of items that bore no imprimatur of Sullivan and whose sellers remitted no licensing fees. When he returned home, Sullivan set his attorney Harry Kopp on the case. See Canemaker, *Felix: The Twisted Tale*.
47. "New in Brief," *Times* (17 April 1924): 9.
48. "Short Reels," *Wid's Filmdom* (5 February 1922): 20.
49. The crowd arrives at the Polo Grounds on cartoon trains that deflate as they empty; Felix arrives on a "real" (photographed) train.
50. Canemaker, "Otto Messmer and Felix the Cat," 34. When *Felix Saves the Day* was distributed to cinemas, it was listed in exhibitor magazines as part of Winkler's states'-rights program (11 February 1922).
51. Canemaker, *Felix: The Twisted Tale*, 66.
52. See Canemaker's chapter 7, passim, in *Felix: The Twisted Tale*.
53. Canemaker, *Felix: The Twisted Tale*, 72–74.
54. Fox, "Felix Remembered," 45.
55. "Loew's State, Boston," *Variety* (16 June 1926): 22.
56. Canemaker, *Felix: The Twisted Tale*, 89. In addition, Canemaker attests, the appearance of a Felix clone in the form of Julius, Disney's Alice series cat, embittered Sullivan—Winkler was distributing the Alice comedies as well.
57. Adamson, *The Walter Lantz Story*, 72.
58. "Winkler Claim Dismissed," *Variety* (28 April 1926): 37.
59. Fox, "Felix Remembered," 48.
60. "Bray-Hurd and Fables Settle Patents Suit," *EH* (11 September 1926): 44.
61. "Bray-Hurd Win Cartoon Suit," *Variety* (8 January 1930): 79.
62. Lutz, *Animated Cartoons*.
63. Barrier, "Silly Stuff," 6. This was precisely what budding filmmakers at Lev Kuleshov's Moscow film workshop had been doing with a print of Griffith's *Intolerance*.
64. Solomon, *ED*, 29.
65. Quoted in Maltin, *OMM*, 126.
66. Solomon, *ED*, 29; see also Hamonic, *Terrytoons*, 70–71.
67. Kanfer, *Serious Business*, 41–42.

68. Hamonic, *Terrytoons*, 79.

69. Hamonic, *Terrytoons*, 81.

70. Hamonic, "Disney Is the Tiffany's," 61–62; quote from George Shorey's review of *20,000 Feats Under the Sea* in *MPN* (14 April 1917): 2361.

71. The same program that featured the debut of Felix (*Feline Follies*), Moser's Bud and Susie cartoons, Bailey's *Silly Hoots*, and Bobby Bumps from Earl Hurd.

72. Maltin, *OMM*, 129.

73. Hamonic, "Disney Is the Tiffany's," 3. A downside was mentioned often—the 1929 Terry cartoons uncomfortably resembled the 1921 cartoons, meaning risk-taking and artistic or subject-matter advances weren't encouraged at Fables.

74. Erickson, *A Van Beuren Production*, 46–47. Many of Terry's surviving cartoons have Japanese subtitles burned into them; Japanese cartoons of the 1930s like *Spring Song* and *Chameko's Day* were clearly influenced by Terry's imported films.

75. Keith was one of the first American vaudeville operations to program films as part of its daily shows (Butsch, *The Making of American Audiences*, 16). See also Balio's *United Artists*, volume 1, 79.

76. Hamonic, *Terrytoons*, 101. Most studios at this time could manage no more than one new title every two weeks.

77. Crafton, *BM*, 191–92.

78. Maltin, *OMM*, 130.

79. Solomon, *ED*, 30.

80. Huemer quoted in Adamson's "Joe Adamson Talks with Dick Huemer," 13.

81. Quoted in Adamson, "Working for the Fleischers," first page.

82. Maltin, *OMM*, 131 (italics added).

83. A technique used several years later by Iwerks at Disney in *Hell's Bells* (1929).

84. Macek, "From *Little Nemo* to *Little Nemo*," 12.

85. Smith, "Early History of Animation," 29.

86. Macek, "From *Little Nemo* to *Little Nemo*," 12.

87. Hamonic, *Terrytoons*, 120–21.

88. *EH* and *MPW* (1 September 1928): 66.

89. This hit the trades on 17 November 1928, the day before *Steamboat Willie* premiered at the Colony. Van Beuren wanted to get ahead of Disney and the cartoon sound story.

90. Adamson, "Suspended Animation," 612. By 1932, the winds had shifted: "Animated cartoons are the most popular [short] subjects on the screen" (Doherty, "This is Where We Came In," 155).

91. Copley Pictures would step in and add sound to some extant titles (fifteen in total) and then commission some sound for twelve new cartoons.

92. Bradley, *The First Hollywood Sound Shorts*, 98.

93. Messmer, not a partner or stakeholder, continued to create the Felix comic strip for many years.

94. Crafton, *BM*, 301.

95. Fox, "Felix Remembered," 48.

96. Crafton, *BM*, 329–38.

CHAPTER 4

1. Disneyfication: "Often used pejoratively, it denotes the company's bowdlerization of literature, myth, and/or history in a simplified, sentimentalized, programmatic way" (Walz, "Charlie Thorson," 51).

2. Finch, *Walt Disney's America*, 41.

3. Bossert, *Oswald the Lucky Rabbit*, 15.

4. If nothing else, the Alice series offered a cat, Julius, and scores of scampering mice—sketched together five years later by Ub and Walt—and Mickey Mouse was born.

5. Mann, "Mickey Mouse's Financial Career," 715. This exposé would give more credit than blame to Pat Powers for trying to make a go of the halting Disney concern; as a businessman, Mann found Disney very much an artist.

6. From a letter handwritten by Walt to Ub, dated 1 June 1924.

7. From a 1928 letter quoted in Thomas's *Walt Disney*, 93. Walt was in New York City, trying to secure a sound system for his Mickey Mouse cartoons and dealing with Pat Powers.

8. Rogers, "Remaking the B Film," 139.

9. Rogers, "Remaking the B Film," 138–39.

10. Winkler had offered $1,500 for each of the first six Alice cartoons.

11. Gabler, *Walt Disney*, 98.

12. Susanin, *Walt Before Mickey*, 153–56. The agreement with Universal meant Disney surrendered ownership of the cartoons and characters for a more favorable payment scheme and better distribution. Mintz had made the deal with Universal—Walt found out about the changes after the fact (Susanin, 154).

13. Universal refused to release *Poor Papa*, so *Trolley Troubles* became the first circulated Oswald cartoon. In 1928, Mintz decided to dust off *Poor Papa* and release it as if it were a normal part of the new Oswald schedule (Iwerks, *Walt Disney's Ultimate Inventor*, 23).

14. Susanin, *Walt Before Mickey*, 157.

15. Bossert, *Oswald the Lucky Rabbit*, 19.

16. Universal was keen to market Oswald, commissioning a line of chocolate bars, novelty buttons, and a children's stencil set—some before the first cartoon appeared in summer 1927 (Merritt and Kaufman, *Walt in Wonderland*, 98).

17. Crafton, *BM*, 295.

18. George Winkler, Margaret's brother, whom Mintz had tasked with monitoring labor and production at the Disney studio (Bossert, *Oswald the Lucky Rabbit*, 16).

19. Gabler, *Walt Disney*, 106.

20. Mosley, *Disney's World*, 96–100; Susanin, *Walt Before Mickey*, 174–76.

21. Gabler, *Walt Disney*, 114.

22. Mintz and Winkler "insisted" Disney make Julius "imitate Felix" more and more as time went on (Bossert, *Oswald the Lucky Rabbit*, 17).

23. Reprinted in Holliss and Sibley, *The Disney Studio Story*, 13.

24. Solomon, *ED*, 26.

25. Canemaker, "Pioneers of Animation," 38.

26. Quoted in Merritt and Merritt's "Mythic Mouse," 62.

27. Merritt and Merritt, "Mythic Mouse," 62.

28. See Gabler, *Walt Disney* (152–55), for the psychoanalyzing Mickey endured across his early life.

29. Les Clark, speaking to Canemaker, *Walt Disney's Nine Old Men*, 21.

30. Not everything came out roses for Mintz. Universal valued the Oswald character, cartoons, and merchandise, meaning that Mintz had to put George Winkler in charge of salvaging the franchise without Iwerks. They released rejected and already-released Oswald titles and commissioned new ones from lesser talents, including Lantz after 1929 (Merritt and Kaufman, *Walt in Wonderland*, 99). The series was never the same.

31. Schickel, *The Disney Version*, 131.

32. Look up Cameraphone, Viviphone, or Synchroscope for a few examples.

33. Quoted often and perhaps apocryphal because it's so nicely stated. See Gabler's *Walt Disney*, 427, for example.

34. Mosley, *Disney's World*, 107–8. Contemporary reviews of *Dinner Time* tended to agree with Disney's assessment (Bradley, *The First Hollywood Sound Shorts*, 94–95).

35. Schickel, *DV*, 131.

36. Gabler, *Walt Disney*, 127.

37. Iwerks and Kenworthy, *The Hand Behind the Mouse*, 65.

38. As opposed to a separate sound-on-disk process favored by much of the industry at the time and used in Warner Bros.'s popular Vitaphone. Fox's Movietone system would improve on other sound-on-film systems soon thereafter.

39. An industry report released in October 1928 outlined seven major shortcomings of the sound-on-disk systems (Geduld, *The Birth of the Talkies*, 228).

40. Schickel, "Bringing Forth the Mouse," 90; Schickel, *DV*, 125–26. The states'-rights approach could channel films into thousands of *independent* theaters—those not owned or controlled by the major studios (Mosley, *Disney's World*, 119). These same theaters would eventually prevail against the monopoly of the major studios when the *United States v. Paramount Pictures, Inc.* case concluded in 1948.

41. Merritt and Kaufman, *Walt in Wonderland*, 120.

42. Schickel, *DV*, 124.

43. Gabler, *Walt Disney*, 128.

44. Schickel, "Bringing Forth," 90.

45. Finch, *The Art of Walt Disney*, 81.

46. Schickel, "Bringing Forth," 93.

47. Stalling had scored the Mickey cartoons *Plane Crazy* and *Gallopin' Gaucho* while still in Kansas City, where he worked as a cinema organist.

48. Gabler, *Walt Disney*, 129–30; see also Thomas, *Walt Disney*, 99–100.

49. Thomas, *Walt Disney*, 100.

50. Theisen, "The History of the Animated Cartoon," 247; see also Gabler, *Walt Disney*, 133.

51. Gabler, *Walt Disney*, 130–32.

52. Thomas, *Walt Disney*, 100; *Life* 97.2524 (20 March 1931): 18.

53. *MPH* (23 April 1932): 66.

54. Schickel notes that the contract that he'd signed with Powers "ran only for one year, with no renewal options," odd oversights in a time of imbalanced contracts (*DV*, 134–35).

55. Solomon, *ED*, 44.

56. Iwerks, *Walt Disney's Ultimate Inventor*, 34.

57. Iwerks and Kenworthy, *The Hand Behind the Mouse*, 56–57; see also Merritt and Kaufman, *Walt in Wonderland*, 121.

58. Ub would maintain that he didn't know Powers was behind the offers until just before he resigned (Iwerks and Kenworthy, *The Hand Behind the Mouse*, 88–89).

59. Iwerks and Kenworthy, *The Hand Behind the Mouse*, 89.

60. Behind only "Comedies" and "Newsreels" (*FD* [6 April 1930]: 3). This same issue (page 17) features a full-page Columbia ad proclaiming Mickey's arrival as well as that of the Silly Symphonies to the Columbia family.

61. The Disneys offered Powers a one-time $50,000 *payment* for all returned rights of all Disney films Powers had handled, the money to be borrowed from Harry Cohn and Columbia. Powers accepted (Mosley, 128–29).

62. Gabler, *Walt Disney*, 137. Mayer's lack of interest was likely due to MGM having already agreed to a secret deal with Powers and Iwerks.

63. Dick, *Columbia Pictures*, 7. Columbia's Frank Capra had encouraged the studio to deal with Disney. Columbia would lose Disney to United Artists and then distribute Mintz cartoons.

64. These and other characters would have more of a life in Mickey's comic-book adventures.

65. Schickel, *DV*, 141–42.

66. "By July 1929," Crafton notes, "Disney cartoons were in lights on the marquees of five Broadway houses" (*The Talkies*, 393).

67. It wouldn't be until Disneyland began to turn a profit that Walt and Roy could finally relax—a bit.

68. Barrier, *Hollywood Cartoons*, 71–73.

69. See "Mickey Mouse's Financial Career," passim.

70. Schickel, *DV*, 142.

71. See Thomas and Johnston's *The Illusion of Life: Disney Animation*.

72. Sklar, *Movie-Made America*, 200.

CHAPTER 5

1. By 1928, McCay was producing editorial illustrations; Cohl had returned to France in 1914 (Crafton, *BM*, 84).

2. *Variety* (28 May 1930): 13.

3. "Record Is Claimed," *Exhibitors Daily Review* (18 September 1930): 6.

4. Crafton, *The Talkies*, 393.

5. *Variety* (28 May 1930): 13.

6. Balio, *United Artists*, volume 1, xxii.

7. *Variety* (28 May 1930): 13.

8. *Variety* (8 October 1930): 55; (22 April 1931): 5.

9. Bragdon, "Mickey Mouse and What He Means," 42.

10. Barrier, "The Careers of Hugh Harman and Rudolf Ising," 46–47.

11. Cohen, "Looney Tunes and Merrie Melodies," 34.

12. "Friz Freleng," *Walt's People*, volume 2 (Bloomington, IN: Xlibris, 2005), 21.

13. Maltin, *OMM*, 224.

14. Furniss, *Chuck Jones Conversations*, 24.

15. See Columbia's 1932 cartoon *The Minstrel Show* for a sample of staged minstrelsy.

16. Bosko's design was more typical of cartoons from the previous decade, when racially stereotyped characters appeared alongside Bobby Bumps and Felix and in many other cartoon series.

17. Lehman, *The Colored Cartoon*, 18.

18. Beck and Friedwald, *Looney Tunes and Merrie Melodies*, iv.

19. Schlesinger personnel would later join in the making of the FDR reelection film *Hell-Bent for Election*.

20. Gomery, *The Hollywood Studio System*, 115–17.

21. Bradley, *The First Hollywood Sound Shorts*, 99–100; see also Beck and Friedwald's entries on these cartoons (Beck and Friedwald, *Looney Tunes and Merrie Melodies*).

22. A partial quotation of Greg Ford found in Scheib's "Tex Arcana," 111.

23. Bradley, *The First Hollywood Sound Shorts*, 99–100.

24. *EDR* (5 December 1930): 3.

25. Foxy and Goopy Geer appeared in three cartoons each but disappeared when Harman-Ising left Warner Bros.

26. Crafton, *The Talkies*, 397.

27. Barrier, "The Careers of Hugh Harman and Rudolf Ising," 47.

28. Maltin, *OMM*, 224.

29. Maltin, *OMM*, 226–27.

30. *MPH* (11 July 1931): 53.

31. *MPH* (30 April 1932): 53.

32. Gomery, *HSS*, 122.

33. Cohen, "Looney Tunes and Merrie Melodies," 33.

34. "Short Subjects," *FDY* (1931): 101.

35. Maltin, *OMM*, 225.

36. Gomery, *HSS*, 122.

37. See Klein's *Seven Minutes* (37–39) for these categories.

38. Solomon, *ED*, 89.

39. Adamson, *Tex Avery: King of Cartoons*, 162–64.

40. Walz, "Charlie Thorson and Temporary Disneyfication," 64.

41. Walz, "Charlie Thorson and Temporary Disneyfication," 51.

42. *BoxOffice* (26 June 1937): 95. Clampett and Jones did much of the work on these titles.

43. Walz, "Charlie Thorson and Temporary Disneyfication," 228n5.

44. Cohen, "Looney Tunes and Merrie Melodies," 34.

45. Ford, "Warner Brothers," 13.

46. Scheib, "Tex Arcana," 112. Ironically, it was Hugh Harman who expressed fascination with Eisenstein and Pudovkin (Barrier, "Silly Stuff," 7–8). It's hard to look at *Swing Wedding* and think of *Strike!* or *Mother*.

47. *The Isle of Pingo Pongo* (1938), a "banned" cartoon not officially claimed by Warner Bros.
48. Adamson, "You Couldn't Get Chaplin in a Milk Bottle," 10.
49. Kanfer, *Serious Business: The Art and Commerce of Animation in America*, 31.
50. Cohen, "Looney Tunes and Merrie Melodies," 34.
51. Gomery, *HSS*, 29.
52. Loew's came through the Depression better than any of the Big Five, never having to reorganize or declare bankruptcy. Of the Big Five, Loew's owned the fewest theaters, meaning its debt burden was comparatively more manageable. See Gomery's third chapter in *HSS*.
53. Gabler, *Walt Disney*, 146–47.
54. Adamakos, "Ub Iwerks," 27.
55. See Adamakos's article in *Mindrot* for that argument.
56. Solomon, Kanfer, and Maltin all cover various *Flip the Frog* titles well, and all come to the same conclusion.
57. Solomon, *ED*, 86.
58. Iwerks and Kenworthy, *The Hand Behind the Mouse*, 92.
59. Titles like *Stratos-Fear* offer surreal characters and hijinks, a sci-fi setting, and clever bits like hammerhead birds that would reappear in Disney's *Alice in Wonderland*.
60. "Poorest Cartoons I Ever Showed," *MPH* (10 February 1934): 64.
61. Some histories claim that Iwerks was ignored by Disney in this last stretch, that Walt kept Ub close to punish him. Thomas, Mosley, Gabler, and Leslie Iwerks disagree.
62. The first two titles were done using two-strip Technicolor and featured the older design of Bosko.
63. *MPH* (19 March 1938): 6.
64. Solomon, *ED*, 108.
65. On the same page, one reviewer gave a hearty thumbs up, while another called the Christmas cartoon "terrible." *MPH* (1 April 1939): 68.
66. Gomery, *HSS*, 98.
67. Gomery, *HSS*, 98.
68. The latter title features the exploding piano key/note gag seen in later Warner Bros. cartoons.
69. In another cartoon, *Pals* (or *Christmas Night*), one of the hobos the Little King brings home has a large NRA tattoo on his chest.
70. Klein, "Cartooning Down Broadway," 62.
71. Bradley, 98.
72. Bendazzi, *Cartoons*, 87.
73. Solomon, *ED*, 90.
74. Adamson, *The Walter Lantz Story*, 106–7.
75. Gomery, *HSS*, 159.
76. The Mickey pictures were being states'-righted by Disney "through independent exchanges" (Crafton, *The Talkies*, 393).
77. Ownership of these theater chains had burdened the Big Five across the Depression, forcing reorganizations, sales of assets, and bankruptcies. See Gomery's *HSS*.

78. Crafton, *The Talkies*, 397.

CHAPTER 6

1. This somewhat disturbing scene might be unfamiliar if you've seen only the scrubbed version of *Steamboat Willie* playing on a loop at Disneyland's Main Street Cinema.

2. From Wells's *Animation and America*, 45.

3. Baker, "Max and Dave Fleischer," 27.

4. Red Seal owned more than fifty theaters, none of them premier sites.

5. *FD* (8 May 1930): 7.

6. Pointer, *The Art and Inventions of Max Fleischer*, 83.

7. This was not the last document signed between the Fleischers and Paramount. Another significant agreement would see to the move to Miami in 1938, with funding provided by the studio. A final, surprise contract, dated 29 May 1941, would demand everything—all films, patents, ownerships, and control—if the Fleischers wanted to avoid missing payroll and entering bankruptcy. Max will be truly over a barrel by then.

8. Langer, "Max and Dave," 48.

9. Betty and Bimbo would change appearance and voice across these early cartoons, meaning model sheets were at best suggestions; Betty's look and sound depended on who supervised production of the cartoon.

10. *FD* (10 January 1932): 10.

11. Kanfer, *Serious Business*, 56.

12. Klein, *SM*, 70–73.

13. Fox, "Felix Remembered," 48.

14. "The Hollywood Scene," *MPH* (9 June 1934): 33.

15. Max had made a preemptive strike—in 1932, he inserted notices into the trade journals, threatening legal action if any Betty Boop clones appeared.

16. Balio, *United Artists* volume 1, 87.

17. Kanfer, *Serious Business*, 83.

18. Almost 8,000 theaters closed between 1929 and 1932 (Eyman, *20th Century-Fox*, 64).

19. Fleischer, *Out of the Inkwell*, 73.

20. Culhane, *Talking Animals*, 36.

21. Arthur Mann, "Mickey Mouse's Financial Career," 719.

22. Max Fleischer in a letter to Culhane, reprinted in *Talking Animals and Other People*, 62.

23. Culhane, *Talking Animals and Other People*, 52.

24. Culhane, *Talking Animals and Other People*, 54.

25. Eyman, *20th Century-Fox*, 64.

26. See Richard Fleischer's assessment of the Code's effect in *Out of the Inkwell*, 103–4.

27. Solomon, *ED*, 77.

28. Agee, "Comedy's Greatest Era," 74.

29. Schickel, *DV*, 163.

30. *Hunky and Spunky* received an Oscar nod in 1938 but lost to Disney's *Ferdinand the Bull*.

31. Produced in Cinecolor, two-strip, and then three-strip Technicolor.

32. Klein, *SM*, 82–83.

33. Klein, *SM*, 83; Maltin, *OMM*, 114.

34. Blackbeard, "The First (Arf, Arf) Superhero of Them All," 100.

35. Fleischer, *Out of the Inkwell*, 55. The deal with King Features Syndicate was one-sided—merchandising rights stayed with King Features Syndicate, and, after ten years, all prints were to be destroyed (54–55).

36. A year later, King Features Syndicate approached Disney with a lucrative Mickey Mouse comic-strip offer (Schickel, *DV*, 163).

37. Deneroff, "Thin Black Line," 5.

38. Merritt and Merritt, "Mythic Mouse," 59.

39. The device was not officially named in its September 1936 patent application.

40. Telotte discusses all three processes in "Ub Iwerks' (Multi)Plain Cinema," 16.

41. "Multiplane Camera for Pinocchio," *International Photographer* (December 1939): 4–5.

42. See Fleischer's *Out of the Inkwell*, chapter 13.

43. See Harvey Deneroff's fine work in this area.

44. Kanfer, *Serious Business*, 98.

45. Kanfer, *Serious Business*, 98.

46. Deneroff, "We Can't Get Much Spinach," 3.

47. Deneroff, *Popeye the Union Man*, 171–72.

48. Adolph Zukor told Max "no" on more than one occasion, allegedly (Fleischer, *Out of the Inkwell*, 93–94). Solomon disagrees, saying "there is no evidence that Max and Dave had any interest in undertaking such enormous projects" (*ED*, 80).

49. Pointer, *The Art and Inventions of Max Fleischer*, 171.

50. See Fleischer's *Out of the Inkwell*, chapter 15.

51. Fleischer, *Out of the Inkwell*, 96.

52. Kanfer, *Serious Business*, 110.

53. Culhane, *Talking Animals and Other People*, 204.

54. Kanfer, *Serious Business*, 112.

55. *Gulliver's Travels* cost about half of what *Snow White* cost but made almost two-thirds less in rentals and certainly didn't generate the scores of millions in merchandising and licensing royalties that *Snow White* enjoyed.

56. The purposely Capra-esque title didn't help matters; Solomon, *ED*, 84–85.

57. *Harrison's Reports* (13 December 1941): 199.

58. *Time* (23 February 1942).

59. Baker, "Max and Dave Fleischer," 35.

60. From a "Critical Summary" appended to a review of Fleischers' *Car-Tune Portrait*, *World Film News* (December 1937): 30.

61. Solomon, *ED*, 43.

62. Erwin Panofsky, "Style and Medium," 23.

63. *Motion Picture Daily* (8 February 1936): 4.

64. Mark Dowling, "Three Little Pigs," *Motion Picture* (January 1934): 52–53, 80.

65. Kaufman, "*Three Little Pigs*—Big Little Picture," 9.

66. Watch Fleischers' *Tree Saps* (1931) for borrowing *from* Fleischer *by* Disney, specifically the recognizable tornado—Grim Natwick and Ted Sears here animating for Fleischer.

67. See Smith's "Beginnings of the Disney Multiplane Camera," 39.

68. In 1934, one-third of Technicolor's business was Disney.

69. Neupert, "A Studio Built of Bricks: Disney and Technicolor," 36. There was collateral damage here. Ted Eshbaugh completed an entire short film—*The Wizard of Oz*—in bright three-strip Technicolor in 1933 and could not distribute it in color after the Disney-Technicolor deal.

70. Schickel, *DV*, 151. The Silly Symphonies titles cost about $50,000 each, meaning that, after a first year of distribution, they hadn't paid for themselves (*DV*, 150–51).

71. Hamonic, "Disney Is the Tiffany's," 34–35; Schickel, *DV*, 146–48; Barrier, *HC*, 94–95.

72. Thomas, *Walt Disney*, 115.

73. Schickel, *DV*, 149.

74. *Variety* (19 July 1932): 45.

75. Theisen, "The History of the Animated Cartoon," 248.

76. Barrier, *HC*, 79.

77. Culhane, *Talking Animals and Other People*, 218.

78. Culhane, *Talking Animals and Other People*, 218.

79. Maltin, *OMM*, 38; Schickel, *DV*, 147–48; Klein, *SM*, 156–57.

80. Schickel, *DV*, 148. Schickel and others credit Smith; Culhane thinks it might have been Ted Sears on the Fleischer film *Swing, You Sinners* (*Talking Animals and Other People*, 36).

81. In a moribund state due to its famous founders' spotty production schedules, United Artists needed Disney in a big way and benefited from the relationship (Balio, *United Artists*, 135–36).

82. Schickel, *DV*, 150.

83. Merritt and Merritt, "Mythic Mouse," 67; see also Culhane's *Talking Animals and Other People*, 94–107, and Gabler, *Walt Disney*, 427.

84. James Cunningham, "Asides and Interludes," *MPH* (21 October 1933): 23.

85. Kanfer, *Serious Business*, 83; Mosley, *Disney's World*, 139–40.

86. Klein, *SM*, 137.

87. Schickel, *DV*, 154–55; see also Sklar, *Movie-Made America*, 204.

88. Robson, *The Film Answers Back*, 262 (italics added).

89. Bragdon, "Mickey Mouse and What He Means," 43.

90. Thomas, *Walt Disney*, 114.

91. Barrier, "Building a Better Mouse," 11.

92. *The New York State Exhibitor* (25 August 1933): 58.

93. Klein, *SM*, 104; see also his chapter 9, "How Money Talks."

94. Klein, *SM*, 122.

95. See Klein's *Seven Minutes*, chapters 9–11, for much more on this transition.

96. "Full" animation might include realistic color, animating at least on the two's, naturalistic backgrounds, and active, personality-based characters. Each "improvement" added costs to the picture (Klein, *SM*, 95–104).
97. Disney said *Three Little Pigs* wasn't a huge moneymaker; he had to keep paying for prints as demand increased and older prints wore out.
98. Klein, *SM*, 106.
99. Mullen, "Master of Cartoons," 11.
100. Gabler, *Walt Disney*, 257–58.
101. Gabler, *Walt Disney*, 258.
102. This is credited to artist Joe Grant (Gabler, *Walt Disney*, 218).
103. Gabler, *Walt Disney*, 218; Thomas, *Walt Disney*, 130.
104. Barrier, "Building a Better Mouse," 16.
105. Gabler, *Walt Disney*, 257–58.
106. Disney had been talking with United Artists about a potential new contract as late as January 1936, with United Artists demanding all TV rights; Walt refused (Gabler, *Walt Disney*, 259–60).
107. Gabler, *Walt Disney*, 260.
108. Allan, "50 Years of Snow White," 158.
109. Solomon, *ED*, 62.
110. Culhane, *Talking Animals and Other People*, 179.
111. *BoxOffice* (19 June 1937): 30.
112. Klein, *SM*, 141–43.
113. Klein, *SM*, 142.
114. Klein, *SM*, 144. A "cult of the *line*" would later characterize UPA's work.
115. The Lynch-Paramount theater circuit in Florida had booked *Snow White*, hoping for a long, profitable run (*MPH* [29 January 1938]: 23). *Snow White* was still showing in the Miami area when the Fleischers broke ground for the new studio.
116. *MPH* (29 January 1938): 22.
117. Rising to $7.70 during the film's run at the Music Hall (*MPH* [12 February 1938]: 13).
118. Barrier, "Building a Better Mouse," 15.
119. Also, *Peter Pan, Cinderella*, and *The Wind in the Willows* (Holliss and Sibley, *The Disney Studio Story*, 33).
120. In the earliest stages, Stokowski wanted a new character created for the short; Walt said it would be Mickey or there would be no film. Roy didn't like the cartoon or Stokowski (Mosley, *Disney's World*, 174).
121. *MPH* (10 August 1935): 10.
122. Feild, *The Art of Walt Disney*, 79.
123. *BoxOffice* (13 April 1940): 13.
124. A new deal would happen, and the Disney-RKO alliance continued until RKO began to fall to pieces thanks to Howard Hughes and *United States v. Paramount Pictures, Inc.*
125. "Lightning War," *MPH* (18 May 1940): 18.
126. Quoted in Shale, *Donald Duck Joins Up*, 20.

127. Holliss and Sibley, *The Disney Studio Story*, 34.

128. Finch, *The Art of Walt Disney*, 199.

129. Mosley, *Disney's World*, 177–79.

130. Kanfer, *Serious Business*, 119.

131. Schickel, *DV*, 232.

132. Mosley, *Disney's World*, 179.

133. Mosley, *Disney's World*, 180–81.

134. Schickel, *DV*, 234.

135. *MPD* (9 February 1940): 12.

136. Thomas, *Walt Disney*, 151.

137. Barrier, *HC*, 272.

138. *BoxOffice* (28 December 1940): 11; Barrier, *HC*, 272–73.

139. *Gone With the Wind* was still on 150 screens and bringing in just under $2 million per week.

140. Gabler, *Walt Disney*, 352–53; also, Iwerks's *Walt Disney's Ultimate Inventor*, 54.

141. Thomas, *Walt Disney*, 153.

142. Finch, *Art of Walt Disney*, 230.

143. Barrier, "Building a Better Mouse," 17.

144. Even Chaplin had succumbed to the sound revolution by the time of 1940's *The Great Dictator*.

145. Or "non-figurative"; Walt allegedly didn't like "abstract" or "abstraction" (Gabler, *Walt Disney*, 316).

146. Solomon, *ED*, 67; Finch, *Art of Walt Disney*, 231.

147. Solomon, *ED*, 67; Gabler, *Walt Disney*, 338.

148. Holliss and Sibley, *The Disney Studio Story*, 40.

149. Finch, *Art of Walt Disney*, 254.

150. From the *New York Herald Tribune*, *The Nation*, and *Look*, respectively.

151. Wells, *Animation and America*, 48.

152. Rogers, "Remaking the B Film 1940s Hollywood," 142–43.

CHAPTER 7

1. Barrier, "Building a Better Mouse," 20.

2. Maltin, *OMM*, 215–16.

3. *Exhibitor* (12 January 1944): 1439.

4. Scheib, "Tex Arcana: The Cartoons of Tex Avery," 112.

5. Hamonic, *Terrytoons*, 206.

6. Rosenbaum, "Dream Masters II," 71.

7. Weinman, *Anvils, Mallets and Dynamite*, 48–49.

8. Hoberman, "Vulgar Modernism," 73.

9. Scheib, "Tex Arcana: The Cartoons of Tex Avery," 110.

10. Ford, "Warner Brothers: Focus on a Studio," 11–12.

11. Gomery, "Disney's Business History," 74.

12. "Walt Disney Reports," *BoxOffice* (28 December 1940): 11.

13. Solomon, *ED*, 71.

14. Ghez, *Walt's People 9*, 90n50.

15. Shale, *Donald Duck Joins Up*, 20.

16. On this same day across the country, Max Fleischer was signing the new contract that would eventually see him out the door of his own studio.

17. Schickel, *DV*, 272; Shale, *Donald Duck Joins Up*, 86–87.

18. Shale, *Donald Duck Joins Up*, 96. Warner Bros. produced 114 short-subject titles from 1941 to 1945 (96).

19. There is little to remark on Terry across the war: "We rarely get a good Terrytoon" (*MPH* [31 October 1942]: 60). There were a few mentionables—*All Out for V*, *Shipyard Symphony*, and some Gandy and Sourpuss cartoons.

20. Shull and Wilt, *Doing Their Bit*, 47.

21. Shull and Wilt, *Doing Their Bit*, 41–44.

22. *BSM* (30 December 1945): 49.

23. *BSM* (30 December 1945): 40.

24. "A Report on the Disney War Effort," in *Film Daily Yearbook* (1942): 201.

25. Culhane, *Talking Animals and Other People*, 274–77.

26. Shale, *Donald Duck Joins Up*, 38.

27. "Disney Values," *The Exhibitor* (29 December 1943): 29.

28. "*The New Spirit*," *STR* (31 January 1942): 24.

29. Shale, *Donald Duck Joins Up*, 15–16.

30. These can be viewed at the National Film Board of Canada's website: https://www.nfb.ca/.

31. Holliss and Sibley, *The Disney Studio Story*, 46–47.

32. Shale, *Donald Duck Joins Up*, 24.

33. Gomery, "Disney's Business History," 74 (italics added).

34. *STR* (5 December 1942): 10.

35. Shale, *Donald Duck Joins Up*, 36.

36. Gabler, *Walt Disney*, 334.

37. Barrier, *HC*, 307.

38. See Maltin for a more complete list (*OMM*, 218).

39. Culhane, *Talking Animals and Other People*, 234.

40. Also used on the bomber in *Blitz Wolf*. The B-19 heavy bomber was much talked about and tested during the war but was never adopted for service.

41. Maltin, *OMM*, 218–19.

42. *Time* (29 December 1942).

43. See the elephants in Tyer and John Foster's *Circus Capers* (1930), for example.

44. Wilmington, "Dumbo," 79. Reprinted in *AAC*, 76–81.

45. Quoted in Schickel, *DV*, 266.

46. Arnold, *Animation and American Imagination*, 108.

47. Maltin, *OMM*, 102.

48. *Variety* (22 April 1942): 20.

49. *Harrison's Reports* (13 December 1941): 199.

50. Shull and Wilt, *Doing Their Bit*, 68.

51. Barrier, *HC*, 501.

52. Shull and Wilt, *Doing Their Bit*, 31.
53. Shull and Wilt, *Doing Their Bit*, 33.
54. Barrier, *HC*, 409.
55. *STR* (26 December 1942): 32–33.
56. Barrier, *HC*, 419.
57. Weinman, *Anvils, Mallets and Dynamite*, 26.
58. Barrier, *HC*, 404–5.
59. *The Exhibitor* (20 January 1943): 19.
60. Shull and Wilt, *Doing Their Bit*, 41.
61. Shull and Wilt, *Doing Their Bit*, 45.
62. Barrier, *HC*, 318.
63. Barrier, "Building a Better Mouse," 16.
64. Erwin Panofsky, "Style and Medium," 146.
65. From Farber's review of the "entirely unpleasant" *Bambi*, *New Republic* (June 1942).
66. "*Bambi*," *Film Bulletin* (1 June 1942): 9.
67. Quoted in *Film Bulletin* (24 August 1942): 25.
68. From Farber's *NR* review (1942).
69. Zipes, *Oxford Companion to Fairy Tales*, 133.
70. Barrier's "Building a Better Mouse," 16; the quote is from animator Eric Larson (Barrier, *HC*, 111).
71. Barrier, *HC*, 314.
72. *MPD* (14 May 1943): 3.
73. Beck and Friedwald, *Looney Tunes and Merrie Melodies*, 133–34.
74. Barrier, *HC*, 444.
75. Beck and Friedwald, *Looney Tunes and Merrie Melodies*, 140.
76. *MPH* (3 July 1943): 49.
77. Schickel, *DV*, 272.
78. Shale, *Donald Duck Joins Up*, 48–49.
79. "Film Is a Weapon," *BSM* (30 December 1945): 78.
80. "Front-Line Pacific Troops," *The Independent* (1 April 1944): 26.
81. "Gen. Osborn Reports," *The Exhibitor* (29 March 1944): 11.
82. Hamonic, *Terrytoons*, 199.
83. Ghez, *Walt's People 2*, 55. UFA was a German film studio and shorthand for an Expressionistic film "style."
84. This "phoney war" talk dealt with the British being seen as Chicken Littles, watching Nazi Germany and crying that the sky was falling.
85. As the baby is being tickled, one of his legs disappears for a few frames—it's there, then gone, and then it returns. As individual cels were photographed, one on top of the other, the camera operator missed a level for a few exposures. They did not reshoot the sequence.
86. *STR* (1 May 1943): 32.
87. Shale, *Donald Duck Joins Up*, 61.
88. *STR* (17 October 1942): 4.
89. Shull and Wilt, *Doing Their Bit*, 45.

90. Shale, *Donald Duck Joins Up*, 63.

91. "May Lengthen *Saludos*," *Variety* (25 November 1942): 5.

92. McGilligan's "Robert Clampett," reprinted in Peary, *AAC*, 152.

93. Schneider, *That's All Folks!*, 71.

94. Putterman, "A Short Critical History," 32–33.

95. Schneider, *That's All Folks!*, 71, 73–74.

96. Weinman, *Anvils, Mallets and Dynamite*, 109.

97. Schneider, *That's All Folks!*, 68

98. Beck and Friedwald, *Looney Tunes and Merrie Melodies*, introduction.

99. Solomon, *ED*, 153.

100. "War Demands," *FD* (21 April 1943): 2.

101. "WB Shorts Lineup," *The Exhibitor* (21 July 1943): 26.

102. Scheib, "Tex Arcana: The Cartoons of Tex Avery," 114.

103. Adamson, *Tex Avery: King of Cartoons*, 68.

104. Lindvall and Melton, "Towards a Post-Modern Animated Discourse," 204.

105. Lindvall and Melton, "Towards a Post-Modern Animated Discourse," 204–5.

106. Shale, *Donald Duck Joins Up*, 77.

107. "Disney Reports," *Variety* (11 January 1944): 1.

108. According to Hamonic, Terry sent family members and employees to theaters to take copious notes on competing cartoons (*Terrytoons*, 220).

109. *MPH* (11 September 1943): 40.

110. Much like *Underdog* twenty-two years later.

111. Shull and Wilt, *Doing Their Bit*, 142.

112. Shull and Wilt, *Doing Their Bit*, 52. An image in *Carmen's Veranda* (1944) of a *hippo* stuffed into a red dress singing an aria alongside her similarly attired *feline* daughter is at least odd.

113. Solomon, *ED*, 138–39.

114. "Give This Little Girl," *STR* (9 October 1943): 27.

115. *The Exhibitor* (14 March 1945): 31.

116. *MPH* (3 July 1943): 49.

117. Beck, *The 50 Greatest Cartoons*, 57.

118. Scott, *The Moose That Roared*, 33–35.

119. Hanna et al., *A Cast of Friends*, 56.

120. For each human puppet character, there were dozens of carved, painted heads ready to switch out, so a character could talk, register surprise, smile, or even blink.

121. *MPH* (31 October 1942): 60.

122. *Time* (13 July 1942).

123. All three were members of the Dewey reelection committee in Hollywood.

124. "Pro-Roosevelt Cartoon," *MPH* (30 September 1944): 16.

125. "*Brotherhood of Man*," *NBR Magazine* (May 1946): 19.

126. Hoberman, "Vulgar Modernism," 72.

127. From John Morreall, *Taking Laughter Seriously* (Albany: SUNY, 1983), 39.

128. "A film by an Antonioni, a Truffaut, a Resnais, even a Stanley Kubrick, owes nothing to anything but the history of the cinema" (Schickel, *DV*, 278).

129. *Photoplay* January–June 1945: 116.
130. Shale, *Donald Duck Joins Up*, 98.
131. "*The Three Caballeros*," *Harrison's Reports* (16 December 1944): 202.
132. Quoted in Shale, *Donald Duck Joins Up*, 106.
133. Deming, "The Artlessness of Walt Disney," 226.
134. Deming, "The Artlessness of Walt Disney," 226.
135. Gabler, *Walt Disney*, 409–10.
136. As of October 1944 (Gabler, *Walt Disney*, 411n).

CHAPTER 8

1. *STR* (6 January 1945): 46.
2. As of January 1945, 81 percent of Disney's market comprised the United States, Canada, and England (*FD* [19 January 1945]: 2).
3. "Music and Color," *MPH* (4 August 1945): 29.
4. "Music and Color," *MPH* (4 August 1945): 29.
5. "Schlesinger," *FD* (21 June 1944).
6. Warner Bros. bought Schlesinger's stake in the studio and put Edward Selzer in charge.
7. Auden's 1948 poem *and* the state of the American mind.
8. "*Brotherhood of Man* and Re-Orientation," *Educational Screen* (March 1947): 152.
9. Thomas, *Walt Disney*, 205.
10. *STR* (21 September 1946): 31.
11. *Variety* (4 December 1946): 25.
12. Maltin, *The Disney Films*, 77–78.
13. Solomon, *ED*, 172.
14. Maltin, *The Disney Films*, 78.
15. The small town here was Loveland, Ohio (*MPH* [10 May 1947]: 49).
16. *BoxOffice* (24 May 1947): 20.
17. "The New Pictures," *Time* (18 November 1946).
18. *FD* (3 December 1946): 3.
19. *MPH* (31 May 1947): 45.
20. *MPH* (19 July 1947): 46.
21. Lardner was one of the blacklisted Hollywood Ten.
22. "*Song of the South*," *Syracuse Post Standard* (21 November 1986): 49.
23. Jasper's design is like the last versions of Bosko as well as Black characters in Messmer's Felix cartoons, all connected to the Black child stereotypes found in older comic panels.
24. Eyman, *20th Century-Fox*, 170.
25. *STR* (9 February 1946): 42.
26. Art direction by Bernice Polifka is striking and suggests a UPA aesthetic. One exhibitor summed it up best after projecting a film that had taken hours, sweat, thought, and care: "A cute little Technicolor short" (*MPH* [6 July 1946]: 61).
27. "Stuffed Duck," *Time* (12 August 1946); also, *Film Bulletin* (5 August 1946): 38.
28. Schickel, *DV*, 281–83.

29. "Disney Profits Off," *STR* (7 December 1946): 12.

30. See Klein's *Seven Minutes.*

31. Gabler, *Walt Disney*, 425.

32. Thomas, *Walt Disney*, 206–7; Farber's essay reprinted in the Pearys' *AAC*, 90–91.

33. Schickel, *DV*, 292.

34. "True-Life Adventures" would win eight Academy Awards.

35. Maltin, *The Disney Films*, 82.

36. *NBR Magazine* (June–July 1946): 9–11.

37. *BoxOffice* (22 May 1948): 13.

38. *Time* (7 June 1948).

39. *Time* (20 October 1947 and 6 May 1946).

40. Gabler, *Walt Disney*, 425.

41. *MPE* (30 October 1957), 4399–400.

42. Schickel, *DV*, 277.

43. Most studios announced increases in short-subject releases for 1947–1948, including reissues (*BoxOffice* [15 November 1947]: 26).

44. *BoxOffice* (24 May 1947): 26.

45. *Variety* (9 June 1948): 4.

46. "Cartoon-Making," *Variety* (28 May 1947): 6.

47. *MPH* (31 May 1947): 46.

48. Oil Can Harry, like Avery's Wolf, drives a stretched getaway car and flees across the country, like the Wolf running from Droopy.

49. On her way to the sawmill, floating on the log, she makes her way down a flume and into the mill, the log bending as the flume bends. This bending gag must've been a particular favorite of Terry's—it appears many times across the years.

50. In other titles from this series, including *Triple Trouble*, Pearl takes a much more active role, physically assaulting Oil Can Harry with everything she can throw.

51. "Lantz Seeks Cost," *FD* (19 February 1948): 1, 4.

52. Hanssen, "Vertical Integration during the Hollywood Studio Era," 519.

53. Dick, *Engulfed*, 39–41.

54. Avery is an uncredited coproducer.

55. *Exhibitor* (30 August 1950): 2915.

56. After two years, the film was to be made available to educators, which is why the film returned to the headlines in 1950.

57. *MPH* (3 July 1948): 4227; *MPH* (11 December 1948): 38.

58. *The Exhibitor* (27 April 1949): 2608.

59. "Along the Rialto," *FD* (2 July 1948): 8.

60. Schickel, *DV*, 293. Full-page ads for the film announced 1950 as "the Cinderella year."

61. Ghez, *Walt's People 2*, 208.

62. Beck, *AMG*, 55.

63. "Shadow Stage," *Photoplay* (February 1950): 23.

64. "*Cinderella*," *NYT* (26 February 1950): x1.

65. Schickel, *DV*, 293.

66. Gabler, *Walt Disney*, 478.

67. *MPD* (16 January 1951): 6.

68. Solomon, *ED*, 188.

69. Ghez, *Walt's People 1*, 104.

CHAPTER 9

1. Abraham, *When Magoo Flew*, 88.

2. Panofsky, "Style and Medium," 23n1.

3. Bragdon championed Disney of the early 1930s and would have frowned at *Snow White* ("Mickey Mouse and What He Means," 42).

4. Sagar, "The UPA Cartoons," 37.

5. Hajdu, *The Ten-Cent Plague*, 10, 12.

6. Before UPA officially existed, the principals struggled to find footing in the commercial cartoon world—when Hubley and pals stooped to conquer, the results were mixed. Columbia title *Professor Small and Mr. Tall*, offering a mismatched comedy duo and gags aplenty, is surprisingly lifeless. As a test to suss out UPA's Mutt and Jeff or Heckle and Jeckle, it failed.

7. Hajdu, *The Ten-Cent Plague*, 21.

8. They made *Brotherhood of Man* and *Flight Safety* films, planned a continuing series of shorts based on Juliet Lowell's work, and hinted at a feature ("Industrial Film," *AC* [August 1945]: 284).

9. Knight, "The New Look in Cartooning," 30.

10. The look of *Hell-Bent for Election* would be borrowed for a 1949 Timken Company commercial cartoon, *Big Tim*. UPA artists hoped that commercial, union, and government work, *not* continuing character cartoons, could keep the company afloat.

11. For other proto-UPA efforts, see Barrier, *HC*, 380–82.

12. Scott, *The Moose That Roared*, 36.

13. Klein, *SM*, 229.

14. Crafton, *BM*, 232.

15. Crafton, *BM*, 235.

16. Klein, *SM*, 231.

17. Much like the state-funded National Film Board in Canada.

18. From Hubley and Schwartz, "Animation Learns," 360.

19. See Bashara's *Cartoon Vision*, 2019.

20. Abraham, *When Magoo Flew*, 44–48.

21. Established by exiles Hilberman and Schwartz in fall 1946 (*MPD* [4 October 1946]: 6).

22. Hubley had worked for Columbia under directors like Tashlin in the early war years.

23. *The Poky Little Puppy*, *The Fire Engine Book*, and *The Tawny Scrawny Lion*, among others. Klein discusses UPA's "cult of the line" in *SM*, 228.

24. For more on this discussion, see Klein, *SM*, 238.

25. Oeri, "UPA," 471–72.

26. Abraham, *When Magoo Flew*, 82. This is what Chuck Jones would derisively describe as the "wallpaper designs" of UPA cartoons. Pete Burness mentioned that background designs came from many sources, including "colored papers, textured and patterned papers, even wallpaper samples" (Rieder, "Memories of Mr. Magoo," 19).

27. Abraham, *When Magoo Flew*, 36.

28. Klein, *SM*, 240.

29. By 1958, animators Gene Deitch, Ernest Pintoff, and then Hubley (as an independent) were garnering these nominations, with cartoons that looked and sounded like the work of UPA.

30. Panofsky, "Style and Medium," 23n1.

31. By the late 1950s, short cartoons cost upward of $70,000, even for non-Disney studios—*double* their cost in 1948 (*Newsweek* [July 1958]).

32. Stocker, "Magnificent Magoo," 129.

33. Hubley and Schwartz, "Animation Learns a New Language," 363.

34. With that renewal, Columbia demanded no artsy, one-off cartoons created without approval—it was to be Magoo cartoons. See the works of Abraham, Barrier, and Bashara for more.

35. Like the slightly earlier Tele-Comics, these were little more than storyboards with narration, but the mold was cast for cartoons on TV.

36. From the testimony of Disney in 1947 and Bernice Fleury in 1951 (Abraham, 128); see also Cohen's "Toontown's Reds," passim, and *Forbidden Animation*, 155–91.

37. Dick, *Columbia Pictures*, 16.

38. *Hollywood Reporter* ran a long series of attacks in this arena beginning in 1946. See, for instance, "Studios Start Purging Staffs," *HR* (28 November 1947).

39. Abraham, *When Magoo Flew*, 126–27.

40. Klein, *SM*, 233.

41. Abraham, *When Magoo Flew*, 49. See also Kepes's mentions in Barrier's *HC*, Amidi's *Cartoon Modern*, and Bottini's dissertation *UPA: Redesigning Animation* (2016).

42. Hubley would use the term "highbrow" when answering questions about the project and the failed funding search (*Variety* [20 February 1952]: 4).

43. "UPA Cartoonery," *Variety* (25 June 1952): 18.

44. In 1952, *Rooty* could command just $200 per week at the Astor, with that amount dropping for the next four weeks and again for the next four weeks. UPA had to agree to a full sixteen weeks to secure this theater (*Variety* [25 June 1952]: 4, 18).

45. Fisher, "Two Premieres," 40–41.

46. See Crowther's "McBoing Boing, Magoo and Bosustow," *NYT* (21 December 1952): 14–15, 23; see also Stocker's "Magnificent Magoo," *American Mercury* 86.131 (April 1958). Since Bosustow was giving the studio's interviews, his name was appearing again and again in relation to UPA's successes—which riled his artists.

47. Fisher, "Two Premieres," 41.

48. Abraham, *When Magoo Flew*, 147.

49. Fisher, "Two Premieres," 40–41.

50. Fox, "Felix Remembered," 48. UPA's designs are akin to the "utter simplicity" of *most* Felix-era animators and styles (Barré, Carlson, Powers), when pen and ink ruled the frame.

51. Crafton outlines these types in *BM*, 274–75.

52. "Cinema: Boing!" *Time* (5 February 1951); Hine, "McBoing Boing and Magoo," 12.

53. "The Screen: Magoo on Magic Carpet," *NYT* (24 December 1959): 13.

54. See Disney's stylized *Toot, Whistle, Plunk and Boom* (1953) and *Pigs Is Pigs* (1954).

55. Quoted in Curtis's "In Betweening," 33.

56. Quoted in Curtis's "In Betweening," 33.

Chapter 10

1. Eyman, *20th Century-Fox*, 182.

2. Leuchtenberg, *A Troubled Feast*, 65–67; Halberstam, *The Fifties*, 195; Hamonic, *Terrytoons*, 255.

3. Film attendance peaked at 65 percent in 1930 (Pautz, "The Decline in Average Weekly Cinema Attendance," 1).

4. Verdict: "Unemployment was the only tangible loss involved in Paramount's shutdown. No one seemed to miss the cartoons. They had made no impact on audiences, and they didn't mean very much to their creators either" (Maltin, *OMM*, 271–76).

5. Thompson, "Meep Meep," 131.

6. Thompson, "Meep Meep," 131.

7. Dick, *Engulfed*, 40–41.

8. "The Shorts Parade," *MPE* (7 December 1960): 25.

9. "The Shorts Parade," *MPE* (7 December 1960): 19.

10. Both men had Warner Bros. backgrounds: David DePatie had been a producer, and Friz Freleng had animated and directed cartoons for three decades.

11. Casper, *Postwar Hollywood*, 74–75.

12. *Variety* (11 January 1956): 26.

13. Klein, *SM*, 209–10.

14. Klein, *SM*, 209.

15. Including Pixar artists, "'all Chuck Jones and violent *Tom and Jerry* cartoon fans'" (Price, *The Pixar Touch*, 108).

16. Perlmutter sets this idea up in *America Toons In*, chapter 3.

17. *Photoplay* (January–June 1960): 79.

18. *Variety* (9 February 1949): 30.

19. Pautz, "The Decline in Average Weekly Cinema Attendance," appendix.

20. Solomon, *ED*, 159.

21. Pratley, "Cartoons in Decay," 35.

22. Barrier, *HC*, 533.

23. The development of 3D technology sent the industry into a tizzy. Warner Bros., not wanting to commit to Cinerama or CinemaScope (widescreen processes), opted to wait and embraced 3D technology with *House of Wax*. Warner Bros. announced a three-month shutdown and laid off scores; the animation unit shutdown followed weeks later. Even so, 3D remained a gimmick.

24. Jones's short (reviewed as "a better than average cartoon") was nominated for an Academy Award but lost to Disney's UPA-ish *Toot, Whistle, Plunk and Boom* (*MPE* [1 December 1954]: 4).

25. Fisher, "Two Premieres: Disney & UPA," 40.

26. Fisher, "Two Premieres: Disney & UPA," 40.

27. *BoxOffice Barometer* (30 January 1954): 32.

28. UPA's *Gerald McBoing-Boing's Symphony* finished eighth on the list.

29. "Disney and A.B.C. Sign Contract," *NYT* (3 April 1954): 19.

30. Ironically, for the nearly invisible Fleischers, Paramount Studio money (profits from forced sales of Paramount theater chains through ABC) helped fund the building of Disneyland (Gomery, "Disney's Business History," 76).

31. Disney licensed this widescreen process from 20th Century-Fox, as did MGM and Columbia.

32. Terry admitted his earlier attempts to sell merchandise had "petered out"; when the cartoons appeared on TV, an upswing in consumer interest followed (*Broadcasting Television* [11 April 1955]: 68).

33. "AAP Envisions Nothing But Money," *Variety* (20 March 1957): 30.

34. This process had begun in November 1953 with an agreement between General Mills and *Bill Barker's Cartoon Show*, where Sugar Jets cereal was the sponsor. Later, Kellogg's was a sponsor of *Disneyland*.

35. *Broadcasting Television* (2 January 1956): 44. Disney's TV exploits paid off; UPA's show lasted less than one season.

36. "WOR-TV $100G for Terrytoons," *Variety* (2 May 1956): 28.

37. "Pix-to-TV Scoreboard," *Variety* (11 January 1956): 43.

38. From "Mousetrap," an article appearing in July 1958 *Newsweek*.

39. Adamson, *The Walter Lantz Story*, 191.

40. And wouldn't restart for thirty years, with *Mickey's Christmas Carol*.

41. It would be twenty-seven years before the next theatrical Bugs cartoon appeared.

42. The first Pink Panther cartoon won an Oscar, and the character's appearances in the eponymous movies were often more appreciated than the movie. Warner Bros. would get back into animation in the 1980s.

43. Korkis and Cawley, *Cartoon Confidential*, 46.

44. "Sleeping Beauty," *New York Times* (18 February 1959): 36.

45. Gould, "Animated Film," 140–47.

46. "Disney 'Beauty' Policy Criticized," *Harrison's Reports* (28 February 1959): 36.

47. Barrier, *HC*, 555, 557; Gabler, *Walt Disney*, 558.

48. Dick, *Engulfed*, 60–61. Paramount's feature films in 1957 grossed about $27 million ($1.35 million each) and in 1958 diminished to $23.4 million, or $974,000 each (63). In 1966, Paramount was gobbled up by Gulf + Western.

49. Casper, *Postwar Hollywood*, 43–44.

50. Dick, *Engulfed*, 72–74. Decca Records had merged with Universal a decade earlier. MCA already owned Paramount's pre-1948 library and considered a takeover of that studio as well (75). The "octopus" MCA at this point comprised Universal Pictures,

Revue Productions (TV), Decca Records, and Columbia Savings and Loan (Dick, *City of Dreams*, 163). To avoid monopoly litigation, MCA sold off its talent business.

51. Nominated for an Oscar.

52. "The Shorts Parade," *MPE* (7 December 1960): 21. By 1968, Terrytoons ceased making theatrical cartoons; Viacom sold the assets in 1972.

53. *MPE* (4 December 1963): 16, 18.

54. University of Southern California grad George Lucas was supposed to start an internship at Warner Bros.'s animation studio in 1963; he didn't (Biskind, *Easy Riders*, 37).

55. Barrier, *HC*, 565–67.

56. *NYT* (26 December 1963): 33. These Disney features have become profitable, thanks to subsequent rereleases and home video. Ironically, it's the dozens of live-action films Disney was so invested in that have faded from the popular consciousness.

57. From John Bright's "Disney's Fantasy Empire," *The Nation* (6 March 1967): 299–303.

58. Adamson, *The Walter Lantz Story*, 213.

59. Biskind, *Easy Riders*, 14. Biskind almost completely ignores Disney and animation in general in his deep dive into 1970s Hollywood.

60. Maltin, *The Disney Films*, 218, 255, 262, 264.

61. Solomon, "Will the Real Walt Disney Please Stand Up?" 50.

62. Culhane, "The Men Behind Dastardly and Muttley," 129.

63. *Aristocats* began life as a potential TV special, while *Robin Hood* was assisted by the reuse of material from *Jungle Book*, *Aristocats*, and *Snow White* (Price, *Pixar Touch*, 50–55).

64. From Amidi's "The Hard Lessons of Kwicky Koala," *Cartoon Brew* (18 January 2008).

65. From Michener's "The Revolution in Middle-Class Values," *NYT* (18 August 1968).

66. Shale, *Donald Duck Joins Up*, 10; Bayer, "Happy 40th, Mickey," 59.

67. Leuchtenberg, *A Troubled Feast*, 271.

68. Rosenbaum, "Dream Masters I: Walt Disney," 65.

69. Biskind, *Easy Riders*, 20.

70. Sito, "Disney's *The Fox and the Hound*."

71. Solomon, "Will the Real Walt Disney Please Stand Up?" 51.

72. *The Hobbit* was animated in Japan at Topcraft.

73. Warner Bros. animation had produced and/or distributed original features from as early as 1962, with Chuck Jones's *Gay Purr-ee*, the hybrid *Mr. Limpet* (1964), two Filmation features a decade later, and even Bakshi's *Hey Good Lookin'* in 1982, sandwiched between compilation films, before *Batman: Mask of the Phantasm* in 1993 and *Space Jam* in 1996.

74. Filmation had to "four wall" the film, meaning see to the distribution and advertising itself, since there was no outside studio funding assistance (Beck, *AMG*, 132).

75. Disney had owned the film rights to *The Lord of the Rings* across the 1960s but allowed them to lapse.

76. Bakshi had been part of the Terrytoons operation until 1967.

77. *NYT* (30 April 1972): D1.

78. And, to a lesser extent, Walter Lantz, too.

79. Miller's unenviable job entailed steering the Disney ship away from choppy waters, so there would be no edgy or adult films, little chance taking. In the same year that the boffo hit *Porky's* appeared elsewhere, Miller did allow for the forward-looking and influential *Tron* to be produced, though, and underperform, so this writer gives him credit. See Masters and Stewart for more details on this period.

CHAPTER 11

1. Maltin, *Disney Films*, 284, 338. Both Bluth and Rich would go out of their way to say they were *not* the next Walt, just happily working under his influence.

2. See Turner's "Disney, Using Cash and Claw," *WSJ* (16 May 1994): A1.

3. Janus-like, the creation of the Academy's Best Animated Feature category in 2002 pleased Katzenberg and other lobbyers; it eased anxiety around Hollywood for those *not* keen on a cartoon taking Best Picture; it also kept cartoons safely distinct from "real" movies, at least in the honorifics.

4. From Horn's "Yeow! It's War in Toon Town," *LAT* (1 June 1997): G82.

5. Dick, *Engulfed*, 150.

6. This was the reasoning for sequels to *Bambi*, *Lion King*, and others as direct-to-video projects—the home-video market was lucrative and the risks small. In just the first weeks of the film's availability, more than six million copies of *Lion King 1½* were sold. The eventual drag on Disney's artistic reputation called those decisions into question.

7. This was true when films were distributed as actual prints and remains true now that DCPs (digital cinema packages) are preferred.

8. Stewart, *Disney War*, 55 and 57.

9. *Sleeping Beauty* was the last (animated) box-office disappointment, frankly.

10. Maltin, *The Disney Films*, 272. Ironically, across Katzenberg's tenure as head of *all* production at Disney, the live-action film "disasters" continued to flounder (Taylor, "The Disney Renaissance Didn't Happen Because of Jeffrey Katzenberg," *Collider* (20 May 2020).

11. Eisner, *Work in Progress*, 91.

12. From Stewart's *Disney War*, 38.

13. Masters, *The Keys to the Kingdom*, 141. *Splash* would arrive in March 1984, from Touchstone, and bolster spirits.

14. *Gallavants*, directed by Art Vitello, a former Bakshi animator.

15. Beck, *AMG*, 243. Beck reminds us that *NIMH* had to compete against both a lackluster platformed release schedule and the Spielberg megahit *E.T.*; Disney's highest-grossing film of the year was cult flop *Tron*, at twenty-sixth.

16. With little overhead and fewer charges against the film, the earning of double the production budget would have been encouraging news to Bluth and partners.

17. Another group of younger animators who'd remained after Bluth's departure, including Kroyer and Brad Bird, left not long after (Sito, "Disney's *The Fox and the Hound*").

18. *Black Cauldron* wasn't all bad news—Disney animators employed their first bits of CG animation (Eilonwy's bauble, for example) in a feature, traditionally animated film. This usage would become a common practice moving forward.

19. Stewart, *Disney War*, 70. *Care Bears* was a Canadian-US coproduction that cost twenty-two times less than *Black Cauldron*.

20. For more, see Taylor's *Storming the Magic Kingdom* and Stewart's *Disney War*.

21. Approaching $1.4 billion at the time of publication.

22. Price, *The Pixar Touch*, 192–93.

23. In 2001, the first *Harry Potter* film led the worldwide box office, followed by *Fellowship of the Ring*, then *Monsters, Inc.*, and then *Shrek*.

24. When factoring in marketing and distribution costs, none of these films made money. (A rerelease of *Lady and the Tramp* for Christmas 1986 eclipsed *Great Mouse Detective*.) Still, banking on the success of *Oliver* at the box office, Disney's Peter Schneider announced there would be a new animated film from Disney yearly ("Disney, Sullivan Studios," *LA Times* [17 August 1987]: B9).

25. Ron Miller had bought the book rights in 1980, another good decision from Walt's son-in-law (Masters, *The Keys to the Kingdom*, 218).

26. Katzenberg really pushed this film forward; it is certainly a thread between the new studio and the good old days (Beck, *AMG*, 226–27).

27. "Robin Hood," *NYT* (17 February 1985): H30.

28. "Disney's Endangered Species," *LAT* (2 July 1978): N25.

29. It would be 1998 before Disney released *Black Cauldron* to video (Beck, *AMG*, 37).

30. This success spurred Katzenberg into animation and eventually to DreamWorks, armed with "the growing realization that Disney had a virtual monopoly in animation and that it could be even more profitable than live action" (Stewart, *Disney War*, 90).

31. Earning about 2.5 times what the cult classic *Heavy Metal* managed four years earlier.

32. For which Roy was relieved; a wider audience accepted the Touchstone film thanks to no Disney branding, embracing the mature subject matter—it wasn't automatically "for kids."

33. Domestically, *Oliver* was eighteenth; *Land Before Time* was twentieth. There was personal animus between these two camps—Disney kept *Oliver* in cinemas longer than "the prehistoric *Bambi*" *Land Before Time*, unwilling to surrender box-office bragging rights to Bluth (Beck, *AMG*, 139).

34. Knockoffs also now appeared with regularity—often using the lucrative direct-to-video method, resulting in the kind of VHS tapes bought by your grandmother, thinking she was getting a Disney original only to discover it was a down-market version made on the cheap.

35. By 1997, Universal had made $375 million from home-video sales of *Land Before Time* titles and was in no rush to finance another feature film ("Yeow!" *LAT* [1 June 1997]: G5).

36. Beck, *AMG*, 20. A second, enjoyable *American Tail* was produced in 1991 by Spielberg but without Bluth. It was released against *Beauty and the Beast*. It lost money.

37. Disney had a habit of scheduling releases against other studios' new work, a canny business practice. Ariel would resurface in theaters in 1997, just when Fox and Bluth's *Anastasia* premiered, as did the Disney live-action *Flubber*, as both *Hercules* and *George of the Jungle* slid into discount cinemas (see Eller's "Draw and Fire: Disney Flexes Financial Muscle," *LAT* [10 October 1997]: OCD1).

38. Price, *The Pixar Touch*, 164.

39. Stewart, *Disney War*, 143.

40. From Warner Bros., Hanna-Barbera/Fox, Amblimation/Universal, Miramax, and Touchstone, respectively.

41. Also known as *Arabian Knight*.

42. 1993 was also the year Disney acquired the independent Miramax. This was still a down year—for the first time since arriving, Eisner took no bonus (Masters, *The Keys to the Kingdom*, 299).

43. There are those in the industry who see Katzenberg as more *self*-important, his influence overstated. A mid-1990s financial writer argued differently, saying Katzenberg was "probably 80 percent responsible" for Disney's stock value increases (quoted in Masters's "The Epic Disney Blow-Up").

44. With visual inspiration drawn from *Lawrence of Arabia*, Doré, and Monet, there was little chance that Happy Meal toys were in the offing (LaPorte, *The Men Who Would Be King*, 116).

45. LaPorte, *The Men Who Would Be King*, 193. The much cheaper *Rugrats* movie from Paramount outperformed *Prince of Egypt* (Masters, *The Keys to the Kingdom*, 404). Hollywood pundits noted that even combining *Antz*, *Prince of Egypt*, and *The Road to El Dorado* didn't match *Lion King*'s box-office success (see Eller and Bates's *LAT* article, 28 April 2000).

46. DreamWorks considered Blue Sky and Rhythm & Hues before settling on PDI (a friendly Pixar competitor), purchasing 40 percent of the firm in spring 1996 (Price, *The Pixar Touch*, 170).

47. Price, *The Pixar Touch*, 173.

48. Bartok was a popular side character from *Anastasia*; Miller, in Beck's *AMG*, 218.

49. It was the billion-dollar success of *Lion King* that spurred new animation endeavors from Warner Bros. (*Space Jam*), Fox (*Anastasia*), and even Turner Pictures (*The Pagemaster*) (LaPorte, *The Men Who Would Be King*, 12).

50. In the mid-1970s, on the way to forming what would become Pixar, founder Ed Catmull had created his first texture map—a Mickey Mouse projection on a moving surface. Catmull and pals worked so "they could be Disney" (Price, *The Pixar Touch*, 15, 27).

51. *Toy Story 2* had been conceived as a direct-to-video production, thanks to tight-fisted studio chief Joe Roth and the runaway success of *The Return of Jafar* (a VHS release). A release to theaters made more sense, given the production cost (Price, *The Pixar Touch*, 175–79).

52. The films were still technically making a profit, though sighs of relief could likely be heard when merchandising and home-video profits began to roll in.

53. When purchased, it became PDI/DreamWorks and was active until 2015.

54. LaPorte, *The Men Who Would Be King*, 119; "good or not" voiced by Pam Kerwin of Pixar (Price, *The Pixar Touch*, 172).

55. LaPorte, *The Men Who Would Be King*, 348.

56. Stewart, *Disney War*, 233. Katzenberg failed at this attempt but would ultimately come away with much more from Disney. He would fight for and win a more than quarter-billion-dollar settlement based on a promised 2 percent payment on Disney projects he'd guided, a golden parachute Eisner had denied existed.

57. Media reports pegged the *Treasure Planet* write-down at about $75 million, taken even before the film could test its legs in wide release. *Treasure Planet* also had to vie with both *Harry Potter* and *Lord of the Rings* films and was soundly spanked, as if it had asked what the Crocodile had for dinner.

58. See Stewart's *Disney War* for more on the volatile period.

59. Maltin, *The Disney Films*, 332–33.

60. Stewart notes that these "soaring overhead costs" were also obviously being "ignored by Eisner" (*Disney War*, 287).

61. *LAT* (28 April 2000): 1. DreamWorks laid off 35 percent of its traditional animators in 2000 (LaPorte, *The Men Who Would be King*, 252).

62. From *Rocky and Bullwinkle* and mentioned by DreamWorks artist Kelly Asbury (LaPorte, *The Men Who Would Be King*, 58).

63. With some added computer-assisted imagery, like recent Disney films.

64. *Shrek 2* easily bested *all* live-action films as well as animated features *Incredibles*, *Shark Tale*, and *Polar Express*.

65. This talk was threaded all over 2003–2004 animation-industry message boards.

66. Katzenberg's *Shrek 2* was the envy of all; *Shark Tale* (DreamWorks's first completely in-house production) underperformed, and yet it made twice as much as Disney's *Home on the Range*.

67. Price, *The Pixar Touch*, 122–23; Stewart, *Disney War*, 480.

68. *Brother Bear* made $250 million while *Home on the Range* lost tens of millions. In the early 2000s, the Pixar deal was contributing up to 45 percent of the Disney studio's total operating income (Stewart, *Disney War*, 411; Price, *The Pixar Touch*, 5).

69. See "Comcast's Decision Brings Disappointment, Relief," *Orlando Sentinel* (29 April 2004): C1. There were other suitors. AOL had talked about buying Disney in the late 1990s but would later merge with Time Warner, to which Disney raised objections.

70. Diane would write directly to board members and Eisner and only hear back from Eisner (Stewart, *Disney War*, 491–93).

71. "Disney Strips Eisner," *Ventura County Star* (3 March 2004).

72. This same refrain would be heard four years later from kids and critics when Disney's *Fox and the Hound* appeared; "average Disney fare best suited for youngsters," said Martin Goodman in Beck's *AMG*, 87. Incidentally, *Pinocchio* would be in theaters again by December 1978, playing with a new Disney short from Bluth and Rich, *The Small One*.

73. Quoted in *Forbes* (1 July 1967): 39–40.

74. Of these films that have been released theatrically (and thence to other platforms), only five have clearly lost money, and six are in the "maybe" category; all the others are easily in the box-office black.

75. The "genuinely troubled" *Road to El Dorado* had been Katzenberg's idea. His Disney bonus trial and arbitration kept him at some distance from the film and the direct competition with Disney's "New World" film *Emperor's New Groove* (LaPorte, *The Men Who Would Be King*, 208–9, 220). Disney's *Emperor's New Groove* wasn't a hit, but DreamWorks's *Road to El Dorado* was a certified flop. Aardman/DreamWorks/Paramount's *Flushed Away* became a $90 million write-off (LaPorte, *The Men Who Would Be King*, 426).

76. A 2022 *Puss in Boots* sequel performed very well (including critically), earning $480 million worldwide, even though it was released to streaming as well.

77. "Disney Hopes Eisner Can Wake Sleeping Beauty," *Newsweek* (17 October 1984): C20.

78. Masters, "Epic Disney Blow-Up," 9 April 2014. These concerns were voiced from the first months of the new DreamWorks SKG, when start-up capital ($400 million a year) was flying out the door (LaPorte, *The Men Who Would Be King*, 127).

79. In 2016, NBCUniversal acquired DreamWorks Animation for almost $4 billion.

80. A third *Spider-Verse* film is set for 2024.

81. The *Ray Gunn* project has been in development since the early 1990s.

82. Stewart, *Disney War*, 363.

83. Stewart, *Disney War*, 299, 321, 363.

84. Martin Goodman, in Beck's *AMG*, 72. *Groove* had begun life as a more serious Mesoamerican-drama-meets-Prince-and-the-Pauper with a Sting-penned soundtrack. It's not that, but it's often hysterical. It managed to make back its production budget and more.

85. Said to have cost $260 million, so a real profit might have eluded Disney.

86. Sequels are likely for all of these, especially given Disney's recent struggles with riskier original material (*Strange World*), struggling Pixar titles (*Lightyear*, *Elemental*), underperforming Lucasfilm and Marvel titles, and the crushing costs of Disney+.

87. Quoted in "Jungle Fever," *WSJ* (16 May 1994): A1.

88. This last includes 2010's *Toy Story 3*, *Shrek 4*, *Tangled*, *Despicable Me*, and *How to Train Your Dragon*; also 2016 and *Finding Dory*, *Zootopia*, *The Jungle Book*, and *The Secret Life of Pets*.

Bibliography

Abraham, Adam. *When Magoo Flew: The Rise and Fall of Animation Studio UPA*. Middletown, CT: Wesleyan, 2012.

Adamakos, Peter. "Ub Iwerks." *Mindrot* 7 (June 1977): 20–24.

Adamson, Joe. "Joe Adamson Talks with Richard Huemer." *American Film Institute Report* 5 (Summer 1974): 10–17.

———. "Suspended Animation." In *Film Theory and Criticism*, edited by Gerald Mast and Marshall Cohen, 606–16. New York: Oxford University Press, 1974.

———. *Tex Avery: King of Cartoons*. New York: Popular Library, 1975.

———. *The Walter Lantz Story*. New York: Putnam's, 1985.

———. "Working for the Fleischers: An Interview with Dick Huemer." *Funnyworld* 16 (Winter 1974–1975): 23–28.

———. "You Couldn't Get Chaplin in a Milk Bottle: An Interview with Tex Avery." *Take One* 2.9 (1970): 10–14.

Agee, James. "Comedy's Greatest Era." *Life* (5 September 1949): 70–88.

Allan, Robin. "50 Years of Snow White." *JPF&T* 15.4 (Winter 1998): 157–63.

Amidi, Amid. *Cartoon Modern: Style and Design in 1950s Animation*. San Francisco, CA: Chronicle, 2006.

Arnold, Gordon B. *Animation and the American Imagination*. Santa Barbara, CA: Praeger, 2017.

Bak, Meredith. *Playful Visions: Optical Toys and the Emergence of Children's Media Culture*. Cambridge, MA: MIT Press, 2020.

Baker, Bob. "Max & Dave Fleischer." *Film Dope* 16 (February 1979): 27–35.

Balio, Tino. *The American Film Industry*. Madison: University of Wisconsin Press, 1985.

———. *United Artists: The Company Built by the Stars*, vols. 1 and 2. Madison: University of Wisconsin Press, 2009.

Barrier, J. Michael. "Building a Better Mouse: Fifty Years of Disney Animation." *Funnyworld* 20 (1979): 6–22.

———. "The Careers of Hugh Harman and Rudolf Ising." *Millimeter* (February 1976): 46–50.

———. *Hollywood Cartoons: American Animation in Its Golden Age*. New York: Oxford University Press, 1999.

———. "Silly Stuff: An Interview with Hugh Harman." *Graffiti* 5.1 (Spring 1984): 6–8, 10–11.

Barrier, Mike, and Milton Gray. "Bob Clampett." *Funnyworld* 12 (Summer 1970): 13–37.

Bashara, Dan. *Cartoon Vision: UPA Animation and Postwar Aesthetics.* Oakland: University of California Press, 2019.

Bayer, Ann. "Happy 40th, Mickey." *Life* (October 1968): 57–59.

Beck, Jerry. *The 50 Greatest Cartoons.* North Dighton, MA: JG Press, 1998.

———. *The Animated Movie Guide.* Chicago: A Cappella, 2005.

Beck, Jerry, and Will Friedwald. *Looney Tunes and Merrie Melodies: A Complete Guide to the Warner Brothers Cartoons.* New York: Henry Holt, 1989.

Bendazzi, Giannalberto. *Cartoons: One Hundred Years of Cinema Animation.* Bloomington: Indiana University Press, 1994.

Biskind, Peter. *Easy Riders, Raging Bulls.* New York: Simon and Schuster, 1998.

Blackbeard, Bill. "The First (Arf, Arf) Superhero of Them All." In *All in Color for a Dime,* edited by Dick Lupoff and Don Thompson. New York: Ace Books, 1970.

Bossert, David. *Oswald the Lucky Rabbit: The Search for the Lost Disney Cartoons.* Los Angeles, CA: Disney Press, 2019.

Bottini, Cinzia. "UPA: Redesigning Animation." PhD diss., Nanyang Technological University, 2016.

Bradley, Edwin M. *The First Hollywood Sound Shorts, 1926–1931.* Jefferson, NC: McFarland, 2005.

Bragdon, Claude. "Mickey Mouse and What He Means." *Scribner's* XCVI.1 (July 1934): 40–43.

Bray, John Randolph. "Development of Animated Cartoons." *Moving Picture World* 33.3 (21 July 1017): 395–97.

Bray, John Randolph, and Earl Hurd. "Bray-Hurd: The Key Animation Patents." *Film History* 2.3 (1988): 229–66.

Butsch, Richard. *The Making of American Audiences.* Cambridge: Cambridge University Press, 2000.

Cabarga, Leslie. *The Fleischer Story.* New York: Da Capo, 1998.

Callahan, David. "Cel Animation: Production and Marginalization in the Animated Film Industry." *Film History* 2 (1988): 223–28.

Canemaker, John. "The Birth of Animation: Reminiscing with John A. Fitzsimmons." *Millimeter* (1975): 14–16.

———. *Felix: The Twisted Tale of the World's Most Famous Cat.* New York: Pantheon, 1991.

———. "Otto Messmer and Felix the Cat." *Millimeter* (September 1976): 34–36, 58–61.

———. "Pioneers of American Animation: J. Stuart Blackton, Winsor McCay, J. R. Bray, Otto Messmer, Disney." *Variety* (7 January 1976): 38.

———. "Profile of a Living Animation Legend: J. R. Bray." *Filmmakers Newsletter* (January 1975): 28–31.

———. *Tex Avery: The MGM Years 1942–1955.* Atlanta, GA: Turner Publishing, 1996.

———. *Walt Disney's Nine Old Men.* New York: Disney Editions, 2001.

———. "Winsor McCay." *Film Comment* 11.1 (January–February 1975): 44–47.

———. *Winsor McCay: His Life and Art.* New York: Abbeville, 1987.

———. "Winsor McCay's *Little Nemo* and *How a Mosquito Operates*—Beginnings of 'Personality Animation.'" In *The Art of the Animated Image*, edited by Charles Solomon, 27–36. Los Angeles, CA: AFI, 1987.

Casper, Drew. *Postwar Hollywood: 1946–1962*. Malden, MA: Blackwell, 2007.

Chute, David. "Keeping Up with the Jones." *Film Comment* 21.6 (November–December 1985): 14–15.

Cohen, Karl F. *Forbidden Animation: Censored Cartoons and Blacklisted Animators in America*. Jefferson, NC: McFarland, 1997.

———. "Toontown's Reds: HUAC's Investigation of Alleged Communists in the Animation Industry." *Film History* 5.2 (June 1993): 190–203.

Cohen, Mitchell. "Looney Tunes and Merrie Melodies." *The Velvet Light Trap* 15 (Fall 1975): 33–37.

Couperie, Pierre, et al. *A History of the Comic Strip*. New York: Crown, 1968.

Crafton, Donald. "American Iconography: The 'Hand of the Artist.'" *Quarterly Review of Film Studies* 4.4 (1979): 409–28.

———. *Before Mickey: The Animated Film 1891–1928*. Cambridge, MA: MIT Press, 1982.

———. *Emile Cohl: Caricature and Film*. Princeton, NJ: Princeton University Press, 1990.

———. *The Talkies: American Cinema's Transition to Sound 1926–1931*. Berkeley: University of California Press, 1997.

———. "Tricks and Animation." In *Oxford History of World Cinema*. Oxford: Oxford University Press, 1997.

Culhane, John. "The Men Behind Dastardly and Muttley." *New York Times Magazine* (23 November 1969): 50+.

Culhane, Shamus. *Talking Animals and Other People*. New York: St. Martin's, 1986.

Curtis, Barry. "In Betweening: An Interview with Irene Kotlarz." *Art History* 18 (March 1995): 24–36.

Deming, Barbara. "The Artlessness of Walt Disney." *Partisan Review* 12 (Spring 1945): 226–31.

Deneroff, Harvey. "Popeye the Union Man: A Historical Study of the Fleischer Strike." PhD diss., University of Southern California, 1985.

———. "The Thin Black Line." *Sight and Sound* 9.6 (June 1999): 22–24.

———. "'We Can't Get Much Spinach!' The Organization and Implementation of the Fleischer Animation Strike." *Film History* 1 (1987): 1–14.

Dewey, Don. *Buccaneer: James Stuart Blackton and the Birth of American Movies*. Lanham, MD: Rowman & Littlefield, 2016.

———. "Man of a Thousand Firsts." *American Film* 15 (November 1990): 44–50.

Dick, Bernard F. *City of Dreams: The Making and Remaking of Universal Pictures*. Lexington: University Press of Kentucky, 1997.

———. *Columbia Pictures: Portrait of a Studio*. Lexington: University Press of Kentucky, 1992.

———. *Engulfed: The Death of Paramount Pictures and the Birth of Corporate Hollywood*. Lexington: University Press of Kentucky, 2001.

Doherty, Thomas. "This Is Where We Came In." In *American Movie Audiences*, edited by Stokes and Maltby, 155. London: BFI, 1999.

Eisner, Michael. *Work in Progress: Risking Failure, Surviving Success*. New York: Hyperion Books, 1999.

Erickson, Hal. *A Van Beuren Production*. Jefferson, NC: McFarland, 2020.

Eyman, Scott. *20th Century-Fox: Darryl F. Zanuck and the Creation of the Modern Film Studio*. Philadelphia: Running Press, 2021.

Feild, Robert. *The Art of Walt Disney*. London: Collins, 1947.

Fell, John L. "Mr. Griffith, Meet Winsor McCay." *Journal of the University Film Association* 23.3 (1971): 74–87.

Finch, Christopher. *The Art of Walt Disney: From Mickey Mouse to the Magic Kingdom*. New York: Abrams, 1988.

———. *Walt Disney's America*. New York: Abbeville, 1978.

Fisher, David. "Two Premieres: Disney & UPA." *Monthly Film Bulletin* (July–September 1953): 40–41.

Fleischer, Richard. *Out of the Inkwell: Max Fleischer and the Animation Revolution*. Lexington: University of Kentucky Press, 2005.

Ford, Greg. "Warner Brothers: Focus on a Studio." *Film Comment* 11.1 (January–February 1975): 10–17, 93, 96.

Fox, Julian. "Felix Remembered." *Films and Filming* (November 1974): 44–51.

Furniss, Maureen. *Chuck Jones Conversations*. Jackson: University Press of Mississippi, 2005.

———. *A New History of Animation*. New York: Thames & Hudson, 2016.

Gabler, Neal. *Walt Disney: The Triumph of the American Imagination*. New York: Vintage Books, 2007.

Geduld, Harry M. *The Birth of the Talkies: From Edison to Jolson*. Bloomington: Indiana University Press, 1975.

Ghez, Didier, ed. *Walt's People*, vols. 1, 2, 9. Bloomington, IN: Xlibris, 2005–2010.

Gomery, Douglas. "Disney's Business History." In *Disney Discourse*, edited by Eric Smoodin. New York: Routledge, 1994.

———. *The Hollywood Studio System*. New York: St. Martin's Press, 1986.

Gould, Michael. "Animated Film." In *Surrealism and the Cinema: Open-Eyed Screening*, 135–47. London: Tantivy, 1976.

Grant, John. *Masters of Animation*. New York: Watson-Guptill, 2001.

Hajdu, David. *The Ten-Cent Plague: The Great Comic-Book Scare and How It Changed America*. New York: Picador, 2008.

Halberstam, David. *The Fifties*. New York: Ballantine, 1993.

Hamonic, W. Gerald. "Disney Is the Tiffany's and I Am the Woolworth's of the Business." PhD diss., Brunel University, 2011.

———. *Terrytoons: The Story of Paul Terry*. London: John Libbey, 2018.

Hampton, Benjamin B. *History of the American Film Industry: From Its Beginnings to 1931*. New York: Dover, 1970 (first printed in 1932).

Hanna, William, Bill Hanna, and Tom Ito. *A Cast of Friends*. United Kingdom: Hachette Books, 2000.

Hanssen, F. Andrew. "Vertical Integration during the Hollywood Studio Era." *Journal of Law & Economics* 53.3 (August 2010): 519–43.

Hearn, Michael Patrick. "The Animated Art of Winsor McCay." *American Artist* (May 1975): 28–33, 63–65.

Hine, Al. "McBoing Boing and Magoo." *Holiday* 9 (1951): 6, 8–9, 11–12.

Hoberman, J. "Vulgar Modernism." *Artforum* (February 1982): 71–76.

Hoffer, Tom W. "From Comic Strips to Animation: Some Perspective on Winsor McCay." *Journal of the University Film Association* XXVIII. 2 (Spring 1976): 23–32.

Holliss, Richard, and Brian Sibley. *The Disney Studio Story*. New York: Crown, 1988.

Hubley, John, and Zachary Schwartz. "Animation Learns a New Language." *Hollywood Quarterly* 1.4 (July 1946): 360–63.

Iwerks, Don. *Walt Disney's Ultimate Inventor: The Genius of Ub Iwerks*. Los Angeles, CA: Disney Editions, 2019.

Iwerks, Leslie, and John Kenworthy. *The Hand Behind the Mouse*. New York: Disney Editions, 2001.

Jameson, Martin. "Cartoonists in Filmland." *Cartoons* 11.1 (1917): 116–24.

Kanfer, Stefan. *Serious Business: The Art and Commerce of Animation in America*. New York: Da Capo, 1997.

Kaufman, J. B. "*The Three Little Pigs*—Big Little Picture." *American Cinematographer* (November 1988): 8–14.

Klein, Isadore. "Cartooning Down Broadway." *Film Comment* (January–February 1975): 62–63.

———. "How I Came to Know the Fabulous Winsor McCay." *Cartoonist Profiles* 30 (June 1977): 49–51.

———. "Pioneer Animated Cartoon Producer Charles R. Bowers." *Cartoonist Profiles* 25–27 (March–June–September 1975): 52–59, 70–73.

Klein, Norman. *Seven Minutes: The Life and Death of the American Cartoon*. London, New York: Verso, 1993.

Knight, Arthur. "The New Look in Cartooning." *Saturday Review of Literature* 34 (April 1951).

Korkis, Jim, and John Cawley. *Cartoon Confidential*. Westlake Village, CA: Malibu Graphics, 1992.

Koszarski, Richard. *An Evening's Entertainment: The Age of the Silent Feature Picture, 1915–1928*. Berkeley: University of California Press, 1990.

Langer, Mark. "Max and Dave Fleischer." *Film Comment* 11.1 (January–February 1975): 48–56.

———. "Regionalism in Disney Animation: Pink Elephants and Dumbo." *Film History* 4 (1990): 305–21.

LaPorte, Nicole. *The Men Who Would Be King*. New York: HMH, 2010.

Lehman, Christopher P. *The Colored Cartoon: Black Representation in American Animated Short Films, 1901–1954*. Amherst: University of Massachusetts Press, 2007.

Lenburg, Jeff. *The Encyclopedia of Animated Cartoons*. 3rd ed. New York: Facts On File, 2009.

Leuchtenberg, William. *A Troubled Feast*. Boston, MA: Little, Brown, 1983.

Lindvall, Terrence, and Matthew Melton. "Towards a Post-Modern Animated Discourse." In *A Reader in Animation Studies*, edited by Jayne Pilling. London: John Libbey & Co., 1997.

Lutz, E. G. *Animated Cartoons: How They Are Made*. New York: Charles Scribner's Sons, 1920.

Macek, Carl. "From *Little Nemo* to *Little Nemo*." *MediaScene* (September–October 1976): 10–13.

Maltin, Leonard. *The Disney Films*. New York: Disney Edition, 2000.

———. *Of Mice and Magic*. New York: New American Library, 1987.

Mann, Arthur. "Mickey Mouse's Financial Career." *Harper's Monthly* 168 (May 1934): 714–21.

Martin, Andre. "In Search of Raoul Barré." International Animated Film Festival, Ottawa, ON (1976): 1, 10–15.

Masters, Kim. "The Epic Disney Blow-Up." *The Hollywood Reporter* (9 April 2014).

———. *The Keys to the Kingdom*. New York: HarperCollins, 2000.

McGilligan, Patrick. "Robert Clampett." In *The American Animated Cartoon: A Critical Anthology*, edited by Gerald Peary and Danny Peary, 150–57. New York: Dutton, 1980.

Merritt, Russell, and J. B. Kaufman. *Walt in Wonderland: The Silent Films of Walt Disney*. Baltimore, MD: Johns Hopkins University Press, 1993.

Merritt, Russell, and Karen Merritt. "Mythic Mouse." *Griffithiana* 11.34 (1988): 58–71.

Morreall, John. *Taking Laughter Seriously*. Albany: State University of New York, 1983.

Mosley, Leonard. *Disney's World*. Lanham, MD: Scarborough House, 1990.

Mullen, Sarah McLean. "Master of Cartoons." *Scholastic* (18 May 1935): 11.

Neupert, Richard. "A Studio Built of Bricks: Disney and Technicolor." *Film Reader* 6 (1985): 33–40.

Nowell-Smith, Geoffrey, ed. *The Oxford History of World Cinema*. Oxford: Oxford University Press, 1997.

Oeri, Georgine. "UPA: A New Dimension for the Comic Strip." *Graphis* 9.50 (1953): 470–79.

O'Sullivan, Judith. "In Search of Winsor McCay." *AFI Report* 4–5.2 (1973): 3–9.

Panofsky, Erwin. "Style and Medium in the Moving Pictures." In *Film: An Anthology*, edited by Daniel Talbot. Berkeley: University of California Press, 1969.

Pautz, Michelle. "The Decline in Average Weekly Cinema Attendance, 1930–2000." *Issues in Political Economy* 11 (Summer 2002).

Peary, Daniel, and Gerald Peary, eds. *The American Animated Cartoon*. New York: Dutton, 1980.

Perlmutter, David. *America Toons In: A History of Television Animation*. Jefferson, NC: McFarland, 2014.

Pointer, Ray. *The Art and Inventions of Max Fleischer*. Jefferson, NC: McFarland, 2017.

Pratley, Gerald. "Cartoons in Decay." *Films in Review* 2.9 (1951): 34–36.

Price, David A. *The Pixar Touch*. New York: Vintage, 2009.

Putterman, Roy. "A Short Critical History of Warner Bros. Cartoons." In *Reading the Rabbit*, edited by Kevin Sandler, 29–37. New Brunswick, NJ: Rutgers University Press, 1998.

Ramsaye, Terry. *A Million and One Nights at the Movies.* New York: Simon and Schuster, 1986 (first printed 1926).

Rieder, Howard. "Memories of Mr. Magoo." *Cinema Journal* 8.2 (1969): 17–24.

Robson, E. W., and M. M. Robson. *The Film Answers Back: An Historical Appreciation of the Cinema.* London: John Lane, 1939.

Rogers, Maureen. "Remaking the B Film 1940s Hollywood." *Film History* 29.2 (Summer 2017): 138–64.

Rosenbaum, Jonathan. "Dream Masters I and II." *Film Comment* 11.1 (January–February 1975): 64–73.

Sagar, Isobel C. "The UPA Cartoons." *Films in Review* 2.9 (1951): 36–37.

Sammond, Nicholas. *Birth of An Industry: Blackface Minstrelsy and the Rise of American Animation.* Durham, NC: Duke University Press, 2015.

Sartin, Hank. "Drawing on Hollywood: Warner Bros. Cartoons and Hollywood, 1930–1960." PhD diss., University of Chicago, 1998.

Scheib, Ronnie. "Tex Arcana: The Cartoons of Tex Avery." In *The American Animated Cartoon: A Critical Anthology*, edited by Gerald Peary and Danny Peary, 110–27. New York: Dutton, 1980.

Schickel, Richard. "Bringing Forth the Mouse." *American Heritage* (April 1968): 24–29, 90–96.

———. *The Disney Version: The Life, Times, Art, and Commerce of Walt Disney.* Chicago: Ivan R. Dee, 1997.

Schneider, Steve. *That's All Folks: The Art of Warner Bros. Animation.* New York: Henry Holt, 1988.

Scott, Keith. *The Moose That Roared: The Story of Jay Ward, Bill Scott, a Flying Squirrel, and a Talking Moose.* New York: St. Martin's, 2000.

Seldes, Gilbert. *The Seven Lively Arts.* New York: Harper, 1924.

Shale, Richard. *Donald Duck Joins Up: The Walt Disney Studio during World War II.* Ann Arbor: UMI Research Press, 1982.

Shay, Don. "Willis O'Brien: Creator of the Impossible." *Focus on Film* 16 (Autumn 1973): 18–47.

Shull, Michael, and David Wilt. *Doing Their Bit.* Jefferson, NC: McFarland, 1987.

Sito, Tom. "Disney's *The Fox and the Hound.*" *Animation World* 3.8 (November 1998).

Sklar, Robert. *Movie-Made America.* New York: Random House, 1975.

Smith, Conrad. "The Early History of Animation: Saturday Morning TV Discovers 1915." *JUFA* 29.3 (Summer 1977): 23–30.

Smith, David R. "Beginnings of the Disney Multiplane Camera." In *The Art of the Animated Image: An Anthology*, edited by Charles Solomon. Los Angeles, CA: AFI, 1987.

Smoodin, Eric. *Disney Discourse: Producing the Magic Kingdom.* New York: Routledge, 1994.

Solomon, Charles, ed. *The Art of the Animated Image: An Anthology*. Los Angeles, CA: AFI, 1987.

———. *Enchanted Drawings: The History of Animation*. New York: Knopf, 1989.

———. "Will the Real Walt Disney Please Stand Up?" *Film Comment* 18.4 (July–August 1982): 49–54.

Stephenson, Ralph. *The Animated Film*. London: Tantivy, 1973.

Stewart, James B. *Disney War: The Battle for the Magic Kingdom*. London: Pocket Books, 2006.

Stocker, Joseph. "Magnificent Magoo." *American Mercury* 86 (April 1958): 129–33.

Stokes, Melvyn, and Richard Maltby, eds. *American Movie Audiences*. London: BFI, 1999.

Susanin, Timothy S. *Walt Before Mickey: Disney's Early Years, 1919–1928*. Jackson: University Press of Mississippi, 2011.

Sypher, Wylie. *Rococo to Cubism in Art and Literature*. New York: Vintage, 1960.

Taylor, Drew. "The Disney Renaissance Didn't Happen Because of Jeffrey Katzenberg." *Collider* (20 May 2020).

Taylor, John. *Storming the Magic Kingdom*. New York: Knopf, 1987.

Telotte, J. P. "Ub Iwerks' (Multi)Plain Cinema." *Animation: An Interdisciplinary Journal* 1.1 (2006): 9–24.

Theisen, Earl. "The History of the Animated Cartoon." *Journal of the Society of Motion Picture Engineers* (September 1933): 239–49.

Thomas, Bob. *Walt Disney: An American Original*. New York: Hyperion, 1994.

Thomas, Frank, and Ollie Johnston. *The Illusion of Life: Disney Animation*. New York: Abbeville, 1981.

Thompson, Richard. "Meep Meep." In *Movies and Methods: An Anthology*, edited by Bill Nichols, 126–35. Berkeley: University of California Press, 1976.

Walz, Gene. "Charlie Thorson and Temporary Disneyfication." In *Reading the Rabbit*, edited by Kevin Sandler, 49–66 (endnotes 228–31). New Brunswick, NJ: Rutgers University Press, 1998.

Weinman, Jaime. *Anvils, Mallets and Dynamite: The Unauthorized Biography of Looney Tunes*. Toronto, ON: Sutherland House, 2021.

Wells, Paul. *Animation and America*. New Brunswick, NJ: Rutgers University Press, 2002.

———. *Understanding Animation*. London: Routledge, 1998.

Wilmington, Michael. "Dumbo." In *The American Animated Cartoon: A Critical Anthology*, edited by Gerald Peary and Danny Peary, 76–81. New York: Dutton, 1980.

Zipes, Jack. *Oxford Companion to Fairy Tales*. Oxford: Oxford University Press, 2015.

INDEX

Note: All short and feature film titles are listed at "films."

offon

Williams, Richard, 236, 239
Winkler, George, 72, 270n18,
271n30
Winkler, Margaret, 6, 49, 50,
54–55, 56, 57, 67, 68–69,
71, 74, 76, 268n50, 268n56,
270n10, 270n22

Woody Woodpecker, 6, 96–97,
139, 188, 227, 232
World War I, 1, 29, 52
World War II, 1, 4, 29, 38, 82, 97,
135–79, 181–83

Zukor, Adolph, 54, 70, 276n48

About the Author

Darl Larsen was born and raised in central California and has been part of the film faculty at Brigham Young University since 1998. He took degrees at University of California, Santa Barbara; Brigham Young University; and Northern Illinois University. He is professor in the Department of Theatre & Media Arts and the Center for Animation at Brigham Young University, teaching film, animation, and screenwriting. *Moving Pictures* is influenced by his classes for animation majors. He has also published extensively in Monty Python studies, looking at Monty Python and English Renaissance drama, *Monty Python's Flying Circus*, and the troupe's three feature films.

www.ingramcontent.com/pod-product-compliance
Lightning Source LLC
Chambersburg PA
CBHW030921150426

42812CB00046B/455